THE SEVEN WONDERS OF THE WORLD

A HISTORY OF THE
MODERN IMAGINATION

John & Elizabeth Romer

First published in Great Britain in 1995 by
Michael O'Mara Books Limited

This hardback edition first published in 2005 by
Seven Dials, Cassell & Co
Wellington House, 125 Strand
London, WC2R 0BB

A CIP catalogue record for this book is available
from the British Library

ISBN 0-297-76391-1

Maps by MapMedia
Designed and typeset by Martin Bristow
Printed and bound in China

CONTENTS

AUTHORS' ACKNOWLEDGEMENTS

Everyone has heard of each of the Seven Wonders of the World, but few have seen all of them for themselves. To do so one has to go abroad . . . Only if you travel the world and get worn out by the effort of the journey will the desire to see all the Wonders of the World be satisfied, and by the time you have done that you will be old and practically dead.

Philo of Byzantium

Our literary journey to the Seven Wonders of the World has been much easier than poor old Philo's, and greatly aided by many people who helped us on our way. As always Mike and Lesley O'Mara provided immense support and good humour; Cathy Randall, unflappable and tactful editing; Martin Bristow, his usual impeccable designs; Hugh Johnstone, limpid translations from the Greek and Latin texts, and most valuable advice.

On the sites of the Wonders, and in the libraries and museums that hold the materials of their history, we also met with much kindness and a great deal of patience. Our debt to the archaeologists and staff of these institutes and institutions is profound. The excavators and their colleagues: Professor Bammer at the Temple of Artemis; Dr Poul Pedersen at the Mausoleum; the curators of the museums and their staffs at Olympia and the Athenian Parthenon in Greece; the Greek and Roman Department of the British Museum, England; the archaeological museums of Istanbul, Ankara, Bodrum and Ephesus in Turkey; the librarians of the University of Heidelberg, Germany and the State Library in Naples, Italy. We thank you all.

Filming *The Seven Wonders* was an extraordinary undertaking. Every film series, indeed, is an adventure for those who make it and each successful film is the product of the skill and energy of many participants working together. Yet only the presenter – the public face of an elaborate enterprise – is ever seen. Nick Barton first saw the idea, and as the series producer guided *The Seven Wonders* through its many, lengthy phases with charm, tact and determination.

At Discovery Communications, Inc., Denise Baddour, Executive in Charge of Production, John Ford, Senior Vice-President, The Learning Channel, Nancy LeBrun, senior producer, Anne Hubbell, associate producer, Linda Guisset, project manager, were never-failing sources of enthusiasm and encouragement. We would also like to thank Karen Brown, commissioning editor, Channel 4, for her pertinent advice.

The series was produced and directed by Peter Spry-Leverton; photography by Peter Greenhalgh and Michael Miles; sound recordist, Rupert Murray; assistant camera operator, Ben Philpott; line producer, Fiona Freed; production assistant, Gina Barrott; film editor, Jonathan Cooke; researcher, Linda Weston; fixers, Roberta Licurgo, Romany and Mary Helmi, Sevim Berker, Leyla Ayas, Hara Palamidi. Our affectionate thanks to all of you.

John and Elizabeth Romer,
Aiola, November 1994

ACKNOWLEDGEMENTS

P. 74 Extract from R. L. Poxon, 'Facts about United States Paper Money', reprinted from *Selections from the Numismatist*, published 1960 by ANA, 818 North Cascade Avenue, Colorado Springs, CO 80903, USA

P. 76 'Oracle of the Potter' adapted from Stanley M. Burstein, *The Hellenistic Age from the Battle of Ipsus to the Death of Kleopatra VII*, CUP, Cambridge, 1985

P. 119 Sumerian hymn reproduced from Wolkstein and Kramer, *Inanna, Queen of Heaven and Earth, Her Stories and Hymns from Sumer*, Hutchinson/Rider, London, 1984

P. 121 First two quotations adapted from Roux, *Ancient Iraq*, Penguin, Harmondsworth, 1964

P. 121 Final quotation adapted from Wiseman, 'Mesopotamian Gardens' from *Anatolian Studies* 33, 1983

Pp. 225–6 Extract reproduced from *The Times*, 14 September, 1991, © Times Newspapers Limited, 1991

P. 227 Extract reproduced from *The Economist*, © The Economist, December 1993

All colour photographs are the authors'.

INTRODUCTION

Everyone has heard of each of the Seven Wonders of the World, but few have seen all of them for themselves. To do so one has to go abroad to Persia, cross the Euphrates river, travel to Egypt, spend some time among the Elians in Greece, go to Halicarnassus in Caria, sail to Rhodes, and see Ephesus in Ionia . . .

Philo of Byzantium, *On the Seven Wonders*, written *c.* 225 BC, in Alexandria, Egypt

Some of the first excavations conducted by Europeans in the Middle East – at the Mausoleum at Halicarnassus in 1856, at Ephesus and the Temple of Artemis in the 1860s – were digging for two of the Seven Wonders of the World. Not only did these expensive enterprises promise the recovery of great works of art, the tangible remains of the ancient Wonders themselves, but also firm evidence of the vanished world that had produced that ardent poetry and prose, that kaleidoscope of exquisite images and strong spare themes, which had fuelled the Western imagination for almost two millenia.

We all of us know a wonder when we see one. Newspapers, indeed, regularly ask their readers to vote on new lists of modern objects of wonder; to list things that arouse the same reactions in us today as the first lists of Seven Wonders did in the age of Philo of Byzantium. At first glance, it seems that the story of the Seven Wonders, the very idea of earthly wonder, is so deeply embedded in us that many people now call it simply 'human nature'. In fact, the apparently innate sense that enables us to sniff out wonders is an inherited sensitivity; the Seven Wonders and the aspirations they embody had finite beginnings. The Seven Wonders of the World, therefore, hold two stories within them: firstly, that of their ancient reality; secondly their later history as symbols of magnificence and competition. This is the real stuff of history, that slow brew suffusing over millenia to form a vast catalogue of past imaginings and future aspirations.

In common with many other popular images and ideas, the precise origin of this list called the Seven Wonders of the World is now lost to us. References to the Seven Wonders abound in classical writings, yet most of these ancient texts are ambiguous in their authorship, disputed in their dates and serve only to underline the impression that the Seven Wonders of the World were as well known and, perhaps, as little recited then, as they are now. Securely dated written evidence shows that the first full modern version of the list of Seven Wonders actually appeared less than four centuries ago, in Italy in 1608, and even after that date the seven constituents of the list were not firmly fixed until the arrival of mass printing and popular education in the last century. These facts, however, confuse essential truths: lists naming the Seven Wonders of the World have been a part of common knowledge in the educated West since the days of Philo of Byzantium in the third century BC. Though the various wonders on those lists may have changed down through the centuries, sometimes, indeed, they have had ten and more wonders in them, all of them were generally awarded the time-honoured title of the 'Seven Wonders of the World'.

Both of the principal ancient texts that describe the Seven Wonders, that of Philo of Byzantium and, some eight centuries and more later, that of Bede of Jarrow, have long been claimed to be the concoctions of lesser authors. In common with all ancient writings, these texts were of course handwritten, individually recopied and probably garbled and embellished in the process. In consequence, little may be proven concerning their original authorship. We rely ultimately, as does so much of our history, upon a consensus of opinion. Whether or not they were actually composed by Bede or Philo, both these documents occupy vital places in the history of the concept of the Seven Wonders, and were certainly first compiled in the approximate time frames of those two illustrious scholars.

Philo's list is certainly the most important of them all. Though conceivably some surviving ancient wonder lists may be even older, none of them remotely compares with his text, not in their length, nor poetry, nor in the information they offer. Philo's splendid essay 'On the Seven Wonders', preserved in a fine Byzantine codex kept in the University of Heidelberg, is given here in the appendix on page 230 in a fresh translation by Hugh Johnstone. Most of the doubts concerning the true authorship of this text revolve around its splendid so-called 'rhetorical flourishes' which seem to some to be inappropriate for Philo's circle in that Hellenistic hothouse, the library of ancient Alexandria. None the less, the text's core seems genuine enough. A close study of a section of it by Dennis Haynes, the first for more than fifty years, led him to comment that: 'Nobody, I think, who reads it with an open mind could fail to admit that it is a surprisingly consistent and credible account to find in the pages of a late antique rhetorician; and it is hard to believe that it does not go back to a good Hellenistic source.' In its day, the essay was persuasive enough to have been taken north from the ancient Library of Alexandria to Byzantium, there to be copied and carried off to Western Europe to be installed successively in the libraries of a Swiss monastery, a Renaissance printer, the courts of Heidelberg and the Vatican, and thence to be carried off again from Rome to Napoleonic Paris and finally, following the Congress of Vienna, to be returned once more to Heidelberg.

Called Philo 'of Byzantium' to distinguish him from all his ancient namesakes, our Philo hailed presumably from his eponymous seaside city on the Bosphorus and crossed the Mediterranean to live in Alexandria in Egypt which, in his day, was the metropolitan centre of the world. He is best described as a librarian engineer; a learned man working inside a strong Alexandrian tradition of scholars specializing in mechanical experiment and written speculation. Philo's mechanical speculations on the Seven Wonders, real 'how to do it' texts, had wide appeal for later ages, fascinated as they were by his vanished ancient world which, it seemed, could build anything it wanted.

In common with all other classical lists of Seven Wonders, Philo does not place the famous lighthouse of his own city, the so-called Pharos of Alexandria, amongst the charmed seven. That joined the now-standard list of wonders with the later Northern European lists of Gregory of Tours and Bede. Most classical lists count the Walls of Babylon as a wonder in their own right, to stand alongside the fabled Hanging Gardens. Even in Philo's day, however, Babylon was a remote dream, the journey of a lifetime. Most of Philo's wonders are set inside his own small world, in the cities that stood around the eastern Mediterranean, the tight rich circle of Hellenistic civilization with civic order at its centre, and chaos, barbarians and dragons at the edges. On the isle of Rhodes, at the centre of the sea lanes, stood one of the two statues on Philo's list of seven marvels: the great Colossus. 60 miles south-east of Rhodes lay Halicarnassus and its Mausoleum, a stalwart of the wonder lists; 60 miles north of that lay Ephesus and its Temple of Artemis, another wonder. Sail 300 miles or so west from Rhodes and you could sight the port close by Olympia, with its great Zeus of ivory and gold, the most admired of all the wonders. Philo's list is like an ancient sailor's tale; an armchair engineer's description of memorable things in nearby seaports laced with some distant desert dreams; the fabled images of all who love to travel. 'The oyster beds of Babylon, beside the Hanging Gardens, the finest seafood in creation, with a pearl in every shell', as a guest at a Greek feast puts it in a volume of recorded table talk.

Philo, an engineer, was never solely interested in technology. For him, mechanics were but a means to wonder. In its day, his list was revolutionary. It underlined a new attitude in the ancient world, marking what was perhaps the greatest transformation the human race had undergone since the first use of metal. His selection of Seven Wonders of the World was the product of a culture occupied in taking wonder itself away from the province of the gods and bringing it down to earth: part of a redefinition of wonder and part of a redefinition of humankind. Philo and his contemporaries were engaged in a kind of cosmic stocktaking, looking around to discover a new place in the universe. In Alexandria, as in all the great trading cities of Philo's day, the king's court was not occupied, as more ancient courts had been, with endless rites and rituals to secure the state's order and success. These new courts were earthly gatherings filled with the personal ambitions of kings, courtiers, bankers and soldiers. Men like Philo held the then novel, now common, belief that human activities like making fortunes, conquering empires, building great buildings and writing great works of literature, might of themselves be wonderful. It was said that King Alexander, the conquering hero of the age, revered above all else the works of Homer, a blind, wandering poet, and kept his own copy of the antique poems in a precious box.

Looking back on those days from the first century after Christ, one ancient writer cleverly observed that though the Greek philosophers created the dream of a well-regulated human-based society, it had taken Alexander to translate their theories into practice.

Every one of the Seven Wonders, indeed, is connected in some way with the legendary image of King Alexander. All of them stood inside the confines of Alexander's short-lived Empire, indeed, they define the extent of it: Alexander founded Egyptian Alexandria, the city of the Pharos; he stormed Halicarnassus, the city of the marble Mausoleum; the Rhodian Colossus was cast in his image; and he died in Babylon, the city of the Hanging Gardens. To find the truth behind the wondrous images of golden temples and hanging gardens, we must go on a part of Alexander's journey. These ancient lists of wonders were made by his people travelling through the ancient world, seeing it with new eyes, judging it afresh.

In some respects, Alexander the Great and his armies were like Columbus and his successors, for they too attempted to impose a new order on another world. The age of the Seven Wonders was also the age of the first clashes between the ancient agrarian societies of the East and the expanding economies of Hellenism. Most of the Seven Wonders, too, were advertisements for this new heroic way of life; they were quite simply the finest examples of the major elements of a brand-new civic architecture, the ancestors of every modern city on the planet. Though most of the Seven Wonders are revealed now only in the precise rectangular pits of archaeologists, their excavation exposes the foundations of a dream so powerful that its images still echo all around us. This, then, is the story of seven ancient things, and of their place in our imagination.

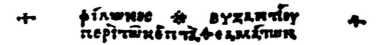

'Philo of Byzantium, On the Seven Wonders', the title lines of the unique ninth-century Byzantine manuscript of Philo's text, now in the library of the University of Heidelberg

Chapter 1

THE
STATUE OF ZEUS

THE SCALE OF ZEUS

The god, made of gold and ivory, sits on a throne. There is a garland on his head made as if of olive shoots. In his right hand he is carrying a Victory [figure], also made of gold and ivory, and this figure is holding a ribbon and has a wreath on its head. In the left hand of the god is a sceptre decorated with every kind of precious metal. The bird perched on the sceptre is the eagle. The sandals of the god are made of gold too, and so is his robe. Embroidered on the robe are figures of animals and white lilies. The crown is ornate with its gold and jewels, ornate with its ebony and ivory.

Pausanias, *Description of Greece*, Book 5, I, xi, 1-2 (*c.* AD 150)

One of the largest indoor sculptures ever made, the Zeus of the Seven Wonders was built at Olympia in southern Greece around 435 BC by the sculptor Pheidias. The statue was made of wooden planks set upon an enormous timber scaffold and was overlaid with ivory and gold in the manner known as chryselephantine, the ivory for the flesh, the gold for drapery. To the Greeks, this vast construction, some 40 feet high, in the sanctuary of their national shrine, stood as a symbol of the unity that their scattered and politically divided culture never actually attained within the real world.

For Romans too, who wove the disparate strands of Greek society into the fabric of their empire, the statue in the temple at Olympia seemed, as Cicero put it, to be inspired by a 'particularly remarkable image of beauty'. It was said that ill-fated emperors themselves dreamed of the seated Zeus on the eve of their assassination. For lesser mortals, though, a dream of the god, 'to see Zeus himself in the form that we imagine him, or to see his statue with Zeus' normal garb is a good thing for a king or a rich man. It strengthens the good fortune of a king and the wealth of a rich man. It foretells recovery for an ill man and is good for other men too.' With such power within it, no one was surprised that when the workmen of the Emperor Caligula came to dismantle the god and carry it off to Rome, it 'guffawed so much that the scaffolds collapsed and the workmen ran away. A certain man called Cassius turned up straightaway and said that he had been commanded in a dream to sacrifice a bull to Zeus'. A few days later, the unstable emperor was himself dismantled, murdered by his uneasy guards. In the hours before his death, he reported that during the previous night he had dreamed that 'he stood in heaven next to Zeus' throne and that he had been kicked with the big toe of Zeus' right foot and sent headlong down to earth.'

Above all other works, the classical world held this Zeus of ivory and gold to be sublime, something that transcended art: an image so overwhelming that it had added to the very nature of religion itself. As Philo of Byzantium said, when writing of the Seven Wonders:

> Whereas we just wonder at the other six wonders, we kneel in front of this one in reverence, because the execution of the skill is as incredible as the image of Zeus is holy. The work brings praise, and the immortality brings honour.
>
> Philo 3, 3

And the creator of this prodigious work was honoured above all other artists. Philo, again:

> Cronus is the father of Zeus in heaven, but Pheidias is the father of Zeus in Elis . . . Those were the good old days for Greece! When her wealth in the world of the gods surpassed any other people's wealth at any subsequent time; when she had an artist who was a creator of immortality unmatched by any that later ages produced; when it was possible to show men how the gods looked – appearances which it was never to be possible for other ages to see. Certainly, Pheidias is the champion over Olympus . . .
>
> Philo 3, 1; 3, 4

No wonder, then, that in Philo's day, this 200-year-old statue was still counted as one of the Seven Wonders, the last of a venerable trio – the others being Babylon's Hanging Gardens and the Egyptian Pyramids – that represent the three centres of most ancient civilization.

In common with most of the other works of its day, Pheidias' sparkling Zeus has long since vanished from the earth. Yet still, like powerful myths, the memory lingers on. Lost statues that have long been regarded in the West as images of perfection, icons of a golden age; magic products of the mind's eye, a miraculous blend of intellect and physicality that the ancient Greeks were believed to have briefly held in perfect balance. Just as the bronze-workers of the Statue of Liberty took ancient descriptions of the Colossus of Rhodes as their model and inspiration, so the literary memorials of Pheidias' Zeus stirred the sculptor of Lincoln's Washington memorial. By that time, though, Western sculptors had competed with these vanished statues for centuries, statues that existed only as ripples of enthusiasm in ancient guidebooks, in the records of plunder auctioned in imperial Rome or in the acquisitive musings of ancient connoisseurs. Even after a century and more of archaeology, the remains of these lost originals could be held in the space of a few small sculpture galleries, three or four of them showing broken fragments of genuine ancient work, six or eight more filled with clumsy later copies of sculptures identified only from ancient written descriptions.

Although not a single sculpture exists that may be confidently attributed to him, the reputation of Pheidias, gilded with ancient praise, has always been high in the academies of the West. Even the most enthusiastic modern commentators, though, have found it hard to find a place of honour for the gigantic seated Zeus that the sculptor himself always counted as his finest work. This, after all, was a monstrous large figure seated in a room so small that, as a lone dissenting visitor, the peripatetic Strabo, complained, with Zeus' head set just below the ceiling's beams 'if he were to stand up, he would unroof the temple'. And this gigantic figure was plated all over with ivory and gold, and enamelled too, with precious stones and flashing glass!

How could these same Greeks, who for so long had been represented as setting the marble-white benchmark of artistic excellence, have regarded such a wildly excessive object as the pinnacle of their achievement? The simplest explanation was that Philo's later list of Wonders was itself inherently vulgar, and showed nothing more than the decadence of the age in which it was compiled – that is, some 200 years after Pheidias' day. As for the Zeus, the flashing statue is often counted as a mere treasure trove of ivory and bullion worked by a famous marble sculptor, an ancient lapse of taste which betrayed the Greeks' Eastern origins – an East that the ancient Greeks themselves usually portrayed as barbarian, effeminate and somewhat childish. Like the slave-filled silver mines that underpinned Athenian democracy, this whole business of beginnings was hardly a proper subject on which to dwell. The Zeus, therefore, gets short shrift in many histories of art.

For all of that, the ancient people, from kings to commoners, genuinely venerated Pheidias' Zeus. To them, it appeared at once noble, balanced, and not a little frightening. For many people, it actually seemed to express a new view of deity itself. 'Blessed is that one person [Pheidias]', writes Philo, 'who saw the king and had the ability to show the Thunderer to others.' By his time, the image in the national shrine had soaked deep into the Greek consciousness. Four centuries after Philo, as angry Christians ran riot through the ancient world, vengefully burning both gods and priests alike, Pheidias' Zeus

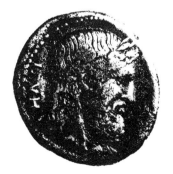 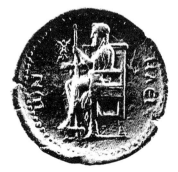

Left: Pheidias' head of Zeus. A bronze coin of the Greek state of Elis, *c.* AD 125
Right: Pheidias' Zeus seated on his throne. Roman imperial coinage *c.* AD 125

still sat high above the fray, shielded by its aura of deity. Indeed, a contemporary writer could still declare that in making such a statue, the pagan Pheidias had contributed to the cause of religion itself. And so he had, and his contribution is with us still. Those awesome Eastern images of Christ as king, that dark-eyed, even-featured, long-haired man that looms in the domes of a thousand Orthodox churches, first found expression in the face of Pheidias' Zeus.

With such an extraordinary artifact, then, one does not simply trace the history of a sculpture, but the birth of one of those rare images, of a presence, of a way of being, that is still with us today. Thus, though the original may have melted like dust into the air, we can revive something of this evanescent statue, and see Zeus for ourselves.

TWO PARTHENONS

The best place to start a search for the vanished Zeus is high up on the sacred Acropolis of Athens. Surviving records describe the 40-year-old Pheidias in the years before he left to work at Olympia supervising the rebuilding of the plundered sacred shrines and the temples of the Athenian Acropolis which had been razed by the Persians when the sculptor was still a child. At this time, Pheidias, a personal friend of the powerful statesman Pericles who had ordered the refurbishment, was at the height of his career. It is often said that he personally supervised both the design and execution of the famous sculptures that once decorated the temple now known as the Parthenon, most of which are called the Elgin Marbles, and are a pretty bone of contention between the British Museum and the Greek Government. In truth, however, the style of these plundered sculptures is varied and inconsistent, and the exact extent of Pheidias' involvement with them is still hotly debated.

Once upon a time, though, the ancient texts tell us, two great freestanding statues by the master himself stood on this same Acropolis; one of them a 30-foot-high bronze of the goddess Athena that was so prominent upon its plinth, of which you may still see a part today, that sailors said the first sight that they saw of Athens as they beat along the coast was the sun flashing on the statue's spear and helmet. She was called the Athena Promachos.

Pheidias' other statue on the Acropolis was also an Athena. Hidden from view, yet 20 feet taller than the Promachos, this was a true colossus, standing relaxed, her weight on one leg, the cheek flaps of her helmet raised, and her spear and shield beside her. Athena Parthenos, she was called, the maiden Athena, and the interior of the Parthenon had been especially designed to hold her. Unlike Christian churches, Greek temples never held rooms for living congregations, but were simply the austere dwellings of the gods themselves. In all probability, Pheidias himself had a hand in the design of the Parthenon, for its interior is unusually wide, planned for the great statue that was to live there. Today, it is still possible to see the ragged hole in the centre of the Parthenon's floor that once held the supporting mast of this colossal statue which, like the later Zeus, was chryselephantine – that is, fashioned of ivory and golden plates all set upon a wooden frame.

As famous as these two Athenas were, however, neither they nor even the Parthenon itself was as anciently renowned as was the Zeus at Olympia and certainly none of them were ever counted as a wonder. People admired the Athena Parthenos above all else in Athens, but she was never afforded the literary awe or respect commonly given to the Zeus. The statues did not capture people's imaginations in the way in which the Seven Wonders did. None the less, there are clues in the Parthenon's deserted shell to provide us with information about Pheidias' Zeus. That hole in the temple's pavement marks the spot where, for the first time in Greek history, a true colossus was erected, and this in a novel and most luxurious medium. Here, Pheidias had been an innovator.

A second clue is to be found in the Parthenon's own architecture, which provides a key to an understanding of the sensibilities that made these ancient things, not merely because of Pheidias' personal involvement with this temple and its renowned statuary. Unlike its myriad imitators and the majority of its predecessors, the Parthenon holds subtleties within it more usually found in fine paintings or great music than in temple architecture. At first glance, the building appears simple enough, a succession of posts and beams, all in good order. In fact, an elaborate and sophisticated set of visual contrivances has enabled these particular lintels and columns to stand in the mind above all others; judgement and skill combined to fill these simple forms with life.

The mystery here is in the details. In reality, the temple's seeming simplicity is highly complex. Never before, or indeed since, has a building been the object of such visual meditations. This is why those simple shapes stay in the mind. Every column, every block of stone, each edge, is considered from a visitor's point of view. What effect does the temple have? How does it appear? Whatever the effort it cost, each stone has been adjusted to achieve a precise sense of balance. Each block is cut as cleanly and precisely as a jewel, with joints so tiny that you may hardly see them and with such visual subtlety that the lines of a 200-foot long stairway may be adjusted to within an inch or so to make a visual difference. Every step and column has been considered from the point of view of an observer. Do the columns at the corner appear thinner because of the light that shines around them? Then we shall make them thicker than the others in the line. Do the straight lines of the steps appear, by an illusion, to bend in the strong Greek sunlight? Then we shall send them in a gentle curve the other way, in an arc so gradual that, were it completed in a single circle, it would join to itself some 3½ miles beneath the temple. Every marble block is shaped differently and to its particular purpose. And the result of all of this is that each and every line of the building holds life and force beyond the simple shape that at first glance it seems to be. The building appears spritely and magnificent, and the spaces that it encompasses seem powerful, balanced and alive. The slight downward curve upon the steps descending to the four corners, for instance, seems to render the building beautifully powerful, set firm upon the cliff; the columns of the two façades as well are tilted slightly inwards to aid this same effect; as you walk towards it then, the building seems lightly rooted on its hill. Held in the shimmering light above the city, it seems to control the entire landscape in which it is set. Like a diamond, its shape transmutes the very air.

When you consider the tremendous effort that these exquisite attentions cost the builders, and the significance therefore that these refinements clearly held for them, you begin to appreciate something of the civic subtlety and perception that was required of Pheidias when he set out to make his Zeus.

Today, the common sensation shared by visitors, especially for those fortunate enough to walk upon the Parthenon's marble floor, is an extraordinary sense of place and of well-being. Perhaps the single most beautiful thing as far as modern people are concerned is the building's exquisite scale. Not its size, which is but middling as far as Greek temples are concerned, but the exact relationship of the building to its visitors, precisely those relationships, in fact, on which its builders worked so assiduously. The Parthenon does not aim to dominate you as the Seven Wonders would later try to do. (That, perhaps, is why it never made the lists of wonders; the Parthenon was too small and by the time those lists were made, a couple of centuries out of date.) Here, though, you feel as if you are walking with the gods; its very scale ennobles. The marble, cut as finely as a turbine, is as warm and translucent as a human body. The building enfolds you. At one and the same time, it is a modest and most splendid thing.

As far as its designers were concerned, however, the careful creation of this most ample sense of scale was only the first act of an unfolding drama that continued inside the building in the presence of the goddess. There, you would have witnessed both the genius and the piety of Pheidias who made the standing figure of Athena Parthenos, and then at Olympia went on to make an even bigger Zeus. Athena, however, has completely disappeared.

There is still a place in the world where you may walk into a temple and experience something of that ancient and alarming confrontation with a god, a confrontation that was a dress rehearsal for the drama of visiting great Zeus in his temple at Olympia. In 1895, in 'the Athens of the South', in Nashville, Tennessee, the good citizens built themselves a plaster Parthenon for a centennial exhibition, and later, in the 1920s, for the edification of its citizens and the amusement of 100,000 visitors a year, cast it again in concrete. And finally, in the 1980s, a reconstruction of Athena Parthenos was set in its proper place.

The first thing you realize at the Nashville Parthenon is what a deep impression the ancient building has left on you. Unlike its ancient original, Nashville's Parthenon is set on a slight rise in a flat and marshy park, yet seen through the concrete columns, the views from its terraces frame spaces of most elegant proportions. Then, as you walk up the front steps to the great bronze doors – the largest made this century – a voice inside you says, yes, these are the proportions of the original in Greece. The ancient building has that strong a flavour: it stays like a melody within the mind.

In Nashville, too, the beautiful scale, the relationship of the Parthenon to its human visitors, is remarkable, unearthly. But when you push open those great bronze doors you find inside a statue so gigantic that your head is hardly level with its sandal straps. Yet here as well, standing under this reconstruction of Athena Parthenos – a third of the height of the Statue of Liberty and currently the largest indoor statue in the world – the temple's architecture is still friendly and accessible, and those small reliefs decorating the plinth and sandals of the great Athena are reassuringly smaller than life-size. Look closer, though, and you realize that the little winged figure of Victory standing on her open hand is larger than a living person. The goddess's scale is awesome.

Here's the trick. Between the statue and the temple, Pheidias has carefully manoeuvred our sense of proportion. First he brought you to a splendid temple carefully tailored to the size of people, then overwhelmed you with the gigantic presence of the god inside it. This drama in two acts, humanity at first enlarged then rendered tiny, must have produced a powerfully humbling effect upon its ancient visitors standing in the presence of their god. And what piety it shows! By all accounts, this was Pheidias' greatest triumph, the dramatic and direct encounter with a god that so impressed the Greeks and Romans and made Zeus at once accessible, ennobling and finally awe-inspiring. As Pausanius said,

> I know that the measurements of the height and breadth of the Zeus at Olympia have been recorded, but I cannot commend those who made the measurements, because the measurements they give fall a long way short of the impression one gets when one looks at the statue . . .

> *Description of Greece*, Book 5, i, xi, 9

Around the same height as a three-storey house, Zeus was the same height as the Athena Parthenos. But as this Zeus was seated on a throne, the figure would have been a third as big again as the Athena. In an older building than the Parthenon, a darker, narrower temple, Pheidias set a heavy brooding sculpture that, from all accounts, completely dominated the interior. Here he played his trick of scale again, and here to its full extent. For most visitors, Zeus seemed to fill the building with his presence. Not only were the proportions majestic, overwhelming, the materials were the richest that

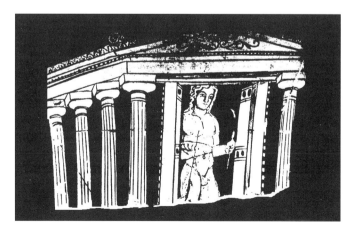

A giant god inside his temple. Greek vase painting from Taranto, Italy, showing the god Apollo, *c.* 385 BC

humankind could offer or imagine. Combined with Pheidias' noble style of sculpture, a manner that held in it a balance between the monumental archaism of the past and a growing tendency towards increasing naturalism, the scale and richness of the figure seemed to have encompassed aspects of the god himself.

THE PURPOSES OF ZEUS

When he had finished his great Zeus, so an ancient tale tells us, Pheidias asked the King of the Gods for a sign if it was pleasing to him, and straightaway a thunderbolt struck and cracked the temple's pavement at his feet – a blemish later concealed by the priests with an artfully positioned pot of bronze, and shown to selected visitors as hard evidence of divine approval. And visitors there were aplenty at Olympia.

> There are many things to see in Greece which are wonderful, and many things to see too. But it is . . . the Olympic games that have a special place in the minds of the gods . . . The historians . . . say that Cronus was the first king in heaven, and that the people of those days, who were called the people of the Golden Age, made a temple for him in Olympia . . . The historians say that Hercules . . . set a running contest, as a game, to his brothers, and crowned the winner with a branch of wild olive. There was, so the historians say, such a quantity of these olive trees that they used to sleep on piles of green foliage from these trees. Hercules is credited with having introduced the wild olive into Greece from the land of the Hyperboreans – people who live further North than the North wind . . . Hercules has the reputation of establishing the games and of calling the games 'Olympic'. He founded the practice that the games should be held every fifth year, because he and his brothers were five in number. Some say that it was in Olympia that Zeus wrestled with Cronus himself for the throne, others that Zeus set up the games in honour of this victory of his. There is a record of other victors, in which Apollo is said to have beaten the competitive god, Hermes, at running and to have beaten Ares at boxing . . .
>
> Pausanias, *Description of Greece*, Book 5, I, x, 1; vi, 6–7, 9–10

Pheidias is thought to have finished his statue of Zeus in about 438 BC – that is, by ancient reckoning, in the third year following the 85th Olympic Games. The Olympiads were the reason that Pheidias had come to work at Olympia: the most celebrated sculptor of his day had been commissioned to make a statue of the king of the gods of Greece for the central shrine at the site of the Greeks' most celebrated festival.

Public festivals, large and small, were a vital part of Greek life. Sometimes they were organized to celebrate a particular event – the 76th Olympiad, for example, was held to mark the defeat of the Persian invasion. Usually, however, festivals were celebrated at regular intervals – the Olympiads taking place every fourth year at a full moon, a week-long religious celebration with accompanying games of racing, jumping, throwing, wrestling and boxing taking place in and around a stadium set beside the sacred precinct of the gods. Under truce, from all around the Mediterranean, each and every city that

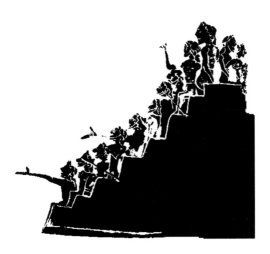

Spectators at the Games. Vase painting from Phasalis, southern Turkey, *c.* 575 BC

was Greek sent athletes: a tense gathering of contentious and competing clans on a fertile plain amidst the pleasant hills that run beside the River Alpheios.

Despite frequent quarrels and on occasion, internecine warfare – in Pheidias' lifetime, Olympia was itself disputed by two local cities and the loser utterly annihilated – the Greeks always understood that they shared a common identity, and believed that to be different from the rest of humankind whom, in imitation of their foreign speech – 'ba–ba, ba–ba, ba–ba' – they called barbarians.

For 700 years, before Roman emperors elbowed their way in, only those whose mother tongue was Greek were allowed to compete at the Olympic Games. On pain of death, slaves and women were not allowed near the games: barbarians could watch but not compete. Trained from boyhood, the Greek athletes arrived from their home cities a year before the festival was due to start, prepared themselves under the eyes of special adjudicators, swore oaths of loyalty to Father Zeus and competed against their fellows as if it were a matter of life or death.

Olympia was never a town, simply a revered shrine set in an enclosure called the Altis. An adjacent stadium whose grassy verges easily accommodated some 20,000 spectators and some other less well-defined areas for throwing competitions and chariot races allowed several athletic events to take place simultaneously. Most of the visitors to the games slept rough along with the athletes; in tents or in the open air, as Hercules and his brothers had done before them. A marketplace was set up to cater for the spectators. Philosophers and other writers gave readings from their work. Groups of city elders, invited to Olympia by the priests of Zeus, held conference together. And at the centre of it all, in the Altis, stood the temples of Zeus and Hera his wife, the shrines of many distant cities, all decked with gleaming plunder and splendid decorations, and Zeus' open altar, a vast archaic mound of blue-grey ash and bone, sending clouds of smoke up into the sky, thank offerings for victories and pledges to secure a triumph. Awarded the palm and crowned with olive, successful athletes were entitled to eat in the house of the priests

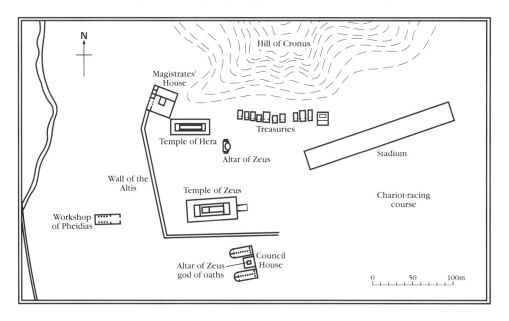

N

Hill of Cronus

Magistrates'
House

Treasuries

Temple of Hera

Altar of Zeus

Stadium

Wall of the
Altis

Temple of Zeus

Chariot-racing
course

Workshop
of Pheidias

Altar of Zeus
god of oaths

Council
House

0   50   100m

The sacred enclosure at Olympia at the time Pheidias was
working on his statue of Zeus, *c.* 440 BC.

of Zeus and to dedicate a statue to the gods. The finest sculptors of Greece made some of these memorials. At the last Olympiad, the 269th, some 3,000 figures of bronze, wood and stone, a millennium of athletes, rulers, warriors and fine and famous horses, stood gathered together in the Altis. And the names of winning athletes, all carved in Greek with their victories listed and signified by little crowns of olive, were cut into the sacred stones like the names of long-forgotten schoolboys, written in gold upon the wooden honour board at school.

There is an obvious temptation to imagine that this ancient world was similar to the modern institutions which have copied from it. The only real connection, however, is the appropriation of some names and a handful of carefully sanitized customs. The faux-Greek manners so assiduously cultivated during the last century, which are still a part of the modern Olympic Games, are now seen to have been a particularly threadbare version of the ancient world: the reality of ancient Olympia and its sacred games was well removed from the custom and belief of nineteenth-century Christendom. Olympia, indeed, was finally closed, after some 1,100 years of activity, upon the orders of a Christian emperor.

Most early Christians clearly saw that before the Kingdom of God could come into being on this earth, most popular notions of sacredness and holiness in the classical world would have to be changed. The Greeks did not differentiate between the sacred and profane world in the same way that Christianity came to do. Enormous numbers of gods lay deep in the classical landscape, at the hearth of every home, at the corner of every field, at every smoking altar, by every tree and stone, at every festival and bacchanalia. Pagan temples were not considered as places for their worship, simply as their local dwellings. Many of these gods were hardly worshipped at all; some were feared, some were shunned, others largely ignored. Together, though, they made up a far fuller pantheon than the realms of the saints and the virgins, and this pantheon underlaid classical society. To change, to redefine this understanding of sacredness , implied a reordering of this society. Pagan festivals therefore were abhorred not simply because they honoured false gods, but because they were central to the classical culture, an order that the Christians had fought so long and hard to overcome.

Most Greek city states promoted a variety of popular festivals both for the glory of the gods and for the good of the cities and their people. Just as the strength of each city's athletes was regarded as part of civic wealth and a sign of harmony, of blessing from the gods, so too was the fertility of its citizens. Brides were often married at public expense, and might be feted like victorious athletes. Strength and sexuality alike were seen as civic assets and were bound by a plethora of convention, both religious and secular together. Powerful pagan festivals like the Olympiads promised fertility, civic strength, community with the gods and, at least to all free male citizens, entertainment, enjoyment and a common bonding.

A powerful part of their redefinition of this most ancient world was the Christians' attitude to the human body. Nudity, which was usual in classical athletic competition, was now seen as an incitement to lewd behaviour, a distraction for the eye from gazing towards heaven. At Olympia, of course, for more than 1,000 years, Greek athletes had competed against each other wearing little more than the hopes of their home towns.

With his fellow sculptors, Pheidias epitomized the millenial Greek love affair with the human body. They spent their lives looking long and hard at the naked body and representing its transient beauty in admiring images of bronze and stone. As you walk through museum galleries and observe Greek sculpture changing through the centuries, you witness the emergence, the creation, of a specifically Greek figure, and one different from anything the world had seen before – a figure that is still within the modern world, as our responses to the Parthenon still prove. In this, statues of trained athletes played a key role; later on, their victorious physiques would be fitted on the portraits of Roman generals and subsequently on the likes of Napoleon and George Washington as well. The generation before Pheidias had made the first statues of athletes at their games, flexed, stretching statues, whose muscles reflected the skills which the athletes had spent such time in practising, and the sculptor's eyes so subtly observed. By Pheidias' day, many sculptors understood the difference between the figure of a man trained to throw the discus or the javelin and that of a runner, in the same way that an eighteenth-century gentleman could sum up the potential of a horse.

The ancient sculptors also understood the processes of aging, the thickening trunk, the changing pose, and produced heroic portraits of middle age. Great Zeus, as everybody knew, threw thunderbolts like javelins, and was usually represented as a bearded man in middle age. We may imagine Pheidias' sculpture of him, then, sitting squarely on his throne with a spare solid body, well-muscled around the pelvis and the pectorals, with a golden cloak thrown over a shining solid shoulder of pure ivory.

TEMPLE AND THRONE

Repeating local gossip, Pausanius relates that when the temple of Zeus' wife, the goddess Hera, was being renovated at Olympia, the mummy of a long-dead soldier was found lying high up on its beams, where he had crawled for protection after being wounded in the final battle between two local towns for the control of Olympia and its games. A battle, so Pausanius relates, that was fought out in the Olympic stadium, in front of a multitude of spectators who had come expecting to see the sacred games.

Both Pheidias' Zeus and the great temple, so people said, had been built from the spoils taken by the people of Elis when they annihilated their rivals in this war; the temple's architect was also said to be a citizen of victorious Elis. But the sheer wealth of the statue alone – over a ton of gold and similar amounts of African ivory – makes it unlikely that the plunder of a single local town could have yielded funds for such a lavish project, and we must therefore imagine that, like the buildings on the Athenian Acropolis, this wealth was drawn from a variety of sources; some Persian plunder perhaps, and partly from the income that the games brought to the people of the fertile Peloponnesian plain. At all events, the product of this extraordinary activity is clear enough; the creation of a national symbol at the very seat of Greece. In every way, therefore, it was a great advantage to the host city, Elis, and it is hardly surprising that drawings of the great Zeus appear upon that city's silver coinage.

As for the house of this amazing symbol, as Pausanius described it: 'Its height up to the pediment is sixty-eight feet, its breadth ninety-five feet, and its length two hundred and thirty . . . The roof-tiles are not made of baked earth, but of Pantelic marble worked to the shape of tiles.'

At Olympia, good building stone was always scarce. Many of the competing cities that built small stone shrines inside the sacred enclosure brought their own stone and terracotta to the site. Zeus' temple, though, was made of local rock, an unsuitable porous limestone studded with sea shells, which had to be finely plastered with a hard white gesso to hold its shape. The plaster today has all but disappeared and left the rough stones blank, bald and strangely grey. A similar temple dedicated to Hera at Paestum in southern Italy, perhaps the best preserved of all ancient temples, shows that in comparison with the later Parthenon at Athens Zeus' temple would have seemed a heavy, rather solid-looking building, if cast in a very splendid Doric order.

In their heyday, temples such as Zeus' did not stand undecorated as they do today, in ruin. Like the sacred precinct of the Altis all around it, the building was hung with valuable dedications and offerings, many of them personal mementoes of famous battles, of great kings and heroes. Our ancient Baedeker, Pausanius, who saw the building at the height of its fortune, describes some of them:

> Of the dedications which are inside the temple or in the porch, there is the throne of Arimnestos, the king of Eretria, who was the first foreigner to make a dedication to Olympian Zeus, and there are bronze horses of Kynisca, the symbols of Olympic victory.

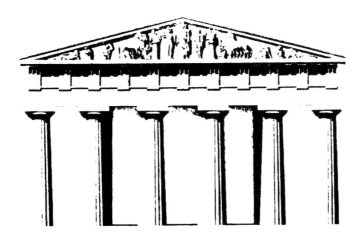

The eastern façade of the temple of Zeus. Reconstruction from Curtius/Adler, 1881

(These are smaller than real horses and stand in the porch on the right as one enters.) There is also the bronze-plated tripod on which, before the invention of the table, the garlands for the winners were displayed. There are statues of emperors . . . Inside the temple there are twenty-five bronze shields too which are what the armed men carry in their race. And there are other monuments standing . . .

As for the building itself, Pausanius is brief:

The style of the temple is Doric and outside it there is a colonnade . . . Pillars stand within the temple, and inside there are porticoes above and the way to the statue is via these. A winding staircase up to the roof has also been made.

Description of Greece, Book 5, I, xii, 5, 8; x, 2–3, 10

And so you came into the presence of the god himself, seated on a vast throne that was so studded with jewellery and mythic incident that ancient scribes generally spilled more ink describing its detail than they did in delineating the features of the unfathomable figure that sat upon it.

The throne is ornate with its gold and jewels, ornate too with its ebony and ivory. There are pictures of animals painted on it and there are worked images: there are four Victory figures in the shape of dancing women at each foot of the throne, and there are a further two at the base of each foot. On each of the two front legs are the Theban children snatched by the sphinxes and below the sphinxes Apollo and Artemis are shooting down the children of Niobe. Between the legs of the throne there are four bars, each one stretching from foot to foot. On the first bar as you approach there are seven images – no-one knows how the eighth disappeared. Perhaps they are pictures of ancient contests, because contests for boys had not been invented in Pheidias' day. People say that the figure tying a ribbon round his head looks like Pantarces. Pantarces, they say, was a teenager from Elis and was Pheidias' boyfriend. Pantarces was also the winner of the wrestling contest for boys in the eighty-sixth Olympic games. On the other bars is the band of men fighting, together with Hercules, against the Amazons. The number of figures is twenty-nine in all . . . The throne is supported not only by legs, but also by the same number of pillars, positioned between the legs. It is impossible to go under the throne . . . There are screens, built like walls, to keep people out . . . [there follows a long description of the decoration on the screens] . . . On the highest parts of the throne, above the head of the statue, Pheidias made the three Graces on one side and the three Seasons on the other. In poetry these six are named among Zeus' daughters. Homer wrote in the *Iliad* that the Seasons were also entrusted with heaven, like guards of a king's court. The stool, which people in Attica call a *thranion*, has golden lions and the battle between Theseus and the Amazons in relief on it – the Athenians' first brave deed that was not directed against their own race. On the pedestal that supports both the throne and the rest of the decoration surrounding Zeus, there are gold figures: the Sun mounted on his chariot, Zeus and Hera . . . and the Moon driving what I take to be a horse. But other people say that the goddess is riding on a mule rather than a horse, and they tell a silly story about the mule.

Description of Greece, Book 5, I, xi, 2–4, 7–8

In Pausanius' time, another singular treasure hung behind the throne framing the figure of the god; a great curtain, in all probability the veil of the Holy Ark, plundered from the Temple at Jerusalem and offered here to Zeus, the god of victories:

In Olympia there is a woollen curtain, dedicated by Antiochus, adorned with Assyrian embroidery and dyed with Phoenician purple . . . This curtain is not pulled upwards to the roof, as happens at the temple of Artemis at Ephesus, but drops down to the ground by the means of cords.

Description of Greece, Book 5, I, xii, 4

The design of the pavement in front of the statue was unique; a shallow pool of oil that served to bar most visitors' approach to the god, and aid the conservation of the ivory. As Pausanius describes it:

The part of the floor in front of the statue is paved in black stone, not white. A border of Parian marble runs round the black paving to hold in the olive oil when it pours out. For olive oil does the statue at Olympia good – it is olive oil that stops the ivory from being damaged by the dank atmosphere of the Altis. On the Acropolis in Athens it is not olive oil but water that preserves the ivory statue called 'The Parthenos'; because of its very great height, the Acropolis is dry and so the ivory statue needs water or moisture. When I asked in Epidauros why they did not pour either water or olive oil on the Asclepius [another composite colossal statue], the attendants at the sanctuary told me that the statue of the god

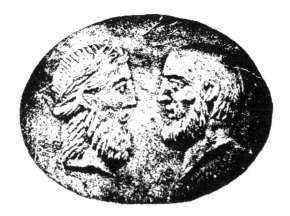

The Zeus faces his creator, Pheidias. Two traditional portraits cut on a Roman gemstone, after Richter/Smith, 1984

and the throne were made over a well . . . [There follows a discussion on whether tusks are to be described as teeth or horns, after which:] . . . In my view, the Greeks who brought ivory back from India and Africa in order to build statues must have prided themselves on honouring the gods to a very great degree, and have been lavish in their expenditure.

And the great statue of Olympia, one of the world's wonders, was made, Pausanias tells us, by Pheidias:

An inscription below Zeus' feet bears witness that Pheidias was the sculptor: 'Athenian Pheidias, the son of Charmides, made me.'

Description of Greece, Book 5, 1, xi, 10–11; xii, 3; x, 2

PHEIDIAS

In the early 1800s, the Elgin Marbles, works that were often claimed to have been by Pheidias himself, were first exhibited to great acclaim in London (this was not the universal view, however, Lord Byron, for example, noting that Lord Elgin had wasted 'useless thousands on his Pheidian freaks'). All of a sudden, Pheidias loomed large in the London fog as a tangible presence, a true artist of the Western school, a Man of Genius. Such visions were easily fostered by apt quotations from ancient authors, texts that were generally held to hold simple and straightforward truths in them, in the manner of British newspapers; Pheidias, the Roman Cicero had written, 'had a particularly remarkable image of beauty in his mind. At this he gazed and on this he concentrated, and he directed his art and his hand to make a likeness of it'. So many ancient authors indeed had written about Pheidias and his work that many European critics now began to follow in their footsteps. They talked about 'the spirit of the man' and of the strains and stresses of his career as if he were as close as Delacroix or Sir Frederick Leighton.

Suddenly, the ancient Greek appeared as a vivid genius in a light-filled studio with a mallet in his hand and inspiration in his head. By the 1880s a Cambridge professor had written an entire book on the man and his art in terms that treated those two literary mirages as if they were the tangible products of a Paris studio: 'The works of Pheidias are ever serene,' he wrote, 'They have coupled with all their greatness the truly Greek element of grace, in which the works of Michelangelo are sometimes wanting.' For most of the last 100 years, certainly for many of those great historians who have painted our broad view of ancient history, this has remained a popular image of Pheidias and his *oeuvre*. As far as anyone can tell, however, the truth of all of this is that not a single authentic piece of Pheidias' own work has survived. We have advanced just far enough in our understanding to recognize that ancient reality was more diverse and more elusive than the Cambridge professor could ever have imagined.

The tremendous leap of imagination that had sent Europe wandering through this Paris of the past had its beginnings in the mid-18th century, in the writings of one J. J. Winckelmann, a German archaeologist and art historian. 'There had been known before him', Madame de Staël later commented on Winckelmann's career, 'learned men who might be consulted like books; but no one had, if I may say so, made himself a pagan for the purpose of penetrating antiquity.' 'Enthusiasm', wrote the highly influential critic Walter Pater in the 1860s in his essay on the German art historian, ' in the broad Platonic sense . . . was the secret of his divinatory power over the Hellenic world. This enthusiasm, dependent as it is to a great degree on bodily temperament, has a power of re-enforcing the purer emotions of the intellect with an almost physical excitement. That his affinity with Hellenism was not merely intellectual, that the subtler threads of temperament were woven in it, is proved by his romantic, fervent friendships with young men . . . bringing him into contact with the pride of human form, and staining his thought with its bloom, perfected his reconciliation to the spirit of Greek sculpture.'

Winckelmann's influence stemmed from his ability to project his own sexual fantasies onto the silent sculptures with great conviction and then to set them acting as characters upon a stage, playing in an extraordinary, novel brew of sexuality, religiosity and humanist sentiment. Here he is in full flow, in 1755, animating the Apollo Belvedere, one of his favourite sculptures, and a popular entertainment for foreign visitors to Rome: 'His height is above that of man and his attitude declares his divine grandeur. An eternal springtime, like that which reigns in the happy fields of Elysium, clothes his body with the charms of youth and softly shines on the proud structure of his limbs . . . Like the soft tendrils of the vine, his beautiful hair flows round his head, as if gently brushed by the breath of the zephyr. It seems to be perfumed by the essence of the gods, and tied with charming care by the hands of the Graces . . . From admiration I pass to ecstasy, I feel my breast dilate and rise as if I were filled with the spirit of prophecy; I am transported to Delos and the sacred groves of Lycia . . . the statue seems to come alive like the beautiful creation of Pygmalion, in the presence of this miracle of art, I forget the whole universe and my soul acquires a loftiness appropriate to its dignity.' It is a pity, perhaps, that such prose has become a part of the roots of that artificial language, that cross between the overheated prose of suppressed sexuality and the chattering of salesmen, with which the modern world discusses the arts. Winckelmann used the sculpture of the Greeks as one would employ the quicksilver of a mirror, to reflect present passions and preoccupation. And in doing that, he has helped obscure the ancient realities underneath.

As for what these were it is most difficult to know. It is particularly difficult, perhaps, in areas where the modern world believes it has found a universal verity; more difficult, that is, on the subject of sexuality than, say, politics. It may be nothing more than an attempted smear on one of the most powerful images of antiquity that an early Christian writer tells us Pheidias inscribed 'I love Pantarkes' on one of the fingers of his Zeus. Pantarkes was a young runner, and a victor at the Olympiad when Pheidias was working there. Yet fragments of erotic drawings found amongst the debris of the artists' workshop at Olympia suggest that the environment in which Pheidias worked was no different from others of his age, when homosexual activity was frequently pictured and discussed. For critics like Winckelmann such spare facts readily form themselves into pictures of a golden age, for others they show a barren world aching for Christian enlightenment; neither of these attitudes help us to recover the past, other than to reinforce the notion that ancient attitudes and opinions may have been as diverse as these modern ones. One thing, though, is sure. There is a common factor shared by the surviving fragments of this past, these fragments of art and architecture and the writing that surrounded this elusive Pheidias; and that is that the lives of men like him were absorbed in a terrific intensity of thought and vision, and a passion for a particular perfection.

As for contemporary reactions to the man and his work, a clue can be gained from the common tale that Pheidias was twice indicted for stealing some of the precious materials with which he made his two gigantic statues; at Athens, he was accused of taking some of the ivory scales from the snake that stood beside Athena Parthenos; at Olympia, of stealing some of the gold of Zeus' cloak. The simplest explanation is that Pheidias was a crook as well as a sculptor. What this meant in terms of ancient Greek society may have been very different to what we generally mean today. The government of Athens after all had raised the funds for building both the Parthenon and Pheidias' Athena Parthenos by similar acts of embezzlement; by appropriating the property of the smaller states which had originally joined in coalition with their powerful neighbour to fight the Persian armies. Pheidias' two crimes, however, are never described as civil offences, but as acts of impiety; it is said that he took the possessions of the gods.

Here Pheidias' relationship with his statues becomes ambivalent; after all, he had created those two deities from whom he was now accused of stealing. It had been his workforce that had transferred and transformed the states' ivory and bullion, had taken it from the city coffers to the temples of the gods. In his writings on the Seven Wonders, Philo of Byzantium understands the contradiction:

> The execution of the skill is as incredible as the image of Zeus is holy. The work brings praise, and the immortality brings honour.

Philo 3, 3

Where, then, did this leave Pheidias? When he first revealed his two powerful new visions of deity, his audience seems to have felt uneasy, felt that by the very power of the image he had made them the god-maker had set himself halfway between heaven and earth. Pheidias' very success was also an impiety: he had indeed taken something from the gods.

As far as is known, no such difficulties had ever afflicted other earlier god-makers. By Pheidias' day, however, the Greeks were in the process of removing themselves from those most ancient ways of thought and, viewing the situation from other points of view as was their wont, had sensed the ambiguity of the sculptor's role. Perhaps the reason why the great Zeus, the foremost of the Seven Wonders and the single most famous sculpture of the classical world, was not much copied or imitated was because such work was in itself thought to be impious. In making a new image of the gods in the shape of human beings, Pheidias seems also to have invented a new image for humankind as well. Perhaps an artist can do no more than that.

FORGING ZEUS

> There is a building outside the Altis and it is called the workshop of Pheidias. It was here that Pheidias worked on each part of the statue.
>
> Pausanias, *Description of Greece,* Book 5, 1, xv, 1

Located by archaeologists late in the last century, Pheidias' workshop was excavated in the 1950s, and the finds were extraordinary. Here we can come as close to Pheidias as is humanly possible. Tools were found; tools to work all the materials used for the Zeus, and even some fragments of the ivory that Pheidias was accused of taking. That these objects were of Pheidias' own place and time was proven by the fragments of pottery that were found in association with the tools. One of these, a small broken cup, had the words *Pheidio eimi* – 'I belong to Pheidias' scratched upon its base. There were others too, with other names upon them, quite possibly the everyday cups of Pheidias' co-workers. Further fragments of pottery, some fine painted shards and some erotic sketches scratched onto a black ground, show that they were made in the 430s BC. This alone settled a lengthy scholarly debate about which of the two colossi, the Athena Parthenos or the Zeus, had been made first; though placed inside an older temple, the Zeus was Pheidias' last known work.

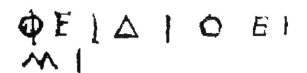

Pheidio eimi, 'I belong to Pheidias'; the small inscription incised on the base of a pot excavated in Pheidias' Olympia studio

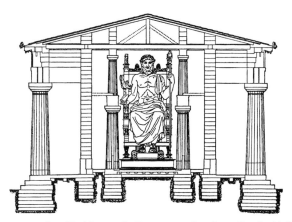

Zeus accommodated in his temple. Reconstruction from Curtius/Adler, 1881

The workshop itself is a fascinating building, great square stone blocks built into massive metre-thick walls, reminding you that the Zeus was also the treasure of the state of Elis. As was the temple, the workshop was a classical Fort Knox. The dimensions of the workshop were the same as those of the interior of the temple, and it was oriented precisely on the selfsame axis, so that it received the same amount and angle of the morning sun. The workshop even had a similar arrangement of columns running through its interior. Here, in all probability, Pheidias solved the problem of lighting his statue in the interior of the dark temple. As the architects of the Lincoln Memorial in Washington, a similarly-seated figure, also came to understand, lighting large statues in small rooms presents great difficulties. When the marble Lincoln was first set in place, the presidential head was seen to disappear into the darkness, and had to be rescued by the judicious lighting of the GEC Corporation. At Olympia, Pheidias was able to mock up the situation of the temple in his workshop, to adjust the height of the lintel of the temple doorway, and to design the unique pool that lay in front of the colossus and reflected sunlight from the doorway up to the god's face. As at the Parthenon, in this workshop we see evidence of an extraordinary intensity and care.

The tools found in the workshop are mostly very small but precisely suitable for working the precious materials of which the statues were made. Here we see that the world's largest indoor statue, this chryselephantine treasure, was made with a jeweller's precision, and mostly with traditional ways and means. The ivory-working chisels that were found in the workshop, for example, are virtually identical to those used in Cretan ivory studios a thousand years earlier, evidence of skills imported from the most ancient centres of civilization far to the East. Homer says that in his Greece, long before the days of Pheidias, women cut and tinted ivory in their homes. Pheidias took this modest tradition, and transformed it into a grand public medium. Homer further tells that in his days, ivory was imported through royal barter or as gifts. Organized trade, which would have been essential for the large amounts of ivory that Pheidias required for his Zeus, started in the centuries immediately before Pheidias' own lifetime. Rhinoceros horn and even water buffalo bone was found inside his workshop; these and most of Zeus' ivory would have come from Africa through Egypt. Philo of Byzantium hints that mother Nature herself had a hand in providing the skin of Zeus:

> But if Zeus is embarrassed to be called the son of Pheidias, skill was the mother of his representation. Nature produced elephants and Africa abounds in herds of elephants just so that Pheidias could cut the tusks of the wild animals and work the matter with his hands into the form that he intended.

Philo 3, 2

Some have said that the Greeks manipulated their ivory in ways that are now lost, stretching and bending it until it assumed the shapes they wanted. If this is so, Pheidias' craftsmen may have employed the large ceramic moulds that were excavated in the workshop as ivory moulds. A possible alternative is that they were the moulds used to cast the golden sheets that Pheidias and his workers employed for Zeus' cloak. Small hammers and tiny iron drills were found that could also have been used in this gold work. Other moulds were certainly made to serve as forms in which were cast the elegant glass lilies that, Pausanius says, decorated the god's great robes. The archaeologists found many iridescent fragments of these lilies, made of white seedy glass, which fitted some of the smaller moulds precisely. Here then is the final irony. The statue is completely described, in words, in praise and in poems. Even the tools, the workshops and the very materials of the statue have been found. More recent excavations have given us a taste of the splendour of these elephantine masterpieces. They were, it seems, not in fearfully bad taste, not vulgar decoration, as previous generations have uncharitably suggested, but careful delicate oppositions of form and texture, as fine as anything the ancients ever made. So the setting is there for us , but the thing itself, the great glittering jewel sitting on its gilded throne, has gone.

The architecture too has all but disappeared. Zeus' temple nowadays is but a mass of tumbled columns. The great rectangle of the temple platform, though, stands straight and firm, a tribute to Libon, its architect, and his understanding of the site. Earthquakes and thunderbolts, both attributes of Zeus, still visit Olympia with regularity, as the stricken pines and fallen columns clearly show. Following one such earthquake in 170 BC, the temple and the statue were badly shaken. Some of the columns had to be dismantled and completely rebuilt. Both façades too were dismantled, and some of the marvellous sculptures that they held had to be restored and replaced. The gold and ivory of Zeus was also cracked; the repair of the statue was undertaken by a sculptor called Damaphon of Messene, who for his pains, seems to have suffered a similar literary fate to that of Daniele da Volterra, who painted bloomers on some of the figures of Michelangelo's Last Judgement.

By this time, the statue was an old familiar masterpiece, like Zeus himself, part of the eternal landscape and regarded as much with affection as with awe. In the second century AD the satirist Lucian of Samosata, using the great old statue as a symbol in a sermon on the state, inadvertently tells us something valuable about the statue's structure – apparently a complex arrangement of inner scaffolding. Kingship, writes Lucian, is all a sham, like those colossal figures that Pheidias and some other later sculptors made.

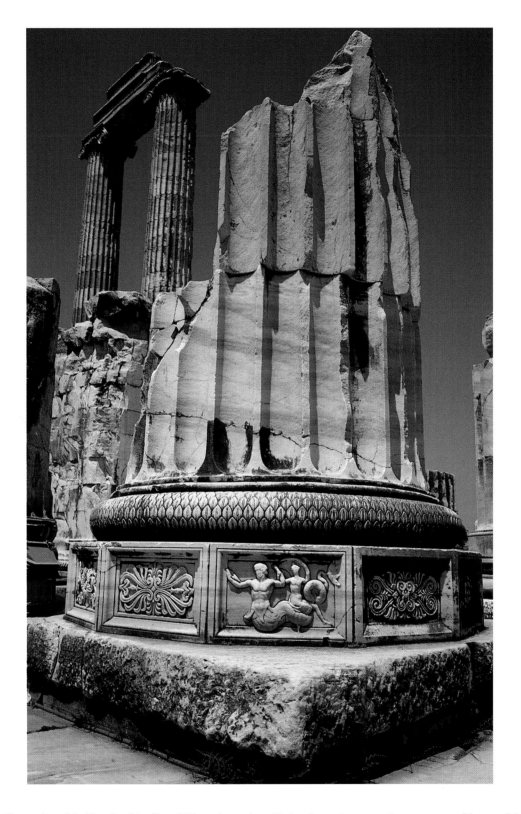

1. These ruins of the Temple of Apollo at Didyma in southern Turkey, begun in 313 BC, give a rare taste of the age of the Seven Wonders. One of the architects who worked at this majestic temple, at once exquisite and gigantic, was also engaged at the Temple of Artemis at Ephesus, one of the Seven Wonders of the World

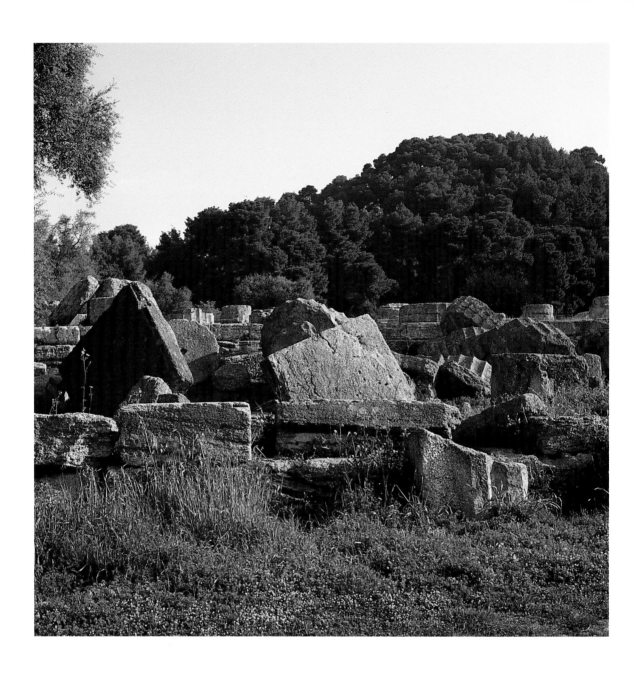

2. The ruins of the Temple of Zeus at Olympia. The temple that housed Pheidias' statue of Zeus was one of the greatest Greek Doric temples, and a wonder in its own right. Started about 468 BC with funds provided from plunder taken in local wars, the temple was quickly built of a soft local stone which, now it has lost its stucco coating, is slowly weathering away

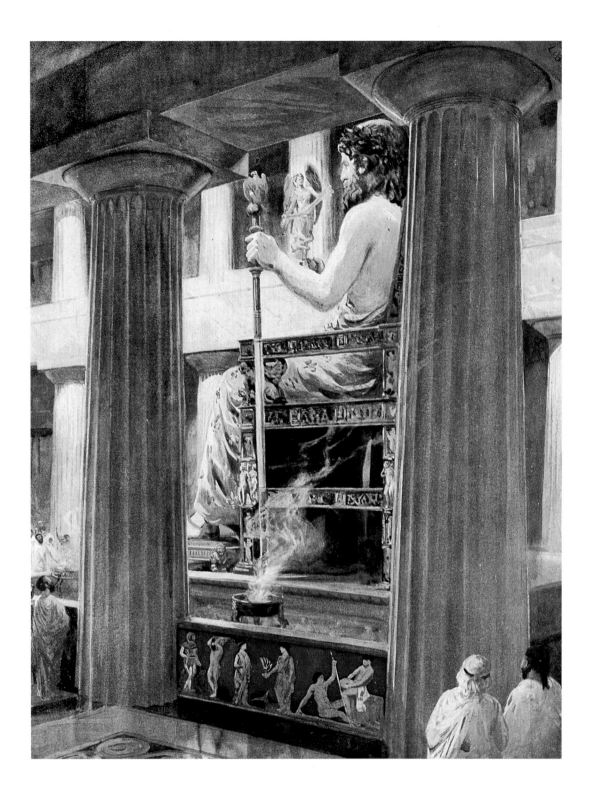

3. A reconstruction of the statue of Zeus. The great statue, perhaps the greatest single wonder of the classical age, was carefully described by many ancient writers. This watercolour by Charles M. Sheldon is one of a set of paintings of the Seven Wonders, commissioned in 1922, which still embodies popular notions of how they once appeared. In reality, the temple's interior was rather gloomy; the statue, a darkly glittering mass of ivory and gold

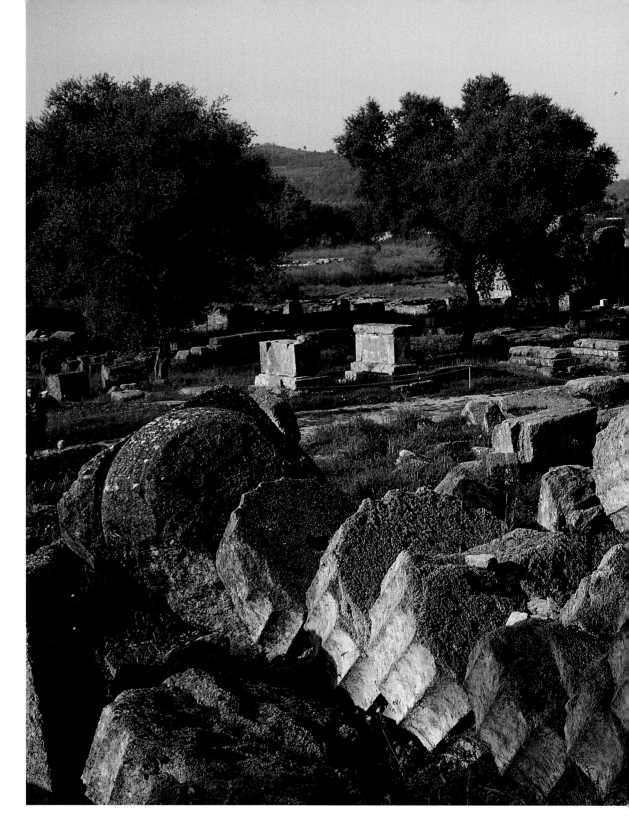

4. The Temple of Zeus, the god of thunderbolts and earthquakes, was itself felled by an earthquake in the 6th century AD.
Buried deep in river silt, these fallen columns were excavated by a pioneering archaeological expedition of the late 19th century,
led by Ernst Curtius of the German Archaeological Institute

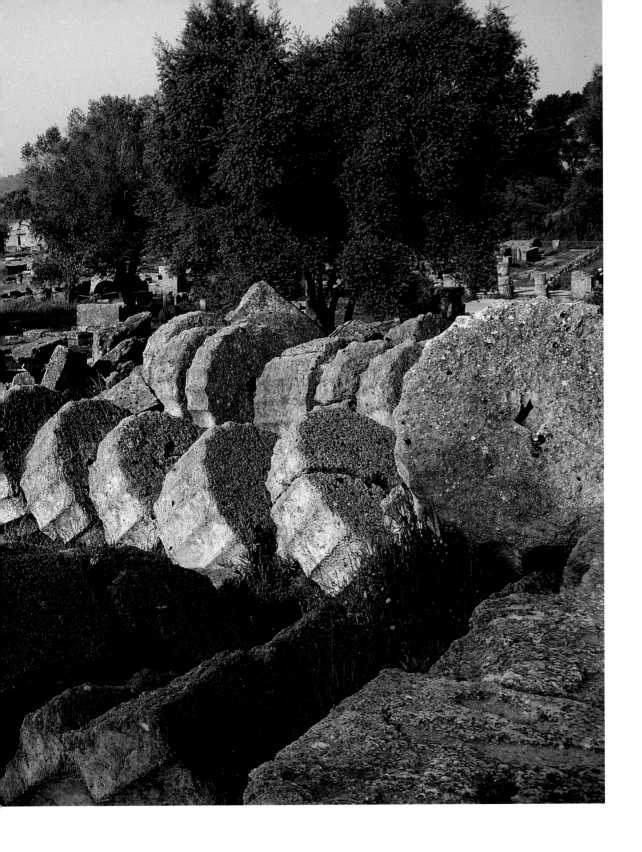

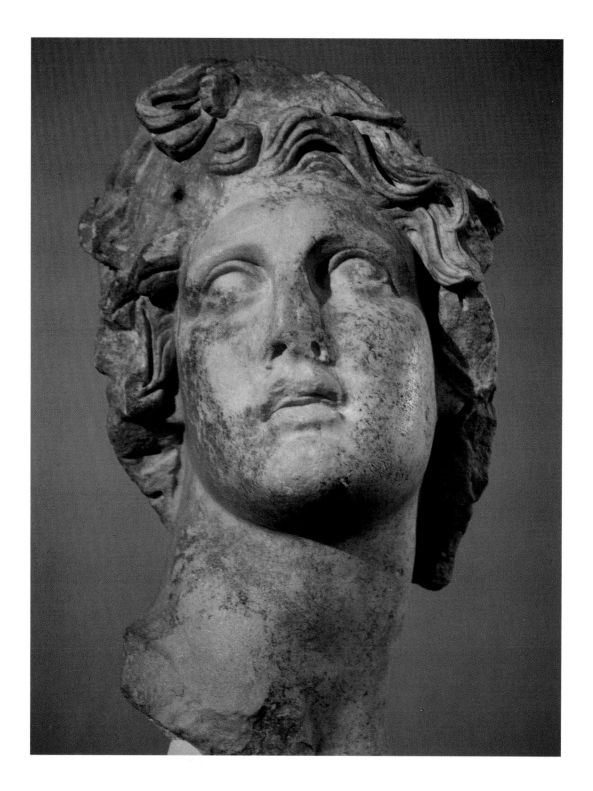

5. A marble head of Alexander the Great found at Rhodes. Holes drilled around this huge head show that it once sported a gilded sunburst like those usually worn in sculptures of Helios, the god of the Colossus. The features of the face, its upward glance and turned neck show the influence of Lysippus' portraits of Alexander the Great, and suggest that Alexander's features also graced the great bronze Helios that was one of the Seven Wonders of the World. Made about the same time as the Colossus, this fine sculpture, about twice life size, is now in Rhodes Archaeological Museum

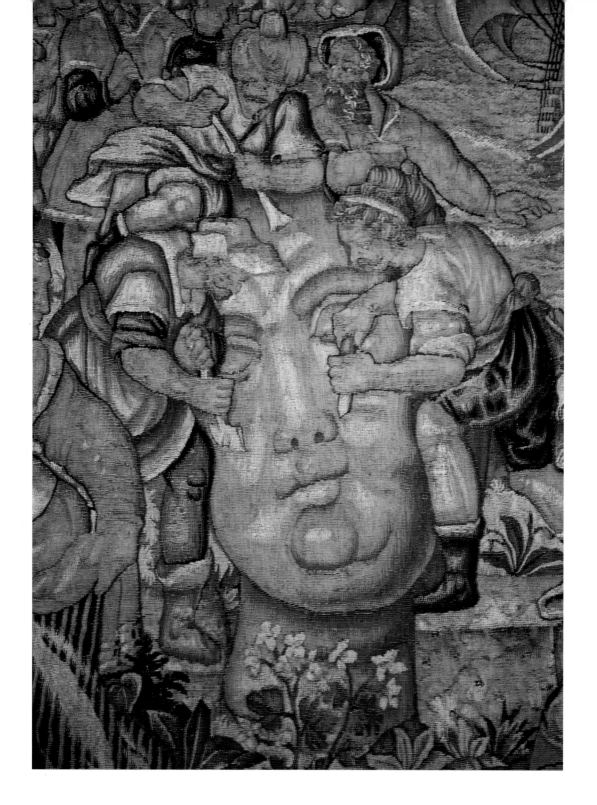

6. The destruction of the Colossus of Rhodes. Engravings of the Seven Wonders of the World made in 1572, after drawings by the Dutch artist Martin von Heemskerck, stand at the beginning of the West's traditional images of the Seven Wonders. In this Brussels tapestry, preserved in the Musée Réattu at Arles, Heemskerck's pretty picture of a group of antique sculptors finishing the head of the Colossus, has been transformed into a frightening image of Turkish soldiers demolishing the great bronze statue, a reflection of the fear that ran through Europe following the Turkish invasions of the early 17th century

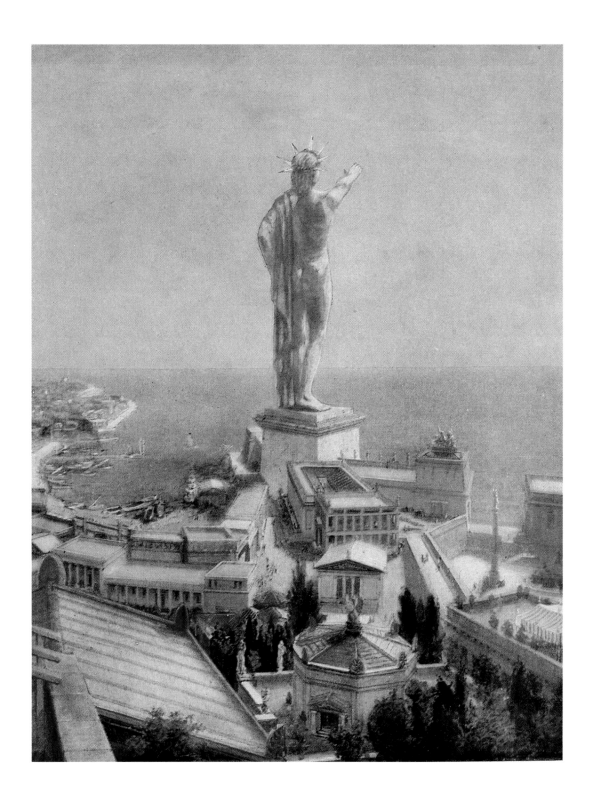

7. A reconstruction of the Colossus of Rhodes: a watercolour by M. Kupka, from the set of pictures of the Seven Wonders commissioned in 1922. Though the artist has drawn the supposed location of the port of Rhodes with care, both the buildings and the pose of the great statue are imaginary. While it is doubtful that the great bronze sun god really was made in the image of a saluting Roman soldier, we still have no idea of the pose or appearance of this vanished statue

'From the outside, each of those statues is a Poseidon or an exquisite Zeus composed of gold and ivory, holding a thunderbolt or a flash of lightening or a trident in his right hand. But if you bend down and look at what is inside, you will see bars, bolts and nails driven right through, beams and wedges, pitch and clay, and general ugliness of this sort lurking within, not to mention the community of numerous mice and rats that sometimes live there. Kingship is just like that.' (Lucian, *The Dream* or *The Cock*, 24)

In truth, mankind did Olympia far more damage than did the force of nature. In the third century AD, fearing an invasion by the savage Heruli from north Germany, the inhabitants of Olympia turned the Altis into a fortress, demolishing the surrounding buildings, the houses and baths of athletes and officials and using their stones to plug the gaps between the temples' columns and to heighten the sacred walls. But the invaders never came and for a while a sort of peace lay on the site again. In the next century, however, Constantine, the first Christian emperor, ordered the gold to be taken from the pagan temples, an order that probably caused the stripping of the two great works of Pheidias in Athens and Olympia down to wood and ivory. During the rest of the century 'in order to deny all the ruined [i.e. pagan] men the opportunity of offending' the gods were under constant threat, the emperors issuing a series of edicts, at first to little effect, 'that, with immediate effect, temples were to be closed, in all places and in all cities' and 'Let superstition cease, let the madness of sacrificing be abolished' (Constantine, *Codex Theodosianus*, XVI, 10, 2, 4).

Most holy emperors, remove your temple treasures. Chop them all down. May your money-making fire and the flame of your metal-works roast those gods. Put all the temple gifts at your own disposal, and control them yourselves. Once the temples have been destroyed, you will be carried forward by the virtue of a greater god.

Firmicius Maternus, *The Error of Profane Religions*, 28, 6

The gods that had lived so joyfully in the minds of men for millennia were not easily dislodged. In AD 381 and 385 severe penalties were enacted for the offering of pagan sacrifice. In AD 393, an edict of the Emperor Theodosius brought the celebration of all pagan festivals, including that of the Olympic Games, to an end and a few years later, the same emperor ordered that 'If there are still any idols in the temples and shrines which have been, or are being, worshipped by pagans anywhere, then may they be torn down from where they are'. In 424 he ordered the burning of the sacred Altis and the plundering of the temples of Zeus and Hera. Shortly afterwards, the firm foundations of Pheidias' studio were serving to support a splendid church. Where the sun had once shone down onto Pheidias' first reflecting pool, there shone the light of God, through a narrow window in the apse behind the altar screen.

At the end, however, Zeus himself destroyed his temple; in the sixth century AD a major earthquake tumbled its columns and cracked its walls and sent the great marble reliefs of the two pediments crashing down to the ground. Armies invading from the east, and plagues as well, then devastated the population of the Peloponnese. Engulfing landslides completed the extinguishing of Olympia. The River Alpheus, carrying huge quantities of yellow silt brought down from the untended terraces of decaying and deserted olive groves and vineyards, laid its alluvium so thickly on the site that the little village there was abandoned, and the ancient name was lost. Its memory confined to the pages of European history books for more than 1,000 years, Olympia itself was recovered late in the 18th century by an English traveller who spotted the inner walls of Zeus' temple sticking out of the gentle pasture beside the lazy Alpheus, and recognized them for what they once had been.

HAUNTING BYZANTIUM

The fate of the great statue was not that of the temple. That most ardent dismantler of the pagan world, the Emperor Theodosius, had appointed an antiquarian as his court chamberlain, a post that gave this official, a eunuch called Lausus, great influence within the empire. Lausus used his power to make a museum in his house in Constantinople.

In itself, there was nothing new in Lausus' hobby. The habit of plundering the classical world to edify the newly-founded city of Constantinople had been started at the city's foundation, a century earlier, by the court officials of Constantine himself. By Lausus' day, and greatly to the dismay of the Fathers of the Church, 'nude brass statues of the most exquisite workmanship' stood everywhere inside the city's walls. The fathers need not have been concerned; the pagan order had been quite destroyed, and the gathered statues stood, as they do today, inside their own small universe, ghosts from another time and place. From the windows of the courtiers' palaces, beside the Imperial Hippodrome, you would have seen row upon row of them culled from every city of the east. Along the centre of the Hippodrome, dividing the two sides of the circuit, stood the most curious of the city's wonders, all of them overshadowed by what once had been the largest obelisk ever to have been raised in ancient Egypt. Shortened now and standing on a pedestal bearing scenes of Theodosius' court, the obelisk was said by some to have been secretly set on four bronze crabs because the city had been founded in the year of the 276th Olympiad, when the sun was in the constellation of the bowman and at an hour dominated by the crab.

Close by, in the courtyard of the Imperial church, stood an enormous twisted tripod. Snake-headed, cast in bronze and brought from Apollo's shrine at Delphi, its archaic text told that this was the very tripod, that holder of the sacred fire, which the Greeks had dedicated to the god Apollo after defeating the Persian armies in 479 BC. In Constantinople, so it is said, its three snake heads had been plumbed so that they spewed refreshment at festivals; water and two kinds of wine, one white, one red. And all around them stood the ancient statues of bronze and marble, courtesans and warriors, colossi and lifelike nudes, and all of them half-feared, half-loved and half-derided by the semi-Christian city-dwellers, who sometimes thought that some held luck within them or, perhaps, the trapped souls of ancient gods themselves, petrified by beams of moonlight into marble.

Near the Hippodrome stood a cavernous public bath, the Baths of Zeuxippus. There, celebrated statues had been placed in tableaux like a modern waxworks, showing incidents from the Trojan War and stories from the *Iliad* and *Odyssey*. But what a waxworks! It was as if the *Mona Lisa*, Piero's *Resurrection*, Gainsborough's *Blue Boy* and Picasso's *Guernica* had been gathered into a single hall, in a single quarter of a single city. Theodosius' punitive edicts allowed the final emptying of the pagan temples of the eastern empire, and Lausus, it seems, had been on hand to take advantage of the opportunity to make a museum for himself. Opposite Zeuxippus' Baths, right beside the Hippodrome, he built a brick palace whose ruins still stand. Today in a civic garden patrolled by rumbling trams you can easily trace the floor of his great round reception hall and, beyond, the long high gallery that held his prized collection from the temples. Once, for a brief while, some of the ancient world's best-known works were lined down these walls: the Lindian Athena from the isle of Rhodes; the Hera from Samos; Praxiteles' own Aphrodite from Cnidos – such a lifelike celebration of the female nude that, as a poet had said, when the goddess herself saw it, she had blushed and said 'Help! when did Praxiteles the sculptor see me naked?' And other statues too, of Eros and Cronus, Hera and the other gods. Lausus of course was a Christian, and a good one. He subsidized the publication of pious works, he prayed and he oversaw the destruction of those great old temples that had led men's souls away from God. So all this splendid pagan nudity, this celebration of a fading world, had to be cast in a brand new light. And so it was. Today, we order our museums in terms of the objects' relative significance, and usually this means an order based on age and beauty, so that the objects jointly tell a single story. Lausus similarly arranged his statues according to the certainties of his own time, so together they told of Christian certainties; told how Christian love conquers both busy time and earthly love. And there, high in the darkness in the apse at the end of the gallery dwarfing all the others stood his triumphant Christian god: Pheidias' own Zeus. These days, the spot is marked, inadvertently, by two plane trees as high as the statue's head. In the shade, boot blacks chatter at their work, and a few scribes type out documents for peasant claimants at the local law courts, which are just across the road, as they have always been.

In Lausus' time, of course, Zeus' cloak of gold and lilies had already gone. People who saw the statue standing in the high dark hall saw only its ivory shining in the lamplight. None the less, it must have dominated all else there, just as it had once filled the dreams of ancient Greece. Lausus had been appointed chamberlain in AD 420. Within a decade he had lost his job and with it the opportunity to collect the sweepings of the classical world, so the Zeus must have been dismantled and packed up at that same time. Lausus lived on, though, with his collection after his retirement, and certainly the Zeus survived him for another 40 or so years. In 475, a fire that destroyed half the city probably consumed its 900-year-old timbers. If it did not, the devastating riots that followed in the succeeding decades surely brought it to its end. Zeus, then, sat at the heart of Byzantium for more than half a century – not long perhaps in the life of that extraordinary city but long enough to haunt the city and fill the imagination of its most Christian state, like the ghosts of the 20,000 rioters the army put to death within the nearby Hippodrome.

Even in its temple at Olympia, Pheidias' Zeus had never seemed to arouse the same scorn and apprehension amongst Christians that other pagan idols did. In one way or another, the statue always seems to have been recognized as a portrait of god; latterly, and most significantly for its survival, of the god who ratified the roles of emperors and kings on earth. In Rome, the Emperor Nero had an image of the Zeus, called by its Roman name of Jupiter the Thunderer, painted on the domed ceiling of the throne room of his palace. Later, in Constantinople, another portrait was similarly placed above the imperial throne but by this time, in this most Christian city, the ancient face was called the face of Christ. Lausus' importation of the original of this imperial icon allowed artists to copy its features anew, and place them, just as the Zeus was placed in the apse of Lausus' sculpture gallery, high up in a thousand churches. Sometimes the Christ/Zeus still sat upon his jewelled throne as he had done at Olympia, sometimes only the head and shoulders were drawn out, but always he had those same distinctive features. 'In the painting,' wrote John of Damascus early in the eighth century, 'he divided the hair into a parting so that his face should not be hidden. For this was the way that the Greeks painted Zeus.' (John of Damascus, *de Imaginibus Oratio*, III, 387).

The use of this pagan image as the face of Christ raised many a dark eyebrow amongst the guardians of the faithful, and a miraculous tale, complete with the necessary Gospel parallels, was summoned to explain how this had come to pass. As James Breckenridge, the scholar who first laid out the details of the story, tells it: 'It was just at this time that there originated a legend which has long intrigued historians of Christian art. In the time of Archbishop Gennadius, who was patriarch of Constantinople from 458 to 471, a certain painter made an icon, at the instigation of a pagan, portraying Christ in the likeness of Zeus; the painter's hand and arm withered in consequence of his blasphemous act, but he was healed miraculously through the intercession of Gennadius.' Thus, the image of Zeus received divine sanction for a second time.

Today, as you stand in one of the great Eastern churches, peering up into the dome, it is difficult at first to see how Pheidias' ivory face could have ever become the dark-eyed soul-raker of Byzantium. Then you remember rare images of Zeus' head with its straight nose and centrally parted hair. And you see the metamorphosis: see how Pheidias' calm Zeus was shot through with the light of heaven and the fires of hell, to haunt us as the face of Christ, sitting in judgement.

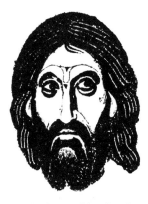

Christ Pantocrator, the mosaic in the dome of the church at Daphni by Athens, *c.* AD 1100

Chapter 2

THE COLOSSUS
OF RHODES

IMAGE AND TRADITION

Rhodes is an island in the sea. It had been hidden below the sea for a long time, but then Helios revealed it, and requested of the gods that the new island be his own. On this island stands a Colossus, one hundred and twenty feet high and representing Helios. The statue is recognizable as being of Helios because it has his distinctive features . . . Perhaps Zeus poured down marvellous wealth on the Rhodians precisely so that they could honour Helios in spending it on the erection of the statue of the god, layer upon layer, from the ground up to the heavens . . . Little by little he [the sculptor] reached the goal of his dream . . . he made his god equal to *the* god. He produced a work outstanding in its boldness, for on the world he set a second Helios facing the first.

Philo 4, 1; 4, 2; 4, 6

The eponymous capital of one of the larger Greek islands, Rhodes has two main harbours; a commercial port, and a smaller one, used nowadays by fishermen and yacht owners. These harbours are divided by a mole running at an angle to the ancient coastline. Ancient blocks in its foundations show that this mole was a part of the first plan of the ancient city, a symmetrical extension of the regular net of roads laid out on the slopes above the bay. Co-founded by three older towns in 408 BC, this purpose built city was an entire success. At the heart of the ancient sea lanes of the eastern Mediterranean, the island city soon established itself as a major trading port, commanding substantial fleets of war ships, and was, as circumstances required, a powerful adversary or ally. The smaller harbour, called Mandraki, the sheep fold, was a renowned shipyard; the larger harbour served as an emporium between Europe and the East. Over the millenia, the rich haven attracted the attentions of a succession of ambitious invaders. It was taken by Arab armies at the ending of antiquity, retaken by the Byzantines and then the Genoese. For two bloody and embattled centuries, Rhodes served as the grim fortress of the Knights Hospitaller, a crusading order from Western Europe, until in 1522 it surrendered to the Turkish armies. And all this time, the city was haunted by the sovereign image of its ancient statue.

> Why, man, he doth bestride the narrow world
> Like a Colossus; and we petty men
> Walk under his huge legs, and peep about . . .

says Shakespeare's conspiratorial Cassius.

> Bastard Margarelon
> Has Doreus prisoner,
> And stands Colossus-wise waving his beam,
> Upon the pashed corpses of the kings . . .

shouts his Renaissance Agamemnon in a call to arms at the siege of Troy, and paints with his single striding figure, spear in hand, the enduring medieval image of this island city and its embattled Knights, defending its trading harbour and its most Christian city from the terrifying Turks.

No trace of the Colossus, that symbol of the ancient Rhodians' wealth and verve, has ever been discovered. Traditionally, it was said to have stood above the harbour called Mandraki, where today the city's history is celebrated, albeit in strong Italian accents, in diverse buildings that stand around the little harbour. (In the years before the First World War, Rhodes was occupied once more by Italian armies and later 'restored' by Il Duce's administrators, in the manner of a film set, as a holiday home for their king.) The Colossus, it was said, looked out to sea, a solitary male figure whose legs bridged the harbour entrance, with one foot planted on the land and the other on the seaward ending of the ancient mole where nowadays there sits a small round fortress of the Knights Hospitaller, restored too by the island's last Italian occupiers.

Along with Pheidias' Zeus, the visual image of a giant statue bestriding the harbour entrance is one of those rare conceits whose beginnings are precisely known. In the decade before Shakespeare was born, a French artist, Jean Cousin the Younger, made 24 engravings to decorate a four-volume book, *Cosmographie de Levant* by the French geographer André Thevet. Today, such books as these are little known or used. Yet for centuries after their publication they were standard works in the libraries of the universities and noble houses of Europe, a standard source of knowledge before the age of the encyclopedia. A German edition of the *Cosmographie*, complete with the original plates, was issued some 60 years after the French original; the latter being still in use by English scholars a century or more after its first release. In those days, knowledge took a long time to go out of date and books like Thevet's, compilations of new and ancient knowledge, had wide and lasting influence. Thevet's work, for example, gave the English language the words *yam* and *toucan*. And his illustrations also gave the West its traditional image of the Rhodian Colossus.

The idea for this illustration of the open-legged statue came from the reports of travellers, especially from pilgrims who had used the fortress of the Hospitallers of Rhodes as a safe haven on their journey to and from the Holy Land. In the shelter of the Rhodian walls, the image of the giant, protecting statue astride the harbour gates was a talisman,

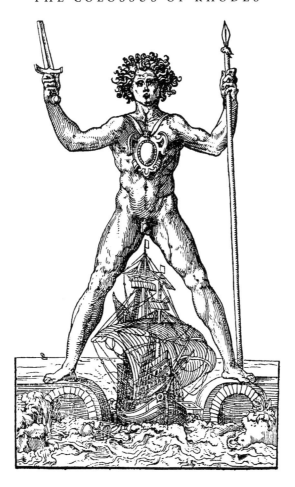

The first image of the striding Colossus: Jean Cousin's woodcut published in Thevet's *Cosmographie de Levant*, Lyon, 1556

and many travellers recorded it. Pictures of the city-fortress of the Knights show its main harbour enclosed by two moles with round fortresses upon them, a chain or wooden bridge blocking the harbour to the Turks. Niccolò di Martoni, a pilgrim lawyer from Capua in southern Italy, wrote down the first recorded version of the tale of the striding Colossus in 1394–5, adding the information that in his time, the site of the statue's right leg, at the ending of the harbour mole, was marked by a small round church called St John of the Colossus. Over the following century, this account was followed by variations of the same tale told by several other people such as a German monk from Ulm called Brother Felix, an anonymous Florentine merchant, a Venetian scholar named Britannico and the learned traveller Cristophoro de'Buondelmonti, who had not only visited the city in the decades after di Martoni, but also found a Rhodian tale 'in a Greek book, of an idol of brass, which had in the middle of its chest a great shining mirror which showed to those who looked, ships which had come from Egypt'. Thevet, who collected the greater part of the information for his books from just such diverse sources had travelled briefly in the eastern Mediterranean just 30 years after the Turks had taken Rhodes, and may have heard some of these same tales for himself, told perhaps by someone who remembered the then-forbidden city under siege.

At all events, stripped to bare essentials, Jean Cousin's image drawn from travellers' tales made an elegant illustration for Thevet's tomes (see p. 27). In fashionable mannerist style, cast in the exquisite tradition of illustrated Italian printed books, the lively, if round-shouldered, figure holds a sword in one hand and a spear in the other. Around its neck hangs an arrangement of Renaissance strap-work, for all the world like a brandy label on a tantalus – an illustration of de'Buondelmonti's mirror. And in the triangle between the statue's legs sails a splendid European boat, like one of those that plied the harbour in the days of the Knights, all drawn in the manner of those contemporary cartographers who filled the oceans of their maps with barques and monsters and round-cheeked, puffing winds. In full sail, the boat is plunging out of the harbour, hitting the rough waves beyond. Quite oblivious, the statue stands upon two harbour moles, and there are two circles of stones underneath its feet. In an aerial view, another of Thevet's plates from the *Cosmologie* shows the entire island, the city, the sea and all its ships. And there, towering over the port of the Knights Hospitaller, is its protecting genius once again, sword in hand. Though the figure is not marked as being Christian, in the manner of the traditional images of Christ and of many of the saints, it has been drawn from that ancient classical heritage that the Renaissance West had taken once more for its own. In the following centuries, this picture of the wondrous, ghostly hero would diffuse right through Western Europe, an image of antiquity that, with its fantastic engineering and its protecting magic, served to underline ancient perfections and a world long lost.

In the decades after Thevet's original illustration of the Colossus, no less than four sets of pictures of the ancient Wonders of the World were published in Europe as loose folios of prints. Three of them used Thevet's potent image of the Colossus and all were widely popular and copied into many different media, from cloth to silverware. In 1606,

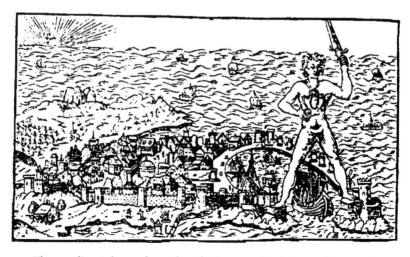

The guardian Colossus, from Thevet's *Cosmographie de Levant*, Lyon, 1556

however, a fresh and dramatic set of pictures of the Seven Wonders by the Florentine Antonio Tempesta pushed the image of the Colossus just a little further. Perhaps, like Thevet, Tempesta had read de'Buondelmonti for himself. Certainly a bibliophile friend told him about other descriptions of the Colossus found in Greek texts long in circulation amongst Byzantine historians, which told how the bronze Colossus had been dismantled by the Arab army that had taken Rhodes in the seventh century, in the years of the first thrusts out of Arabia. Tempesta illustrated this scene and the novelty of his plates was that the figure compositions he placed around his drawings of the wonders told something of their history. By Tempesta's day, however, the Turks and not the Arabs had become the main threat, a major power constantly warring with the Christian kingdoms. Tempesta, therefore, often shows the Seven Wonders under attack not from ancient Arab armies but at the hands of contemporary invading Turks, swathed in silk, wearing turbans and wielding curved swords. More conventional than Thevet, Tempesta stands the Rhodian Colossus on a single, land-bound base, and draws the statue as if it were a Roman senator. And he shows us the evil Turk chiselling at its fallen head, at the command of the Vizier.

At the end of the day, though, the older, more dramatic image proved to be the most popular, woven willy-nilly into Flemish tapestries and written histories. And still, in 1949, a new edition of Lemprière's *Classical Dictionary* was describing Thevet's Colossus as if it were a real ancient statue: 'its feet were on two moles which formed the entrance to the harbour, and ships passed full sail between its legs . . .' By that time, it had been through many transformations, passed through many different schools of art and been rendered in every medium from the gentle hand-tinted plates of the Dutch baroque mapmakers to the garish 'artist's reconstructions' of the Seven Wonders so popular in history books before the age of television. In 1960 the 450-year-old 'French' Colossus starred along with Rory Calhoun in Sergio Leone's SuperTotalScope movie, *Colossus of Rhodes*, 'in 300 BC a huge statue doubles as a fortress . . .', which critics called a good-looking spectacle with the usual muddled script. Yet more recently, the Colossus featured in a lavish set of computer graphics made for a TV campaign to advertise the Danish National Telephone Corporation.

The history of this image is not the history of the ancient statue, nor could it ever be so. A colossus spanning even the smallest harbour entrance must needs be of truly titanic proportions, a feat well beyond the bounds of ancient probabilities. Not surprisingly, no trace of such a statue has ever been found at Rhodes; moreover, none of the classical writers who describe and discuss the Rhodian Colossus ever say it bridged the entrance to a harbour. Several of them, however, give the statue's height, and the joint concordance in their measurements and their most practical discussions of the work gives the strong impression that the information is fairly accurate. They tell us that the Colossus of Rhodes stood about 110 feet high; that the sculptors built themselves an earthen ramp to enclose the statue and enable access. This arrangement would have been as high as the capital of Nelson's column. As for the figure itself, it was some 60 feet around the chest and 20 feet across the armpits, with 11-foot thighs and 5-foot ankles. Even so, all of this would still have been some 40 feet shorter than the Statue of Liberty and, certainly, no boat much larger than a dinghy could ever sail under the arch of that lady's legs. How and where, then, did this vanished statue stand, and what could it have looked like?

THE SITE OF THE COLOSSUS

Classical writers say that the Colossus was made by a sculptor named Chares, and that it was set up by the citizens of Rhodes as a thank offering to the city god, Helios, after the abandonment of a siege of their city by a Syrian king. In his *Naturae historiarum, Natural History*, the Roman Pliny tells us that the statue fell 56 years after it was finished, and that the Rhodians did not dare to re-erect it as the oracle of Delphi told them not to do so. Now, the Syrian siege of Rhodes took place in the winter of 306–5 BC, and two devastating earthquakes hit the city in 227 and 224 BC. Chares must therefore have been building his Colossus between 292 and 280 BC.

The first place to look for a statue such as this, one made as an offering to a god, is at the usual location of such offerings. As at Olympia, that would be in the sanctuary of the god to whom the offering was made. In most classical cities, the gods' sanctuaries were usually at the oldest, highest and most central parts of town. At Rhodes, this leads us to the top of the hill above the port, near the restored Castle of the Knights Hospitaller and the site of their great church of St John. And here indeed, in recent excavations in the pretty, narrow streets, you can see Turkish stonework still standing on ancient Byzantine pebble pavements, which in their turn stand on yet older walls, made with the large distinctive stones cut in the age of the Colossus. Did a temple of Helios stand on this hill, under the Knights' great church? Tantalizingly, inscriptions of some of the god's priests have been found on reused blocks of stone within this general area. It would therefore be reasonable to imagine that the temple and even the Colossus stood somewhere in this vicinity. Here, the later, tragic history of the city serves to aid the search.

In November 1856, after six months without rain, an evening storm broke over Rhodes. Lightning struck a church tower on the hilltop, and a tremendous explosion occurred – the detonation, it was later supposed, of a long-forgotten store of gunpowder abandoned by the Knights Hospitaller after the siege of 1522. In the course of the long summer, the ancient powder in the crypt of their great church seems to have dried and then to have been ignited by way of the lightning conductor on the church's steeple. The explosion was extraordinarily severe. The local paper reports that some 800 people died that night. Not only did it demolish the foursquare castle of the Knights, the governor's residence and the town library, but a great part of the city's housing, too. At the centre of the blast, the Knights' church, which just a few months earlier had been badly damaged in an earthquake, had largely vanished. All that remained were the lower parts of the walls of the undercroft with fragments of the funerary vaults of the Masters of the Knights. In the most ancient area of Rhodes, the millenial accretions of the city had just been blown away. This disaster served to open a window onto a deeply buried history to which in normal circumstances no archaeologist could ever hope to gain access.

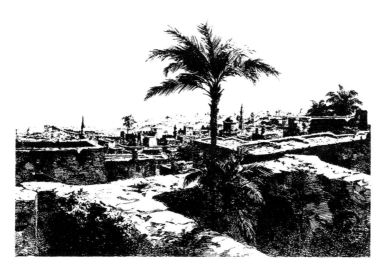

The old town of Rhodes, from the Castle of the Knights. Lithograph from Flandin's *L'Orient*, Paris, 1853

Both the Italian occupiers and then the Greeks themselves have excavated widely in this area, work that continues to this day. It might be anticipated that, if it had once stood in this area, traces of the vanished statue would remain. Such an enormous enterprise as the making of a bronze colossus would leave many signs for archaeologists. Remnants of its base perhaps, which, on the soft earth of this hill, would have had to have been enormous and carefully engineered; and other scraps too, such as tiny pieces of the statue's bronze from the era of its destruction. Certainly, there would be debris from the workshops, fragments of the enormous clay moulds; stains from the fires of the furnaces, from the huge amount of ash and brick and clinker that Chares and his workmen would have produced as they fired the kilns in which the statue's bronze was mixed and cast. Yet, as far as is known, nothing, no trace of the statue, nor of its architecture, nor of the processes of its manufacture, has ever come to light. Upon the hill of Rhodes, the trail seems to be cold.

Ancient precedent allows one further possibility for the location of the ancient statue. As if by law of custom, several classical authors assume in their writings that the Rhodian Colossus stood by the sea; that simply seemed to them to be the proper place for such a thing. This location was selected too by the designers of the colossus standing on the seaboard of the entrance to New York. Dressed in Greek costume, the lady in the harbour also has Helios' sunburst upon her head! Two thousand five hundred years earlier – and two centuries before the Rhodian Colossus – the Greek playwright Aeschylus wrote of another colossus that stood by an entrance: of Helen looming in Agamemnon's memory at the doorway of his palace. In ancient Egypt too, the ageless birthplace of colossal statues, they were always set at the doorways, at the entrances of temples. The Greeks, of course, knew such ancient statues well. The two colossi that they thought were memorials to Memnon, king of Ethiopia, who fought at Troy with Agamemnon, became as famous as the Seven Wonders. Standing at the entrance of an ancient Theban temple, one of these was said to sing and groan each morning, as the sun first lit its face. Of course, the Greeks also knew that the kings of Egypt, whom these statues usually represented, were identified with the sun and its great burning orb, as was the Greek god Helios.

Statues were not the only things that were considered to be suitable decorations for the entrances to cities. The Pharos of Alexandria for example, another of the Seven Wonders, was built at the entrance of the harbour of Egyptian Alexandria some 400 miles to the south of Rhodes and at the same time that Chares was working on the Colossus. Alexandria, indeed, was a great ally of Rhodes, and situated at a equally vital point on the east Mediterranean trade routes. By Roman times, when harbours on the pattern of the ones of Rhodes and Alexandria were built at ports throughout the empire, great statues and lighthouses were often set up upon the artificial harbour walls, as benefits and blessings to the sailors of the empire and as the monumental guardians of the port. At the port of Caesarea in Palestine, Herod the Great built another celebrated colossus, a portrait of Augustus, at the end of the brand-new harbour; in Calais too, and Ostia, imperial architects built enormous lighthouses on the harbour moles. Though these have mostly disappeared, their literary trail must lead us back again through the narrow streets of Rhodes, down to the glittering sea.

Where then would be the most appropriate seaside site for the Colossus? The place that gains immediate attention from both land and sea and the one therefore of most practical use to sailors and most visible from land, is the tip of the mole that divides Mandraki from the commercial harbour: the spot where the small round fortress of St Nicholas now stands at the harbour mouth. This area was once the larger of the two artificial sea walls of the ancient city, the mole nearest the island's most northern point; the place where, the medieval legend says, the right foot of the striding Colossus once touched upon the ground. Certainly, the site of the fortress, solidly based upon an outcrop of good hard rock, could comfortably take the colossal weight of a giant statue, and provide a conveniently stable outcrop for its elevation at the same time. In its day, the medieval fortress was a key emplacement in many of the city's wars and sieges; the Knights Hospitaller fought their most bloody and important battles upon this promontory, and there is no reason to imagine that it was any the less vital to the city's defences in earlier times. Equally tough fighting took place there during the siege, whose lifting, so the ancient texts have told us, caused the Rhodians to commission Chares to make a Colossus as a thank offering to Helios, the island's god.

Attracted by the legends and its prominent position by the sea, several archaeologists over the last century or so have visited this fortress and most of them have wondered at the amounts of ancient marble embedded in the sandstone walls, used at almost every point where extra strength might be required; on window and door sills, at gateways and to hold the wheels of the cannon in their gun emplacements. And a few of these stones have inscriptions on them.

One of the archaeologists, Albert Gabriel, also noticed that many of these reused stones were first cut in precisely the same period as the Colossus – that is, many of these marble blocks had carefully and distinctively chiselled borders and were of quite different sizes from the rest. Gabriel also noticed that the longer sides of many of these same stones were cut in subtle curves; in segments of a circle about 55 feet in diameter, that is, a circle with the same diameter as the medieval castle's central keep. More recently, work deep inside the fortress has revealed enormous building blocks of sandstone laid in a circle – this, too, probably from the era of the Seven Wonders. The core of this fortress, then, appears to be built upon a circular classical structure of similar dimensions; this was hardly a part of a classical fortified tower, as these were usually rectangular and, though carefully constructed, were seldom decorated with finely finished marble. Gabriel suggested that these marble blocks may be the base of the age-old Colossus. And indeed, it is true that the ancient Rhodians seem to have provided an unusually large number of their statues with rounded plinths, rather than the more usual cubic ones. Pictures of some of the later ancient colossi show that circular bases were used for them as well.

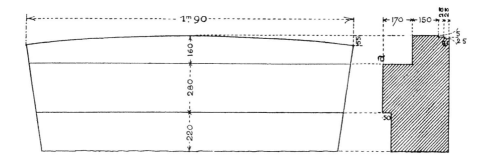

Gabriel's drawing of one of the curved blocks from St Nicholas' fortress, from Gabriel, 1932

Gabriel also noticed that there were many other marble blocks of the most unusual shapes and sizes reused in the fortress and these, he suggested, could well have been made for the interior of the Colossus which several ancient texts described as being filled with blocks of stone, all bound together with iron. What Gabriel proposed was that he had found some of the materials left over from the Colossus after the stripping of its metal skin. Here then is something tangible that could perhaps be connected to the long-lost statue. The proof, though, if it still exists, is to be found in connecting the ancient descriptions of the statue's manufacture with the remaining stones on the mole of Mandraki. How then was the Colossus made?

THE MAKING AND UNMAKING OF A WONDER

280 BC: COLOSSUS BUILT

The artist secured it firmly from the inside with iron frames and squared blocks of stone, of which the horizontal bars exhibit hammer-work in the Cyclopean fashion. The hidden part of the work is bigger than the visible parts. Further questions strike the admiring spectator: what kind of fire-tongs were used, what size were the bases of the anvils, with what workforce was such a weight of poles forged? The artist used a quantity of bronze that might have exhausted the mines, for the molten image of the structure was the bronze-work of the world.

A base of white marble was laid down, and on this he first set the feet of the Colossus up to the ankle-bones. He had already conceived in his mind the proportions in which the one-hundred-and-twenty-foot god was going to be built. Since the soles of the feet on the base were already at a greater height than other statues, it was impossible to lift up the rest and set it on top. The ankles had to be cast on top and, just as happens in building houses, the whole work had to rise on top of itself.

And for this reason, in the case of other statues, artists first make a mould, then divide it into parts, cast them, and finally put them all togther and erect the statue. But the artist of the Colossus cast the first part and then moulded the second part on the first and, when the second part had been cast in bronze, built the third part on top of that. He used the same method of construction for the remaining parts. For it was not possible to move the metal parts.

When the casting had been done on the earlier worked parts, the intervals of the bars and the joints of the framework were taken care of, and the structure was held steady with stones that had been put inside. So that throughout the construction he might retain his conception unshaken, he continually poured an immense mound of earth round the finished parts of the Colossus, hiding what had already been worked on underground, and carried out the next stage of casting on the flat surface of what was underneath.

Philo 4, 2; 4, 1; 4, 3–5

75 BC: COLOSSUS FALLEN

Sixty-six years after its erection the statue fell over in an earthquake, but even lying down it is a marvel. Few people can get their arms round one of its thumbs, and its fingers are bigger than most statues. Where the limbs have been broken off, there are huge gaping cavities. Inside it, one can see rocks of enormous size which Chares had used to stabilize it when he was building it. It is said that it took twelve years to build at an expense of three hundred talents . . . There are a hundred other colossi, all smaller than this one, in the same city, and each one of these would have been sufficient to make the site of its erection famous, no matter where else it had been put. Besides these there are five statues of gods . . .

Pliny, *Natural History*, XXXIV 18, 41–2 (*c.* AD 50)

AD 654 : COLOSSUS SOLD

This man [the Caliph 'Uthman] took Africa in a war and, after he had arranged the matter of taxes with the Africans, returned. His general was called Mavias, and it was he who overturned the Colossus of Rhodes . . . and stripped it of its bronze and, taking it to Syria, put it up for sale for anyone who wanted it . . . A Jewish merchant from Edessa bought it, and loaded the bronze onto 900 camels . . .

Constantine Porphorygenitus, *de administrando imperio* 20, 1–3; 21, 63–4; 20, 8–10

At the time that the Colossus was made, there was a tradition of bronze-working in the eastern Mediterranean stretching back more than 2,000 years. Today, the oldest known metal statue, itself a colossus, larger than life-size and demonstrating great skill of craftsmanship, is that of the Egyptian pharaoh Pepi II. Like the Statue of Liberty, Pepi's statue is made of sheets of metal that were first hammered individually to shape, then riveted together. When hammered, bronze and copper are tempered and become quite hard and therefore very rigid.

At a conservative estimate, at the time of the making of the Colossus there were some 20,000 bronzes standing in the marble cities of the eastern Mediterranean. Though none of these approached the size of Helios, many of them were very large indeed. Rhodes, Athens, Olympia, Delphi, each had around 3,000 statues in them, according to Pliny. One sculptor alone, Lysippus – in whose studio Chares got his training – made some 1,500 pieces. At Rhodes, so Pliny says, there were 100 other colossal statues, five of these by Bryaxis, another of Lysippus'pupils. Alas, though such bronzes were common enough in antiquity, most of them have disappeared today. Like gold, bronze was a commodity in itself; though the Arabs who raided Rhodes in the seventh century were only on the island for short periods of time, they saw the value of the fallen giant and occupied themselves in rendering it into portable pieces to ship and sell abroad. The value of bronze did not change much through millenia. In the medieval archives of Barletta in southern Italy, for instance, there is record of a dispensation awarded to townspeople during a celebratory holiday that allowed them to strip pieces from the ancient statue of an emperor standing in their city.

By Pliny's day, the size of some of these colossi exceeded even that of the Colossus of Rhodes. The largest ever built, he tells us, was made in France by a sculptor named Zenodorus, who in consequence was called to Rome to make a colossus of the Emperor Nero. This was a famous statue in its day and stood close to the Colosseum, the celebrated amphitheatre being named after the now forgotten statue. After Zenodorus, many Roman emperors continued the tradition of having colossal statues of themselves erected, and many of the singular fragments littered Rome until they were collected up by archaeologists. How were these later statues made? Certainly, their surviving pieces show that, like the colossal Zeus of Pheidias, they were made piecemeal, of many different materials. Sometimes the emperor's skin – his head and hands and feet – were made of marble, at other times they were cast in bronze. As evidence, two such heads survive.

Most life-sized bronze statues, both past and present, have been cast in a single piece. The most accurate method, and one widely used by ancient people, is called the 'lost wax process' and consists of modelling the figure first in wax upon a solid core. A mould of plaster or clay is put around this finished figure, and all of it is then heated and hardened so that the modelled wax runs out from the inside – it is 'lost'. Liquid bronze is then poured into that gap between the statue's core and the inside of the mould. Casting in 'lost wax', Egyptian foundries of the time of the Rhodian Colossus used iron bars to strengthen the statues and to hold their core in place as the bronze was being cast. Here then we have hints of processes that sound like those that Philo is describing in his text.

Immediately, however, a range of problems threatens to confuse us. The first and most basic of these lies with the author, with Philo himself. From his text, it is easy to gain the impression of someone musing on these Seven Wonders and proposing ideas on how they had been made. After all, several of the Wonders were already old or ancient in his time; he could not have witnessed their manufacture. And how much, indeed, did he really know about the construction of contemporary wonders? Philo was celebrated for his writings upon the making of assault catapults and mechanical amusements, upon siphons and siege engines, the theoretic action of air and water. His practical abilities are unknown. Perhaps he was indulging in scholarly debate in the manner of modern academics. Or, like a bored custodian of scientific documents, he was idling away a happy hour with a list of wonders, in much the same way as many scientists today set themselves the amusing task of trying to discover how the pyramids were built.

Whatever the case may be, Philo has some tremendously important things to tell us. He was from the same world as the sculptor Chares. He understood the constraints of his own time, the aesthetics of ancient method and procedure. We can see in his writings something of the limitations and the possibilities of that lost age. Chares worked in a millenial technological tradition, one infinitely longer than our own. He and his men possessed skills that we no longer know or care about. Neither were they bound by many of the 'practical' criteria which govern most modern assessments of their work – criteria, that is, concerning what is 'sensible' or 'economic'. Usually, these terms imply restraints of time or expense: 'they would never have done that, it would have taken too long/too much effort' is their usual tone. Pliny, though, who was also a part of that same ancient world, says that the Colossus took 12 years to build, that is, it rose by 6–8 feet a year; hardly a rate of working a modern city council would endure. Philo tells us that 'the hidden part of the work is bigger than the visible parts' and that would hardly be 'practical' in the modern sense of the word, where everyone wants a big bang for their bucks. It is as if Kennedy had said that he would put mankind on the moon in just two centuries by slowly building a gigantic ladder up from the North Pole.

Modern people cannot easily appreciate what mass labour can achieve, nor indeed do they know how to organize so fluid and intelligent a source of peasant power and skill as the ancient world contained. Like the Chinese rulers of the Great Leap Forward, people such as Chares understood about the organization of large public works, it was a commonplace. In his own studio, in buildings, temples, cities and harbours and even in the mechanics of war, skilled craftsmen and organizers worked with vast masses of the population. King Demetrius Poliorcetes, the besieger of Rhodes whose defeat led to the construction of the Colossus, had a siege tower in operation on the island that was quite as tall as the Colossus, and half as long in the length of its base. The tower ran on wheels.

It took vast numbers of people, it was said, to pull it around. And skill too, of a type that we have completely lost; the manoeuvring of similarly large objects today is achieved with steering wheels and buttons. This great tower, it was said, had nine storeys, with stone walls on its lowest decks and catapults on its upper levels. For protection, it had water tanks at every storey to douse fires and was clad in iron and hides. It also held offensive battering rams and bridges. And King Demetrius, it may once again be observed, was on the side that lost.

That then is the broad scope of ancient possibility and accomplishment. How does all this square with the texts describing Chares and his work? In their mass, there is great discordance. Philo, for example, says that just 12.5 tons of bronze was used in the Colossus. This would allow a statue about as thick as cardboard and would require just 70 camels to carry away its residue, not the 900-odd that Constantine Porphyrygenitus says were used for the task. The data, then, is not what modern engineers would wish for. Amongst the ancient words, there is no guarantee of fact. In their mass, they represent a sort of poetry; information must flow from the evidence rather than from its manipulation. And always, there remain questions with no finite answer. What exactly were these ancient texts for? Are they true? Are they even genuine? Does Philo's text, for example, really date from the age of the Colossus, that is, from that 50-year span before the statue fell? There are even problems in the words themselves, which are ambiguous and allow diverse interpretations.

'Do let us at least try to understand what Philo actually said,' remarks Dr Haynes of the British Museum at the ending of a retranslation of Philo's description of the making of the Colossus – a rebuttal of a translation used by the sculptor Herbert Maryon to show that the Colossus had not been cast at all, but was constructed of plates of beaten bronze. The version of the text that Maryon used, Haynes asserted, was inaccurate and, further, a key word had been wrongly translated which, when retranslated, proves that the Colossus had been cast. These are statements with which other, later, scholars are generally in agreement.

Yet Haynes is mistaken when he comes to give us his own version of the making of the Colossus. You cannot cast bronze statues piecemeal in the way that he asserts, casting one section upon another. Pouring molten bronze against cold bronze does not result, as he assumes it does, in 'fusion', whatever an ancient text might say. The philological alternatives – Haynes' use of 'cast upon' against Maryon's 'filled in' – hold further alternatives in them; if Haynes is right, then Philo was quite wrong or again, the phrase 'cast upon' seems as ambiguous as something being 'cast upon' the waters.

One thing is sure: the Colossus was not made like the smaller bronzes of the day, in a single pour, a single piece. Cast with just 1-inch thickness of bronze, at a 100 feet and more, the Colossus would have weighed some 200 tons (thus employing some 1,150 camels to carry it away). Even if modern-day technology could enable such a folly to be made, it is doubtful whether the resulting figure would even stand under its own weight. As much as anything, the parameters that govern the scientific truths in all these ancient texts are physical constraints such as the pressure of wind upon the towering bulk and the problem of sustaining such tremendous weight, even in times of calm. The limits of possibility have to be set against the insinuations of the ancient texts.

For never do these texts tell us a single way of proceeding. Once again we bump against the difference between modern and ancient methods of procedure. Haynes' and Maryon's disagreement about whether the statue was cast or made of plates is just such a modern distinction. Today, we automatically think in terms of modern trades and processes – these after all are the most 'sensible' divisions of time and material. If, for example, we want a staircase for our house, we choose the material – wood, stone or metal – and three completely different types of specialists arrive for the installation. Maryon's account of the building of the statue is bound by a single method. He seems to think that Chares worked rather like a Herbert Maryon would if commissioned to make a colossus of Queen Victoria at Delhi, that is with the aid of a thousand workers and a lot of pencilled diagrams. Such was not the case. The prospect becomes even less likely with Haynes' impractical proposal, as he knows less about the properties of bronze than does the sculptor Maryon. Here, the diversity of the fragments found in Pheidias' workshop should warn us that such separation of technique did not necessarily exist within the ancient world. As for the Colossus itself, Pliny even tells us that Lysippus, Chares' master, had started his metalworking as a coppersmith, a beater of copper. Of the 1,500 statues that he made in his life, some were of metal and others were of stone.

Everyone at least seems to agree about the interpretation of that simple single phrase of Philo's that described the building of the Colossus: '. . . just as happens in building houses, the whole work had to rise on top of itself'. Like ours today, the houses of Philo's time were not cast piece by piece on top of each other, but fitted together. A wide range of different techniques and materials had to be assembled by a single builder. Similarly, Pheidias' Zeus had been made with half-a-dozen techniques and more, all brought together by a multi-skilled workforce, one not constricted by the rules of a union or a production line.

Given that, as Philo says, the work of the inside of the statue was as great a task as that of its exterior; and that the Colossus was neither cast of bronze in one section, nor fused section by section one upon the other, it is most reasonable to opt for a diversity of process. Philo says that the statue's core, of stones and iron all bound together, gave as much work as its final skin. Pliny tells us that in its fallen state the great stones of the interior were visible between the opened sheets of bronze. We may imagine, then, that these stones, '. . . secured firmly from the inside with iron frames . . . exhibited hammer-work in the Cyclopean fashion' (Philo) were the true structure of the Colossus, and that its skin of bronze was part embedded in this construction and partly hung from it in sheets.

Here, perhaps, another text of Constantine Porphorygenitus can serve to help us. The text is carved upon an obelisk in Istanbul, one of the surviving wonders from Byzantium, standing quite close to the walls of Lausus' palace. This obelisk is built of blocks of stone and once was placed as a counterpart to the great Egyptian obelisk of Seti I, standing on the spine of the Hippodrome.

The four-sided wonder of the heavens, now destroyed by age, Emperor Constantine, father of Romanus, the glory of command, renovates to a better standard than the old spectacle. For the Colossus was an object of wonder in Rhodes, and this bronze [structure] is an object of wonder here.

In other words, this old stone obelisk, which was looking its age, was covered in bronze by the Emperor Constantine, who wished it to be considered as much a wonder as the Colossus of Rhodes, that vanished statue that had fallen down almost 1,100 years before! This Emperor Constantine is the same one who first recorded the fate of the Colossus in his history of Byzantium. Emperor from childhood, he was a learned man who, while regents ruled, spent much of his time in writing and research aided by a staff of scholars. The text upon the obelisk is of much the same tenor as the writings of the Emperor himself. Here is someone who believed the Colossus was formed of brazen plates. For as you stand before this stony obelisk, you may still see the holes for the studs which held the emperor's sheets of bronze in place, bronze that was to be taken a century later by the crusaders, just as the Colossus' bronze was taken by the Arabs.

Such a relatively economic use of bronze would enable an approximate correspondence with Philo's sum of the total amount involved. It would also account for the reason why no fragments of the statue have ever been recovered; the bronze sheets were already cut in sections, were fairly thin and their removal therefore was clean and relatively convenient. Dismantling a cast statue would have been much more difficult. Messy and time consuming, it would also have created a deal of refuse, charcoal, bronze fragments and splintered stones and all the rest. Neither need the philological distinctions between cast and sheet metal detain us further: in the ancient world, sheet bronze such as it existed would have been produced by casting the liquid metal onto a smooth surface, and not by rolling in a modern mill. The distinction is largely a modern one. The most important thing, however, is that there is no need to imagine that Chares used a single method of construction for his statue. Pheidias' Zeus, whose body was plated with sheets of ivory, seems to have had cast locks of solid gold upon its head and sheet gold for its cloak. It is difficult to imagine that Chares' Colossus did not also have different parts of it made in different ways; a colossal brazen statue such as the world had never seen, held together with good craftsmanship and with experience that reached back for millenia to the beginnings of history.

THE HEAD OF HELIOS

There are no known ancient pictures of the Colossus, nor other statues that are models of its figure. Apart from the stones that may be the fragments of its base, all that is left is the dedication poem that was once inscribed upon its base and has been preserved in a book of ancient verse.

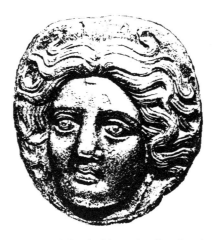

Rhodian silver coin with head of the god Helios, fourth century BC

To you, Helios, yes to you the people of Dorian Rhodes raised this colossus high up to heaven, after they had calmed the bronze wave of war, and crowned their country with spoils won from the enemy. Not only over the sea but also on land they set up the bright light of unfettered freedom.

Anon, *Palatine Anthology*, VI, 171

What Chares' statue looked like, how it stood or what, if anything, it wore, nobody knows. One thing though, is sure. For the Colossus to have been identified as the sun god, the Rhodian Helios, it must have carried the signs, the icons of that deity. Above all else, at Rhodes, this consisted of an aureole, a burst of pointed flames, symmetrical, flat and gilded, blazing round the god's head just as, in later centuries, a Christian halo would decorate the saints. Many portraits of Helios have been found on Rhodes, in marble, in ceramic, both as modelled clay and drawn by painters onto pots, and, most commonly of all, on silver, for the islanders put the features of their god upon their coins. In Chares' time, many of these portraits share common features; over and over again, they show us the same face.

A particularly splendid illustration of the face of Helios is a grandiose marble head, currently one of the finest pieces in the collections of the Rhodes Museum. Right around it, in the curls of its hair and cut deep into the marble, is a ring of equidistant holes which once held bronze or silver studs. If the angles of these holes are extended outwards, they form a perfectly symmetrical burst of rays: they are the roots of Helios' aureole. Here, then, is Helios: a young man, head turned, hair ruffled, alert, a splendid image of the head of a new type of figure developed from older traditional sculptures. Almost certainly, these same features were also shared by the Colossus, perhaps even its pose; for it is typical of a new type of figure, one developed by Lysippus, in whose studio Chares had received his training. Simply by building his Colossus, Chares continued the tradition of his most influential teacher, who had reintroduced colossal statues and brought a brand-new high theatricality into the sculpture of his time. In the image of this young man, Lysippus had also created the most potent image of his time, and in so doing, had become the most famous sculptor of the period and, as time has shown, as influential an artist as any who has ever lived.

The head turns on the marble neck as if somebody has touched his shoulder; the stony eyes peer towards a far horizon; like real hair, the chiselled locks blow in the wind (see pl. 5). Here, the sculptor is working hard, working to make a theatrical event, a moment of time. With its slight translucence this stone is perfect for the task, and half-polished, marble resembles human skin. Its surface texture holds the light like real flesh. Helios' cheeks are cut so that they seem to have real weight, they seem to lie upon the skull. The sculptor draws out weight and surface, draws skin, stretching it over bone and muscle, right across the face, draws the way the muscle comes down beside the nose, the way the edges of the lips move, freed of the tension of the rest of the face. One feels that if a fly settled on this piece of marble it would twitch like a horse's flank. The sculptor has made for us a human moment, a moment of time. And this is the first time almost in human history that sculptors have concerned themselves with such a thing. It is the time and style of the Colossus.

Before Lysippus, even in the time of Pheidias, sculptors made still and solemn figures of timeless and eternal forms which, though lifelike and sometimes even vigorous, seem to inhabit quite a different world from ours. Between us and these ancient people, the people even of the time of Pheidias' Zeus there is indeed, a vast chasm – a transformation of mentality. Then the gods that ruled, that rose each day with the sun, that flooded rivers, that sprouted wheat, lived outside of human lifespans. Cyclical things, like the seasons and the sun, gave life. A fly upon a horse's flank, a mere passing moment on the earth, had no significance for the sculptors or their clients and therefore hardly needed to be celebrated in bronze and marble.

Most of the Seven Wonders were made at the time that the ancient world was changing; the age when time itself seemed to pass under human control, the time in which the chasm between the present and the distant past first opened: when man himself took charge of his own destiny, when the achievements of humankind – including the Seven Wonders – began to seem more important than the holy mysteries of shooting stars, of sprouting grain and the rising of the sun and moon. Here then, in the age of Lysippus and the Colossus, sculpture changes; begins to work in time, to live inside the human moment. It was as if one of those ancient colossi, one of those gigantic figures at the temples' doorways, got up and left the confines of the sacred compound. At Rhodes, the sun god Helios, 'Almighty Ruler, Spirit of the World, Power of the World, Light of the World' was revealed for all the world to see. And this, in the manner of Lysippus, and in his image of the new man. For here humanity itself becomes the wonder. Its struggles with the earth and sea, with the gods, with its own kind, were taken as the main part of a new and rather tragic history. Not surprisingly, many of Lysippus' revolutionary sculptures showed the gods at ease, at rest, tired, frail and almost human.

This image of the new man was the image of a king, of Alexander, King of Macedon. His great march from Greece to India inaugurated this brave new world; a world where history was made and measured by erratic events; a world counted in human history, not in the movements of the moon. Alexander and his armies had marched through vivid geographies of strange and wonderful landscapes inhabited by wild, exotic, alien cultures. And just as the architects of the Parthenon had done, they stood back and saw this ancient world working like a clock. In amongst this ancient universe, they transformed old cities and set up new ones; multi-cultural, multi-ethnic trading cities like Alexandria, Pergamum, Miletus and Rhodes. The icons of these cities, the signs of the new age, were the images of Alexander made by Lysippus and his pupils; these were the first international propagandists, and also the makers of the Colossus. The Seven Wonders indeed are haunted by Alexander. He died at Babylon, the city of the Hanging Gardens; he founded Egyptian Alexandria, the city of the Pharos; he stormed Halicarnassus, the city of the Mausoleum and, half a century after his death, the Rhodian Colossus was cast in his image – the image of the superhuman man who had brought wonder down to earth.

Alexander, became the icon of a brand-new world with brand-new aspirations, with cash and careers to think about, with slaves and mobile populations, with plotting kings and bankers, and a vast disquieted prosperity. This is the age in which the Seven Wonders lists were first compiled, the age in which a new image of humanity was born. And the list of Seven Wonders is looking at the ancient world and judging it afresh and changing it for ever. That is why Lysippus' image of a new man was so appropriate. A brand-new figure for a brand-new age: the beginning of the modern world.

ALEXANDER'S SCULPTOR

As Plutarch later commented, 'Zeno[the Greek Stoic philosopher] had a dream, or an image, of a well-ordered and philosophical state, but Alexander put the theory into practice.' With his march to India, Alexander had put human affairs at the front of history – a new sort of history, governed by the actions of men and women. With the careful propagation of an international image in words and pictures and great sculpture, Alexander became his own colossus; a Man of Destiny.

There is, of course, a distinction to be made between the man and his statue. This young king, Alexander III, was not unique. Almost everything he ever said or did had been said or done by someone else before him. There have been other great conquerors and travellers too, who, lacking biographers, are quite forgotten. What is so significant about Alexander is the image that built up around him. This image it is that makes the hero: not deeds, but the descriptions of the deeds. Like the Rhodian Colossus itself, the powerful physical image of Alexander hailed from the workshops of Lysippus.

Along with the painter Apelles, and the jeweller and coin-maker Pyrogoteles, Lysippus seems to have been especially chosen as Alexander's artist. From around 365 BC, throughout a very long career, a stream of works left the studios of this most applauded sculptor, celebrating everything from the dead members of one of Alexander's cavalry charges to pensive portraits of gods and philosophers. Contemporary writers say that Alexander himself picked Lysippus as his sculptor because he alone could capture his manly yet lion-like appearance, his soft yet piercing eyes. According to Pliny, the sculptor himself used to say that his predecessors had made men as they were, whereas he made them as they appeared. And there perhaps lay the root of his success. Just as he created a theatre-in-time for his sculpture, so he also concerned himself with creating the precise theatre, the precise image, that his clients wanted to project. Alexander was surrounded by hagiographers from early in his career: it is easy to imagine the Macedonians' enthusiasm for such a sculptor as Lysippus. It is not surprising that when the sculptor portrayed the senior gods, he showed them at rest, their work done, powerful old warriors leaning on their spears and clubs, and when he made images of the younger ones, he made them in the image of his new hero. Pheidias' Zeus has stood up and left the temple; the hidden god was revealed as a Colossus; the Colossus as a human being; the human being as the one true hero.

Just as literary tales about Alexander's life and loves proliferated in libraries from Germany to India, so Lysippus' invention of this youthful and heroic image promoted copies in their thousands. On coins and sculptures Alexander was often pictured wearing a lion's skin, the head above his own – hence at Rhodes, the wild mane upon the head of Helios. In a copy of a figure painted by Apelles, the same young man sits on Zeus' throne, abrogating Pheidias' dark and bearded king. In other paintings and mosaics, the eyes flash dangerously, an armoured arm hurls lethal spears. This Man of Destiny, of course, was made. Just as Hitler had Leni Riefenstahl, and Garbo Hollywood, so, amongst many others, Alexander had Lysippus, the sculptor who was not only a master crafts-man, but something of a poet, too.

Alexander, so his biographers say, really did have long hair, despite the fact that Greeks thought the style effeminate. He also appears to have been rather short, perhaps a bit short-sighted, too. Lysippus' matinée idol image, the rumpled hair, the mouth and teeth just slightly opened, the neck vigorously, questioningly turned, made personal idiosyn-crasies of posture into the Man of Action. A slight craning of the neck, a little twist, becomes dynamic, as if the marble was directing armies. And that in turn, of course, would cause the mouth to curl and open too. Naturally, the long hair becomes a lion's mane. The distinctive crinkle in the forehead becomes like the furry furrows of a lion's brow. Alexander's family nose, both straight and long, is made magnificent, wider, straighter, leonine. The eyes, defocused, have indeed become liquid, soft and penetrat-ing orbs, the object of many an academic musing. What Lysippus makes, of course, is poetry; it is also the first image of a modern pin-up. Just as, for millenia, the gods had taken on something of the appearance of the king who served them, so that on occasion it is difficult to tell the difference between a god and a king, a goddess or a queen, so this fabulous confection based on Alexander became a heroic face for all mankind.

As for Alexander's body, Lysippus' aim to make the young king 'as he appeared to be' affected even the proportions of his sculptured torso. Traditionally, the Greeks had fitted the head into the body at a ration of seven to one. Lysippus made the body bigger, fitting the splendid image of his Alexandrine face onto a larger bulk of body than ever before. To older sculptors, the new Alexander must have seemed grotesque, something like an American football player or a Mr Universe. Other sculptors, though, enjoyed the vigorous effect, and it stayed popular for many centuries. Lysippus was also famous for the three-dimensionality of his sculpture. Pliny says that he had started as a metalworker, and perhaps it was the extra sense of freedom in that light and flexible medium that made him push the stone and bronze further than ever it had moved before. Here then is the beginning of those extraordinary complex tableaux, with men and animals and gods combined in a single complicated piece of stone – sculpture at the movies. For Lysippus' figures moved in space like real people. Unlike older works, they did not bear the traces of the blocks from which they had been cut. Lysippus took the gentle curves of earlier sculpture and thrust them into sharper poses. In Alexander's statues, the traditional pose with one leg gently taking the weight of the torso is pushed into such vigorous shape that, from the navel to the neck, the body moves in an elegant elongated S. Even the athletes' highly-developed muscles above the pelvis, which had long been exaggerated in sculpture of athletes, now appeared to be clamped down hard onto the bone in yet more energetic movement.

The result of all of this, the shrinking of the head, the turning and tuning of the body, was that Alexander, and presumably the Colossus too, had an appearance like nothing ever before. This too has gripped imaginations up to the present day. In Lysippus' portraits, Alexander looked so grand now, so magnificent, that Alexander said to Zeus, according to a Greek poet, 'The earth is mine. Have Olympus as your own, Zeus.' Via Michelangelo to Hollywood, this colossal and heroic figure remains much the same; though the original Colossus may long have disappeared, it lives on in a thousand echoes, some of them, with tinkling spurs, walking down the main street of a Western set, a ghostly image of our time.

As for the Colossus, Greek artists also represented the sun god as horse wrangler, a charioteer dressed in a long robe, driving his team across the sky and sometimes carrying the sun along with him as well. Often the god appeared with his right hand raised in benediction, his left perhaps holding an orb or whip or thunderbolt, and in addition even a sceptre crowned by a sphere or some fruit. Not implausibly, it has been suggested that the Chares Colossus too stood in a chariot, and though the theory cannot now be proven wrong, there is nothing, not a hint in the ancient silence, to say that it had not been so. Alternatively, the Colossus may have been a seated figure. The largest Greek statue known to have been made before the Colossus, a famous 60-foot statue of Zeus, was built by Lysippus for the town of Taranto in southern Italy, and this was a seated, rather sprawling, figure. Other alternatives exist as well; perhaps he stood like the young Alexander, a mighty athlete in a single robe – a figure with a considerable twist within the body, and a third leg of support, a robe perhaps, a club or spear. Here, Lysippus'statue of Hercules leaning on his club – described by one authority as 'a repulsive bag of muscles' – might have provided the model for the subject. But then, Helios is usually young, not old like Hercules. And so eventually we are led back to the

Alexander image in the Museum, leaning perhaps with a spear or carrying a robe that touches the ground to lend the great Colossus extra strength against the winds and earthquakes.

HELIOS AT THE VATICAN

An assortment of sun gods – Helios, Apollo, Mithras, Elah-Gabal – rose to power and precedence in the Hellenistic cities, such as Rhodes and Pergamum, and in Emesa too, where later, it would be said, there stood a huge temple of the sun god. When the East became Roman, these Eastern religions travelled to Rome, where for a while the cult of the sun god became a major state religion and the sun god's various attributes became part of the generic trappings of divinity – so much so indeed that in the first three centuries of Western Christianity, before the image of Christ became that of Pheidias' Zeus – that dark-haired bearded man with piercing eyes – Jesus was sometimes portrayed as a blonde-haired straight-nosed man in classical pose. Thus the face of Alexander's Helios, eyes now focused firmly on heaven, became one of the oldest images of Christ, and Christ became, like Helios, the 'Light of the World'.

With its Seven Seals, Seven Sleepers, Seven Cities, and the Seven Names of God, Christianity too was a product of the Hellenistic East, along with all those sun gods from the great cities founded or enriched by Alexander and his Macedonians. Indeed, one of Christianity's immediate attractions was that it showed how the wisdom of more ancient faiths could be applied in this brand-new age in which everything that was new was good, and could be bought and sold – a new ethic for a money economy and for fluid populations. The novel life of these great cities itself engendered many new religions, some of them esoteric astral mysticisms imbued with notions of the sun god's omnipotence. And so it was that in the first centuries of Christianity, many religious movements were decorated with solar motives and from the third century on the image of the sun became one of the most popular and effective metaphors in the Christian church. To this day, indeed, it has its place in the liturgy, in sermons and in hymns. To the early converts though, it was more than a metaphor, it was an invocation of the deepest currents of most ancient faiths. Thus several of these solar gods gave early Christianity many features. Sunday, the day of worship, was the sun's own day; the birthday of Mithras, born like Jesus, of a virgin in a cave, was celebrated on December 25. Like Jesus in the Book of Revelations and the Hebrew prophets too, several of the sun gods were borne to heaven in a tempest or in a chariot. The church, though, gave the sun a moral aspect. Sol Invictus, the pagan sun of Victory worshipped by Constantine the first Christian Emperor, became a Sol Iustitiae, the risen judging Lord. The substitution was not difficult to accomplish. Notions of judgement were rooted in the ancient faiths of Babylon and Egypt, in Greco-Roman mythology and Hebrew prophecy as well. Like Jesus, Helios had been an approachable, understanding god and had also taken on the role of judge. And did not the prophet Malachi himself declare 'unto you that fear my name shall the Sun of righteousness arise . . .' Modern people may take such sentiments as a simple metaphor; but like Alexander's image, for many centuries they held an aspect of reality. Early popes had to ban people walking backwards up the steps of old St Peter's on their way to pray, which they did for fear of offending the rising Sunday morning sun, and St Augustine fiercely warned that identifying Christ with the sun god risked a relapse into paganism. Though this relapse never took place, Helios has stayed, and the image of the young sun god too, right through Christian history in the West.

Deep underneath the Vatican, a few yards from St Peter's tomb, there is a burial chapel of the third century whose ceiling is laid with fine mosaics. There, amidst the tendrils of a vine, is the figure of Christ, riding across a blazing golden sky in Helios' fiery chariot. He wears the aureole of the Colossus around his head, he has the long straight nose of Alexander's portraits, the upward gaze, the mop of hair and the briskly turned neck. In the same pose that the sun god Sol strikes on the coins of pagan Roman emperors, and in the self-same century, Christ Helios is carried up to heaven through the celestial vine in the same chariot that carries Ezekiel up to heaven in early Christian art. A thousand years on, Giotto's great fresco cycle at Assisi showed precisely this same scene: the ghost of the Colossus rising in apotheosis.

In 1499, one Anton Koberger wrote a poem to accompany one of Dürer's etchings that provides an epitome of Helios' career, and Alexander's too, in their extraordinary afterlife:

> As the sun, when in the centre of his orbit, that is to say, at the midday point, is hottest, so shall Christ be when He shall appear in the centre of heaven and earth, that is to say, in Judgement . . . In summer, when he is in the Lion, the sun withers the herbs, which have blossomed in the spring, by his heat. So shall Christ, in that heat of the Judgement, appear as a man fierce and leonine; He shall wither the sinners and shall destroy the prosperity of men which they had enjoyed in the world.

The imagination of the Middle Ages was greatly troubled by such visions, filled with the images revived from Hellenistic astrology. By that time, the sun that earlier Christians

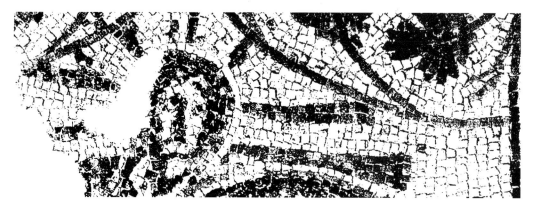

Christ Helios in mosaic in the catacombs under St Peter's, Rome

had visualized in simple Apollonian beauty, like the Lysippan vision of Alexander Helios, had assumed the aspect of a lion-like demon, a terrifying judge. Two thousand years earlier, he had stood beside the lapping waters of the Mandraki, a true wonder for the world, and one that although now is lost from view, yet lingers in the ghostly presence of its half-forgotten image in the churches and cinemas of every town.

To you, Helios, yes to you the people of Dorian Rhodes raised this colossus high up to heaven, after they had calmed the bronze wave of war, and crowned their country with spoils won from the enemy. Not only over the sea but also on land they set up the bright light of unfettered freedom.

Chapter 3

THE PHAROS
OF ALEXANDRIA

SAILING INTO ALEXANDRIA

The day had been very cloudy, with a wind at N. E. which freshened as we got under way. Our master, a sailor of some experience upon this coast, ran before it to the westward with all the sails he could set, trusting to a sign which he saw, that he called a bank, resembling a dark cloud on the horizon, he guessed the wind was to be from that quarter on the next day.

Accordingly, on the 18th, a little before twelve o'clock, a very fresh and favourable breeze came from the N. W. and we pointed our prow directly, as we thought, upon Alexandria.

The coast of Egypt is exceedingly low, and, if the weather is not clear, you often are close in with the land before you discover it. A strong current sets constantly to the eastward; and the way the masters of vessels pretend to know their approach to the coast is by a black mud, which they find upon the plummet at the end of their sounding line, about seven leagues distant from land. Our master pretended at midnight he had found that black sand, and therefore, although the wind was very fair, he chose to lie to, till morning, as thinking himself near the coast; although his reckoning, as he said, did not agree with what he inferred from his soundings . . .

The 20th of June, early in the morning, we had a distant prospect of Alexandria rising from the sea . . . It is in this point of view the town appears most to advantage. The mixture of old monuments, such as the column of Pompey, with the high moorish towers and steeples, raise our expectations of the sequence of the ruins we are to find . . .

There are two ports, the Old and the New. The entrance into the latter is both difficult and dangerous; having a bar before it; it is the least of the two, though it is what is called the Great Port, by Strabo. Here only the European ships can lie; and, even when here, they are not in safety; as numbers of vessels are constantly lost, though at anchor. Above forty were cast ashore and dashed to pieces in March 1773, when I was on my return home, mostly belonging to Ragusa, and the small ports in Provence, while little harm was done to ships of any nation accustomed to the ocean.

The other port is the Eunostus and is to the westward of the Pharos. It was also the Port of Africa; is much larger than the former . . . but in time it will be filled up . . . and posterity may probably, following the system of Herodotus (if it should be still fashionable) call this, as they have done the rest of Egypt, *the Gift of the Nile*.

James Bruce (1768)

This beautiful record by the Scottish explorer James Bruce serves to describe the experiences of most earlier voyagers who had sailed into Alexandria during the previous 2,000 years or more. On the Egyptian coast, sailors needed to employ caution and experience, and not a little skill. The port was difficult to find on the flat coastline, the surf savage, the currents strong, the rocks and sand banks numerous, the winds both fast and changeable. No wonder then, some seven centuries before Christ, the sailors of Homer's *Odyssey* also found that 'the journey to Egypt is long and troublesome'. Without modern navigational aids and charts, both Bruce's captain and Odysseus belonged to a single tradition of Mediterranean seamanship, a tradition of seasonal, short, preferably daytime, voyages, anchoring at night, hopping from port to port along convenient coasts, stripping through the bays, inlets and islands of the inland sea. In this tradition, lines of sight were vital, and knowledge of the features of the seaboard landscape was essential.

Surviving fragments of Hellenistic sailing guides give careful descriptions of the coastline on either side of ancient Alexandria, and underline its barrenness and dangers:

From Calameum [on the Western coast] to the Old Woman's Knee is eight miles. The promontory is rough and on the top there is a rock, and a tree grows on the beach. There is a harbour and water laps right up to the tree. Be careful of the south wind.

Anon, *Stadiasmus of the Great Sea*, 18

Not surprisingly, the adjective 'clear-seen' is a most favourable epithet of coastal landscapes in Homer's poems. So carefully, indeed, did he describe the features of the shoreline that the voyages of his heroes can still be accurately mapped from the ancient texts, just as can the voyages of other bygone travellers, voyages described by poets, geographers and by the Bible's saints.

Though at first glance the precision of these writings may seem surprising, you soon realize that in their accuracy may lie the difference between a safe homecoming and death by drowning. It is the same acuteness of observation typical of the practicalities of most ancient writings that draw immediate distinction between the romance of their stories and the realities of the landscape in which they are usually set. Pliny, for example, tells us that precisely on the summer solstice, the shadow of Mount Athos' peak, that most dangerous seaside promontory, fell upon a village marketplace on the island of Lemnos some 40 miles away. So when Homer describes a view on another mountain peak upon the isle of Samothrace as taking in the distant Hellespont and Troy itself, 'the city of Priam and the ships of the Greeks', we may be sure that this is so. Similarly, when it is observed that from the top of the highest mountain of Rhodes, a peak sacred to great

49

Zeus, it is possible to see Mount Ida in Crete, the god's own birthplace; though this is more than 100 miles away, on clear days the statement is true.

Before compasses and wireless, knowledge of such lines of sight was widespread, and such markers were far more numerous than most people today, used to modern navigation aids, might credit. Just as it was recorded that on a clear day, you may see the Taurus Mountains above the coasts of Turkey from the isle of Cyprus and sail your boat accordingly, so similarly you may sometimes see the coast of Africa from the peaks of Sicily; Corsica looms up from the shores of Tuscany, and Sardinia is seen to be less than 200 miles from Tunis, this latter an unusually long Mediterranean journey broken by just a few islands. Sitting between Sicily and the coast of north Africa, lonely little Pantellaria, always a point of rest for migrating flocks of birds, was as important an ancient navigational marker on the sea lanes to Africa as its radar beacons are for air traffic today. In reality, inside the well-established ancient sea lanes, sailors were hardly ever more than 40 miles or so from shore and the lay of land and the disposition of Mediterranean winds seldom required that they should be so. The poet Aeschylus, for example, describes the news of the fall of Troy being conveniently flashed across the Mediterranean by fire signals from point to point, from island to island, from the Hellespont in Asia Minor right across the Aegean Sea, back to mainland Greece and on to the colonies of southern Italy.

Generally speaking, then, in the Hellenistic age, high land was counted as useful; the gods lived on mountain tops, and many temples too were built there; shepherds and farmers worked on their slopes, and boat timber was cut from forests on the mountain sides. And volcanoes too, as well as gods, might play a role in navigation. It was recorded, for example, that the clouds above Mount Etna by the port of Naples were sometimes visible for over 120 miles, especially when the top was lit by fume and fire.

In constrast, low and featureless coasts like that of Egypt were widely feared. The wide delta flat lands were framed by long low desert. The geographer Diodorus reports that, other than a little single cove sheltered by the rocky isle of Pharos – that same island that had sheltered Homer's ancient heroes, 'an island in the surging sea . . . a harbour with good anchorage' – the entire Egyptian coast displayed no seaside features for 500 miles and more, and that the flat fast-running sea that pounded hard upon its lonely beaches was studded with low rocks and sandbanks. All river deltas, not just the silty outlets of the Nile but also the Po, the Rhone, the Tiber and many of the rivers running out of Asia Minor, had sinister reputations. Here man-made marks were sometimes created specially to aid the traffic of the sea.

Long before the rise of Greece and Rome, the Egyptian pharaohs had already turned away from their traditional kingdom in the valley of the Nile and moved their palaces and capitals out of that narrow riverine oasis and into the soft, wet river delta. Access to the Mediterranean, which they had previously simply called 'the great green' and which had little role in the ancient inward-looking kingdom, took on increasing importance. Connected by river and by canal, the harbours of these splendid delta capitals filled with sea-going craft. The ancient kingdom opened up and in the last centuries of its independence, Egypt became a Mediterranean power. Though dangerous and slow, the desert road to Canaan and the north became increasingly important. Access to and from the rivers of the delta, those watercourses that split the Nile's single stream into a dozen different outflows, was always difficult for sailors. By one watercourse, ancient writers noted, a Greek temple stood, by another, a fortified naval station, by a third, a high tower that the Greeks had named the Tower of Perseus. And all of these were remembered and hopefully anticipated, for these were the low marks on the horizon that showed ship captains where they had fetched up on the coast of Africa.

Of all these safety signs along this coast, the most famous, most beloved and most eagerly awaited by all sea-goers was the one celebrated as one of the Seven Wonders of the World; the great tower that stood before the city that Alexander founded on the coast of Egypt; the city that, like so many others, he called eponymously Alexandria. This tower, the lighthouse, was named after the small island on which it had been built, the Isle of Pharos.

> Another tower made by a king is glorified – the one on Pharos, the island that dominates the harbour of Alexandria. People say that it cost eight hundred talents. To complete the account, we should add that it was through the generosity of King Ptolemy that permission was granted for the name of Sostratus of Cnidos, the architect, to be inscribed on the structure itself. Its function is to shine with beacons for ships as they make voyages by night – to warn them off from the shallow waters and to reveal the entrance to the harbour.
>
> Pliny, *Natural History*, XXXVI, 83

THE PHAROS ON ITS ISLAND

So celebrated was the ancient Pharos that in most Western languages the island's name has stood from time to time not only as a term for any lighthouse or beacon to direct mariners, but for any bright light or lantern, a candelabrum in a room, a guiding torch and, by association, an inspiring leader, a nice surprise, a flashing line of poetry or prose.

> A great name there is, of a tower built by one of the kings of Egypt within the Island Pharos, and it keepeth and commaundeth the haven of Alexandria.
>
> Philemon Holland's translation from Pliny, 1601 (*Natural History*, XXXVI, 83)

Yet the Pharos was not named in the earliest-known lists of Seven Wonders; not even those drawn up in ancient Alexandria, the city that it served. In the Hellenistic lists, the Pharos' place is usually occupied by the towering Walls of Babylon that, alongside the Hanging Gardens, were counted as separate wonders in their own right. Not until the sixth century, in the cold and distant landscapes of northern Europe, was the Pharos placed in that charmed category of wonder, by followers of Bede and other monkish scholars. This, one must suspect, was the result of the reputation that the Pharos enjoyed

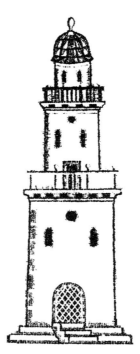

The Pharos in its later days, with a domed mosque upon its top. Twelfth-century mosaic
in St Mark's, Venice

amongst many of the Mediterranean authors that provided the northern writers with
their sources of southern wisdom and the material for their compilations. In truth, in
Bede's time, the old tower of Alexandria still really was a wonder. Then the Pharos stood
above the ancient city as it had done for almost a millennium, its light flashing 50 miles
across the sea – the same light that five centuries before, a Roman writer had complained,
might easily be mistaken for a star or planet set low down in the sky. A star, then, that
had been counted as a wonder by the ancient Greek writers as the power of their state
waned before the rise of Rome; a star still counted as a wonder by Amr and his Arab
army as they galloped through the marble streets of the trembling city that the Byzantines
had left the day before, sailing out of the ancient harbour at dawn on the day of the Holy
Cross, 14 September 641, carrying all their treasures and their taxes, sailing for the last
time past the great tower of Pharos that still advertised the power and vision of their
forefathers.

Of all the Seven Wonders, the Pharos was the most practical aid to humankind. For
the most part, it was this, its reputation for utility and longevity, that led it to be counted
as a wonder. In modern lists of wonders – those, that is, compiled since the days of the
Renaissance – the beacon is described as a marvellous example of ancient common sense
and splendid engineering. And so it stood indeed, marking the entrance to the
Mediterranean's greatest city for 17 centuries.

In a legendary dispatch to the Caliph Omar, the Islamic general Amr allegedly reported
that he had captured a city 'of which I can but say that it contains 4,000 palaces, 4,000

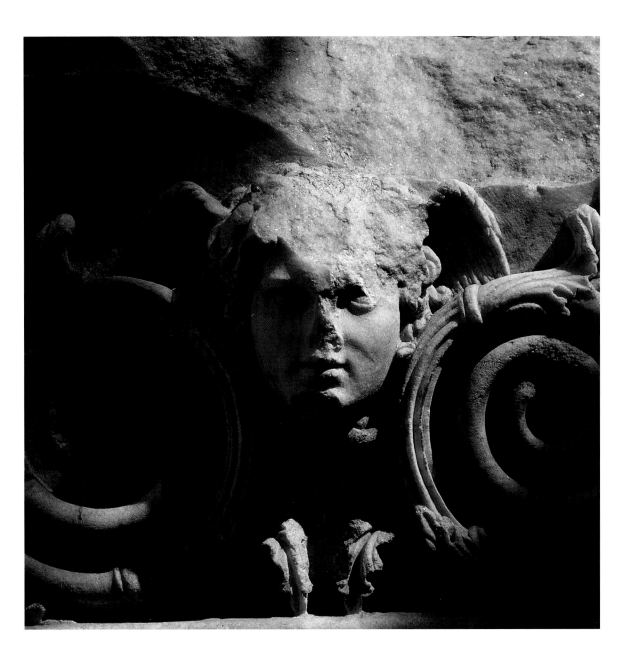

8. A column top from ancient Alexandria. This magnificent head carved amongst the decoration on a square column top from an unknown building, is now in the courtyard of the Greco-Roman Museum at Alexandria. Made in the first and finest age of Hellenistic Alexandria, the age that also saw the building of the Pharos, the capital is cut from imported marble, and shows that the city's early rulers employed the greatest foreign craftsmen and the best materials to beautify their public monuments

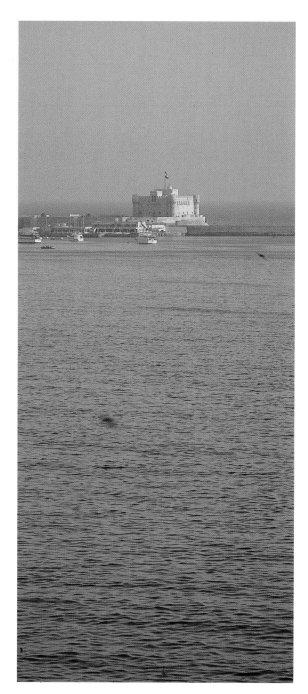

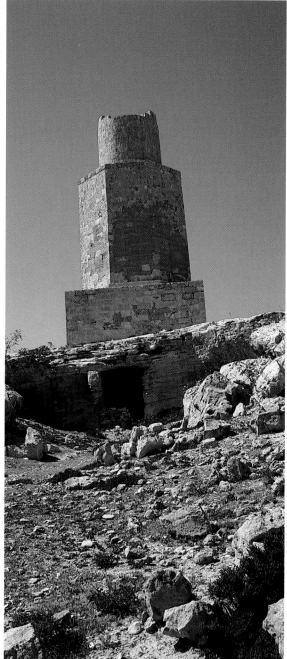

9. (*Left*) The fortress of Kait Bey. Built in the 15th century at the sea gate of Egypt, the Egyptian fortress stands directly on the foundations of the ancient Pharos, fragments of whose marble and granite masonry still stud the sea walls round about. The fortress, however, is only about one fifth of the height of the ancient lighthouse, which was one of the tallest buildings of its day

10. (*Right*) The Pharos of Abusir. This ancient lighthouse at Abusir, some thirty miles from Alexandria, was part of the same navigation system as the Pharos, a marker tower that also served to locate the port of Taposiris on the Lake of Mareotis behind the port of Alexandria. Partially reconstructed in the 1930s, it gives a good idea of how its bigger brother once appeared

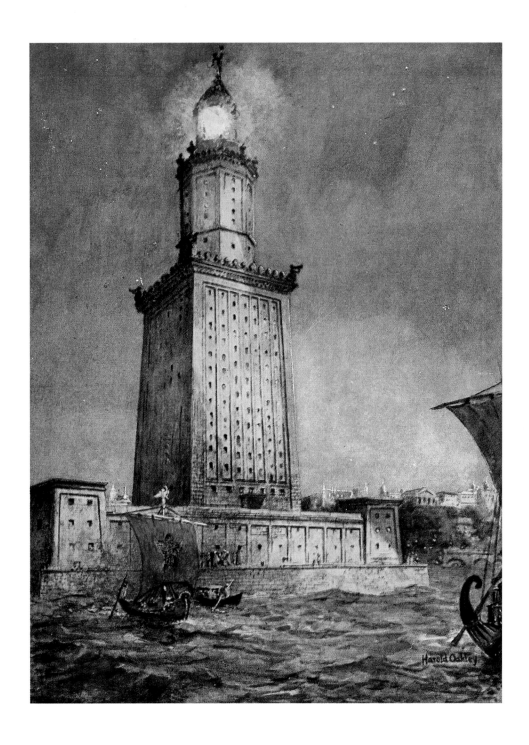

11. A reconstruction of the Pharos. This watercolour, by Harold Oakley, is based on the famous reconstruction of the Pharos made at the turn of the century by the German scholar Hermann Thiersch. Classed as 'science fiction' by one modern scholar, Thiersch's restoration yet remains the most popular image of the ancient original. In its day, it inspired architectural imitations from Kensington to California

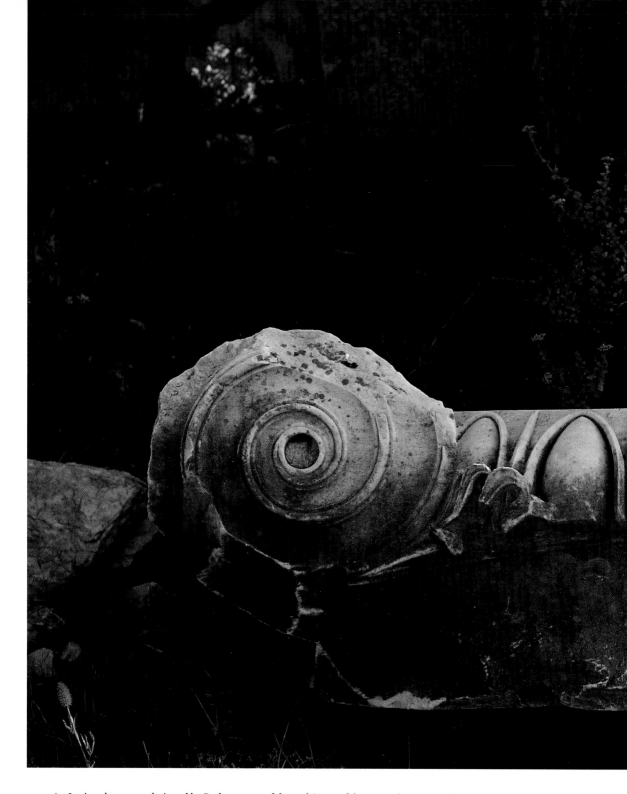

12. An Ionic column top designed by Pytheos, one of the architects of the Mausoleum at Halicarnassus. Ancient writers tell that Pytheos also worked on the Temple of Athena in the city of Priene. A superlative example of an Ionic column top and very similar to surviving fragments from the Mausoleum, this huge capital, lying upside down in Priene's temple ruins, prompts the memory that Pytheos was also famous as the author of a book about this same architectural order. The clumps of wild oregano growing beside the fallen capital are fresh examples of the herb once used by the ancient priests in burnt offerings at the temple's altar

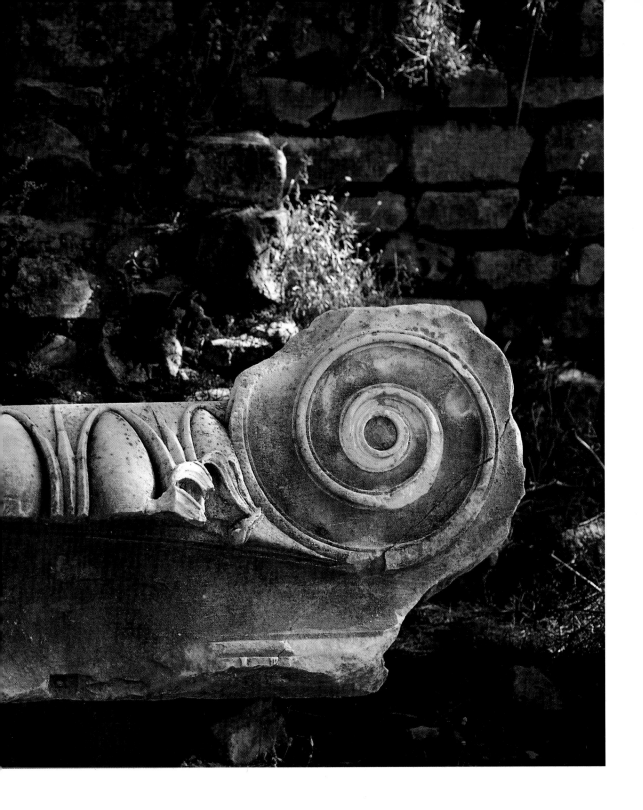

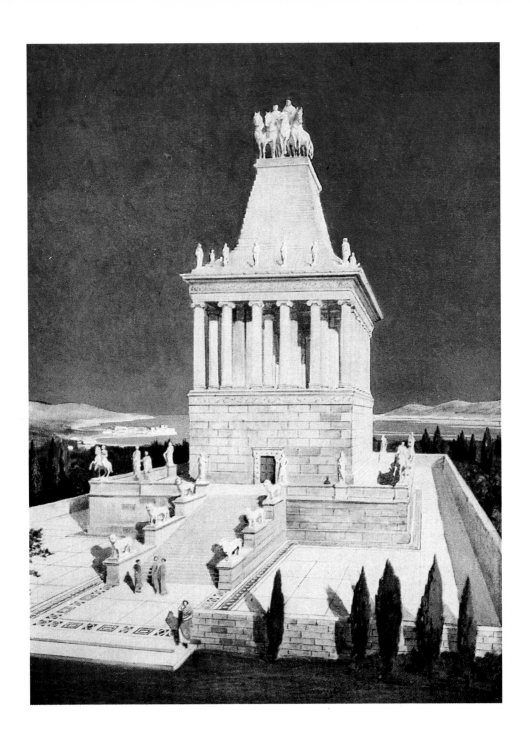

13. A reconstruction of the Mausoleum. Using the line of the sweeping bay of Bodrum, the glare of fine marble and the building's slanting silhouette, A. J. Stevenson's restoration gives a taste of the ancient wonder. We now know however, that the Mausoleum's enclosure was larger than Stevenson shows, and fine colossal statues once stood between the tall Ionic columns

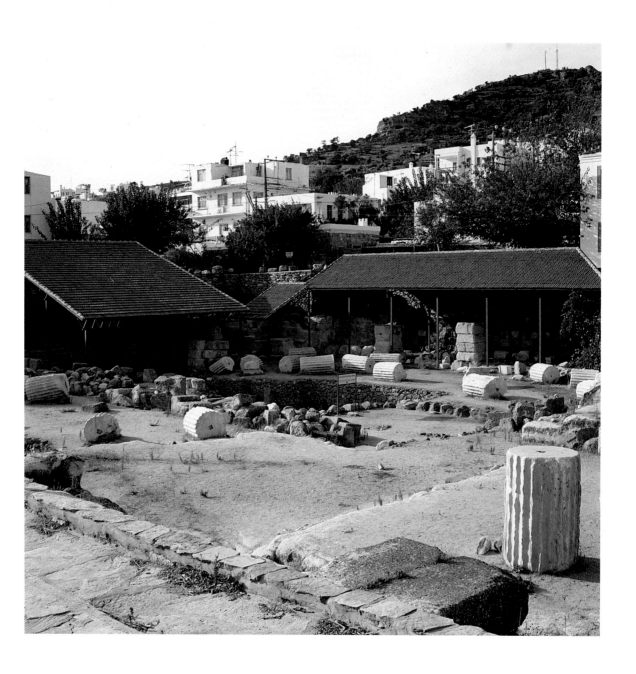

14. The site of the Mausoleum. Re-excavation in the 1970s by an expedition led by Professor Kristian Jeppesen of Aarhus University served to emphasize the Mausoleum's utter devastation at the hands of the medieval Knights of Rhodes. New red roofs now shelter the stairs that lead to Mausolus' burial chamber, once set deep under the marble monument but now a blank pit lying open to the sky

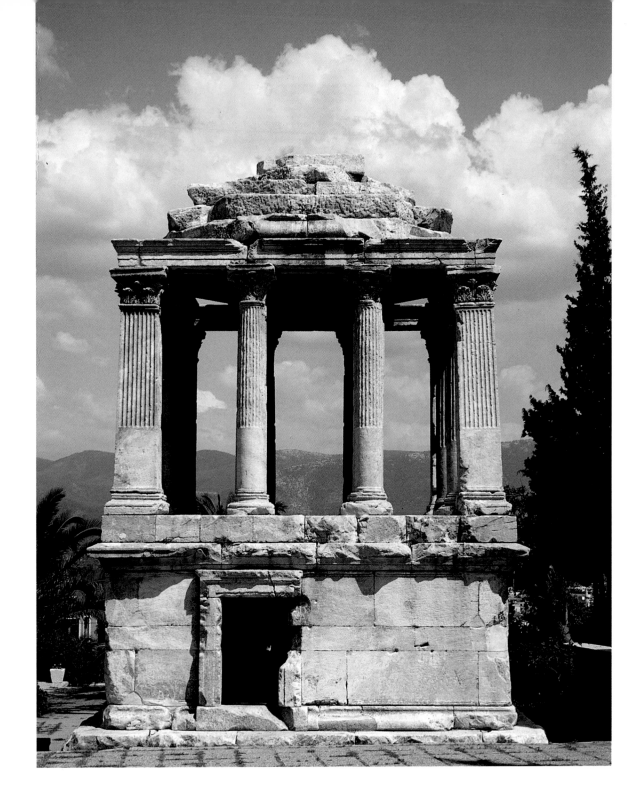

15. A Roman tomb at Mylasa. Several ancient monuments were built in emulation of the Mausoleum, the least ruined of which is this Roman tomb, made for an unknown inhabitant of the city of Mylasa, the ancient capital of Caria. Supported on rows of columns, the beautifully corbelled roof, a distant echo of Pytheos' ancient original, brings to mind a Roman poet's comment that the Mausoleum had seemed to 'float in the open air'

baths, 400 theatres, 12,000 greengrocers and 40,000 tributary Jews'. With alterations and amendments, with care and conservation, the Pharos stood and served the transmuted city for nearly eight more centuries, until it was finally overthrown by earthquakes.

Even as the Arab armies travelled through the East, and throughout the following centuries, Christian pilgrims freely came to Alexandria to pray beside its holy places and wonder too at the mighty Pharos and its guiding light.

To the West, four days away, is the city of Alexandria. There Saint Mark the Apostle and Evangelist lies buried, Athanasius the Great, Troilus the Holy, Saint John the Merciful, Saint Peter the last of the Martyrs, Apolinarius the Orthodox, Holy Vitalius, and the five Virgins that were modelled on the Five Wise Virgins. At the harbour of Alexandria stands the tower called 'Pharas' [sic], the first Wonder. It is held together by glass and lead, and is 600 yards high. About nine miles to the West of Alexandria Saint Menas is buried. A further nine miles on, Saint Theodora, who changed her name to Theodorus and who was condemned, is buried. To the South of Alexandria, six days away, Saint Macarius the Great is buried . . . About four days from Saint Macarius are the granaries of Joseph [the pyramids, another Wonder] – thirty-six in all. From them one crosses the river . . . on a bridge held up by eighty boats. From there one goes into the big [city of] Babylon, to the palace of Pharaoh. About six miles to the East of Babylon Saint Arsenius the Great is buried.

Epiphanius the Monk, *Description of Palestine*, v, 20–, 19 (*c.* AD 750–800)

In the 12th century, the Spanish writer el-Badawi el-Andalusi gave a detailed description of the Pharos, complete with measurements, in a travel encyclopedia, *Kitab Alif Ba – The ABC Book* that he wrote at his home in Malaga for his son Abd al Rahim. This shows that in AD 1166 , the year of his trip to Egypt, the better part of the classical Pharos still existed. El-Andalusi understood the similarity between the Pharos and some of the oldest and largest of the mosque towers – called minarets by Westerners – from which the faithful are called to prayer. Centuries before, ghosts of the Pharos had travelled with the Arab armies along the coasts of Africa and into Spain.

Certainly, the silhouettes of the great minarets of the mosques of Cordoba and Qairawan, which el-Andalusi also visited, and many of their architectural details too are reminiscent of the forms of the ancient lighthouse. The shape of the traditional Egyptian minaret as well, square at the bottom, octagonal in its central section and round at the top, shares this same architectural arrangement with the Pharos. Other parts of the Pharos' architecture that today we know only from Arab authors – its spiral staircases, the vaulted halls and chambers at its base – may also have played a role in the designs of some of the early mosques. With its grand architecture, with its palaces and churches, Alexandria was a major prize of Islam's beginnings and it is hardly surprising that, when the desert Arabs began to build the first great ceremonial buildings of Islam, they took forms from its impressive architecture. Indeed, it may be that the word minaret is itself derived from the Arab name for the Pharos – *manara* means 'a place where fire burns'.

Thus, though it may never be proven that the Pharos was itself a major catalyst of mosque design, one thing is sure: the first Islamic architects derived their forms from the age in which they lived; and a wonder of that age was the ancient lighthouse on the rock of Pharos.

Islamic writers down through the ages were fascinated by the great Pharos. Just as many Greek travel writers had done before them, most of these authors considered that as well as to inform their readers, their job was also to tell a good tale. So wonderfully tall stories were told about the Pharos, conflated from a variety of ancient texts and local legend. In them we discover that Alexander built the Pharos upon a giant crab of glass through which you might fall to your death; that at its top, it held a lens to focus burning beams upon attacking foreign fleets; that another similarly situated lens of 'Chinese iron' showed panoramic images of the streets of faraway Byzantium; that the tower itself was built of Roman stones all joined with lead, and that there were so many chambers at its foot and so confusing were they that without a guide to point the way you could despair of ever getting out of them, and die there of vexation.

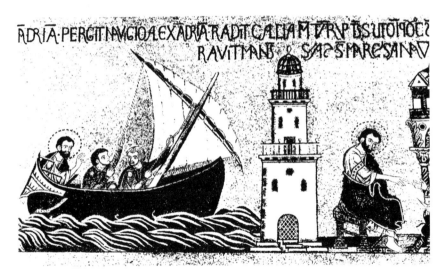

St Mark sails into Alexandria harbour; the Pharos drawn in the mosaics of St Mark's, Venice, c. AD 1200

As well as numerous literary pictures, such as images of visitors splashing their way from the city to the island lighthouse at low tide and watching donkey trains carrying the fuel for the lantern at its summit, there are also a few glimpses of it late in its life. The most famous of them is a mosaic from St Mark's in Venice showing the Venetian's patron saint, Mark the apostle, arriving at Alexandria and sailing past the Pharos in its harbour. Here you can see the doorway and steps at its bottom, the three stages of the tower, and its windows which, we are told, lit the donkey trains on their way to the top. In the mosaic the Pharos sports a little dome as did many minarets; this is one of several crowns built upon the tower after the ancient upper storey had been shaken by earthquakes.

54

The Arab writers also describe the slow processes of the tower's erosion. Here is an extract from the journals of Abu Abd Allah Mohammed Ibn Battuta, a travelling scholar of the first half of the 14th century:

At length on April 5th [1326] we reached Alexandria. It is a beautiful city, well-built and fortified with four gates and a magnificent port. Among all the ports in the world I have seen none to equal it except Kawlam and Calicut in India, the port of the infidels [the Genoese] at Sudaq in the land of the Turks, and the port of Zaytun in China . . . I went to see the lighthouse on this occasion and found one of its faces in ruins. It is a very high square building, and its door is above the level of the earth . . . Inside the door is a place for the lighthouse keeper, and within the lighthouse there are many chambers. . . It is situated on a high mound and lies three miles [sic] from the city on a long tongue of land which juts out into the sea from close by the city wall, so that the lighthouse cannot be reached by land except from the city.

On my return to the West in the year 750 [1349] I visited the lighthouse again, and found that it had fallen into so ruinous a condition that it was not possible to enter it or climb up to the door. El-Malik an-Nasir had started to build a similar lighthouse alongside it but was prevented by death from completing the work.

Egyptian records state that the Pharos was finally shaken down to its base by an earthquake in 1375, and that a century later, the embattled Burji Mameluk Sultan Qaitbay ordered that a fortress be built on its foundations. This is the same handsome building, enlarged, refined and rather battered by its would-be conquerors, that still stands in the bay beside the noisy city. Interestingly, three of the Seven Wonders have been incorporated in such fairy-tale fortresses.

At the heart of the Mameluk fortress, deep in the ancient foundations of the Pharos, is a mosque, orientated not to Mecca as is usual but to the Pharos' original alignment, the four points of the compass. The fortress is lit from lantern windows in the roof, the sunlight slashing down through the building onto the mosque's splendid inlaid floor. As you stand on the ground floor of the fortress, looking up into its centre, a space like a great high tower, it does not require a large stretch of the imagination to see in the mind's eye, the ancient ramps of the Pharos winding up towards its lantern, and the patient donkeys too, with their drivers, carrying the fuel for the light up the full height of the tower.

ALEXANDRIA-BY-EGYPT

Long before the building of the Pharos lighthouse, the little island where it would stand had served to shelter the boats of a fishing village on its lee-shore. This was the village where, so Homer says, as they were sailing home from Troy, Helen and Agamemnon once walked upon the white strand and wondered at the basking seals. On either side of the sheltered bay, running to the low horizon, lay dangerous steep beaches and pounding bright blue surf. If, then, in 332 BC you had wanted to found a city close to Egypt, as

Alexander had, the half-drowned rock of Pharos Island and the little sheltered village behind it would have been as good a place to start as any.

One story tells that the great king entrusted the planning of the city to one Dinocrates, from all accounts a man of lively imagination.

When Alexander was ruler of the world, Dinocrates, an architect who was assured in his ideas and in his skill, set out from Macedonia to the army, keen to win royal approval. He took with him from his own country letters written by relatives and friends to the top officials in order to facilitate access. After he had been courteously received by those officials, he asked to be introduced to Alexander at his earliest convenience. They promised to do this but, as they waited for the right moment to ask, were quite slow. So Dinocrates, suspecting that they were not taking him seriously, resorted to his own devices. He was a big, handsome man, very good looking and distinguished, and so, relying on his natural gifts, he got undressed in an inn, anointed himself with oil, put a crown of poplar leaves on his head, draped a lion skin over his left shoulder and took hold of a club in his right hand. He then went to the tribunal opposite, where the king was administering justice.

When this novel sight had attracted the attention of the people, Alexander caught sight of him. Admiring him, he commanded the people to make way for him to approach, and asked him who he was. He replied, 'I am Dinocrates, a Macedonian architect. I bring ideas and designs fitting for someone of your renown. For I have designed Mount Athos in the shape of a human statue. In its left hand I have marked out the walls of a substantial city and in its right a bowl to collect the water from all the rivers which exist in that mountain, so that the water can be poured out from it into the sea.

Alexander was delighted at the sort of thing designed, and immediately asked whether there were fields nearby which would reasonably be expected to be able to supply the city with corn. When he found out that it was only possible to achieve this if the corn was shipped in from across the sea, he said, 'Dinocrates, I am aware of the outstanding conception of your design, and I am delighted with it, but I think that if someone were to set up a colony there, their judgement might well be held at fault. For, just as a newborn child cannot be nourished nor proceed to grow up if it is deprived of breast-milk, similarly a city cannot grow if it does not have fields and crops in abundance within its walls; it cannot come to have a big population if there is no ready supply of food; it cannot supply its people without a harvest. Therefore, while I think your design commendable, I believe that the site [you choose] is open to criticism. I want you to come with me because I am going to use your services.'

From that moment Dinocrates did not leave the king's side and followed him to Egypt. Alexander noticed that the harbour there was by nature safe, that it was an outstanding place for trade, that there were corn fields all over Egypt and that there were great benefits in the huge river Nile. Then he commissioned him to build the city of Alexandria named after himself. This was how Dinocrates progressed from someone who was handsome to look at and of distinguished build, to someone of such renown.

Vitruvius, *On Architecture*, II, Preface, 1–4

Arrian, a Roman historian, tells us that Alexandria had been laid out in the shape of a Macedonian cloak. Two harbours lay on either side of the island, separated by a causeway running from Pharos island to the shore, and this hammer-shaped structure provided the collar of the cloak; the mainland city, outlined by its oblong walls, formed its substance. Right from its beginnings, this was a city for settlers. Large numbers of Jews came to the new town, Macedonians too and Greeks as well, many of them veterans of protracted military campaigns, of which King Alexander's expedition into Asia had been the last. Of course, there were the native Egyptians in the city too, drawn from the hinterland of Egypt; they ministered to the foreigners and formed that essential bureaucratic link between the brand-new city and the ancient land that provided its food and water, its heating and most of its raw materials too. Inside the city walls, each culture had its own district, its own portion of the cloak, each with its own temples, its own gods, and its individual identity.

The sailor's marker on the isle of Pharos, that wondrous tower built upon the harbour hazard, was started early in the city's life. If the port was to prosper, the tower was essential to ensure safe passage for ships. Later it served to advertise the city's wealth and grand potential, and to impress the city's splendour on its visitors, above all upon those ruling dynasts, all of them Macedonian, who had fought alongside Alexander across the plains of Asia and then fought with each other on his death. General Ptolemy, the general who chose Egypt for his kingdom, had taken Alexander's body and made a tomb for it right at the centre of Egyptian Alexandria.

When, like Menelaus, Alexander and his architects went walking on the beach, however, Ptolemy's plans for Alexander's tomb were 10 years off.

> Alexander thought that the place was an ideal one in which to found a city, and he expected the city to be prosperous. A passion for the project seized him and he placed markers to indicate whereabouts in the city the market-place should be built, how many temples there should be, to which gods they were to be dedicated – some were to be for Greek gods, another for the Egyptian goddess, Isis – and where the surrounding wall was to be built.

> Arrian, *Anabasis* III, 1 (*c*. AD 150)

Alexander offered sacrifices and obtained the necessary favourable omens. Then, on a proper and auspicious day, a day marked out by millenial astrological formulas, guiding the traditional wooden plough, he cut long furrows in the land behind the bay and sprinkled salt and barley meal in them to mark the confines of the city, shaped like his military cloak. Trade had been his first concern. 'Just as a newborn child cannot be nourished nor proceed to grow up if it is deprived of breast-milk,' he had informed Dinocrates 'similarly a city cannot grow if it does not have fields and crops in abundance within its walls.' So trade would be the city's blood. On the low and empty hills, set precariously between a marshy lake at the Nile's ending and the roaring sea, the markets were laid out to stand beside the port, the walls and gates were set and named according to the sun and moon and an arched causeway was projected to join Pharos island to the shore. Surely the great tower of the Pharos must also have been planned at this same time.

In the early days, before Ptolemy and the Greeks had taken proper stock of their dominion in the Nile valley, the Alexandrians had exported things that had always been to hand: ships' rope, spices, drugs and Africa's age-old products, leopard skins, ivory and ebony. Later, though, this most novel entrepôt took to itself the produce of the most fertile land on earth, exporting the bulk of it to cities all around the eastern Mediterranean, and latterly, of course, to Rome. It is a measure of the astuteness of the city's founder that half a millennium after Alexander walked the beach behind his wooden plough, Egypt and its exploiting port were still deemed so essential to imperial government that both were designated as parts of the emperors' personal estate.

The city's street plan followed the usual Greek grid system; a regular lattice of streets in which every function of city life was carefully contained. Most of the ancient cities that Alexander took for himself had a single focus in them, the locus of a god or ruler, around which the city, as organic and as sprawling as an ant hill, had grown up; their streets were narrow and there were few public spaces. From their very beginnings, though, the gridded Hellenistic cities gave their human populations undreamed-of areas of open space; space inside the confines of the walls and later, of course, the possibilities of extension into the landscape.

The new spaces of these cities – novel public areas – fulfilled a number of requirements. They offered room for trade and for debate, for exhibition and display – for propaganda, then, politics, and public entertainment and all this on a scale unknown in earlier times. For the first time in history, cities became the salons of their free citizens, just as their successors have remained down to this day. For the first time, cities had public walkways in them, and paved and arcaded roads and squares, in which the citizens could stroll and talk and simply admire each other and their possessions. Statues filled these cities too, set up on plinths in almost every city space, emphasizing the beauty and consistency of the Greek body image, the heroic figures of the cities' founders. Most of them were statues of human beings and not gods. For the real-life attainment of the physical perfection that they advertised, there were expensive public gymnasia enclosing huge amounts of space, and public baths and promenades. Amongst the marketplaces, council chambers, temples for local and for foreign gods, the tombs of the cities' founders, the palaces of its rulers, and parks and gardens, shops, theatres and stadia, were many different versions of the Seven Wonders, most of which were simply the most splendid examples of the usual urban features of these revolutionary cities.

The people of the age of the Seven Wonders occupied a different space from their predecessors. They lived in different ways, in brand-new cities, and so essential were the buildings of the Seven Wonders to the identity of these cities that models of them, or diffused images and conflated images of them, have became a part of the public furniture of successive cities down to this day. So, as most modern cities still follow the outlines of these Hellenistic foundations, we find the ghosts of wonder haunting modern cities too: from St Peter's Square in Rome to Washington and Delhi and Sydney in

Australia, echoes of the ancient wonders still fill the modern urban landscape. And this is why, though they themselves have gone, the ancient things have fascination still, and meaning: their images provide a repertoire of urban form. The Seven Wonders seem to have become part of the perfect city, the necessary city, the human city. Such enduring influence tells of the extraordinary contemporary significance of these Hellenistic cities, and also of the period in which they were born.

Inside Alexandria's squared-off cloak was everything to make and hold a city-dweller's fortune. No wonder, then, that this settlement upon the outer rim of Egypt, a storehouse of people, money and success, was girded with stout walls. Nor is it surprising that, far away in Babylon, the city where Alexander died, the mighty mud-brick city walls, the largest that the Greeks had ever seen or could yet imagine, were also counted as one of the wonders of the world. They were what a modern city really needed.

Semiramis was rich in royal inventiveness. So when she died, she left a treasure of a wonder behind: she laid down foundations forty-one miles long and walled Babylon. The perimeter wall is long enough to exhaust a long-distance runner. The wall is striking not only on account of its length, but also on account of the solidity of its structure and of the width of the recesses inside it. For it is built from baked brick and bitumen.

The wall is more than eighty feet high and four four-horsed chariots can simultaneously ride [on top] along the width of the circular track. There are consecutive multi-storeyed towers [along the wall] which are capable of housing a whole army. The city is, thus, the advanced fortification of Persia. From the outside you would not guess that it encloses within itself a habitation.

Thousands and thousands of men live inside the city's round wall! The size of the land outside the walls which is farmed is hardly bigger than the built up area in Babylon, and the farmers outside the walls are as foreigners to those people living within the wall.

Philo 5, 1–3

The Hellenistic cities – and there were dozens of them along the roads from Greece to India like Alexandria-by-Egypt, 17 of them bearing Alexander's name – did not just hold the wealth of trade within them, but a new idea that has been so successful as to mark the human race in its entirety. Multi-ethnic, multi-lingual, multi-cultural, these cities owed allegiance only to themselves and to Alexander's notion of internationalism.

Even the gods of these strange new cities were new, constructed from older faiths. Though their forms seemed familiar, the goddesses Isis and Athena, brave Hercules and Horus, Jehovah, the gods of Persia and the distant East, they too, like the human inhabitants of these brave new cities, had undergone a vast if subtle change. This was a world where the gods of Egypt might be fused with the gods of Greece to make brand-new patchwork deities. This is the urban world that Jesus Christ would enter, reshaping an ancient faith and formulating a morality for situations and economies that more ancient worlds had never known. At Alexandria, too, the Jews turned a fresh eye to their ancient faith, invented the idea of the synagogue and had their ancient holy books translated into Greek, so it was said, by 70 scholars in 70 huts, sitting on the isle of Pharos. These Hellenistic cities, then, were where such replanted faiths were born again. Some, though, required fresh explanations of the experience of life and death, and they now turned to magic keys of wisdom, keys held and understood by just a few initiates, and these selected by unknown gods in subterranean conclave. Here then is a world of urban alienation, a world where ancient wisdom often turned into a cosmic parlour game, where murderous mobs ran riot on the streets, and where the streets were paved with marble paid for by the rich solely out of civic pride. These cities, the cities of the Seven Wonders, were some of the most beautiful, the most extraordinary, and the most bizarre the world has ever known. Certainly, they were a thousand miles away from most popular Western conceptions of the nature of the ancient Greeks.

With all their grids and planned perfections, it is hardly surprising that the endless repetition of the same sweet forms bred a strange new world. As if sensing something was at an end, Alexandria held the greatest library of the world, one that attempted to preserve, for such was its ambition, all human knowledge. Beside it and above it stood the Pharos. Beside the Pharos stood the markets and the wharfs and warehouses. Beside them, the tomb of Alexander, then the palaces of the brother/sister kings and queens, the world's first synagogues, mystic meeting houses of the sects, the merchants' counting rooms, the brothels and the shops, the perfect whitened palaces of richer citizens and, later on, rows of great churches each with quarrelsome monks and martyrs' bones, and one with the relics of St Mark himself. And all the while, the great devouring city ran as fast as a machine upon its daily course, and ran much harder and much further than most older cities. In its day, and its day was very long, Alexandria was the most exciting place on earth. Of all those cities Alexander founded, Alexandria-by-Egypt was the greatest of them all. As Caesar himself wrote (and Caesar fought and nearly died in Alexandria), the gate of Egypt was the Pharos, that towering lighthouse that stood symbol of the city's trade and energy, and symbol too of the convulsive urban order that Alexander planted through the ancient East.

Today, the Pharos has gone and much of ancient Alexandria is sunken in the waters of the two expanded harbours. Of the parts that remain on dry land, almost nothing remains of the city of the Pharos. Such is the residual energy of the place that every ancient thing has been broken up, replaced or changed or carried off. There is an ingenious plan to close and drain the western harbour, and revive its sea-washed streets. All one could really ever hope to find, however, is what archaeologists have found in other more conveniently situated cities of the same period. Above all, Alexandria survives in words; it lives as a literary city.

My child, for how long have you been separated from your man, wearing out a double bed with a single body? Mandris has not sent you a single word from the moment he went to Egypt, ten months ago. No, he has forgotten you and is drinking from a new fountain. Aphrodite lives there, and everything that exists or was ever made is in Egypt: wealth, wrestling schools, power, peacefulness, fame, spectacles, philosophers, gold, young men, the shrine of the sister/brother gods, our excellent king, the Museum, wine – everything one could possibly want – as many women, by Persephone, as the number of stars that heaven can boast as its own . . . Look elsewhere. Focus your attention on someone else for two or three days. Make yourself attractive to another man. Ships need two anchors to sail safely, not one.

Herodas, Mimes I, 21–33, 39–42 (third century BC)

When they first edged their way down the coast of Africa, the ancient sailors saw the mountains of the Sierra Nevada in Spain and, so it is said, the mountains seemed to beckon to them. For them and for their successors on the seas, the world was gauged by such measured lines of sight. Centuries after, the geographer Strabo still described the world in distances, as points between such coastal markers – he locates the island of Crete, for example, by telling us the distances of its various promontories from Egypt, Africa and Greece. In Alexandria, Ptolemy the geographer turned all these old sea guides into a map with latitude and longitude. But then, in Alexandria, this new geography grew to include the shape of the cosmos, atomic physics and foreign races and religions; the human body and the soul, the stars and their strange music, and the spirits of this new-found universe; the four seasons, the four temperaments and the Seven Wonders, too. And over all of this, there stood the flashing lighthouse.

LIGHTHOUSE

In the sixth century, in a town by the sand sea of the Calansho Desert in central Libya, a certain Bishop Makarios built a church, and on its floor he set a large mosaic with fifty picture panels in it. Though they were working for a Christian, the mosaic artists, who

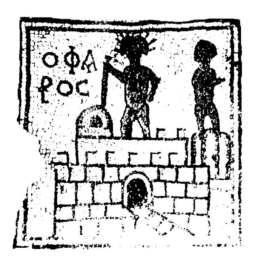

The Pharos named in a Cyrenaican mosaic, AD 539. The statue at its top is identified as Helios by his sunburst and sword. After Goodchild, 1961

were probably Egyptian, used a basic pagan repertoire; pictures of paradise, some river gods and lots of naked nymphs, and all drawn with such earnest clumsiness that you can almost see the tip of the artist's tongue protruding from his mouth as he draws his figures out in coloured tesseræ.

One of the subjects of these fifty panels is the Pharos – of this we are quite sure, because the artist wrote the word PHAROS in big bold letters in the picture (see p. 61). If confirmation were needed, the high doorway on the building in the picture confirms that this is indeed the Alexandrian Pharos and no other, for other pictures of the tower share many of the same features. Here the Pharos is drawn with battlements and walls of heavy stone and, surprisingly, with a colossal figure standing on its top, holding a sword. The simple rays around the figure's head tell us that this is Helios, the god of the Rhodian Colossus. Behind him, separated by a flow of water and standing on another plinth, is another figure, this one without Helios' sunburst. Far away in the Libyan desert, our artists were drawing pictures of the great green sea, and the gods that studded its shores.

From Ras Mohammed at the tip of Sinai in the Red Sea to Cape St Vincent on the Atlantic seaboard at the southern tip of Portugal, ancient sailors and their cities built monuments both large and small. The sea ports and many maritime hazards too had fates and deities watching over the sailors and their ships, guarding against dangerous currents, strong winds and shipwreck and granting them safe homecoming. Most of the trade route headlands had special sanctuaries on them, each one dedicated to a god or hero. Some 200 of these are known today, and they include some of the most famous Greek temples, those for example at Didyma, Sunion and the port of Ephesus. Some of these promontories were taken to be the very thrones of major gods like Poseidon, Castor and Pollux, Venus and Astarte. Quite correctly, after he won the sea battle of Actium, punctilious Augustus rebuilt an ancient nearby temple of Apollo as a victory offering. And still, on many Mediterranean coasts today, in shrines built on these self-same points, Christian saints and the Virgin Mary, Stella Maris, look out across the blue sea towards the village fishing boats.

> On land and on sea, pray towards the shrine of Aphrodite-Arsinoe. Callicrates, the sea cap-
> tain, was the man who positioned the temple in a commanding position, blown by the West
> wind, on the shore. If you pray to her, she will grant fair sailing and, in the middle of win-
> ter, she will make the ocean smooth.
>
> Poseidippus, *Greek Anthology*, Book VII, 10 (*c.* 280 BC)

Like Rhodes, the port of Alexandria was made by Hellenistic engineers. If then, like Rhodes, the artificial harbour required an artificial promontory, it required its own gods, too. The Libyan mosaic artists knew that well. They have drawn us two statues, not simply because they liked statues, but because they are the gods of the places that they want us to see – and the gods, of course, give each place its own distinctive character. So just as Rhodes harbour had its Helios, the isle of Pharos had a seaside temple of the goddess Isis. The lighthouse too held a respectable gathering of deities, for the figures on the

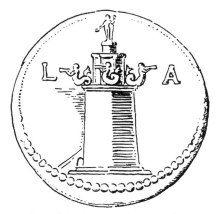

The Pharos and its statues. Alexandrian bronze coin, second century AD, from Thiersch, 1909

Pharos were not mere decoration, but images which, like scenes inside a Christian church, had appropriate significance.

The lighthouse had deity built into its very ornament; tritons, sea sprites as ancient, mysterious and capricious as the sea herself, tamed though at the Pharos to sit upon the building's corners, blowing on marble conch horns. The harbour's protecting deity, Isis Pharia, the Isis of the Pharos, had a separate temple that seems to have stood close to the tower. The granite columns built into the walls of Sultan Qaitbay's fortress seem to have come from her temple, as does the enormous sea-worn statue of her that was dredged up from beside the island and lies now in an Alexandrian garden. One of those extraordinary Hellenistic hybrids, as her name betrays, Isis Pharia was drawn from the ancient Egyptian pantheon, where she had been the wife of Osiris. Naturally enough, in Alexandria she wears Greek dress, though she appears on coins and statues still wearing an ancient headdress and carrying a magic rattle used in the rituals of Egyptian temples. Isis Pharia may be identified from all other Isises by her special pose. At Alexandria she was usually drawn as an elegantly striding woman, leaning forward to grasp and steady the masts of the boats as they sailed in and out of the windy, rocky harbour by the Pharos.

Scholarly argument rages like the sea when the identity of the god or gods whose statue once stood on the Pharos' top is considered. Although the original upper sections of the tower were toppled by earthquakes quite early in its long existence – and this forever begs the question of the Pharos' original height – one thing is sure; it was originally topped by a giant statue, just as the Libyan mosaic artists drew. Was this statue really one of Helios, though? Or did the desert artists simply scramble up the names of the two harbour deities, Rhodian and Alexandrian? The pictures and models of the statue on the Pharos provide different alternatives. The earliest writings say that the statue was of Zeus Soter, Zeus the protector, and this may well be another hybrid deity, for the first Macedonian king of Egypt, the ruler who seems to have commissioned the Tower of Pharos, was known as Ptolemy Soter. Other sources claim the figure as Poseidon, the Greek god of the sea and, appropriately enough, of earthquakes, too. Later in history, when the Romans took the port, they may also have changed whatever god they found

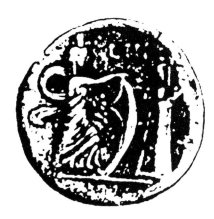

Isis Pharia holding a wind-filled sail beside the Pharos. Alexandrian bronze coin, second century AD

there on the Pharos to one more sympathetic to their cause. One is reminded of those ancient Roman statues that over the millenia have had their heads cut off and changed about as various emperors and gods have slipped in and out of power and favour. Such perhaps was the fate of the figure on the Pharos. One thing is sure, though; until the coming of the monotheistic Arabs, some kind of genius overlooked this port; in the minds of Alexandrians, in bronze, in stone or even in the stars. For it was sometimes said that the Pharos was dedicated to Castor and Pollux, the heavenly twins who were the saviour gods of navigators. And then again, King Ptolemy Soter and his queen were also known as Saviour Gods and heavenly twins, and this returns us to our beginning. Sometimes, the subtle ways of deity are not easily discriminated.

Happily, though, the general appearance of the Pharos is well known. Drawings of it have been found in mosaic and relief, its image was stamped on Alexandrian coins and there are models of it, some made like little lamps and even a glass engraving upon a beaker, found in faraway Afghanistan. All this not only shows us how Hellenistic people saw the Pharos but also, by the widespread of the evidence, just how much of a wonder it was really thought to be.

Behind all this accumulated evidence looms the encyclopedic labours of several 19th-century scholars and cataloguers. One of them, Hermann Thiersch, gathered and sifted all the ancient data available at the time, and supervised the production of lifelike reconstructions of the ancient Pharos, these in the manner of the realistic historical painting of his day. Reproduced over and over until today – historical movies, after all, are but the natural inheritors of that once-popular academic school – these lifelike visions of the ancient lighthouse remain the most potent pictures of the Pharos that we have. They show us a vast tower with an enormous beam of light cast from its lantern, the whole looking much like an early American skyscraper (in turn, Thiersch's Pharos had great influence on contemporary architecture, including many of the skyscrapers of the 1920s and 1930s). Today though, with all its classical details and sculpture scaled to a size appropriate to the Belle Epoque, Thiersch's reconstruction appears like the central tower of a gigantic Hanseatic railway station.

There are practical objections to Thiersch's reconstruction, too, one of which is the recent realization that in its original design the Pharos was not a lighthouse at all, but simply a tower to provide a traditional sailor's marker. Though they all considered it to be remarkable, no writer who described the Pharos in the first three centuries of its existence ever mentioned a light within it. There are ancient literary references to watchtowers with fire signals, and fire signals too on hills by harbours, but there is no evidence that a regular systematic system of night beacons for shipping was ever in place before the Roman period. It was only in the first century AD that several ports with traffic heavy enough to require night-time sailing on a large scale – Boulogne, for example, on the English Channel, the Roman port of embarkation for recently subdued England, and Ostia, the port of Rome itself – were provided with fire beacons. The idea was so successful that a dozen other lighthouses were quickly built. It was probably at this same time, when the Pharos was three centuries old, that it was first equipped with a beacon, that beacon which Pliny, the Roman writer of the period, complained could easily be mistaken for a winking star. So famous was the Pharos, though, that its name came to be used for many of the later lighthouses that the Romans built in harbours all around the Mediterranean, a tradition continued both by the Byzantines and Arabs, who also built more lighthouses. And so in many European languages the word Pharos still stands for all and any guiding light.

Thiersch also used his painstakingly assembled research material to produce scientific explanations for all the maritime paraphernalia of the lighthouse that the ancient sources hint at or describe, attacking the problem in the same way that contemporary engineers

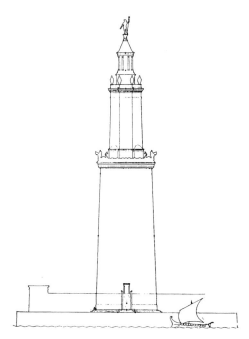

The latest reconstruction of the Pharos, by Otero, who estimated its height at 445 feet.
From *Proceedings of the British Academy*, 1933

were addressing the questions of designing power stations and railway trains with results that some recent authorities have described as 'more or less fantasies' or 'simple science fiction'. The drawings, however, are still quoted and reproduced; elaborate interior systems of vaults and staircases that would allow the tower to qualify as an early industrial masterpiece; gigantic fog horns whose doleful tones issue, in the best 19th-century manner, from well-documented statues; huge and ingenious systems of illumination and observation with lenses and mirrors.

The truth is, though, that the ancient Alexandrians had little in common with Thiersch and most of his contemporaries, who usually considered what we now think of as the real roots of ancient experience as mere 'superstition'. There should be little doubt however, that many ancient Alexandrians were as clever as anyone today; Alexandria was the intellectual centre of the ancient Mediterranean. Yet such was the shape of Hellenistic urban society that even theoretical engineers seldom undertook practical work, or bothered with practical applications of their novel and occasionally brilliant theories.

Though trade and industry continued apace in Alexandria and its great sister cities, and this to the delight of its inhabitants, the most basic work, the titanic task of feeding the populations of these cities, and of constructing their buildings, was done by slaves. It has been estimated that behind every free citizen of this city society stood a minimum of eight slaves in addition to the unknown numbers of farmers and peasants working the lands around – these often the original inhabitants of the area who might speak indigenous languages and worship local gods. These farmers lived close to the land, and generally survived while emperors and armies came and went.

It is no coincidence that the idea of liberty is commonly credited to the Greeks, for they were the first Mediterranean society in which slavery was an important economic element. Slaves were everywhere, most of them obviously and relentlessly oppressed. In consequence, they continuously presented free citizens with a terrifying alternative existence, and one right at the centre of their own daily life. So though they were an equally essential economic component of Hellenistic urban society, free citizens kept the majority of their slaves at a psychological distance. Roman society, which to a greater extent than the earlier cities of the Hellenistic East was built on slavery, called slaves, the real wealth of that devouring empire, 'implements that talked'; in an earlier century, Alexander's teacher Aristotle had referred to them simply as 'animated tools'. One of the effects of this strange separation was that for the greater part of classical history, the very idea of intelligent practical work on the part of a free citizen, or even working to improve the methods employed by farmers and builders, was hardly ever considered. That, after all, was the domain of the slaves. Allied to a deep-seated conviction that the world, indeed the entire universe, was a closed and constant system and one without the possibility of development, such attitudes meant that though men like Philo of Byzantium might sit in the great library at Alexandria and write wide-ranging speculations on the nature of matter and the construction of the Seven Wonders of the World, though they might calculate the circumference of the earth and the parabolas of stones thrown by siege catapults to batter down a city's walls, they would hardly ever put their speculations to practical use. Thus, though Alexandrians invented the steam turbine, its power was used only as a parlour trick; though they designed and made complex geared mechanisms that showed the movements of the heavens – mechanisms so sophisticated, so precise, that the year of their manufacture may be calculated from the specifications of their cogwheels – these elaborate devices were never utilized for the demands of transport or navigation nor to gear the simplest clockwork. Even Archimedes, the patron of inventors and a man who had many friends in Alexandria, was reported to consider 'science that has to do with need as ignoble and base'. His own research, he proudly said, was 'uncontaminated with necessities'.

Though several of the Seven Wonders of the World may be claimed as remarkable feats of technology, they were born of a completely separate environment from the exquisite world of the Alexandrian academies. There was a practical technology of metal and stone handling derived directly from the revolutionary, though completely undocumented, breakthroughs that occurred at the ending of the Stone Age, and upon which all later Mediterranean cultures directly depended; techniques of agriculture and metalworking, of stonecutting and animal husbandry. Thousands of years later, the classical world was still a culture in which technical innovation was virtually nonexistent and where physical achievements like the Seven Wonders were but triumphs of logistics, feats of applying ancient technologies on a previously unknown scale, of mobilizing vast masses of people and resources. Thus we should properly dispense with the notion that the fire of the Pharos was magnified in some extraordinary manner by systems of clever lenses, or that vast foghorns really did sound the alarm in times of sea fog. That is the reasoning of 19th-century Hamburg, not ancient Alexandria. What we may properly imagine, however, is that the Pharos' light was organized like any other Roman lighthouse. The fuel, though, would not have been of wooden logs, as Egypt has little of that material. Probably the flame was fed with oil and reflected out to sea by sheets of polished iron or bronze.

The best surviving image of an ancient Pharos is a large stone tower that stands on the western coast of Egypt, just 30 miles from Alexandria and in a good state of conservation. A graffito found nearby (now lost) seemed to mention this tower and it was written in a mid-Ptolemaic hand. The tower then must be virtually of the same century as the Pharos itself. Like the Pharos, it is a simple if deceptively subtle building, a three-storey structure, square rising through an octagon then to a cylinder, and about one-fifth the size of the original Pharos. As ancient drawings of the Pharos show, apart from its statues and its decorated balconies, these two buildings must have been very similar; great blank elegant towers whose fine stonework looked back to the Pharaonic tradition and forward to the exquisitely proportioned architecture of Islamic Egypt.

This lone tower stands in a prominent and useful place, one not only convenient for a sailor's first sighting of the dangerous sea shore, a marker to show that the full-sized Pharos and Alexandria lay on the port side, but also as the marker of another hidden harbour, one set on a huge lake that lay behind the coastline, the Lake of Mareotis, fed by the western branches of the Nile. This tower marked the port from which the oil, wine, dates and beer of the western delta and oases were shipped down the lake to Alexandria and its harbour. As the ruins by the lake still show, this trade supported a prosperous community from the time of the arrival to the delta of Greek settlers during the sixth century BC to the departure of the Byzantines more than a millennium later.

Excavations conducted in the 1940s showed that this tower had a function other than aiding commercial shipping. It is built in the centre of the town's huge cemetery, a stony catacomb and graveyard, rectangles cut into the top of the ridge of the petrified sand dunes that form the barrier to the sea. The tower stands over the largest subterranean tomb in the graveyard, a monument that looks down towards the lakeside port, with a wide, long courtyard and a doorway at its rear with a large, dark chamber set beyond for interments. It is not difficult to imagine that this was the tomb of a rich family, perhaps merchants, shipowners or a sea captain. Linked by a common axis in the architecture, the tower looms high over the courtyard of the tomb.

Other Greek towns in Egypt have similar Pharos in them, albeit none quite as splendid as this. All of them, though, were a Pharos of the soul, a mystic light to guide the spirits of the dead back over the land and sea to the land of shades. Here, then, is the Pharos' second identity. Never simply a navigation aid – for what ancient king would ever have devoted such a lavish and enormous enterprise on those poor souls who merely worked – the Pharos was as well a light to guide human souls toward eternity.

THE PHAROS OF THOTH

In the city he built a castle which had four gates, one for each quarter of the city. On the East Gate he made a figure of an eagle, on the West Gate one of a bull, on the South Gate one of a lion, and on the North Gate one of a dog. He caused spirits to enter these figures, spirits that spoke with resonant voices. And nobody could pass through the gates without their assent . . . On top of the castle he ordered men to build a tower fifty feet high. On top of this he put a globe, whose colour changed every seven days. So, after seven days it was the same colour as it had been on the first day. Every day of the week the city was lit up with a different colour.

The Book of Picatrix (Latin Version) IV, 3, 5–16

This city is Hermopolis, its creator the god Thoth. This is the place where, according to certain Egyptian doctrines, the world began; where the claw of Atum, the god of creation, killed the cosmic serpent and put an end to formless chaos. And the sign of this city is a slippery serpent, joined around itself, its mouth eating its tail in endless cycles of rebirth. Greek texts tell us that the different quarters of the city were each divided around a central point, and at this centre was a great tower, shining seven coloured lights into the city and its various communities. Just as at Alexandria, the different communities had different temperaments. To many Alexandrians, Hermopolis, the first and perfect city, seemed just like home.

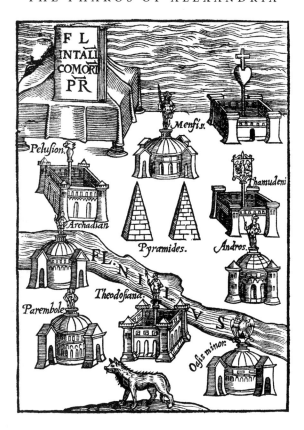

Magic Egypt, a European woodcut of a fourth-century map of Egypt, the *Notitia Dignitatum*,
showing a series of walled cities with high towers standing at their centre, from Leone, 1593

This then is a different light shining out of Alexandria. *The Book of Picatrix*, known
and used by several medieval Islamic writers, was written, it seems, in Greek and translated into medieval Latin, via Spanish, from Arabic in Islamic Spain. Its origins are
obscure, its message diffuse, its authors ancient and mysterious. Several similar
Hellenistic texts, however, also take the image of a spiritual Pharos and mix it with the
age-old faith of Egypt, much as the makers of Isis Pharia had done. In these writings,
Thoth became Greek Hermes, and Hermes was transmuted into Hermes Trismegistus,
who was neither Greek nor Egyptian, but perfectly Alexandrian. He it is who holds the
secret meanings of the world. Just as Plato had before him, Picatrix observes that 'speech
is the most beautiful kind of theoretical magic'. And in the verbal landscapes of these
mystic explanations looms a great high light, a beacon sending its magic light into the
dark of ignorance.

I heard that . . . one of the ancient gods in Egypt has the sacred bird called Ibis dedicated
to him. The name of this deity is Thoth and I am told that it was he who first invented numbers and calculation, geometry and astronomy and, furthermore, draughts and dice and,
finally, letters of the alphabet. Now, at that time Thamos was king of all of Egypt and he

lived in the big city of Upper Egypt which the Greeks call Egyptian Thebes. They call Thamos 'Ammon'. Thoth went to him, showed him his inventions and said that they should be made public to the other Egyptians. Thamos asked what good each one did, and when Thoth explained, he criticized and blamed the ideas depending on the merit he thought each one had . . . It would take too long to run through all the pros and cons Thamos raised about each invention. But when Thoth reached the letters of the alphabet, he said, 'King, this subject will make the Egyptians wiser and improve their memory. The drug of memory and of wisdom has been discovered.' Thamos replied, 'Most skilful Thoth, the man who has the ability to invent the objects of science and the man who can judge the extent of damage or good that those objects will bring about in those who will use them are not one and the same. Now, through fondness for your invention of letters, you, their inventor, ascribed to them the opposite capacity from the capacity they in fact have. This, you see, will cause forgetfulness in the minds of people who learn them because they will not practise using their memory – if they rely on writing, they will be reminded from the outside, by external characters, not from the inside, by themselves. What you have discovered is a drug not of memory but of reminding. You are providing those who learn your letters what seems to be wisdom, but is not real wisdom. If they are very attentive to you, then without teaching they will seem to be very knowledgeable, but they will as a rule be ignorant and hard to get on with because they are apparently wise instead of really wise.

Plato, *Phaedrus* 274c5-275b2 (*c.* 360 BC)

Set apart from the certainties of the ancient communities from which they came, many Alexandrians sought a subtle wisdom that would embrace all the different aspects of their synthetic city. Underneath each of the city's various populations, underneath each of their religions too, ran common themes of life and death. Though by themselves the truths that each separate community held as eternal might appear as limited and limiting; together, if the proper light was shed on them, they could be seen as universal. Every element of this mixed society, therefore, could be taken as symbol for something else. Lift the stones of these base realities and underneath true wisdom might be found.

Egyptian Thoth, the ancient guide to these investigations, had once been a sort of vizierial god, the secretary of Re. Thoth, lord of magic, great in knowing and compassion, had healed the injured eye of Horus. The first month of the Egyptian year was called Thoth, and his bird was the Ibis, intelligent and handsome, who had measured out the ancient land with pecks of his elegant beak. He had measured out the years of pharaoh's rule as well, and the deeds of the dead.

Over the centuries the Alexandrians' story of the primal city of Hermopolis became a metaphor for their own. Thoth, after all, had brought numbers and counting into Egypt. At time's beginning, he had regulated the calendar and the Nile in correspondence with the movements of the moon and stars. It was fitting then that this regulating god should found the first and perfect city. Just as Alexander and his priests had laid out Alexandria, so was Hermopolis structured according to precise and ancient astrological standards. And at its centre stood the lighthouse whose great glass lantern illuminated the darkness and confusions of the world.

So Thoth tells his initiates:

> When I wanted to understand and to reveal the secrets of the world and of its nature, I stood above a very deep, dark well, out of which a fierce wind blew. I could not look down into it because of the darkness. As soon as I lowered a lit candle into it, it was blown out by the wind. Then a handsome man [who later turns out to be Nature], powerful and authoritative, appeared to me in a dream, and said: 'take the lit candle and put it in a glass lantern so that it is not blown out by the force of the wind. Lower the lantern down into the well . . .'

The Book of Picatrix (Latin Version) III, 6, 13

This is another science, an alternative method of scientific thought. This is the beginning of the search for alkahest, the universal solvent; the search for panacea, the universal remedy: and the discipline of alchemy which, in later days, transformed itself into a simple search for the formula that turns base metal into gold. In Alexandria, however, alchemy involved a search for both wealth and for the true wisdom, a combination that for many Alexandrians was endlessly appealing. Such people saw their lives as a mysterious voyage on seas marked and posted, for those who could see the true light, by the magic pharoi of an ancient god.

As you go around the ruins of Hellenistic cities such as Alexandria, their marble bones seem to have set out to meet you, white columns lying far across the landscapes of the surrounding countrysides. Though it may be your first visit, when you arrive, each city seems familiar. For every individual one of them is composed of the self-same elements – each has its theatres, gymnasia, markets, temples, statues, council offices, walls and gateways and public water supply. And each of these stony elements embodies aspects of the new Greek civic life. Just like the Alexandrians, many of the inhabitants of these other cities believed that this strange new urban landscape held mythic pathways to the gods. For them, the walls and gates defined enclosures that were sacred, the spiralling theatres were allegories of the cosmos, the lighthouses were transmitters of salvation, the founders' mausoleums, like the colossal statues of the gods, were built to link the human soul to heaven. In these cities the Seven Wonders were not only seen as splendid expressions of urban institutions, but could also be regarded as symbols on the path toward alchemical enlightenment.

> This mysterious fire . . . all fire, all nape-of-neck, all sigh, all plaint, all . . . that you forge in this stove of fire, breathe it also into the heart and the liver, into the woman's loins and belly. Lead her into the house of the man, and let her give to his hand what is in her hand, to his mouth what is in her mouth, to his body what is in her body, to his wand what is in her womb. Quick, quick, at once, at once.

Greco-Egyptian Magical papyrus

So ancient Thoth became the guide of alchemists. 'Here the spell is of love' he says, and uses metallurgical metaphor to bring about the sexual fusion of two lovers that in its turn produces pure golden drops of undiluted wisdom.

THE CARESSING FLAME

Another alchemy sustained these great Greek cities, the alchemy of trade. And that, for its success, required the realization of the dream of every medieval alchemist: to make perfect, pure and therefore standard gold, an abstract unit from which everything could take its value. When in about 600 BC this dream was first accomplished and the world's first guaranteed coinage of silver and gold was issued, the invention of the 'free market' system followed immediately – in all probability originating in quite small grain sales to foreign mercenaries. In a single century, millionaires, misers and merchant bankers all came into being. Most important, though, the market places, the agoræ, that focused all these Hellenistic cities also came into being. So important were they that Alexander put an agora at the hub of all his cities: men and their activities stood at the centre now, not the gods. Merchants, the *agoraioi*, the traders of the marketplace, were able to set prices that were valid from Italy to India.

This new phenomenon held something within it yet more important than the invention of banking and even of capitalism itself: for the very way that people thought had changed forever. Listen, for example, to the words of Heraclitus of Ephesus, one of the inventors of Western scientific theory in the fifth century BC. As he described his theoretic unit of all matter, which he calls the atom and he says is made of heat – 'everything comes through struggle' – Heraclitus describes the very motions of the universe as working like a marketplace:

> Neither did any god nor any man create the world, nor likewise anything else, but it was, is and will be an ever-living fire . . . All things are an exchange for fire, and fire an exchange for all things, just as money is an exchange for gold and gold for money.

> Heraclitus of Ephesus (*c.* 500 BC)

The invention of pure gold, therefore, was an invention of a new wheel within the human mind, one that made the power of metaphor run as it had never done before.

The Pactolus, a pretty stream that flows beside the village of Sart Mustapha in western Turkey, once held so much alluvial gold within it that the ancient state of Lydia through which it coursed was known as the richest kingdom in the world. Here it was, at Sardis, the capital of Lydia, with gold like sand and kings like the fabled Croesus, 'Who to his Gods, did Gold-walled Temples build' that the gold standard was established.

Archaeologists started to excavate at Sardis around a century ago. They have not yet found King Croesus' golden city, but things much more interesting; the very workshops where the modern world was forged. At Sardis in the 1960s they found the city's gold-refining workshops and the very temple of the goddess who controlled the processes of refinement, and whose picture, on small fragments of the smelted metal, make the world's first coinage.

When modern archaeologists dig sites like Sardis, they sieve the earth they excavate. At Sardis, to their surprise, they found little pearls of pure gold, small splashed pellets of the precious metal, rolling in their sieves. What they had discovered were some of the smelting places where the yellow dust and nuggets panned from the Pactolus had been melted down and purified. At first, this alluvial alloy, mostly gold but mixed with lead and silver, was placed in a depression in the bank beside the stream, a small clay hearth, lined with a thin layer of bone ash. This furnace was filled with a mix of charcoal and alluvial electrum dust and fired up with wood and bellows. The lead would have melted first, and was either burned away or scraped away as scum from the top of the liquid alloy. Then the fire would be doused and from the bottom of the hearth the goldsmith would retrieve a lens-shaped slab of pure electrum. Now, similar techniques to this had been practised for thousands of years in many different countries. What happened next, however, beside this little river, was a very different alchemy, and one completely revolutionary. For the smelted alloy was broken down into its component parts of gold and silver. First the electrum from the hearth was beaten into thin sheets, and these were placed in layers in a large pot, each layer separated by bits of crushed brick and salt. Then the pot was sealed and heated up for days. In the mysteries of this fire, the silver then embraced the salts and left the gold alone and pure. What had been sheets of bright electrum were now transformed into sheets of pure, if spongy, gold. For the first time in human history, these goldsmiths by the river could precisely control the content of their materials. One of the small huts on the river bank, built just like the others and standing at their centre, was a little temple, guarded by two stone lions and dedicated to a goddess known in Sardis as Kybele and to the Greeks as Artemis, whose temple at nearby Ephesus was one of the Seven Wonders of the World. Here it was that the pure gold was cut precisely into pieces of identical weight, and these were stamped with the image of the goddess' lions to make the world's first coins. When the goddess Kybele was stamped on equal amounts of Croesus' gold, people knew that what they held in their hand was an absolute, eternal unit. Within 50 years there were not only banks, misers and merchants but coin debasement too – that is, the clipping of a percentage of the precious metal of a coin and mixing the remainder with dross.

Like most Greeks, Alexandrians believed that the elements of the world were very few in number and that the transmutation of one element to another, especially the manufacture of pure gold, had already occurred in nature, as the natural occurrence of gold clearly showed. Hermes/Thoth the alchemist became the guide in the laboratories devoted to this esoteric science. Hermes' text suggests that gold is made by cooling liquid metals, and explains the theory by observations on the oxidation of lead.

Metal must be heated, cooled, washed, purified and sieved according to the correct formulas and procedures, the process being repeated thousands upon thousands of times, with an intensity of care similar to meditation. The spirits produced in these processes, explains our guide, are the gods of the metals they hold in subjection. Slowly, with prayer and heat, all these are manipulated and cleared away. The sun and stars, the very seasons are brought to bear. And this becomes a lifetime's process, the path of self-knowing. Above all, the motive of the alchemist must be above reproach; the spirit must be clean. At its ending, the alchemist will find both gold and wisdom in his crucible; the yellow metal, like the gold cooked on the banks of the Pactolus, as soft and spongy as acacia gum.

Today, money is minted on sheets of specially refined paper, designed and printed so that forgers cannot copy the subtleties of the state. Other gods now rule the currencies. Kybele is no longer there, but Zeus' eagle still stands upon the dollar bill, clutching the lightning bolts that he once loosed at the feet of Pheidias to express his pleasure at his golden statue. The numismatist R. L. Poxon describes:

> Our present One Dollar Silver Certificate, Series 1935–A, is printed in black on the obverse of face side. The fine lines in the border that cross and recross are clear and distinct. The printing on the hill is perfectly spaced and of equal height. The portrait of Washington, which appears only on the One Dollar denomination, is very lifelike. The eyes are clear and look directly at you. The background around the head is clear and even. The fine lines that form the small squares of the background are very noticeable; to the right of the portrait the words, 'ONE DOLLAR' . . .
>
> The back of our present One Dollar Bill is printed in green . . . Between the reverse and obverse of the Great Seal of the United States is the word 'ONE' on a ruled face Roman letter having a ruled shadow. This word is approximately 1⅞" long, and ¹¹⁄₁₆" in height . . . The obverse of the Great Seal is on the right center, and the reverse is on the left center . . . The obverse of the Great Seal is described as follows: 'Arms; Paleways of thirteen pieces argent and gules; a chief, azure; the escutcheon on the breast of the American Eagle displayed proper, holding in his dexter talon an olive branch of thirteen leaves and olives and in his sinister a bundle of thirteen arrows' . . . The olive branch and arrows denote the power of peace and war which is vested in Congress . . . The reverse of the Great Seal shows a pyramid unfinished, its thirteen courses being the thirteen original states of the union. In the zenith an eye in a triangle, surrounded with a glory, proper. Over the eye these words, Annuit Coeptis (meaning, Prosper our Beginnings). On the base of the pyramid, the numerical letters MDCCLXXVI and underneath the following motto, ('Novus Ordo Seclorum'; A New Order of the Ages).

The light that issues from this pyramid is the light of providence; the same light that Alexandrians saw beaming from their mystic Pharos. As are our cities, the money of the modern world is filled with venerable symbolism; we are the inheritors of this strange and ancient state.

Everything that exists or was ever made is in Egypt: wealth, wrestling schools, power, peacefulness, fame, spectacles, philosophers, gold, young men, the shrine of the sister-brother gods, our excellent king, the Museum, wine – everything one could possibly want – as many women, by Persephone, as the number of stars that heaven can boast as its own, as beautiful to the eye as the goddesses who, once upon a time, came to Paris to be judged in their beauty-contest.

Herodas, *Mimes* I, 26–35 (third century BC)

Settlers from points all around the Mediterranean flocked to Alexandria, this El Dorado on the Nile as it has been called. They came from France, from south Russia, from Italy and Greece, from India and Malta. On the quays of Alexandria, you might meet Buddhist missionaries from India and Sri Lanka, and ships from further east as well. The ancient and mysterious land of Egypt now became a great emporium, and a place to live the good life.

Rich, aristocratic, stratified and exploitative, Alexandria was so large and so diverse that the individuals of its constituent groupings might never even see each other. A society, then, with social distrust built into it. Though there was intense organization there was little stability. As Alexander himself had demonstrated, individual human history was now the dynamo.

Behind Alexandria, behind the lakes and delta of the Nile, lived an ancient nation whose lives and faith were harnessed to the rhythms of the land. Here, the gods of nature were the people's heroes and their temples stood at the centre of each and every city. In Alexandria, a market not a temple stood at the centre of the town, and a great lighthouse with the names of its architects written on its side guided foreign boats towards it. This was a city of human heroes which thrived on competition and disequilibrium. Here Thoth the ancient measurer of land and fields became Hermes Trismegistus, a secret spirit who told men how to make pure gold with spells and potions.

When these citizens of the Greek cities – Girdlewearers, the Egyptians sometimes called them – looked at the indigenous inhabitants they saw barbarians, weak and lazy foreigners. Untrustworthy too; people clearly marching to a very different drum. None the less, these ancient people were an essential element of Alexander's brave new world and were forced to participate in it. There was of course a devastating culture clash. Time and time again the Egyptians rebelled against the foreigners, and were beaten on the field of battle. Their most ancient cities were torn down, the temples ground and broken. As it is usually only the victors who write history such tense and terrible contacts go largely unrecorded. In Egypt, though, there is a single text, 'The Oracle of the Potter', written in Egyptian some four centuries after Alexander's day and surviving only in texts written in the foreigners' Greek. Using traditional Egyptian story lines, it is quite simply the local voice of every ancient culture that has ever railed against invaders. It prophesies, it longs, it dreams, that the very elements of the holy land – the sun, the river's annual flood, the seasons of the year – will rise up together, an invisible choir against Alexandria-by-Egypt, the city by the sea. And then, its fortune giving way, the ancient gods will abandon Alexandria to failure and to brave illusion.

. . . Speech of the potter to King Amenophis, translated as accurately as possible, concerning what will happen in Egypt . . .

. . . In the time of the foreigners [people will say] 'Wretched Egypt, [who has been] mistreated by malefactors, who have committed evil against you . . .

The river, [will not have] sufficient water, [and will flood], but so little that [the land] will be badly scorched . . . And the sun will darken as it will not be willing to observe these Egyptian evils. The earth will not respond to seeds, and this will be part of its blight. [The] farmer will be taxed for what he did not plant. There will be fighting in Egypt because people will be hungry. What one person planted, [another] will reap and carry off and so, there will be [war and slaughter] which [will kill] brothers and wives.

[And these things will happen] when the great god . . . desires to return to the [city], and the foreigners will kill each other and evil will be done. And the great god will pursue (them) on foot [to the] sea [in] wrath and destroy many of them because [they are] impious . . . The city will later be deserted. The children will be made weak, and the country will be in confusion, and many of the inhabitants of Egypt will abandon their homes (and) travel to foreign places.

Then there will be slaughter among friends; and people will lament their own problems although they are less than those of others. Men will die at the hands of each other; two of them will come to the same place to aid one. Among women who are pregnant, death will also be common. The foreigners will kill themselves. Then the gods will abandon the city and enter Memphis. And the city of foreigners, which had been founded, will be deserted. This will happen at the end of the evils when there came to Egypt a crowd of foreigners. The city of the foreigners will be abandoned like my kiln [the prophet is a potter] because of the crimes which they committed against Egypt.

The cult images, which had been transported there [to the city], will be brought back again to Egypt; and the city by the sea will be a refuge for fishermen . . .

Then Egypt will flourish and the generous fifty-five-year ruler will appear, the king descended from the sun god [Horus], the giver of good things, the one installed by the greatest [Isis], so that the living will pray that the dead might arise to share the prosperity. Finally the leaves will fall, and the Nile, which had lacked water, will be full and winter, which had changed its orderly ways, will run its proper course and then summer will resume its own track, and normal will be the wind's breezes which previously had been weak . . . And Egypt . . .

Having spoken clearly up to this point, he fell silent [i.e. the potter died]. King Amenophis, who was grieved by the many disasters he had recounted, buried him in Heliopolis and placed the book in the sacred archives there, and unselfishly revealed it to all men.

Chapter 4

THE
MAUSOLEUM

THE CITY AND THE KING

Though they are no longer included in the modern lists of Seven Wonders, it is no surprise to find that in ancient times several legendary city walls – the pylons of Homer's hundred-gated Thebes in Egypt, the titanic defences of far-off Babylon – were counted amongst the world's great achievements. Of all the great Hellenistic cities, only Alexandria-by-Egypt, protected by the desert and the sea, was not heavily fortified. Most of the others were surrounded by elaborate engineering; high walls of huge stone blocks stretching for mile after mile, up hill and down dale, across the landscape around the cities. After the invention of the ram, the siege tower and terrifyingly powerful catapults, these walls were needed to command the high ground in the event of siege. Such walls were part of the essence of Alexander's brave new world; high blockades to circumscribe the land, to guard the farms and harbours, walls so large that, manned or not, they presented a considerable barrier against invading armies. Stone walls to show, by their very bulk and engineering, and the slave labour they denoted, the ruler's authority and ruthless power.

Semiramis, a naturally ambitious person who was eager to surpass the renown of her predecessor on the throne, decided to found a city in Babylon. She selected a group of architects and craftsmen from every quarter and secured the other necessary resources, and then gathered together two million men from her entire kingdom to execute her plan. Taking the Euphrates river as the centre, she ran a wall with many big towers along it around the city. The wall was three hundred and sixty stades long [forty and a half miles], according to Ctesias of Cnidos, but Cleitarchus and some of those who later crossed over to Asia with Alexander recorded that its length was three hundred and sixty-five stades long [forty-one miles]. These people suggest that she was keen to match the number of days in the year with the number of stades. Using baked bricks on bitumen, she built a wall whose height was fifty fathoms [300 feet], according to Ctesias (but fifty cubits [75 feet], according to the reports of some of the more modern writers), and whose width was more than ample for two chariots to ride along the top side by side. There were two hundred and fifty towers in all and their height and width was proportional to the impressive scale of the wall . . .

Diodorus Siculus, *The Library of History*, II, 7, 2–4

77

Nothing had impressed Alexander's army and biographers quite as much as Babylon on the Euphrates, a sight for which the enthusiastic, if not always entirely accurate, descriptions of earlier Greek historians had well prepared them. What thrilled their imaginations was the idea of its size. For the Greeks, Babylon, the distant work of mighty monarchs, was the most titanic of cities, with walls that were the largest in the world. In reality, the first Greek geographers lived at the end of an era in which most of the city of Babylon, as ancient as any in the world, had been speedily rebuilt. It had been this quick labour-intensive work, mainly in mud brick, that at first had filled the East with stories, and these it was that eventually fired the Greeks' imagination. In turn, the Greeks had then conflated a grand tale of a mythic queen called Semiramis who, filled with ambition, the love of gold and other passions that the Greeks found entirely congenial, had founded the largest city ever made.

Diodorus tells us that before she founded Babylon, Semiramis had buried her beloved husband, Ninus, the king of Assyria, in the nearby city of Nineveh, which he had himself founded.

> Semiramis buried Ninus in the palace and built an enormous mound over him, a mile high and just over a mile wide, according to Ctesias. So, as the city lay on a plane by the Euphrates, the mound could be seen from many miles away, like an acropolis. This mound still remains today, so they say . . .

> Diodorus Siculus, *The Library of History*, ii, 7, 1–2

The very thought of dead bodies residing with the living in their city was an idea generally abhorrent to the Greeks. Cemeteries, for kings and commoners alike, were all outside the city gates, and often lined the ancient roads with their most mournful monuments. Exception might be made if the dead person had been directly connected with the spirit of the city and could somehow aid communion between the city and its gods. Like the Babylonians, on rare occasions the Greeks might bury the founder of their city at its centre, often in a special enclosure close by the marketplace, a low and sacred tomb, bounded by a wall. Occasionally, too, a similar space might be made for a city hero; a warrior buried in his armour, a poet or a hunter, even an athlete or a handsome boy. When King Ptolemy Soter buried Alexander himself at the centre crossroads of Alexandria, he was grandly following a custom of Greek city life, though one a native Egyptian would not have understood at all. Here too is another aspect of the profound break between Alexander's age and the more distant past; Egyptian tombs were chiefly made to aid and support the living spirits of the dead; Alexander's monument memorialized a king who was no more, and provided political legitimacy for the living family of a general who would be a king. Ptolemy's tomb for Alexander was a fitting frame for this self-conscious hero-king who shrewdly followed in the footsteps of the ancient heroes.

Just as Alexander had obtained both his army and his ambition from his murdered father, so in many aspects of his city founding he also followed the customs of the previous generation. As far as synthetic bright new cities were concerned, however,

Alexander's prototype seems not to have been his father Philip, but rather an older contemporary monarch, one Mausolus of Caria, a ruler of a Persian province in what is now south-western Turkey, close to the isle of Rhodes. In Alexander's day this area was the very heartland of Magna Græcia, the heartland too of the world of the Seven Wonders; three of them are situated within 100 miles of each other on the same beautiful coastline.

As Alexander would do after him, Mausolus had carefully united different races into his kingdom, mixing native Carians with Greek culture in his cities, each one with vast walls, marketplaces and Greek temples and, at their centre, a hero's tomb. Philip, Alexander's father, a greater warrior than Mausolus and greater statesman too, never indulged in such multi-culturalism and at the beginning, Alexander seems set to have followed in his father's footsteps. Before starting on his Asian adventure, for example, he buried his father at Aigai, the capital of Macedon, in the usual modest Macedonian manner, in the city's ancient cemetery at the edge of town. After he embarked upon his journey through the ancient world however, Alexander's vision changed entirely. Like Mausolus, he part-expressed these novel earthly ambitions in the foundation of splendid Greek-styled multi-cultural cities, the basic plans of which were laid like those of Mausolus, each with their various Greek elements on a grid, and all laid out inside long and splendid walls. When at the ending of Alexander's long journey to India and back he found to his great grief that his friend Haephestion had died, he called Dinocrates his architect to make a tomb at Babylon larger than any monument that had ever held a Macedonian king, a tomb so large and lavish that a great part of the centre of that city, and part of its fabled walls as well, had to be demolished for its accommodation.

Ten years earlier, when Alexander had fought his way down the coast of western Turkey, Mausolus' great capital of Halicarnassus had caused him to stop and fight a long besieging war. There, each and every day, he would have seen the white shining tomb of Mausolus himself, at the city's centre soaring high above the walls; and at the centre too of the bright blue bay beyond. A beautifully columned rectangle with a pyramid-shaped roof and rooftop sculptures, it stood calmly over the city walls that Alexander so impatiently besieged; the same great building that, four centuries later, a Roman poet would describe as 'poised in empty air'; the fabled Mausoleum.

Like Ninus' tomb at Nineveh, the Mausoleum was visible from many sides and from a great distance. From the sea it would have presented itself much like the Pharos and the Rhodian Colossus, a gigantic marker for the island-hopping sailors. When Alexander captured the city in 334 BC it had been finished for less than 20 years. A century later, the tomb was already counted one of the greatest wonders of the world. The Greeks considered its architecture extraordinary; its sculpture too was reckoned amongst the finest. In short, the Mausoleum was the greatest funerary monument of its day, impressing both young Alexander and succeeding generations. Indeed, it was the durable ancestor of thousands of tombs, the inheritors of its very name, from those built for African princes on the coasts of Libya to the tombs made for the emperors of Rome who called them after the old monument of Mausolus, the ancient ruler of distant Caria. In the 12th century after Christ, the Bishop of Thessalonika was writing about the ancient pagan tomb 'the Mausoleum was, and is, a wonder still'.

If the Pharos was the architectural centrepiece of Alexandria, then the tomb of Mausolus was planned as Halicarnassus' centrepiece. Set inside its grand enclosure, it was exactly at the city's hub, at the point where the city's roads crossed. At Alexandria, Alexander's tomb would be set in just the same location. And both these tombs became an emblem for their cities and held a portion of their city's individual identity.

In placing his tomb at the centre of the living city, Mausolus not only followed the inclinations of the Greeks, but local custom too. Many of the old cities of Caria had just such magic monuments at their centres. Mausolus himself, indeed, incorporated several fine archaic tombs into other cities that he either founded or re-formed. At the magical site of ancient Heracleia where the mountains that rise from the waterside are like the mountains of the moon, he built a sanctuary at the town centre for Endymion, a mythical young man who was loved by Selene the moon goddess. To keep him prisoner she cast him into a protracted slumber on the very mountain over Heracleia. It was said that in the course of Endymion's long and fretful sleep inside the city he gave the goddess some 50 daughters. As for Mausolus' own great monument, a later story tells that his queen and sister, Artemisia, had been so consumed by grief at his untimely, unexpected death that she had made the great white marble monument for him and drunk his very ashes too, dissolved in wine, before she expired in grief for her lord and brother. In so doing, Artemisia became a lady of medieval renown, a symbol of wifely devotion and plump heroine of a thousand tapestries, whose cheerful air daintily skirts the unseemliness of consanguineous marriage.

Mausolus does not seem to have employed hagiographers to decorate his reign as Alexander and his successors did, and so we know little enough of the man. In essence, he was a noble who had inherited a small principality as the administrator, a satrap, of the kings of Persia. His links to the East, however, were never very binding. Mausolus saw himself as a Hellene. Over the years, he made clever coalitions with the other cities of the region until his province grew to the size where it threatened even the power of Athens. As it would with Alexander, such ambition had strong and original architectural expression. Mausolus seems to have employed the finest architects and sculptors of his day, and kept many of them in his retinue for years.

The careful planning of Mausolus' religious sanctuaries and cities, their great walls, their founders' tombs setting history at the cities' brand new centres, all this shows architectural pretension decorating political and dynastic ambitions, and all cut short perhaps by Mausolus' unexpected death. Notwithstanding the story of his sister Artemisia, he could hardly have organized his own eternity in any better way; his name is with us still. As for his earthly life, at Halicarnassus he built four fine walls and gates for his new city, and populated it with Carians culled from nearby towns and villages. He built two main city roads that intersected at a central crossroads, beside the Mausoleum. He made two great harbours by the marketplace, one smaller and behind the other, from which warships might sally forth upon an unsuspecting enemy. Beside these harbours, he built an arsenal with a fortress to protect the city's spring. And on the opposing spit of land across the bay he built a palace so rich and famous that three centuries later Vitruvius, the Imperial Roman architect, still talked of it respectfully. Here is something of the root of Roman grandeur:

> The palace of the powerful king, Mausolus, at Halicarnassus is decorated throughout with Proconnesian marble, but nevertheless has brick walls. These walls have maintained their excellent solidity up to the present day; they have been so finely burnished that they are as translucent as glass to look at. The king did not do this out of poverty – he ruled over the whole of Caria and so was inundated with tax revenue.

> Vitruvius, *On Architecture*, II, 8, 10

As if to underline Mausolus' influence on Alexander, Vitruvius continues his description of the city and its king as if the two were one and indivisible.

> A word, then, on Mausolus' shrewdness and skill in preparing for building: born in Mylasa, noticing that at Halicarnassus the situation was naturally well-fortified and that it was just right as a trading centre, and that the harbour there served a purpose, he set up a home for himself there. The place was curved like a theatre, so the market was positioned at the bottom along the harbour. A very broad road was constructed half-way up the curving slope along a recess in the hill, and in the middle of this road the Mausoleum was built with such extraordinary skill that it is numbered among the Seven Wonders of the World.

> *On Architecture*, II, 8, 11

THE DARK TUNNEL

Thus speaks Diogenes, in the words of Lucian, the Roman poet:

> When Mausolus remembers the things above the soil, the things he thought his happiness consisted in, he will groan, but Diogenes will laugh at him. Mausolus will mention his tomb in Halicarnassus built by his wife and sister, Artemisia, but Diogenes does not know whether his body has any tomb at all. He did not care about that. He left behind for future generations a treatment of this subject, and lived a life of a man – a life that was loftier, you most servile of Carians, than your memorial – and it was built on safer foundations.

> *Dialogues of the Dead*, 24, 431

As the Alexandrians discovered, when you abandon the ancient rhythms of the agricultural calendar, when you abandon history made by timeless gods as Alexander did, and enter human time, erratic histories topped and tailed by earthly events, you quickly lose many of the old securities. As life changes, so does the fate of the dead. After Alexander's time, tombs changed from serving as the eternal dwellings of the dead to being the markers and memorials of those who had died. Though centuries later Christianity would partly reinstate an eternal afterlife, in the interim death was filled with a multiplicity of possibilities. Nothing if not inventive, the Greeks now imagined the afterlife as holding everything from the black horror of stench, worms and pure decay, through a sort of grey Hades in which the souls of the dead vainly flapped about 'squeaking like bats' to the sweet realms of pure white light and the Isles of the Blessed, a marine Elysian Fields where you would finally beach your boat. 'Good sailing', indeed, was a proper funerary salutation, and inscribed on marble monuments.

So, in the second century AD, the Roman writer-scholar Lucian considered some of these diverse destinies in an underworld debate conjured up between Diogenes the old Greek Cynic, and Mausolus of Caria:

'Carian,' asks Diogenes, 'why are you so proud, and why do you think that you should be honoured above all of us?'

'First,' replies Mausolus, '. . . because I was king . . . , secondly because I was tall and handsome and powerful in war but, most importantly, because I have a huge memorial lying above me in Halicarnassus, bigger than any other dead person's, more beautifully worked too: horses and heroes are represented most accurately in the finest marble . . .'

Clearly unimpressed, Diogenes points out that worldly attributes all die with the individual and that he really cannot see why, if they were to hold a beauty contest 'your skull would be thought preferable to mine. Both are bald . . . , we have both lost our eyes . . . And your tomb and those highly wrought blocks of marble may well provide the people of Halicarnassus with something to show off, and something they can boast about to visitors . . . But I do not see what pleasure it gives you, dear fellow, except that you can say that you carry a greater weight than us, because you are weighed down by all that marble.'

'Are all those things useless to me then?' asks an understandably chagrined Mausolus. 'Will Mausolus and Diogenes be equally honoured?' And then at last, we see the intention of Lucian, held in Diogenes' reply, which is to express his conviction that the one true path to eternity is to be a scholar and write essays!

Excavations undertaken by a Danish team at the Mausoleum in the 1970s, show that 500 years before Lucian, Mausolus and his contemporaries had very different views upon the afterlife. In an area close to where the Mausoleum had once stood, the excavators found a rocky covering of stone placed over a stairway that led down to the doorway of the burial chamber. At the time of Mausolus' funeral in 352 BC, after the burial chamber door was finally closed, a flock of sheep, five oxen, eight lambs and two dozen farmyard birds were slaughtered and butchered on this stairway. Hens' eggs were then carefully placed upon the joints of meat, the victuals arranged neatly on the shallow steps as if in readiness for the cooking of a great feast. At the time of the sacrifice, the animals' blood must have run down these steps and formed into a great dark pool at the entrance of the burial chamber.

The fastidious excavation of this offering provided a great deal of new information about the simple facts of butchering in the days of Mausolus. The scholarly world has

traditionally occupied itself with topics such as international politics and works of architecture, and comparatively little is known about the practical details of the stuff of daily
life. For urban Greeks, however, butchering and sacrifice played an essential role in all
their lives. Before every major event, before battle, the building of a temple, the founding of a city, or the appointment of its rulers and magistrates, sacrifices were conducted.
So essential indeed was the sacrifice that, so the Greeks said, all you needed to found a
city was a roasting spit, a boiling cauldron and a fire. The Greeks' relationship with their
gods was conducted through sacrifice. The act, then, gave shape and meaning to all their
social activities. This was not mere butchering but part of a complex social activity, surrounded by rites and customs that were vital to the Greek identity. And here, at
Mausolus' tomb, the bones of ancient sacrifice still lay undisturbed.

The first thing the excavators discovered was that, as in modern butchery, all the animals killed at Mausolus' funeral had been dismembered in a standard way. Examination
of the many small knife marks on their bones, showed that the animals had been slaughtered by having their throats cut, followed by complete decapitation. The larger animals
had been hamstrung before they were slaughtered; the subsequent collapse had damaged their leg joints as they fell down onto the ground.

So precise was the animals' dismemberment that excavators thought that the ancient
butchers must have worked on a specially made flat surface; this, in all probability a
butcher's table, similar to the ones drawn on Greek vases. The direction of the chop and
cut markings on the bones also showed that just like these ancient pictures of sacrifice
on Greek vases, Mausolus' butchers had turned the carcass belly-up before they began.
Small knife cuts on the interior of the animals' ribcages showed that they were completely eviscerated in this position; further tiny nicks on the exterior bones bore witness
to the fact that they had been carefully skinned. The carcasses of three animals had been
left at this stage of the work and were placed near the burial chamber doors. Most of the
other animals, though, had been carefully butchered. Shoulders had been removed,
chests cut open, and ribs and spines briskly chopped apart. With the larger carcasses,
this butchering had been hard work and the resulting joints of meat, gargantuan. The
softer, younger carcasses seemed to have encouraged the butchers to make Mausolus
some daintier cuts for his eternal table. So, buried in the soft soil, the archaeologists
found crowns of lamb and the remains of succulent small joints of leg and rump. This
in itself was fascinating, for though many ancient texts refer to cuts of meat by name,
today we have lost all means of their anatomical identification. Some parts of the animals, however, the skin, the heads and feet and entrails, were not found by the excavators. These, so inscriptions tell us, were often claimed by the butchers as their fee, a
custom still practised in some slaughterhouses to this day. Pottery decoration sometimes
shows butchers and their servants gleefully carrying away their share of the proceeds
from the sacrifice.

This large pool of blood lapping at the centre of the Seven Wonders brings home the
absurdity of that cliché of the pure rationality of Hellenic culture. Though supporters
of the view might well claim that this unusual offering was 'native Carian' practice –

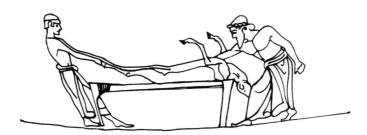

Greek butchers at work. Detail of an Attic red figure vase, after Detienne, 1989

'native', as is usual in such observations, implying a tendency to savagery – in fact we have no knowledge at all of such practices in Caria. One might also add that Hellenic society was of its nature heterogeneous. Unlike prize poodles and budgerigars, the Greeks themselves were not thoroughbreds; their culture was rooted in many different lands.

The rite of sacrifice, however, was almost universal. As you approached a Greek city then, you would have seen a thin wisp of black smoke rising daily from the altars of the gods – an excellent example of ritual equating practicality, for the ritual act of offering also provided each city with its daily meat. After the initial sacrifice, some pieces of the animals, the thigh bones wrapped in fat perhaps, the gall and sinews, were burnt upon the sacrificial altars. This was the smoke that hung over Greek towns, a genuine signal of their wealth and well-being. After butchering, the meat was then taken for the use of the offerers and for the priests. In sundry cities, the animals' intestines would be wrapped on skewers and roasted in the manner of the modern Greek dish *kokoretsi*, and the oregano used to flavour this gamey delicacy still grows wild by the ruins of many of the ancient altars. Other cuts of meat were first boiled and then roasted.

To deny that constant and bloody sacrifice was at the very heart of Greek society, feeding both its people and its gods, is a natural enough reaction for Christian scholars. Unlike most religions, Christianity admits only the sacrifice of the Son of God as having religious significance; the death of all other living things is denied any hallowed significance, and so we have lost a common area of sacredness within the ancient world. When any animal is killed or dies, its spirit leaves it, and this it was supposed then joined the world of gods and shades, who can also exist without possessing a physical reality. Sacrifice then, the human ordering of a contact between this world and the next, was a prime connecting point between humankind and their gods. Though the Greeks and Romans always considered the Mausoleum to be one of the greatest of ancient memorials, in its own time it had also catered for Mausolus' spirit as well.

There is very little left to see of the Mausoleum today. You enter an archaeological site through a small iron doorway in a narrow lane of whitewashed walls that follows the ancient east-west thoroughfare of Mausolus' city. Beyond the gate is a small flat field. Set around its edge are the sparely spaced stones of the Mausoleum's low enclosure wall and some modern tiled shelters, the largest of which shadows the staircase that once led down to Mausolus' tomb. Today, the fresh red tiles lead the eye down to a regular, rectangular pit lying in the sun, its sides supported by modern drystone walls. This pit held the vanished stones of the walls of King Mausolus' burial chamber. Running around and away from it, snaking through the natural rock that used to support the Mausoleum's bulk, are tunnels wide and high enough to hold a person. Some of these, their excavators say, were cut before the Mausoleum was built, and this may suggest that Mausolus made his tomb in an older cemetery. Most of them though, are a part of the Mausoleum's elaborate drainage facilities. Most ancient Greek stone buildings made provision to contain and direct the large amounts of rainwater that build up quickly in Mediterranean storms – the enormous structure of the Mausoleum would have collected considerable amounts. Hardly anything remains of the Mausoleum; a chessboard of quadrangular greenish slabs of stone, about 3 feet across and 1 foot deep, that were once the base of the building's core; a few indeterminate standing stones, and some elegantly fluted shining column drums lying loosely about the site in the positions into which they had fallen and rolled; these are the remains of this celebrated Wonder of the World. The sparkling marble, the sunshine and flowers, and the pink paintwork of a nearby house, save the spot from gloom. One is left in simple puzzlement; where on earth has this colossal building gone?

As you would suspect from the totality of its destruction, the Mausoleum was demolished intentionally, quarried away at the turn of the 16th century. The soft green lava stone of the building's core was directly reused as building blocks. The fine exterior marbles were broken up, hauled away, and mostly burnt and rendered into lime to make fine mortar. In the following centuries, though this brutal activity left a considerable mound of chippings lying all over the ground, the very site of the Mausoleum was forgotten, as was indeed the location of the ancient city of Halicarnassus. The Turkish inhabitants called their town, a pretty little fishing port, Bodrum, and they built small houses and some little gardens in and around the mound of chippings, and sank wells down through them to tap the sweet water in the rock below. In November 1856, however, armed with an imperial firman from the Turkish sultan permitting excavation and backed by the cannon of HMS *Gorgon* anchored in the bay, HM Acting Consul at Rhodes, Charles Thomas Newton, late of the British Museum, started digging for the ancient Mausoleum.

Above all, Newton was after sculpture. The Mausoleum was famed for its sculptures, this largely because Pliny's description of it, the best surviving ancient description of the Mausoleum, was part of an essay whose subject, in Pliny's own words, was 'sculptors in marble and highly esteemed artists'. As for the Mausoleum, Pliny was nothing if not enthusiastic:

Scopas had rivals in his day – Bryaxis, Timotheus and Leochares – and we must discuss these together with him, because they were just as much involved in carving the Mausoleum. This tomb was built for Mausolus, king of Caria, by his wife, Artemisia . . . These artists worked so hard on the work that it became one of the Seven Wonders . . . Before they completed the project, the queen died. But they did not abandon the incomplete work; already they saw it as a monument to their individual glory and skill. Today too they vie with each other. A fifth artist also entered the running . . . At the top there is a four-horse marble chariot which Pytheos made.

Pliny, *Natural History*, XXXVI, 30–1

Newton believed that he knew where this famous monument had stood. Clearly, such famous works of art were well worth digging for, and it had not been difficult to interest several of the offices of the British Government in work that held the promise of the acquisition of such long-lost masterpieces for the national museum.

Newton had long been preparing for this work. Years before, while working at the British Museum, he had seen some marble sculptures sent to the Museum from Bodrum by the British ambassador in Constantinople, Lord Stratford de Redcliffe. 'The great Elchi', as Redcliffe was known, was one of a succession of powerful British ambassadors to the Sublime Porte at Constantinople, many of them deeply involved in the acquisition of antiquities from inside the vast and crumbling Ottoman Empire, an involvement that had earlier resulted in the Museum's acquisition of the Elgin Marbles and later would result in very many more additions to Britain's collections. The Bodrum reliefs, which had been taken from buildings in the town, were Hellenistic in style and were generally believed to have come from the Mausoleum. Newton, recently down from Oxford and an assistant in the Museum's Antiquities Department with a good eye for classical sculpture, had traced similar pieces of relief in Genoa and Rhodes, and thought there must be more of them, and who could say what else, at the site of the Mausoleum itself. Consulting the records of earlier travellers to the isolated fishing port, he believed that he could easily locate the great tomb in the town and then, as he put it, the famous sculptures could be 'rescued from their perilous and obscure situation'. At the instigation of the great Elchi himself, at the age of 36, Newton had resigned his post at the British Museum and taken a series of minor diplomatic appointments in the south Aegean to enable him to make a broad archaeological survey of the islands and coastal cities of the region. Though British travellers had researched widely in the area for a century and more, there was still a great deal of territory to cover and large numbers of untouched ancient sites to examine and identify. The 18th-century explorers moreover had been happy to study the ancient monuments that they found in situ. Newton's explorations were specifically collecting trips for the expanding Museum. In 1855, with funds supplied especially by Lord Stratford de Redcliffe, he had visited Bodrum for himself, and recognized more fragments of fine sculpture buried in the walls of later buildings. He informed the ambassador at Constantinople and, addressing a memorandum to the Foreign Secretary in London, successfully applied for a government grant of £2,000 to secure the Mausoleum sculptures for the British Museum. For Newton, the excavation at the site of the Mausoleum promised to be the climax of his career.

Newton was provided with a naval corvette for the work at Bodrum; HMS *Gorgon* with a full company of 150 men, a mess of archaeologically inclined officers, and, as he had especially requested, a lieutenant from the Royal Engineers with four sappers – a smith, a stonemason, a photographer, and a senior NCO. Newton also enjoyed the company of three young incipient Pre-Raphaelite artists, and a London architect of growing reputation and gothic inclinations, Richard Popplewell Pullan.

The site, which was most promising, was a series of low mounds set amidst the houses and gardens of the town where earlier travellers had seen great marble column drums sticking from the ground, and Newton himself had found marble splinters buried in the soil, splinters whose surviving carving, he had noted, closely resembled the sculptures taken to London. Before he could begin excavating the area, however, he had first to buy a group of small Turkish houses and their gardens from their reluctant owners and then demolish them, a business which took him two months or more. Undaunted, in the meantime he engaged some local townsfolk as his labourers and soon they were all hard at work, digging in an open area a few hundred yards to the west of the mounds of chippings, further down Mausolus' old high street. Here they soon came across some fine mosaic floors, part of a large Roman villa. These they first mapped and recorded, then lifted, packed in wooden crates, and stowed aboard the *Gorgon*. Not only were the mosaics drawn in situ by the three young artists but they were also photographed by an amateur photographer, Officer Edgeworth, the ship's surgeon. This revolutionary act, the first use of photography on a Middle Eastern excavation, made the artists' efforts instantly redundant, a feeling that must have been creeping over them as soon as Corporal Spackman of the Royal Engineers, the expedition's official photographer, had unpacked his cameras to make some pictures of the *Gorgon* tied up in Bodrum Harbour. Before long, two of the artists, Val Prinsep and his friend G. F. Watts, retired to the mild celebrity of croquet and tea parties in Little Holland House in Kensington. Years later, Watts was to bask in the immense celebrity of his *Hope* and *Physical Energy*, the latter an alarming bronze colossus. All his life, Watts believed that his work lay in continuing the traditions of classical art. Certainly the notion of a Mausoleum stayed with him, for he made another, for himself; a modest enough folly in the English countryside at Farnham, Surrey.

Newton started work on the mounds of chippings on New Year's Day 1857 and in less than a week he had found fragments similar to the sculptures in London. Now he was confident that he was digging in the right place. For the most part, Newton spent his days sifting through the rubble of the ancient demolition gangs, the daily haul being small fragments of fine marble sculpture; reliefs, morsels of marble lions and tantalizing fragments of superb Ionic architecture. The Mausoleum had been completely pulverized. So thorough indeed had been its demolition that, like their Danish successors at the site, neither Newton nor his architect was able to trace the merest outline of the building's exterior. Judging from Newton's own account of the work, where he describes the excavation as consisting of 'mines' and 'galleries', he set his gangs digging through the mounds of chippings in the manner of Victorian railway engineers and their teams of navvies, back-filling their colossal holes and trenches as they slowly dug their way across the bedrock that underlaid the mounds, a procedure that somewhat dismayed the

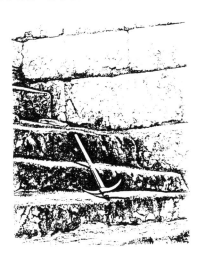

The steps of the Mausoleum, after Newton, 1862

architect Pullan. When he first arrived to map the excavation, he found it mostly reburied under brand-new mounds of Newton's own confection.

It is easy to decry such methods today. In the 1850s, however, the profession of archaeology lacked both established techniques and a basic corpus of knowledge. This was a time when archaic Greek objects in European collections were either unclassified or identified as being 'from the graves of slaves', or similar. Newton was digging before Schliemann conducted his celebrated excavation at Mycenæ, and certainly before the Germans began work at Olympia and set the international standard for such enterprises in their publications.

By early April, Newton had dug out a part of the soft wide staircase leading down to Mausolus' burial chamber. In the process he had also unwittingly disturbed part of Mausolus' great funerary feast, though, judging the protective layer of stone upon it to be the debris of a fallen wall, he later reburied the entire area in discarded excavation debris. Close by the Mausoleum's door sill, deep in the chippings at the bottom of the steps, he uncovered, along with some of the sacrificial animal bones, a cache of small statues and some splendid alabaster vases, one of which bore inscriptions in Egyptian hieroglyphs and Mesopotamian cuneiform, mentioning the name of Xerxes, king of Persia. Though hardly what one might have expected to uncover in a village in southwestern Turkey, the presence of these sumptuous and regal vases amongst the chippings confirmed Newton's conviction that this low hill really was the site of Mausolus' fabled tomb. He still had not found a trace of the ancient building, however, and once again he had to stop work to buy more of the houses so that he might continue the excavation. Then, cutting further into the fill, he found the Mausoleum's entrance corridor, now open to the sky, and came across the gigantic slab of lava stone that once had closed the Mausoleum's burial chamber. Until Newton turned it over to discover if there was anything underneath, the huge block had lain where its ancient architects had intended it to, closing a deep corridor that led now to an enormous pit. In the days when the

Mausoleum still stood, this block had been attacked with chisels but its sheer bulk had resisted the ancient intruders. However, no architectural ingenuity can protect a building from total demolition: Newton found the area where the burial chamber had been excavated completely bare and empty.

Although interesting enough in itself, Newton's expensive enterprise had precious little to show for itself. Though a corporal of the Royal Engineers had carved on every large block of marble, including the fine column drums, the squat arrow that denotes the property of the British War Department, and these could easily and quite legally be carried off to Britain, damaged column drums, however fine, were hardly what the Museum wanted or what the Foreign Secretary's committee had anticipated for their considerable outlay. Sadly, it was clear that the ancient sculptures had been methodically rendered into fragments with chisels and sledgehammers. Though Newton took virtually every piece of marble with an ancient surface on it from the site and loaded it into shipping crates, though he paid his workmen bonuses for joining any two of these sorry fragments back together, there was precious little in it all to interest London connoisseurs who were used to antiquities of the size and quality of the Parthenon frieze.

All Newton had to put on exhibition, then, was a beautiful though badly mutilated fragment of a Persian on a horse, a shattered capital of uncommon elegance, and three heavily damaged slabs of classical relief which he had found early on, covering up a modern drain. Nevertheless, the modest haul inspired one of the *Gorgon*'s officers to send some drawings to the *Illustrated London News*, 'from sketches obligingly communicated by Lieut. Michell, HMS *Gorgon* . . . The interesting ruins . . . in parts of Asia Minor, at length aroused sufficient attention to induce our Government to direct an expedition of discovery; and the first result has been the "Gorgon" collection of marbles from Bodrum . . . These sculptures like those of the Elgin Collections, have come to us just as they were dug out of the ruins, without having suffered by passing through the hands of the mender and restorer of sculptures. All that is requisite will be to join the pieces together, and it may be that we shall find some continuation of groups in the frieze

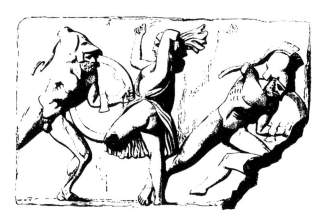

'From sketches obligingly communicated by Lieut. Michell, H.M.S. *Gorgon*':
a block of Mausoleum sculpture, from the *Illustrated London News*, 24 October, 1857

perhaps some corner stone – which may afford assurance that we possess the work of more than one of the celebrated artists to whom the mausoleum is attributed.' The lieutenant was overly optimistic. A century and a quarter on, officials of the British Museum are puzzling over the same smashed fragments, their major recent discovery being that most of Newton's joins-for-bonuses were false – 'membra disjectanda' as the scholarly communication puts it.

In late April, Newton's luck changed. Right at the northern edge of the site, underneath the little garden of one of the houses he had already demolished, close by the whitewashed lane, he found a soft area of earth covered by a heap of marble slabs. These, happily, had escaped the limekilns; clearly, the area had not seen the light of day for a very long time. And here at last, buried in the thin red soil, was fine sculpture, badly broken it was true, but at least fragments that were pieces of the same figures. From their disposition, lying shattered at the bottom of where the north wall of the Mausoleum had once stood, Newton theorized that in deep antiquity, the building had been shaken by an earthquake whose shocks had sent the topmost sculptures crashing down the side of the pitched roof, smashing through balustrades and knocking some of the lower sculptures off their bases as they fell, before finally smashing on the ground, 120 feet below. So there they lay, figures of people, chariots and snarling lions, accompanied by the architectural debris of their destructive fall. At this point in the enclosure, a large level platform cut into the gentle slope of the hill above the bay, the sheer wall of the Mausoleum had stood just a few feet from the courtyard wall, and the fallen statues in this small area had been quickly covered with soft earth brought down by rain from the slope above. And there they had lain, until Newton and his labourers excavated them. Some of them, the splendid remnants of a chariot and its four horses, with fragments of their bronze bits and bridles still attached to them, could properly be claimed to be part of the famous group that the ancient architect and sculptor Pytheos had made, just as Pliny had described it.

Though Newton continued buying more houses and sifting the chipping heaps for sculptures and searching for the building's plan, this cache of sculpture on the north side of the Mausoleum contained the best things he would find. By 11 May, all the sculptures from the site of the Mausoleum had been crated, and the sailors had stowed 197 cases on board the *Gorgon*. 'The hold is nearly full,' Newton wrote in his log 'but there is still room for more sculpture on the decks. It will, perhaps, be necessary to land the guns at Malta.' And so it proved to be. Though many of the large WD marked column drums were left behind, the marines still kept on loading more crates. By 24 June there were 218 aboard, and the *Gorgon* cast off for the naval dockyard at Woolwich.

With a lugubrious plate the engravers of the *Illustrated London News* celebrated the arrival of the sculptures of one of the Seven Wonders of the World at the British Museum. 'For some time past marbles of the rarest interest, not only from their high artistic merits, but also in consequence of their being examples of the progress of art, have continued to arrive at the British Museum . . . The arrival of the remains of the tomb of Mausolus at the British Museum not only illustrates an event in the history of English art, but also suggests the necessity which exists for the immediate enlargement

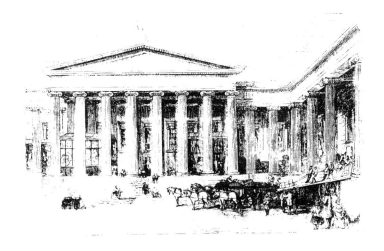

The Mausoleum's marbles arrive at the British Museum.
From the *Illustrated London News*, 22 January, 1859

of our great national institution.' So crowded was the Museum, indeed, that Newton's sculptures had to be temporarily accommodated under the eastern wing of the Museum's façade in a sort of a greenhouse. And so it was that the Mausoleum's grand Ionic capitals, a little battered now and carved with the arrow of the War Department, came to rest in the grand Ionic temple of the Museum in Great Russell Street. Sir Robert Smirke, the British Museum's first great architect, had modelled the Ionic order of his imposing façade upon the ancient order of the Erectheum on the Acropolis of Athens, just as Mausolus' architect had done 2,000 years before him.

In the event, the battered fragments assured Newton of a triumphal return to the Museum where he became head of a newly founded department and eventually was knighted after a long career as the elder figure of British Hellenic studies. And after years of intensive restoration and enlargement, Baedeker awarded a total of three stars to the Mausoleum sculptures at the Museum, all cleaned and plastered now, and set into a brand-new gallery.

We now descend the steps on the left to the Mausoleum Room, added in 1882, containing remains from the **Mausoleum at Halicarnassus, discovered by Newton in 1857.

This celebrated monument . . . among the remains of it preserved in the British Museum are the following: Wheel from the chariot of Mausolus restored in harmony with the fragments that have been found; fore and hind quarters of one of the colossal horses attached to the chariot of Mausolus; a female figure found under the ruins of the pyramid, *Statue of Mausolus, restored from 77 fragments . . . among other fragments is a frieze, in bad preservation, representing races and the battle of the Greeks with the Centaurs. Female torso; eight lions; fragment of an equestrian figure in Persian garb; part of a colossal ram; fragments of columns from the Mausoleum . . . at the north end of the room is a reproduction of the cornice of the Mausoleum.

Above such hollow 19th-century pomp, however, still floated the elusive if enduring image of the long-lost Mausoleum, an image that was strangely heightened by the pathetic fragments that Newton had brought home with him. This abiding image though, was not one conjured from the galleries of a museum where the scant remains of the Mausoleum seemed no more or less than any other dusty fragment, but was born of the enthusiasm of the ancient texts themselves, whose images were held in the imagination of the West for more than two millennia.

THE MAUSOLEUM IN THE CASTLE

It was the enduring literary image of the Mausoleum, a far distant tomb set grandly by a bright blue sea, that had prompted the Victorians to invest large sums of money in excavating those smashed sculptures from a remote town in western Turkey. This literary Mausoleum, more grandiose than reality could ever be, was the archetypal Western European funerary monument. Elizabethan poets conjured images of their 'brave erect Mausolian monument', German knights placed pictures of the tomb upon their coats of arms and the deep poetry of its ruin filled the fevered dreams of Venetian monks. This Mausoleum, this 'most sumptuous Mausole . . . graced with flattering verse', it was that so affected architects from Hadrian, emperor of Rome, and Michelangelo to Lutyens and John Russell Pope.

The dream had its roots in the enthusiastic descriptions of the Mausoleum in the works of Greek and Roman writers – in Aulus Gellius, Eusebius, Pliny, in Martial's epigram, Pausanius, Vitruvius and Lucian – and later on, the Byzantines Gregory of Nazianzus and Constantine Porphorygenitus. And all that while, the first Mausoleum had stood in its courtyard in the Bay of Bodrum. 'It was, and is, a wonder,' remarked Bishop Eustathius of Thessalonika of the Mausoleum, in the 12th century AD. There is even a fanciful Byzantine picture of it from this same date, a Greek saint's tomb with a columned canopy by a billowing sea, and opposite, upon the isle of Rhodes, the great Colossus standing gilded on a plinth.

Long isolated from the reality of the ancient East, European dreams of the Mausoleum were rather more diffuse, a mixture of classic texts and gothic form. Only in the early Renaissance, with the revival of interest in antique monuments, did people begin again to wonder what the tomb of Mausolus had really looked like, a long and whimsical investigation that began in an odd book said to have been written by a Venetian priest, the friar Francesco Colonna, who describes his night-time wanderings in a magic wood, where he comes across the ruins of an ancient Mausoleum, of which he gives a magnificent woodcut illustration and a beautiful picture too in words;

On every side there lay fallen downe smoothe round pieces of serpent spotted Marble, purple and red diverse couloured. Fragments of strange histories, Pangyphic and Heiroglyphic compendiousy caracterized, showing the excellencie thereof, undoubtedly accusing our age, that the perfection of such an art is forgotten . . . I behelde the straunge manner of the

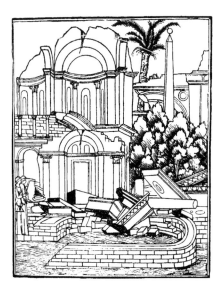

The pleasure of ruins, from the *Hypnerotomachia*, Venice, 1499

arte, the hugenesse of the frame, and the woonderfull excellencie of the woorkmanship. Marvelling and considering the compasse and largenesse off this broken and decayed object, made of the pure glittering marble of Paros. The squared stones joyned together without anye cement, and the pointed quadrangulate corner stones streightlye fitted and smoothlye pollished . . . so as betwixte the joynts, even the enemie to the woorke (if ever there were anye) could not devise to hide the point of the smallest Spanish needle used of the best work women . . . pillers small upon great, with their excellent heads of an exact most perfect clos-ing, crowned battelments, embost carvings, bearing forth like embroderie, arched beames, mightie mettaline images over throwne and broken in sunder . . . infinite fragments of notable woorkmanship, far different and inferiour from that they were, in their perfection, but now brought back as it were to their first unshapelines, being fallen and cast downe, some heere, some there, upon the earth . . . And in the myld red places of broken walles grew Howslike, and the hanging Cymbalaria bryers, and pricking brambles, among the which crept Swifts and Lyzarts which I sawe crawling among the overgrowne stones . . .

There follows Europe's first flash of archaeologic speculation:

What should moove and cause such a pride & burning desire in any man, to fetch from far, and gather together so mightie stones, with so great travell: With what carriage, who were the conveyers and porters, with what manner of wheeles, and rowling devices, and uphold-ing supporters, so great large and innumerable a sort of stones, should be brought thither, and of what matter theyr cement that joyned and held them together, was made the heyth of the Obelisk and stalinesse of the Pyramides, exceeding the imagined conceit of Dinocrates proposed to Alexander the great, about a worke to be performed upon the hill Athos . . .

Hypnerotomachia Poliphili (English trans, 1592)

Fra. Francesco used Vitruvius and Pliny as his nocturnal guides. Twenty years later, there were several printed editions of these two Roman authors in the bookshops, and architects and artists were preparing less feverish reconstructions to illustrate their written texts. Ironically, at this very same period, at the same time that scholars were disinterring the literary Mausoleum from 2,000 years of accumulated hyperbole, the real ancient building in the town of Bodrum that was the root of all those images was being demolished. The Knights Hospitaller, an order of military monks sworn to work for the succour and protection of poor Christian pilgrims, needed stone and mortar to strengthen the great castle that they had built upon the ruins of Mausolus' ruined palace on Bodrum Bay. The story of the Mausoleum's ending is not difficult to trace; there is record of it in the account books of the Knights at Malta that even list the sums paid for the wood that fired the kilns in which the Mausoleum's marbles were rendered into lime. There are as well the sometimes despairing accounts of travellers, many of them the self-same people – scholars and pilgrims – who also recorded the legends of the ancient Colossus upon the nearby isle of Rhodes, which at this same time was the headquarters of the Grand Master of the Knights.

Briefly then, in the first quarter of the 15th century, two visions of the antique past ran side by side in Europe. One, the traditional view held by the Knights, was that the ruins of the antique past were pagan and therefore dangerous, but though they were beyond polite conversation, they might provide a useful quarry for new buildings – the destruction of ancient Rome, for example, continued throughout the 15th century. The other, more modern, view was that the ruins of the past were both beautiful and precious, a heritage and exemplar, just as the dreaming friar had described. When the Knights were smashing up the sculptures of the Mausoleum and burning them in kilns on Bodrum beach, close by, at Rhodes, an antiquarian was writing poems to some ancient statues that he had found there in the Garden of the Knights, and was tying his verses with coloured ribbons around their crumbling stony necks. As Fra. Sabba di Castiglione reported to his patron, Isabella d' Este, at home in Mantua: 'They lie around despised, abused and so little valued that they are exposed to wind and rain, snow and storm which miserably consume and waste them so that pity for their cruel fate moved me, just as if I had seen my father's unburied bones; I improvised a little sonnet on them, which I am sending to your Ladyship . . .' The following month, Fra. Sabba wrote to Isabella that there was talk of a major find at Bodrum:

It is four or six days since we have letters from the Captain of the Castle of St Peter, where the city of Halicarnassus used to be. Near the place where one can still see venerable ruins of the famous sepulchre of Mausolus, a new burial has been found under the earth . . . the sculpture is of finest marble, and all of one piece, and its cover is five spans high and also of one piece . . . I hope, God willing, to go and see it soon, but one fear holds me back. That is that Monsignor our most reverend Grand Master will write to the Captain telling him to break the tomb for lime, because the most reverend lord is naturally hostile to . . . antiquity . . .

The embattled Knights had built their fortress in the Bay of Bodrum a century before Fra. Sabba's time, thinking, as they put it, to 'control Asia' – or, as we might say, as part of a plan to control the ships that sailed the ancient trade routes of the eastern Mediterranean. Schlegelholt, a German Knight, first planned the outpost to command a narrow strait, and complement another on the opposing isle of Kos. When they began to build, no Westerner had known that the little Turkish town beside their fortress stood on the site of Mausolus' great city. But even had they known, it is doubtful that they would have given a fig. As was usual for these fighting monks, the order was being pushed ever further from the holy places that it was sworn to protect and hold, and was fighting to retain a toehold on the eastern seaboard. During the 15th century, as Constantinople fell and Turkish armies reached ever deeper into Europe, the Castle of St Peter, the Knights' last Asian outpost, was continuously and somewhat frenetically enlarged. And right throughout that same time, the embattled Knights must have seen the ancient Mausoleum, standing broken half a mile away, high and white above the Turkish town. Something of its presence, too, may be found in the tales of the travellers who used the castle's armoured port as their point of entry on their journey to the holy places. There is a pilgrim legend that in ancient times Bodrum had been Tarsus, the city of St Paul, and that before their removal to Cologne, the Three Wise Men had been buried there together. Their tombs, so it was said, were 'large and tall' and therefore, one imagines, highly visible.

Usually the Castle garrison consisted of around 150 Knights of various Western European nationalities, each one of which had built its own tower for eating and accommodation, and had its own section of the castle wall to guard and hold. Accompanied by their squires and servants and by many mercenaries, the garrison made up a sizable community on the edge of a hostile continent. Relations with the Turkish town were generally difficult. Sometimes the two communities were openly at war, and the Knights had to take care behind their battlements to dodge the casual arrows of archers in the town. Then the Knights would terrorize the townsfolk with destructive armoured forays and with ferocious packs of dogs that were released by day and gathered in at night for feeding by blasts from the garrison trumpeters. Usually, though, a wary peace prevailed. Then the Knights bought their water, food and firewood from the merchants of the town, sometimes ransomed the occasional Christian slave and conducted a brisk trade in local carpets. There were, of course, the usual garrison scandals.

Two major events changed this vertiginous existence upon the edge of Asia. The first was the defection of the Sultan's brother Djem to Rhodes in 1482 which, though it had initially caused all hostility to cease between the Hospitallers and the Turks, had provoked open warfare when the prince was sent to Rome as hostage to aid the Pope's project for a new crusade. The second was the appearance in the Turkish armies of cannon capable of knocking down the castle's walls. All at once, the Grand Master at Rhodes was sending architects and engineers to all Hospitallers' island outposts charged with refortifying the castles' walls so as to withstand the massive cannonballs. At Bodrum, armed parties foraged from the castle each day hunting for building stone and buying wood to feed the limekilns that produced the mortar. Throughout the last quarter of the 15th century, the Knights sucked the best part of the stone of Mausolus' ancient capital into the castle walls, where today most of the surviving remnants of the city are still buried. Framed by rougher, darker blocks, the fine marbles from the city temples are displayed, reused and recut to bear the crests, titles and nationalities of the Knights. Naturally, at first the Knights took the stones lying nearest to their castle, but gradually they moved further afield.

Around 1522, the stonemasons finally arrived at the enclosure of the Mausoleum, 'steps of white marble . . . in the middle of a level field' it is called in the melancholy chronicle made some 50 years later by the Lyonnais Claude Guichard, one of many citizens of that city who had served in St Peter's Castle.

> In the year 1522, when Sultan Suleyman was preparing to attack Rhodes, the Grand Master, knowing the importance of the Castle of St Peter, and being aware that the Turks would seize it easily at the first assault, sent some Knights to repair the fortress and make all due preparations to resist the enemy. Among the number of those sent was the Commandeur de la Tourette Lyonnaise, a Lyonnais Knight, who was afterwards present at the taking of Rhodes, and came to France, where he related what I am now about to narrate to M. d'Alechamps, a person sufficiently known by his learned writings, and whose name I mention here only for the purpose of publishing my authority for so singular a story.
>
> When these Knights had arrived at Mesy [the Knights' name for Bodrum], they at once commenced fortifying the castle; and looking about for stones wherewith to make lime, found no more suitable or more easily got at than some steps of white marble, raised in the form of a terrace in the middle of a level field near the port, which had formerly been the great square of Halicarnassus. They therefore pulled down and took away these marble steps, and, finding the stone good, proceeded, after having destroyed the little masonry remaining above ground, to dig lower down, in the hope of finding more.
>
> In this they had great success, for in a short time they saw that the deeper they went, the more the structure was enlarged, supplying them not only with stone for making lime, but also for building. After four or five days, having laid bare a great space one afternoon, they saw an opening as into a cellar. Taking a candle, they let themselves down through this opening, and found that it led into a fine large square apartment, ornamented all round with columns of marble, with their bases, capitals, architrave, frieze, and cornices, engraved and sculptured in half-relief. The space between the columns was lined with slabs and bands of marbles of different colours, ornamented with mouldings and sculptures, in harmony with the rest of the work, and inserted in the white ground of the wall, where battle-scenes were represented sculptured in relief.
>
> Having at first admired these works, and entertained their fancy with the singularity of the sculpture, they pulled it to pieces, and broke up the whole of it, applying it to the same purpose as the rest.
>
> Beyond this apartment, they found a very low doorway, which led into another apartment, serving as an antechamber, where was a sepulchre, with decorated column tops and

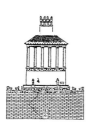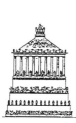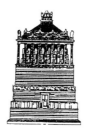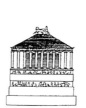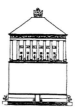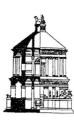

Various European Mausoleum reconstructions, from 1858 to 1989

a tympanum of white marble, very beautiful, and of marvellous lustre. For want of time, they did not open this sepulchre, the retreat having already sounded. The day after, when they returned, they found the tomb opened, and the earth all round strewn with fragments of cloth of gold, and spangles of the same metal, which made them suppose that the pirates, who hovered along this coast, having some inkling of what had been discovered, had visited the place during the night, and had removed the lid of the sepulchre. It is supposed that they discovered in it much treasure.

It was thus, that this magnificent tomb, which ranked among the Seven Wonders of the World, after having escaped the fury of the barbarians, and remained standing for the space of 2,247 years, was discovered and destroyed to repair the Castle of St Peter by the Knights of Rhodes, who immediately after this were driven completely out of Asia by the Turks.

The Knights had come across the Mausoleum half-buried on its gentle slope, and as they took it down stone by stone and dug into the debris and soil surrounding it, to their surprise, they found that the building became larger as it neared its foundations, a statement that, so modern scholars have deduced, shows that the walls of the Mausoleum were either stepped or battered. The Knights had already found other tombs in earlier years and treasures too, as Fra. Sabba had reported, and it is indeed surprising, if not incredible, that when they happened upon the largest tomb of all in Bodrum they did not quickly plunder it, despite the castle trumpeters having sounded the retreat. Here, after all, was a treasure lying within arms' reach and all that was required to take it was the opening of a sarcophagus and perhaps some other boxes too; a work of minutes. This part of the story, that tells us that it was the Turks – the 'pirates' as the Commandeur de la Tourette Lyonnaise calls them – and not the Knights that plundered the tomb, has the effect of keeping the names of the treasure's holders a secret. Such stories are common enough in this period and gave rise to the legends of the Hospitallers' great wealth; a legend marvellously employed by Dashiell Hammett and John Houston in *The Maltese Falcon*.

Written at a distance of 50 years, not all of Guichard's details may be accurate, but there is no good reason to discount his outline. Some details indeed are proved by recent discoveries. When the Danish archaeologists were working in the area of the burial chamber, for example, they too, like the Knights on their return next day, found a small dispersed treasure, 'the earth all round strewn with fragments of cloth of gold, and spangles of the same metal'. The Danish finds were of a few beads of stone and variegated glass, some gold beads and 40 or so rosettes, most of them 1 inch wide, and cut from thin gold sheet, their edges pieced with holes; embossed rosettes such as were sewn onto the robes of Middle Eastern potentates millennia before and after Mausolus' day. These items, in all probability, were the last remaining fragments of Mausolus' burial, although we may never know for sure. Mausolus' burial probably contained similar riches to that of his contemporary, Philip of Macedon, Alexander's father, whose undisturbed tomb was recovered, filled with fine things, in 1977 at the Macedonian royal burying grounds.

Newton's excavations show that the Knights had rendered much of the Mausoleum's marbles into kiln-sized chunks, breaking the inconveniently shaped sculptures down on site before transporting the fragments to the kilns close to the castle, where the fuel for firing them was stored. The surviving accounts of the Grand Knights, part of the records of the castle's endless rebuilding programme, contain mention, on various dates, of the wood used to fire the kilns. Presumably these kilns, the *forni della calcina*, were the ovens that burnt the celebrated antique sculptures as Guichard says they did, leaving us only those sad fragments that Newton excavated.

Some of the more whimsical Knights used a few of the Mausoleum's reliefs as elements of decoration on the fortress walls. For several hundred years, Mausolus' battle frieze of Amazons and Greeks served to stir the blood of sentries standing at the castle gate. And on the English tower, the Plantagenet arms were embellished with some of the fine Greek Mausoleum lions, an extraordinary mix of style and culture, and of course an extraordinarily heraldic symmetry, too. Over the centuries, these sculptures in the grand old castle became well known to travellers, and in the 1840s, Lord Stratford de Redcliffe asked the sultan's permission to remove them to England. An imperial firman was subsequently written, and 13 damaged and eroded slabs were 'rescued from their perilous and obscure situation at Bodrum and brought to England' by the commander of HMS *Siren*. Unfortunately, the good captain left no records of the places whence he had removed them. So, despite the fact that they were often pictured in early travel books – drawings that are not accurate but picturesque – their provenance is lost to us. That is a shame, for the information would have greatly aided the study of the Mausoleum.

It was the arrival of these blocks at the British Museum that stirred Newton's interest in the Mausoleum and inspired his thesis that there should be further sculptures still buried at the ancient site. First he asked the Admiralty to authorize some mapping surveys of Bodrum hoping that the naval officers would find traces of the Mausoleum, which they duly did. When he arrived in Bodrum a few years later and went to the castle to look for more sculpture, he found to his surprise, as he walked in through the door, splendid lions still built into the walls, and he 'had no hesitation in at once recognizing these as part of the Mausoleum'. At the same time as he started his excavations at Bodrum, he had these sculptures taken down; most of them went to England, and one splendid example was sent to the imperial collections in Constantinople.

Recent studies in the fortress have revealed further slabs of relief buried in its walls. The same studies have also shown that entire walls of the fortifications, some of them of colossal dimensions, are built wholly of the Mausoleum's stones. The two churches in the fortress too, one for the Greek and one for the Latin rite, are principally built of large blocks of hard grey limestone whose carefully chiselled edges show them to be of the time of Mausolus. Yet more of these impressive ancient blocks form the corners and the turret stones of some of the last of the castle walls to be erected. Other large sections of the castle, which are also dated to the precise period of the Mausoleum's destruction are constructed, or sometimes sheathed, in precisely the same type of blocks of soft green lava stone that to this day still line the base of the Mausoleum's core. The fortress architects seem to have judged this soft stone to be especially resistant to the sharp hard shocks of cannonballs. Many of these slabs are angled on the tops of ramparts to provide a platform that is almost insurmountable for attacking troops, and a pillbox-like defence against the Turkish cannon. Numbers of these same clean, easily recognizable stones are also used in pavements and in staircases.

The final battles, though, the battles that for 20 years or so the Knights at Bodrum had expected and for which they had rearmed their castle, actually took place at Rhodes, in precisely the same year, 1522, during which, so Guichard says, the Mausoleum was destroyed. Shortly after a desperate resistance, the Knights sailed away from Rhodes under truce, to settle at Valetta on the isle of Malta. The superb Castle of St Peter at Bodrum, filled with the remnants of the ancient Mausoleum, was handed over to the Turkish armies without a cannon being fired.

The fortress is still a picturesque palimpsest of the ancient city from which it was made. Sections of the walls of Mausolus' lost palace protrude from flowerbeds. Fragments of otherwise unrecorded temples sit high up on its walls, shielding the splendid crests that still decorate its towers. Blocks of shining anciently imported marble bear the names of the Knights and the blazons of their nationalities. Inevitably, one wonders if amongst the mass of stone there are not more pieces of Mausolus' fabled tomb still set there in the walls, medieval texts now inscribed upon their backs; fighting Greeks and Amazons encrusted with builder's lime standing hidden in the dark thickness of the wall. Outside in the sunlight, the Knights' domestic architecture still holds fragments of the Mausoleum's marvellous marble architecture, serving as sills and doorways. Faint marks on some of these stones have recently provided many of the dimensions of the Mausoleum that were previously quite unknown; the precise spacing of the colonnade that seemed to be 'poised in empty air', the size of its stepped roof as it rose to its final point beneath Pytheos' chariot; details of the genuine building that centuries of European scholarship and fantasy never knew.

In AD 382, the great Byzantine scholar Gregory of Nazianzus briefly mentioned the Mausoleum in a poem. It is one of the wonders of the world, he tells us, 'The tomb of Mausolus is gigantic but it is honoured by the Carians; no tomb-wrecker's hand is there.' On another day, though, the poet had a change of heart, and then he wrote as if the ancient building by the sea had a mind and spirit and was looking back upon its life;

'I was a wall,' he wrote, 'a wall, set upon bases and rising upright, then flat, with flanks which met together at a point, a tomb, a hill upon a hill. But what did that mean? Nothing to the gold lovers who shook me from top to bottom.'

PYTHEOS, MAUSOLEUM ARCHITECT

Most of Newton's gleanings are stored at the British Museum in crates and cabinets in vaulted storerooms, something like those of the *Raiders of the Lost Ark*. Above them, just as Baedeker describes, a selection of the largest is exhibited in a tiny public gallery. Recent scholarship concerns itself with sorting these fragments into different groups and some scholars even try to link the fragments to the four sculptors that Pliny names as having worked upon the Mausoleum. Other scholars attempt to reconstruct the Mausoleum's architecture; combined with Pliny's literary ambiguities, the fragments have provided generations of historians with fonts of inspiration and debate.

The most intriguing question though about the Mausoleum lies elsewhere: why above all others, of all the beauteous and bulky buildings of antiquity, was this tomb considered to be a wonder of the ancient world? Whoever it was who made them, the surviving reliefs are not especially powerful works of art, nor are they large nor especially well made. Neither were they revolutionary nor influential in their own time. Without the benefit of their most romantic provenance, indeed, it is doubtful if they would justify the public gallery space allotted to them. As for the Mausoleum's architecture, that curious construction, like a columned temple on a giant podium topped with a marble pyramid, was always an oddity. In ancient times, only one other tomb of similar design and quality was copied from it. What, then, was the attraction of the thing?

By ancient standards, it is true, the Mausoleum was very large – so large that many people thought that it reflected an altogether immodest claim on immortality, as the Roman Lucian said (see p. 82). Building sizes, though, were generally greater in Asia Minor than in Hellenistic Europe – the very word 'colossal' was an Asian importation into Greek. And then again, the Mausoleum was rather something of a local wonder too. The Rhodian Colossus and the Temple of Artemis at Ephesus were both two comfortable sailing days out of Bodrum on the ancient shipping routes. Perhaps the three of them were close to the list-maker's hometown.

Yet, despite the fact that the Mausoleum was neither the largest Hellenistic monument nor the finest, it never left the ancient lists of wonders. There was something at Halicarnassus that excited Hellenistic people, and the later Romans too. Perhaps the innocence of the Renaissance scholars, who read the ancient texts without the luggage of accumulated scholarship, can give a clue to what this was: 'Of this temple', writes Cesariano in his commentary upon Vitruvius published in 1521, 'some have written its interior had 36 columns and amongst them were marvellous sculptures of poets and other excellent men displaying their erudition, and tragedy as well . . .'

The wonder lay in the statues, then – 'the statues of the superb mausoleum, of gypsous alabaster'. Not the reliefs, in which it is difficult to discern any special quality, but

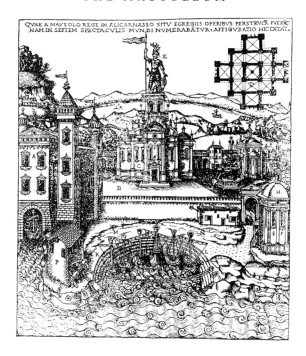

Cesariano's Mausoleum, an illustration from his translation of *Vitruvius*, Como, 1521

the figures that stood amidst the building's architecture. Of these, just two have been preserved in anything like their original condition; the two colossi found by Newton beside the Mausoleum's northern wall. The man especially is fine. Unlike the woman, his sculpture still has a face, and that face is near perfect; a thick-set, moustached individual, with his legs swinging in a pose such as Lysippus and his followers were exploring at about this same time. The figure's clothing is cut around his powerful body in a particularly splendid way; vigorously gouged and pleated and gathered grandly all around the waist. By any standards, it is a remarkable piece of sculpture. So vivid is the head – 'the first great individualized Greek portrait', it has been called – that with no firm evidence at all, it is usually considered to be either a portrait of Mausolus himself or of one of his dynastic ancestors. Though this giant man is as idealized as Lysippus' later Alexander portraits, this is no god, no abstract hero, but a person walking in his own time. The woman too, though more broken than the man, holds much of the same strong quality. She also is an individual, holding a living pose and, with the dramatic stretch of her drapery, gathered as elegantly as the man's, we are shown that familiarly proportioned torso, breasts, pelvis, hips, that reminds us that this work was made at the beginning of that admiring age when Greek sculptors began to produce those impudently sensual images of women that are still a popular part of Western sexuality.

Newton always claimed that the two great statues were portraits of Mausolus and Artemisia, his sister-wife, and suggested that they had stood inside the four-horsed chariot that topped the Mausoleum, the remains of which he found mixed in the same cache of sculpture. Yet Newton found other sculptures in that cache, which clearly had not

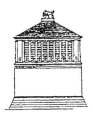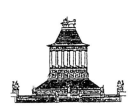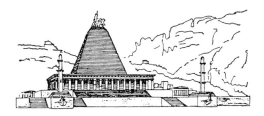

Various European Mausoleum reconstructions, from 1858 to 1989

come down from the quadriga, but had been brought down by its fall. Today, it is widely recognized that the poses of the two figures are not those used by the Greeks for charioteers. There are, moreover, similar fragments from other figures at the Mausoleum. It is most likely that these two grand statues stood along with many others of a similar quality as part of two long series of freestanding sculptures that were set, as their fragmentary architectural fixings show, either between the rows of columns on the colonnade, or amongst another row of standing statues lower down on the monument.

One thing is sure. In its heyday, the Mausoleum had at least 100 of these sculptures, and in all probability many more. Fine, powerful marble portraits of large, personable people strolling amongst the columns standing row upon row; crowds of these recently developed Greek portraits, colossal statues like the gods, but made like individual humans en masse. When it was new, the effect must have been as electric as was the cinema when it began. Suddenly, there was another human presence in the world, one larger and more perfect than real life, a gathering of human individuals 'poised in empty air' above the world, a human Parnassus; the beginning of the image of the heroic individual that would come to full flower in the works of Alexander's iconographers. Here then, in this wonder of the world, the power of this new sculpture, this new way of seeing humankind, first found expression.

Pheidias had made his great ivory and gold Zeus, the sculpture that was generally considered to be the supreme image of the classical world, less than a century before the building of the Mausoleum. All the ancient authors, Greek and Roman alike, who wrote on sculpture pay homage to the masterpiece, where Pheidias had used the scale and size of the temple's interior to produce a precise effect, to make the theatre, indeed, that he wanted for his work. At the Mausoleum, Pheidias' internal space was turned outwards to the world, taken out of the closed darkened world of the gods, and brought into the daylight, into the bay by the bright blue sea. The gods had left their temples and their high pediments and come down into the marketplace to walk between the columns. The grand figures had been given their proscenium, their role and pose, their size and majesty, by the architecture of the tomb. The majestic columns of the Mausoleum framed carefully scaled heroes. It was a new model for the Greeks; and they would run with it, alongside Alexander, right through the East, exalting in the new-found role. The wonder of the Mausoleum was not held in either the actors or their scenery, but in their relationship together.

Pliny describes this in his full text. Though he begins by telling us that it was the sculptures that made the Mausoleum wonderful, he carefully threads his description of them through a precise account, even including measurements, of the tomb's architecture, the only time in his essay upon sculpture that he does such a thing.

Scopas had rivals in his day – Bryaxis, Timotheus and Leochares – and we must discuss these together with him, because they were just as much involved in carving the Mausoleum. This tomb was built for Mausolus, king of Caria, by his wife, Artemisia. Mausolus died in the second year of the 107th Olympiad [351 BC]. These artists worked so hard on the work that it became one of the Seven Wonders. The length of the North and South sides is sixty-three feet, the length of the front and back is less, the whole perimeter being four hundred and forty feet. Its height is forty feet and it is surrounded by thirty-six columns. People called the surrounding colonnade 'pteron' [Greek for a wing]. Scopas carved on the east side, Bryaxis on the north, Timotheus on the south and Leochares on the west. And before they completed the project, the queen died. But they did not abandon the incomplete work; already they saw it as a monument to their individual glory and skill. Today too they vie with each other. A fifth artist also entered the running. For above the pteron there is a pyramid of a height equal to the lower structure, and in twenty-four steps it tapers to a point. At the top there is a four-horse marble chariot which Pytheos made. Including the addition on top, the whole work is one hundred and forty feet high.

Pliny, *Natural History*, XXXVI, 30–1

The influence of all this on Greek architecture and sculpture was profound. The grandeur and immediacy of such sculpture set in architecture was taken up in a number of sarcophagi, on altars and on shrines, where rows of sculptures were now divided by carefully designed columns measuring and always magnifying the sculptures' scale. And linked to this great grand chorus were other figures, both in relief and in the round, placed close to the Mausoleum's human visitors, where the full power of their human personality, their individual faces, would have their full effect. The new style, though, often placed the sculptures in more vulnerable positions than the high-set sculptures of the older temples, and many of the new monuments, such as the Phillippeion, a round temple at Olympia that held a series of life-sized sculptures of Alexander's family by Leochares who also worked upon the Mausoleum, have not been well preserved.

The Mausoleum's greatest influence, though, is deep in the grandest buildings of the Hellenistic East. Its imposing new conception of size and space, colonnades with heroes walking in between them, is propelled into Hellenistic marketplaces, and into each and every public monument. Most spectacularly of all, perhaps, it is seen at Pergamum and its great majestic altar. It was not the Mausoleum's shape that particularly influenced the designers of this altar, but its use of sculpture and architecture together to create a new environment for both these elements, and for their human viewers. A recent

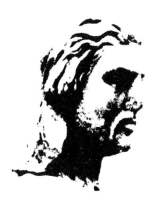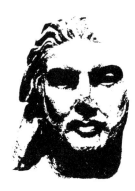

'Head of Mausolus' found by Newton in the ruins of the Mausoleum

reconstruction of the altar has changed earlier notions of its appearance. Now we see that the rhythms of the massive low reliefs, those extraordinary sculptures that sprawl across the steps to meet you, are echoed in the splendid standing figures set above them in the building's lengthy colonnades. And as you walk past these two great wings, up the steps towards the sacrificial altar, you are surrounded by a genuine heroic environment; giant humans and monstrous gods, gigantic emotions and the most human pain. Just as Pheidias pushed his sculptural concept of a gigantic god to maximum effect inside the darkness of his temple, so the architects of this great altar have taken the lesson of the Mausoleum and have manipulated the traditional elements of Greek architecture to extremity.

Inside this great square building, surrounding the altar slab, a long low frieze depicts the exploits of the hero Telephos, a mythical Pergamene king. The first continuous narrative known in Greek art, it is the predecessor of all comic strips and movies and it so clearly shows that absorption with human time that so vivifies the standing figures from the Mausoleum. Here too, all around the altar, are human-sized statues, dying warriors slowly lying down, bleeding to death, a poignant memorial to the defeat of a tribe of Gauls who had threatened Pergamum. We are reminded that altars were the city slaughterhouses. Amid the smell of blood and the great black plume of sacrificial smoke, set amongst these gods and heroes, is this new view of humankind, more tragic now perhaps than when it first found form in Mausolus' great monument, but still produced by the same trick of enlargement and engagement, of showing the visitor a new way of being, a new size and way of standing in the world.

Who was the person then, who made King Mausolus' extraordinary tomb? Apart from Pliny's short list, various ancient texts name some other sculptors as working on the monument; Praxiteles, who made softly sensual flowing sculptures; even the great Lysippus. Ancient additions that, for simplicity's sake perhaps, are usually considered as antique slips of the pen. One individual though stands out in all of this and as the weight of recent scholarship shows, his role as both architect and sculptor may have been decisive. This man is the artist who, so Pliny says, made the quadriga that topped the Mausoleum: the sculptor Pytheos.

A man called Pytheos, so the Roman architect Vitruvius tells, also designed an Ionic temple in the city of Priene, close to Halicarnassus, and wrote a book about his work as well. The book is lost now, but Vitruvius goes on to tell us something of its contents. Pytheos, he seems to say, believed that architects should accomplish much more in their work than 'those who, through their dedication and experience, have brought particular subjects to the highest renown.' He believed, therefore, in a unity of the arts. Vitruvius also tells us that he considered the Doric order ugly and took as his model the slender Ionic order of the Erectheum on the Acropolis of Athens. The Temple of Athena at Priene shows that Pytheos' rendering of the Ionic order was another masterwork; the fragments of its decoration, lying all around the temple platform, are things of great beauty in themselves. Pytheos was also an innovator. At Priene he took the traditional, rather simple, form of marble ceiling used to shelter a temple's colonnade and transformed it into a richly elaborate structure of corbelled marble slabs. Not only was this novel, it was also widely influential.

Vitruvius also tells us that a man called Pytheos part-wrote a book about the building of the Mausoleum, which was carried out just before the construction of the Athena temple in the nearby town of Priene. That book too is lost to us. Interestingly enough, though, the Mausoleum shares the design of much of its architectural detail with the Athena temple. The elaborate coffering, for example, is seen for the first time in the Mausoleum and in a slightly less advanced form than the Athena temple. The beautiful Ionic capitals of the two monuments as well are very similar, as are the measurements and proportions of the classical façades, which show a close mathematical relationship. Sculptures too, colossal human portraits from the sanctuary of the Athena temple, are of identical style and material to the colossal figures of the Mausoleum. One of these is similar to the male figure in the British Museum. Certainly, Mausolus and his family also played a part in Priene's history. These two buildings then, temple and tomb, have a great deal in common. Bearing all of this in mind, we may reasonably be justified in assuming that the Mausoleum's architect was the sculptor Pytheos.

As the years go by, and more sites are excavated in Caria, a broader vision of Mausolus' building activities has begun to emerge. Typical elements of Pytheos' architecture may now be found in many ancient sites including a regional temple called the Panionion, and Mausolus' buildings at the palace of Labranda. His influence has even been detected in another of the Seven Wonders of the World; the Temple of the goddess Artemis in Ephesus.

If this is so, and we may take it that such shared details of measurement and design are as specific as an artist's signature, then the shadowy character of a true master architect, this man called Pytheos, starts to emerge. True, Vitruvius did not think of him as in any way supreme, but then he did not understand Pytheos' remark about the architect's role in building, either. '. . . [his] analysis is not true to the facts . . .' he says. Yet there are hints, in fragments of papyrus and other surviving architectural texts too, that the name of Pytheos was widely known, and even honoured, as much as any architect of Greek society – which preferred to discuss the artists who made the statues of the gods rather than the architects who made their temples. Further hints show that he may even have been the father of Apelles, Alexander's greatest portraitist. Slowly, then, this 'Pytheos' is beginning to appear as a truly revolutionary artist, and certainly someone of considerable influence. Someone indeed with a new vision for humanity, someone who, like Michelangelo, brought sculpture and architecture together to produce a new stage for humankind to walk upon.

Though never widely imitated in a narrow sense, the Mausoleum really was a wonder. At a stroke, by mixing Greek sculpture and Greek architecture in a new relationship, it gave a new dimension to the Greeks themselves. King Mausolus, however, had also made a tomb standing in a direct line of succession to the local monuments of earlier rulers on this coast, where traditionally tombs had been like houses, with pyramidal roofs and set on high-standing plinths. Tombs that were houses for the dead, where offerings were made, where ancestors might be brought together in a common house. The Mausoleum was made in this age-old form and for these age-old purposes, but it was also built with the sophisticated vision of the finest sculptors and architects of international Greece. It was hardly necessary for later Greeks to imitate the Mausoleum's rather clumsy local forms, or for later sculptors to reproduce the gestures, the haircuts or the costume of its statuary. It was the space between these elements, the manufactured space that made humankind heroic, that was so exhilarating.

Similarly, it was the savour of this grand new scale that affected Renaissance artists too. This was a large part of what they experienced when they viewed and drew the classic fragments that they excavated. For the generations of Raphael and Michelangelo, the classic past was held in the works of Rome and especially, of Alexander's Hellenism, works that were greatly influenced by this new 'Pythean scale'. This was born again in the Sistine Chapel and in Raphael's great frescoes in the Vatican – not in the shimmering image of an ancient tomb standing by the sea, but in the scale and majesty of that long-lost monument and its fragmented sculpture.

Chapter 5

THE
HANGING GARDENS

THE DUST OF BABYLON

In 302 BC, just two decades after Alexander's death, one of his erstwhile generals, now the King Seleucus ruling an empire stretching from Afghanistan to Syria, sent a certain Megasthenes as ambassador to India. He went to Patna, the capital of Chandragupta's empire, and from there he travelled on across India, reporting as he journeyed travellers' stories of northern nomads who traded in Chinese silk, of the Tamil nation to the south, and of Tibet and the gold mines of the Himalayas. What most impressed this peripatetic Greek though, were Chandragupta's own gardens in the royal palace of Pataliputra. These, he says, were even more magnificent than those of the emperors of Persia:

> Tame peacocks and pheasants are kept, and they live in the cultivated shrubs which the royal gardeners care for. As well as this, there are shady groves with green plants growing in them too, and the boughs are interwoven by the wood man's art . . . The trees are a sort of the evergreen, and their leaves never grow old and fall. Some of them are indigenous, others have been imported from abroad.

'Megasthenes' (*c.* 290 BC), adapted from McCrindle, 1877

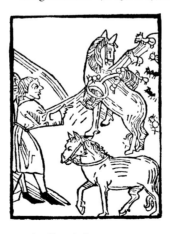

Gold-mining ants loading their nuggets onto pack donkeys,
from Sir John Mandeville's *Travels*, 1482 edition

Megasthenes also recorded the most marvellous travellers' tales, of gold-mining ants, of sweet stones that when you sucked them tasted like figs, of countries where there were no shadows at all and of snakes whose urine generated instant skin-rot. Here was a man who certainly knew a wonder when he saw one and, to the disgust of less imaginative colleagues, usually wrote about them when he got the chance. Yet though Megasthenes must have lived at Babylon and known its palaces and, as his remarks on Pataliputra clearly show, he was very fond of gardens, he never seems to have written on the Hanging Gardens in that same city; or if he did, no trace of his text has ever been detected. Where, then, are its fabled wonders to be found?

> The so-called Hanging Garden with its plants above the ground grows in the air. The roots of trees above form a roof over the ground. Stone pillars stand under the garden to support it and the whole area beneath the garden is occupied with engraved bases of the pillars.
>
> Philo 1, 1

> . . . it was built not by Semiramis but by a later Syrian king for one of his concubines. For they say that she was of Persian race and that, as she missed the meadows in the rolling hill-side, she asked the king to imitate the distinctive features of her native Persia by means of a wonderfully designed garden.
>
> Diodorus Siculus, *The Library of History*, II, 10, 1

As he introduces his list of Seven Wonders, Philo, just for a moment, just for a sentence or two, pauses to think of the effect that he wants his essay to have on his readers:

> But if a man investigates in verbal form the things to wonder at and the execution of their construction, and if he contemplates, as though looking at a mirror image, the whole skilful work, he keeps the impressions of each picture indelible in his mind. The reason for this is that he has seen amazing things with his mind.
>
> What I say will be shown to be reliable if my words make a clear description of each of the Seven Wonders, and persuade the listener to acknowledge that he has got an idea of the spectacle. Of course, only the Seven Wonders are commonly described as praiseworthy, in so far as other sights can be seen just as much as these, but the admiration provoked for the Seven Wonders and for other sights is different. For beauty, like the sun, makes it impossible to see other things when it is itself radiant.
>
> Philo, *Introduction*, 2–3

Today, perhaps, Philo would be surprised at the precision of his prophecy. His Seven Wonders, impressive enough perhaps when they stood upon the earth, have become enduring literary images; seven magical, unattainable things, the reality of which 'can be seen just as much' at other sites. Yet the real power of these Seven Wonders, the power of the ancient words, is seen to its best effect in the image Philo created of the Hanging

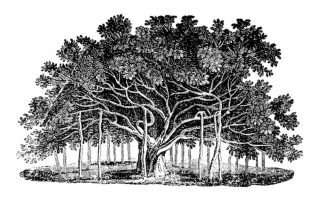

The Banyan Tree, from *Remarkable Trees and Shrubs*, London, 1836

Gardens, far away in distant Babylon. They have hung now, in the imagination of the West, for over 2,000 years.

In its day, Babylon, the city of the Hanging Gardens, had a similarly fabled reputation in the Mediterranean world. Philo, for example, counts the city's walls – the largest ever made – as an equal to the Hanging Gardens, and lists them separately in his catalogue of seven. In many ancient lists of Seven Wonders, indeed, the entire city is itself numbered as a wonder, the Hanging Gardens, the great walls and obelisks and temples, all counted as elements of that magic distant place. This same city, though, meant different things to different peoples. For the Mesopotamians, for example, the people of the land of the two rivers on which the city stood, it was a holy place. For the people of ancient Jerusalem, on the other hand, it was the city of the Biblical Exile; and they wept by the waters of Babylon. This city, on the muddy ruins of its unfathomable predecessors, became the city of the monster king Nebuchadnezzar, part-man, part-bull, part-ox, resembling the ceramic monsters on his city gates and terrifying even the writers of the Book of Revelations. In their various heydays, cities from Rome to Las Vegas have been called Babylons; Babylon, the scarlet whore, the gigantic all-consuming heartless every-city, an oriental pit of hell, all-pleasure, all-riches, all-corruption, all-whores, all-gold, all-gods, all your heart could desire or your mind might imagine. This Babylon stood in the half zone between sleep and Christian wakefulness, this city at the edge of earth, the city of a hundred gods and ancient hero kings, and the place where at the end, great Alexander himself, had come to die. And as he lay upon his deathbed in the antique royal palace, it is said he would have seen the Hanging Gardens, laid out for a long-dead queen, amidst the towers of Babylon.

To his eternal fame, three centuries earlier, the Babylonian King Nebuchadnezzar II rebuilt both this palace and the better part of Babylon as well '. . . and he did this by setting three walls around the inner city and another three around the outer city . . . After he had completed these remarkable fortifications of the city and decorated the gateways with sacred images, he added another palace to that of his father, right next to it. It would take too long to describe its height and its extravagant workmanship – except to say that despite its size and its splendour it was completed in fifteen days.

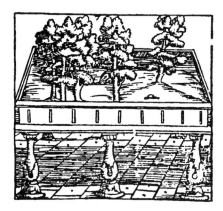

The Hanging Gardens, from Steven Münster's *Cosmographie*, 1550

'In the palace he built lofty stone terraces, made a vista as if of mountains, and planted all sorts of trees.' . . . 'The approach to the garden is mountainous and it is built tier upon tier. The result is that it looks like a theatre . . . On the roof enough earth had been spread for roots of the biggest trees [to grow in]. Once the ground had been levelled, it was filled with trees of every kind . . .' . . . 'On top grow broad-leaved trees and garden trees, and there are varied flowers of all kinds – in short everything that is most pleasing to the eye and most enjoyable. The area is cultivated just as happens on ground level. In much the same way as on normal ground, it sees the work of people who plant shoots: ploughing goes on above those wandering through the supporting colonnade.' . . . 'Although no one can see from the outside what is happening, there are machines for irrigation: a great amount of water is brought up from the river by these machines.' . . . 'From above, aqueducts carry in running water: along one way the stream follows a wide downhill course, along the other way the water runs up, under pressure, in a screw; the necessary mechanisms of the contraption make the water run round and round in a spiral. The water goes up into many large receptacles and irrigates the whole garden. It dampens the roots of the plants deep in the earth and keeps the earth moist . . .' (extracted from Josephus, Diodorus and Philo)

Like the legends surrounding Alexander, these Hanging Gardens are the strangest, the most intangible, the most wonderful wonder of them all. Of all the Seven Wonders they are the one that everyone first names, but they are also the one that is most insubstantial and elusive. The image of a floating garden is perhaps the apotheosis of Philo's wonders; it is the first wonder in his list of seven and his description of it follows on the heels of his words about the power of writing and of images held in the mind's eye. Today, it seems that his images of the Hanging Gardens were conjured entirely from words, for there never was such a thing in Babylon; not, that is, in the sense that Philo and the other authors of the wonder lists would have you believe.

The first and most obvious objection to the common image is one of translation. When, from the ancient distant East, tales came to Greece of perfumed gardens filled with herbs and apricots and holy wisdom, scholars would naturally have described them as sitting on terraces, for these were the usual utilitarian arrangements for farming the hilly Greek countryside. The word 'hanging', then, is probably a misunderstood translation of the Greek term for a farmer's terrace. As for gardens hanging or otherwise amidst the ruins of Babylon, there are objections to them as well.

In 1899, after centuries of haphazard digging and destruction, the mounds of Babylon were given over to one of the first scientific archaeological expeditions to be mounted in the Middle East. For nearly two decades, Dr Robert Koldewey of the Deutsche Orient-Gesellschaft led an expedition that excavated the plan of the ancient city, mostly that of its later and grandest phases; its temples, palaces, houses, magazines and processional roads, its gates, bridges, and the vast encircling walls which, after the great Wall of China, were the longest ever made. The work was accomplished in a brilliant application of the newly emerged scientific archaeological methodology that had been developed over the previous decades by German expeditions working at sites in Greece, Italy and Turkey. Koldewey was amongst the first to employ such methods on an ancient Middle Eastern site, and the excavation at Babylon was of a size and scope appropriate to the enormous venerable city. At its enforced ending, after some 18 years – a British Expeditionary Force was shelling Baghdad and at nearby Babylon the German archaeologists were daily threatened – Koldewey finally left, for Berlin. From then until his death eight years later, he produced a flood of books and plans and restorations that gave the world a new vision of ancient Babylon and, as it turned out, of its Hanging Gardens too. For even the German professor, trained in the iciest of scholarships, fell under the spell of the Seven Wonders, and went looking for them amongst the dust and pots and archaeological plans. And, inspired by the ancient texts, he found them. Without texts like Philo's as a guide of course, no one would have dreamed of identifying part of the vast brick ruin of Babylon as an ancient garden on a terrace. None the less, the garden was located in a corner of Nebuchadnezzar's great southern palace, equipped with high stone vaults and a unique and ingenious irrigation system. It was, however, set back from the Euphrates River.

Koldewey devoted an entire chapter of his best-known book to this discovery. Like a prosecuting attorney, he leads us through his evidence, piece by piece, with careful plans and diagrams and then, at the ending, leaves the argument with a scholarly caveat; the theory, he says 'bristles with difficulties', but then he adds, given the nature of the ancient texts, that is hardly surprising and bids us 'rejoice' when the 'discoveries of the present day' are seen to be in accordance with 'ancient statements of fact'.

As Philo knew well, words are powerful things. Add Koldewey's considerable reputation to this text, to his selective scholarly descriptions and the scientific plans that so ingeniously underlie his imaginative drawing of the Hanging Gardens, and they appear imbued with real authority. To the reader, Koldewey's caveat appears to be the usual caution of a careful scholar. No wonder that his splendid plates and plans still decorate so many children's books on the Seven Wonders, and are presented as an accurate scientific 'reconstruction'.

The truth, though, is that Koldewey's identification has crumbled and fallen away just as surely as have the vast walls his expedition exposed. Modern archaeologists now say

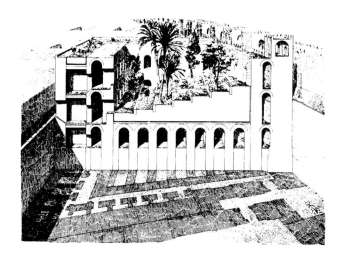

Archaeology and fantasy: Babylon's Hanging Gardens, from Koldewey, 1914

that Koldewey placed his Hanging Gardens in a part of the palace that was not made for recreation but administration; that the view there was prosaic, the ambience plebian. Further, the whole dull place is too far from the river. Moving a daily mass of water to gardens on this site would have been a gigantic labour in itself. And those high stone vaults, the grand arcades that Koldewey tells us are unique and held the fabled garden terraces, have been shown by their re–excavation to have served primarily as buttresses for a great processional way that passed above them – the marching ground of Nebuchadnezzar's armies. There is another snag too, one more horticultural; even in the first decades of its existence, the roots of the trees and plants of a hanging garden made like Koldewey's would have quickly damaged its supporting terraces and eventually even threatened to open and displace the stone arches underneath. Alexander would have seen a ruin from his deathbed.

Finally, some 20 years after the excavations had finished, an epigrapher examining some of the fragile clay tablets that Koldewey had excavated from those same stone vaults recognized that the fragmentary inscriptions were ration lists of oil; oil that had been issued, amazingly enough, to the court of Jehoiachin, the captive king of Judah. Though a genuine sensation for Biblical scholarship – such specific substantiation of any of the Bible's texts is very rare – it was bad news for Koldewey's Hanging Gardens. For the basements of these great stone buttresses had either served as an oil store or a record office, and though both of these were appropriate to the administrative area of a palace, they would have been improbable and inappropriate in the moist atmosphere under a royal pleasure garden.

Other scholars have since taken up the same challenge of finding the Hanging Gardens in the plans of Babylon. Common sense and practicality and modern aesthetic preference, they say, would all locate the Hanging Gardens closer to the river, beside a palace that exists to the north. New reconstructions of the gardens have been made based not on Koldewey's archaeological plans, but on the evidence, pictorial and archaeological, of other ancient gardens in the Middle East. The scholars however, accustomed to the parks and gardens of more temperate climates, have made new reconstructions dotting the trees over open grassy slopes. But there, exposed to the full fierce sun, they would have scorched in the heat of a single Iraqi afternoon. The Greek writers at least, knew how such things had to be done; their trees are planted densely, so that 'their broad leaves nearly touching, help foster the Garden'.

At Babylon itself, no one since Koldewey's day has found a stick or stone of any ancient garden. The game then remains entirely in the ancient texts that describe it to us. As Philo hints, the location of such a fabled paradise is in the manuscripts. There alone, in the mind's eye, will we find true visions of these magic gardens, 'each single image, never to be destroyed. Like the sun, their beauty dazzling in its brilliance.' This image, though, was not invented in the age of Hellenism, by Philo and his friends, but was one of the oldest dreams of humankind, from the heartland of the most ancient civilization in the world.

EACH SINGLE IMAGE

Along with his contemporaries, Alexander knew that there were fabulous gardens in the ancient kingdoms of the East long before he set off on his journey. The distant dream had been sung since the days of Homer; even the *Odyssey*, indelibly Greek, hides traces of it in the description of a palace garden on the isle of King Alcinous:

> Outside the courtyard, near the palace doors, is a large garden – four acres in all – surrounded by a fence. There are tall blossoming trees in the garden: pear-trees, pomegranates, apple trees with their gleaming fruit, sweet figs and blooming olive trees. Their fruit never die nor cease to grow all year long, winter and summer . . . A prolific vineyard has been planted in the garden: here is a flat place for drying the grapes in the sun; other grapes are being gathered in and yet others are being trodden; in front are unripe grapes shedding their blossom; others are just growing dark. In the garden, beyond the farthest row, grow tidy flower-beds which are for ever in bud. There are two springs in the garden . . . Such were the beautiful gifts of the gods to Alcinous.
>
> Homer, *Odyssey*, VII, 112–8, 122–9, 132

The literary archaeology of the Hanging Gardens is like a mirage: the closer in time the texts are to the gardens they describe, the thinner and more diffuse the vision of them seems until they disappear completely two centuries away from the reign of Nebuchadnezzar II, the king who, so later texts assert, built the Hanging Gardens for his queen. The oldest records of the city, for example Babylon's own cuneiform inscriptions, the historical records of the city precisely impressed word by word into pillows of fine clay, do not mention them at all. What they do tell us, however, is that the greater part of the ancient city that Koldewey excavated was built during the long reign of that same king, Nebuchadnezzar.

The tale begins in 689 BC, when, as Lord Byron says, the Assyrian came down like a wolf on the fold – came down, that is, from their cities on the River Tigris, and devastated Babylon. As you might expect, the archives of the Assyrian king Sennacherib put a somewhat different spin on the tale in his report to the state god Ashur; 'As a hurricane proceeds, I attacked it and, like a storm, I overthrew it . . . Its inhabitants, young and old, I did not spare and with their corpses I filled the streets of the city . . . The town itself and its houses, from their foundations to their roofs I devastated, I destroyed, by fire I overthrew . . . In order that in future even the soil of its temples be forgotten, by water I ravaged it, I turned it into pastures. To quiet the heart of Ashur, my lord, that peoples should bow in submission before his exalted might, I removed the dust of Babylon for presents and . . . I stored some in a covered jar.'

Eighty years later, though, Ashur's gleaming cohorts had been swept away just as the Israelite prophets had said they would be and in their turn, the armies of the Medes and the Babylonians had destroyed every major city in Assyria. As Koldewey proved in his excavations, this was a resurgent period of Babylonian history, the period of the city's great rebuilding, with vast new defensive walls and gates enclosing a 200-acre city, with a grand moat transforming the whole thing into a fortified triangular island. Ruling for some 45 years, Nebuchadnezzar was the longest-lived king of this new Babylonian dynasty, and it is to be expected therefore that the greater part of the inscriptions that Koldewey excavated would be written in his name. In the manner of such ancient records, however, cuneiform texts describing the king himself are few and far between. To give the character some flesh, historians generally mix the rare ancient fragments with later literary accounts, usually those of the Greeks and Hebrews.

These same texts, however – and Koldewey excavated approximately 25,000 tablets at Babylon, many of which have not yet been studied – offer tremendous detail about Nebuchadnezzar's building projects. The great clay cylinders covered with the tiny pick marks of the Babylonian scribes tell of the city's vast new walls that no army should ever pass again, of the moats whose entrances were bound with 'bars of shining iron', of the massive new city gates and river harbours, of the great bridges and temples, and of the refounding of what is believed to have been the Biblical Tower of Babel, the central Babylonian temple said to have first been built by the hands of the gods themselves. But they never mention a single royal garden.

Avid historians of mighty cities and heroic rulers, the later Greek writers shared a common view of Babylon. For them, fighting wars, founding and rebuilding cities and ordering colossal public works were all signs of great rulers. They included ancient Middle Eastern monuments in their histories and in their lists of wonders because, like their own great cities, such colossal things were the clear residue of great, heroic deeds. From this point of view, the age-old custom of Babylonian and Egyptian kings building their monuments, as the inscriptions often say, 'for their gods', seemed to offer confirmation that such superhuman achievements put their mighty makers in the vicinity of the gods. This attitude alone would have assured Nebuchadnezzar's Babylon a place in their history books. So magnificent was its reputation, indeed, that the city itself became a legend in the lands of the distant Mediterranean. At the same time that the Greeks were labo-riously developing their own distinctive style of art and architecture, Nebuchadnezzar had rebuilt the world's most ancient city and it became the largest and most splendid in the world. Though Babylon was taken by the Persian kings in 539 BC, the selfsame Persians who were enemies of Greece, its heroic builders, its ancient kings and queens, were always counted as great rulers.

'The most powerful and famous city in Assyria was Babylon,' reports the sagest of Greek historians, Herodotus of Halicarnassus, in the fifth century BC, '. . . Babylon lies on a large plain in the shape of a square, each side of which is about fourteen miles long. The total circumference of the city is about fifty-six miles. Such is the size of the city of Babylon, and it is decorated in a way that surpasses all other cities we know.' Herodotus lived about a century after the Persian conquest and gives the impression that he travelled to Babylon himself and is reporting what he saw. In fact, there is little agreement between scholars as to whether he did so or not; in common with many other classical writers, he may have simply reworked and recopied other older texts. At the outset of his descriptions of the Seven Wonders, Philo states directly that he is aiming to give you the impression of visiting the Wonders without the fatigue of actually doing so. To achieve this effect, just like many novelists today, Philo and Herodotus both provide you with a mass of idiosyncratic detail that paints their subject with a varnish of veracity. The use of the written word to make 'indelible impressions in the mind', as Philo says, was part of the ancient joy of writing, a new-felt power in the Greek world. And this, of course, is still true in more modern times as well; Koldewey, for example, is employing the selfsame mechanism when he draws his Hanging Gardens reconstruction over his scientific excavation maps.

Whether Herodotus saw Babylon by the Euphrates or not, he still has a great deal to say about it. His lively account of the city, the vast walls, its huge temples with their smoking altars, and those sensual Eastern rites that so intrigued the later historians, is the first Greek record that has survived. However, he has nothing at all to say about the Hanging Gardens nor even of King Nebuchadnezzar – both subjects ideally suited to Greek descriptions of mighty kings and all their works. Like many later Greek histories of Babylonia, Herodotus' story of the city revolves around the tales of two semi-legendary queens, Semiramis and Nitocris, who rule like Amazons and build like daemons. But never once do they make a garden.

Indeed, in all of these surviving records, in each and every tongue, written in the cen-tury and a half or so following Nebuchadnezzar's death in 562 BC, there is no mention at all of Hanging Gardens at Babylon; gardens that had been made, so later records say, for Princess Amytis, a daughter of the Median king, whose marriage to Nebuchadnezzar had soldered the vital alliance between Media and Babylonia that had broken Assyria for ever and prompted Babylon's rebuilding.

The first hint of the Hanging Gardens is found in a small surviving fragment of a 24-volume Greek history called the *Persika*, written by a doctor at the Persian court about 400 BC, one Ctesias from Asia Minor. Later on in antiquity, no one professed to think much of Ctesias' books – another of his fragments, for example, tells us that, though he was enslaved, a prisoner of war, the Persian king, who 'always dressed in women's clothes', sent him 150 slave girls to dance for him at dinner every day. When they proved helpful and seemed plausible, though, like most writings, bits of Ctesias' works were taken up and used by other authors and this piecemeal selection it is that has enabled snippets of his work to survive embalmed in later descriptions of the Hanging Gardens.

This indeed is how all the early records of the Hanging Gardens are preserved, as quotes in the writings of later classical historians. All these authors, however, both the quoters and the quoted, lived centuries after Nebuchadnezzar's day, and frequently contradict each other. Diodorus Siculus, for example, writing in the first century BC, describes the rebuilding of Babylon by quoting two earlier texts:

> Taking the Euphrates river as the centre, she [Queen Semiramis] ran a wall with many big towers along it around the city. The wall was three hundred and sixty stades long [forty and a half miles], according to Ctesias of Cnidos, but Cleitarchus and some of those who later crossed over to Asia with Alexander recorded that its length was three hundred and sixty-five stades long [forty-one miles] . . . The so-called hanging garden was by the Acropolis, built not by Semiramis but by a later Syrian king for one of his concubines. For they say that she was of Persian race and that, as she missed the meadows in the rolling hillside, she asked the king to imitate the distinctive features of her native Persia by means of a wonderfully designed garden.

> Diodorus Siculus, *The Library of History*, II 7, 3; II 10,1

The writings of several of Alexander's hagiographers had earlier mentioned the Hanging Gardens and the homesick queen. One of them, the Alexandrian historian Cleitarchus, who owes his present modest fame entirely to the fact that his works are preserved in copies and paraphrases of later writers, himself gleaned his texts from other older works. Cleitarchus lived and wrote around 275 BC and never seems to have travelled much at all; the sources of his information on Babylon were probably some of the veterans who had fought with Alexander. Similarly, though both ancient and modern scholars generally consider his writing to be unreliable, the description of Babylon and its gardens by the sea captain Onesicritus, who is supposed to have sailed down the River Jhelum in India with Alexander, may also have reflected some first-hand knowledge of the city. We know of Onesicritus' account, however, only because it is quoted by Strabo, a geographer of slightly later date than Diodorus:

> The Hanging Garden is in the shape of a square, each side four hundred feet long. It is surrounded by arched vaults which are positioned, one after the other, on cube-shaped boxes. The hollow boxes are filled with earth so that the biggest trees can grow in them. The slabs themselves, the vaults and the arches are all made from baked brick and bitumen. To get to the very top of the roof there are staircases and, running alongside these, there are spiral

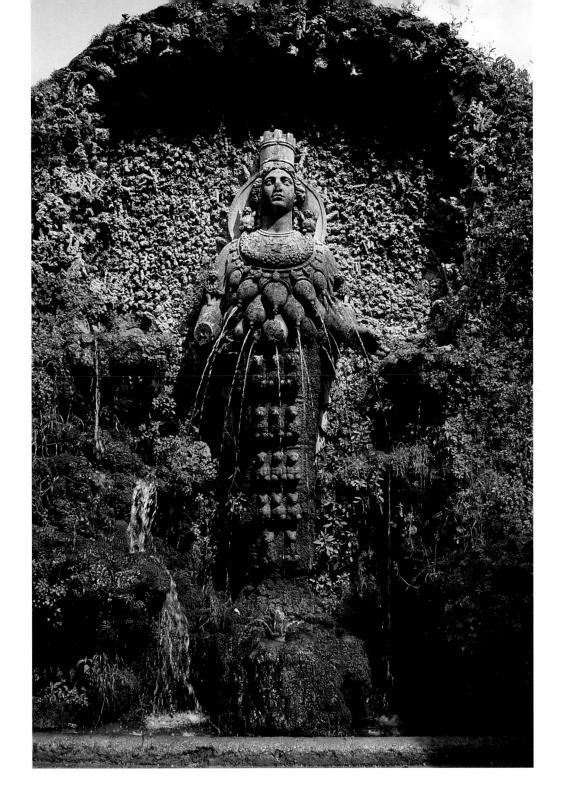

16. A statue of Artemis at Villa d'Este, Tivoli. During the Renaissance, renewed interest in antiquity saw the rebirth of its most ancient gods. In the 1550s, the image of Artemis, whose temple at Ephesus had been one of the Seven Wonders of the World, was used as a grandiose garden ornament, designed by Pirro Ligorio for Cardinal d'Este's wondrous gardens near Rome. Later prudishness has since demoted the once-great goddess, moving her from the garden's central axis where she symbolized abundant nature, to a leafy pathway on a side walk

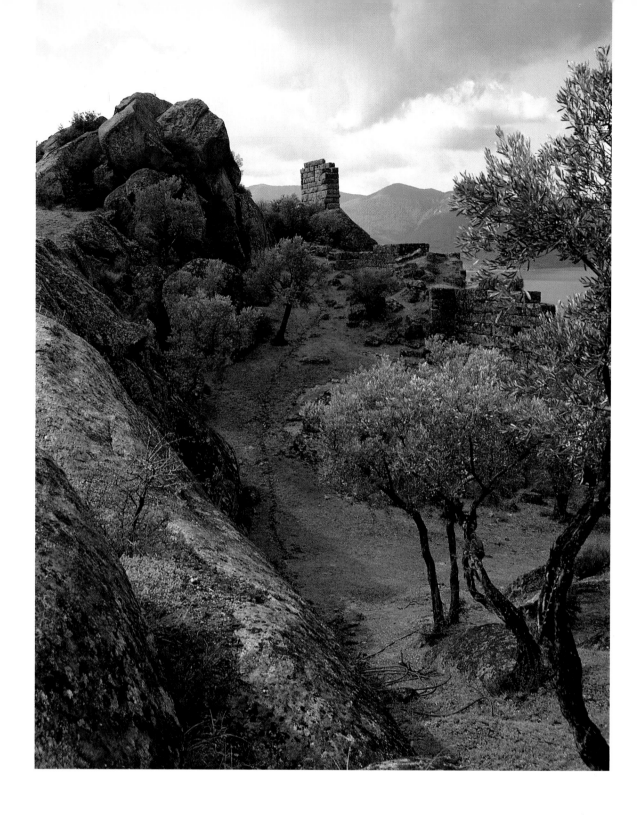

17. An olive grove at Heracleia under Latmus. For ancient Greeks, 'hanging' gardens were terraces like these at the ancient city of Heracleia. On the stony uplands of greater Greece, such terraces were used for cultivating everything from olives to wheat. To such hardy farmers, the lush terraces of the old Assyrian gardens and the Persian hunting parks set on the broad well-watered plain of Mesopotamia, really must have seemed like paradise

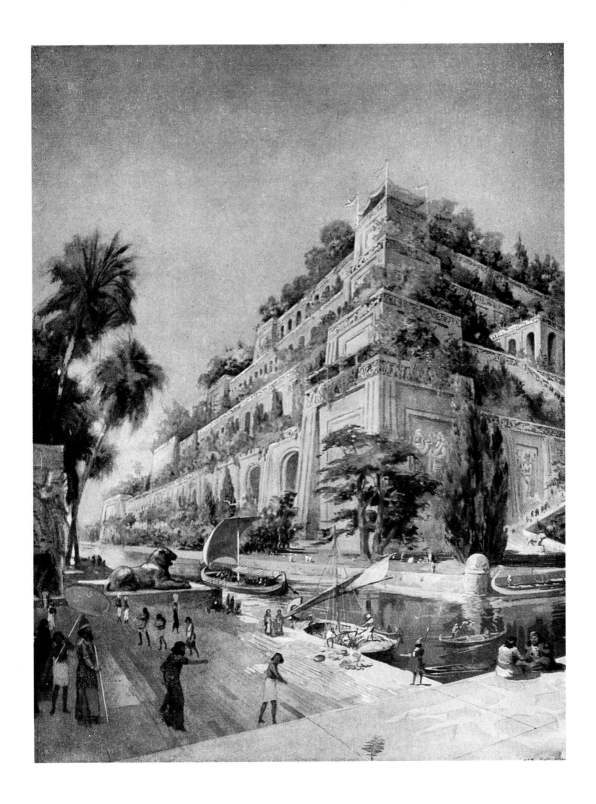

18. The Hanging Gardens of Babylon, a standard image of the ancient wonder, painted by Charles Sheldon and published in 1924. The design simply plants rows of trees upon the terraces of a ziggurat, in reality, an ancient temple whose loose mud bricks could never have sustained such arboreal fantasies. The dream though, is a compelling one, part of that powerful nineteenth-century vision of Biblical Babylonia

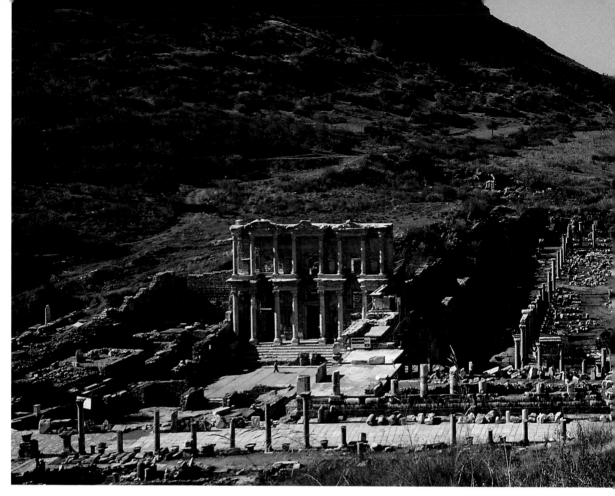

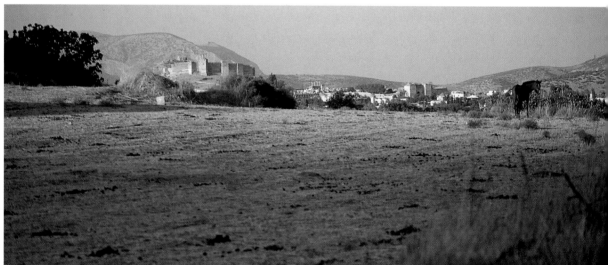

19. (*Top*) Ancient Ephesus from the Amphitheatre. John Turtle Wood started his marathon search for the Temple of Artemis, one of the Seven Wonders of the World, by excavating the length of this great marble street, a part of the centre of ancient Ephesus

20. (*Above*) The ancient road to the Temple of Artemis. Continuing his excavations outside the city gates, Wood cut a continuous trench some twelve feet deep through these beautiful fields, heading in the direction of the castle that still stands above the town of Seljuk

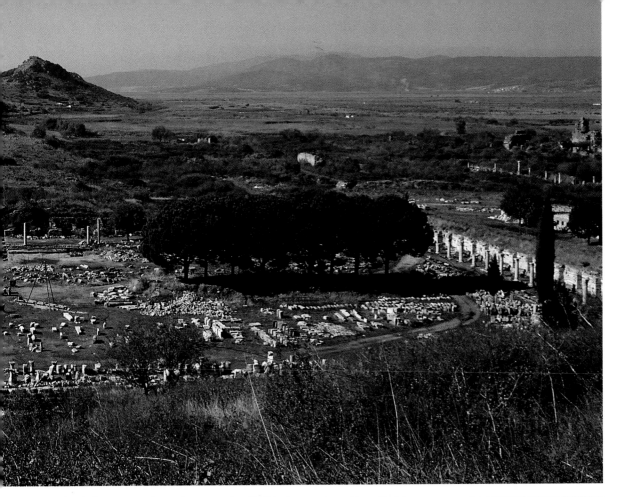

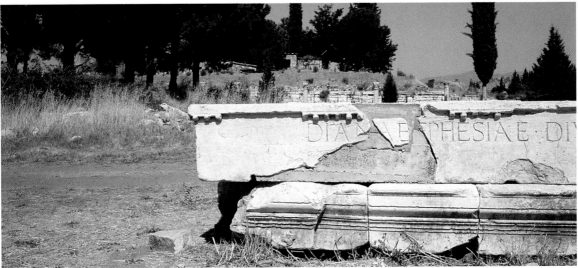

21. (*Above*) An inscription from an ancient arcade. Wood's most consistent clues were the fragments of ancient arcades that he found buried in the fields. Such arcades had served to shelter the statue of Artemis on her processions around ancient Ephesus, and led Wood to the buried temple. These marble fragments spell out the goddess' Roman name, Diana, the name also used by the Book of Acts

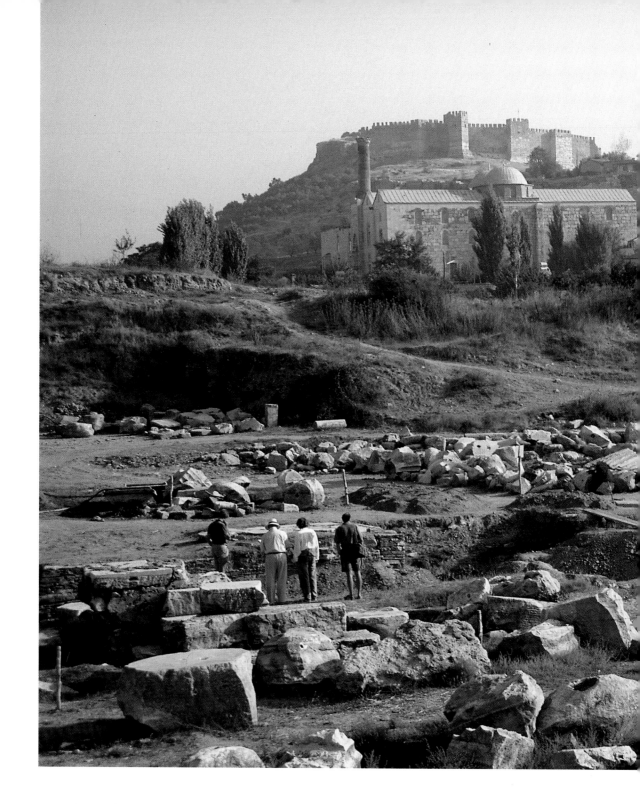

22. The site of the Temple of Artemis at Ephesus. The great temple was buried in 15 feet of river silt. Still ringed by Wood's enormous excavation, today the site looks stark, despite its location beneath the ancient Mosque of Isa Bey and the church of St John. The continuing excavations, however, are one of the great modern archaeological dramas: Professor Anton Bammer of the Austrian Institute has uncovered the oldest-known Greek columned temple, and the archaic jewels of Artemis herself, buried deep beneath the fragments of later marble temples

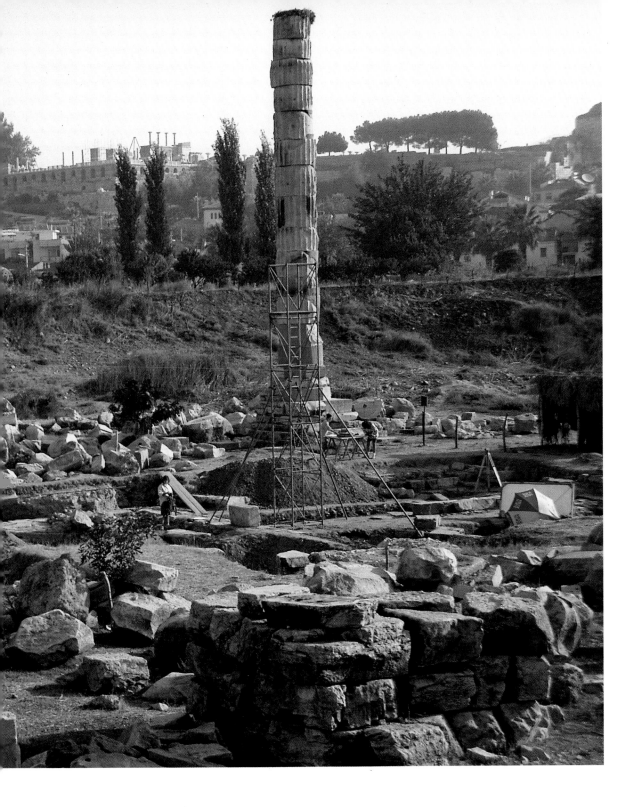

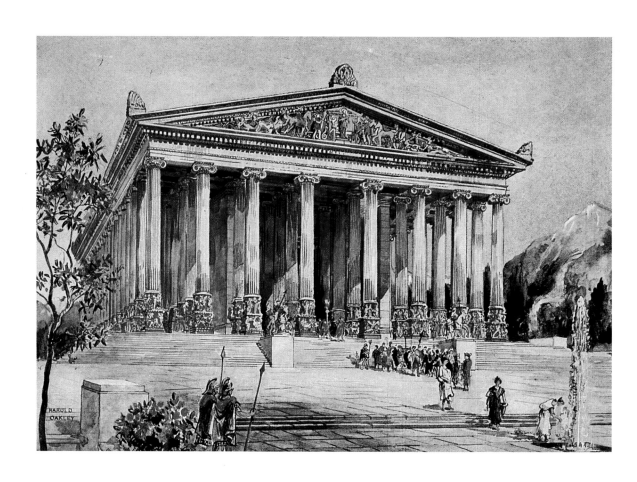

23. A reconstruction of the last temple of Artemis at Ephesus. This 70-year-old watercolour gives a fairly accurate impression of how the Temple of Artemis appeared in the later days of its prosperity. One of the most ancient religious shrines of the Greek world, the last temple of Artemis was a superb example of the florid Ionic order so beloved of Asian Greeks. The ruins of the Temple at Didyma (*see* plate 1) gives some idea of our loss; most of Artemis' great temple was quarried for its stone or burnt for building lime screws. Those whose job it was continually brought up water to the garden from the Euphrates through these screws. For . . . the garden is on the bank of the river.

Strabo, *Geography*, XVI, 1, 5

None of the later, more picturesque, descriptions – paraphrased on p. 110 – add any real information to the spare facts of these three ghostly records of the Hanging Gardens. In this exotic Hellenistic world, Babylon was as remote, as magnificent a mirage as the legend of Semiramis, or for that matter as Nebuchadnezzar, and the Hanging Gardens formed but a tiny part of the city's identity. A city, it was said, as rich as Sardis, with oysters and red waters in its river, perfumed wine called nectar, fine incense, and perfumes (so Aristotle believed) that will make your hair turn grey, and orchards heavy with Alexander's favourite apples.

Just as did Megasthenes, who had really been to India yet still wrote of its gold-mining ants and people with ears strong enough to rip trees out of the ground, these writers knew their audience. Such a grand city clearly had heroic kings, and they must have made the finest of those gardens that were an ingredient of all such Eastern cities. So these Hellenistic writers take the short descriptions of the earlier texts and fill them up with speculation, their main interest seemingly, as far as the Hanging Gardens are concerned, being armchair gardening on the grand scale; working out the theoretical mechanics of making waterproof terraces, and wondering how aerial roots can best be watered and sustained, or what this astonishing literary concoction would look like, floating high above the plain of an imaginary desert. Of one thing we may be sure; none of these gentlemen had practical experience of either gardening or engineering, and in all probability none of them had ever been to Babylon.

Like his accounts of some of the other wonders, Philo's explanation of the Hanging Gardens is rather that of an imaginative engineer – in this, he is similar to those modern specialists who speculate on how the ancient Egyptians built their pyramids; though they know little of the ancient world, their modern expertise endows their calculations with spurious authenticity. Similarly Philo, who did not see the Seven Wonders being built, offers contemporary Alexandrian solutions to the problem of their construction. Thus, the descriptions of the irrigation channels in his Hanging Gardens bear great similarity to the hydraulic experiments of his contemporaries in Egyptian Alexandria: '. . . the water runs up, under pressure, in a screw; the necessary mechanisms of the contraption make the water run round and round in a spiral'. It would be naive indeed to imagine that here Philo is attempting to provide us with a modern functional explanation of an ancient wonder, or to imagine that he was writing for us today and not for the world in which he lived.

In spite of this wonderful melange of information, there yet remains a unique ancient document which, though it has been preserved in the same piecemeal fashion as the others, has an authenticity that is difficult to deny. This text, of great age and the most intriguing pedigree, once a part of a history dedicated to Seleucus' son, was called the

Babylonica. It was written in Greek in the third century BC by a priest of Babylon called Berosus who lived on the Greek island of Kos, close by Halicarnassus. Like a similar work of Manetho, an Egyptian priest, the *Babylonica* was partly an attempt by a learned man to explain his national heritage to the Macedonian conquerors. Just as Manetho had access to hieroglyphic texts, so Berosus had access to the ancient Babylonian cuneiform records and, as one would expect of a priest of Babylon, he could probably read them for himself as well. He wrote on everything: on Babylonian astronomy, on the fundamental stories of his faith, and he compiled a history of his city from the creation of the world, starting with the great Creation stories and the Epic of Gilgamesh and continuing the account with lists of the dynasties of ancient kings and countries, and all of this in the form and language of a Greek history. At its ending, Berosus gave a brief history of Nebuchadnezzar's dynasty, and this is the most accurate record of it to have survived, with many unique details. As he tells again the old story of Babylon's renewal, tells how Nebuchadnezzar rebuilt and enlarged the city and made gigantic walls 'to prevent the city being sacked in the future', he also tells us of the Hanging Gardens. First he gives an account of the materials that Nebuchadnezzar used in his rebuilding programme, then he describes the great new palace in which Alexander would come to die. This is the palace, he tells us, with all its high balconies and terraces, that Nebuchadnezzar made in 15 days. Then he continues, 'In the palace he built lofty stone terraces, made a vista as if of mountains, and planted all sorts of trees. He built the so-called hanging paradise, because his wife, who had been brought up in the area around Media, wanted mountain scenery.' (Berosus, cited twice in Josephus, *Against Apion*, I, 139, 141, *Jewish Antiquities*, X, 224, 226)

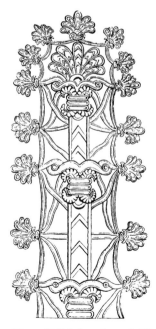

An Assyrian 'Tree of Life', from Layard, *Nineveh*, 1867

Here then, at last, shorn of Philo's imaginative mechanics, the free-running imagination of the gardening Greeks and the deadly hands of later editors, are the Hanging Gardens of Babylon. We move closer to the ancient truth of things: ever since the gods first made the land there had been gardens in great Babylon.

THE ROOTS OF PARADISE

In the first days, in the very first days,
In the first nights, in the very first nights,
In the first years, in the very first years . . .
When heaven had moved away from earth,
And earth had separated from heaven . . .

At that time, a tree, a single tree, a *huluppu* tree
was planted by the banks of the Euphrates.
The tree was nurtured by the waters of the Euphrates.
The whirling South Wind arose, pulling at its roots
And ripping at its branches
Until the waters of the Euphrates carried it away.

A woman who walked in fear of the word of the Sky God, An,
Who walked in fear of the word of the Air God, Enlil,
Plucked the tree from the river and spoke:

'I shall bring this tree to Uruk.
I shall plant this tree in my holy garden.'

Inanna cared for the tree with her hand.
She settled the earth around the tree with her foot . . .

From an anonymous Sumerian Hymn (*c.* 2400 BC)

Inanna's garden is described again, as the hero Gilgamesh passes through it in his search for the elixir of life.

After he has travelled twelve double-hours, it is light.
Before him stand shrubs of precious stones,
he sees them as he draws nigh.
The carnelian bears its fruit;
vines hang from it, good to look at.
The lapis lazuli also bears fruit; pleasant to behold.

For thorns and thistles there were hematite and rare stones,
agate, and pearls from the sea.

And Gilgamesh walked in the garden.

Mesopotamia (third millennium BC)

Long before the Hanging Gardens gained celebrity, in the age of Sumer, in the tales of Gilgamesh, this great garden had four streams, and perfumed trees and luscious fruit, and walls around it. Here are the roots of Paradise. No mountains, though, are mentioned yet, no terraces or vaults are raised. Part of this man-made landscape begins to appear however, when the Old Testament, a later text than those of ancient Sumer's, takes up the selfsame story.

Now, the first garden, made for Adam, lies in Eden away to the east and, so the Prophets and the Book of Genesis tell us, is stocked with trees whose fruits are blazing jewels. One of these trees is the Tree of the Knowledge of Good and Evil. A river flows down from Eden to feed four streams. On leaving Eden, one of them waters the land where gold, gum resin and onyx are found; another encircles eastern Africa; the third is the River Tigris, the river of Assyria; the fourth is Babylon's river, the Euphrates.

With its trees and rivers, Eden is that rare thing, a common legend. Deep inside the faiths of Judaism, Christianity and Islam there stands this single Mesopotamian garden surrounded by a high wall, backed by water-bearing mountains, with four crossing rivers, perfumed trees and luscious fruits and birds and animals. Outside the garden there is wild nature, for hunting and planting. Inside the gates, however, nature is ordered, the air is perfumed, moist and shaded and the fruit is always ripe. The four rivers of Eden flow through Genesis, through Augustine's City of God, they flow through Milton and Mesopotamian myth alike. They are Iranian and Iraqi, they are English and Californian. And the garden is filled with saints and djinns and houris, with prophets and fruit and flowers and heroes and fine horses and ease and all delight, this high-walled paradise from which we were expelled.

Just as the old rabbis dreamily wondered how Adam and Eve appeared before they saw their nakedness (one suggestion was that they had been sheathed in fine white light, like a lustrous pearl) so this garden too had shadowed, sensual charms. The fruits and flowers in it wore the blush and forms of the human body, as Solomon celebrated in the Song of Songs. And even wise Solomon, the Bible says, boasted of his own high-walled garden at his palace at Jerusalem, set beside a city gate and watered from the high hill of Siloam. In Syria too, in Armenia, and the land of Urartu, such gardens, laden with fruits and grapes, were an ephemeral amenity of many different cities. On the Euphrates in Babylon at the same time as Solomon, the gods themselves granted the same horticultural boon; 'Gardens enhance the pride of the city' sings the refrain of a Babylonian hymn.

The Assyrians, those ferocious holy warriors from the cities of the northern Tigris, were especially keen gardeners. They planted huge orchards in their cities with thousands upon thousands of fruit trees for the citizens, orchards that also provided timber for boats and for the city gates, and supported perfume-makers, pharmaceutical industries and market gardens.

In 877 BC, Ashurnasirpal II went on a collecting trip, a ferocious *razzia* across Iraq to Syria and down the coast and back again in a burning circle of destruction which was recorded in the annals of the reign:

> I built a pillar by the city gate and I flayed all the chiefs who had revolted, and I covered the pillar with their skin. Some I walled up within the pillar, some I impaled upon the pillar on stakes, and others I bound to stakes round about the pillar . . .
>
> I burned many captives. From some I cut off their noses, their ears and their fingers, of many I put out the eyes. I made one pillar of the living and another of heads, and I bound their heads to tree trunks round about the city. Their young men and maidens I burned in the fire . . .

Even as he fought the holy war, he kept a keen eye out for roots and cuttings, and for specialist gardeners too. When he returned to the city of Nimrud, after suitable celebrations, he planted a huge souvenir garden, watered from a canal cut off the Tigris, and was very proud of it:

> From lands in which I travelled, and the mountains I have passed, I saw and I collected: cedar, cypress, box, prickly cedar, myrtle, juniper, almond, date palm, ebony, sissoo, olive, tamarind, oak, terebinth, nuts, ash, firs, nightshade, oak from Kanis, willow, pomegranate, plum, pear, quince, fig, grapevine . . . [other unidentified names in the list may include pear, acacia, rhododendron, azalea, castor oil plant and frankincense].

For its maintenance in the baking summer heat of Nimrud, the setting of this great botanical garden had to be most carefully planned. The text tells us that the king's men created a luscious and fertile environment, one heavy from the humidity of its fountains, and filled with the shade and scents of its trees and plants. The key to such a garden's charm and fertility would have been an elevation sufficient to maintain waterfalls and provide the base for a gradient that gave a swift passage for the garden's irrigation, as the single source of water divided to run down through its orchards and its vines. Such a garden would also need high walls, so that the cool moist atmosphere so carefully produced was held inside its shaded glades. The result was a beautiful delight on the flat hot plains of north Iraq, and one most enthusiastically and accurately described:

> The canal water comes flowing down from above to the gardens: the paths are full of scent; the waterfalls glisten like the stars of heaven in the garden of pleasure. The pomegranate trees are clothed with clusters of fruit like vines, and enrich the breezes in the garden of delights. Ashurnasirpal gathers fruit continuously in the garden of joys like someone who is starving.

These gardens were highly successful and sufficiently long-lived to allow Ashurnasirpal to use his synthetic orchards as a source of precious woods to decorate his palaces. In his building inscriptions, there is talk of doors of cedar, cyprus, juniper and mulberry, boxwood, pistachio and tamarisk. Many of the gardens' plants also served special purposes, rendering medicines and aromatics and even frankincense for use at the temple. On occasion, the rare fruits of the gardens were themselves offered to the gods. As well as this, the gardens were used for religious ceremonies and sometimes the regal pleasure pavilions saw the enactment of the affairs of state.

Further descriptions of Assyrian gardens confirm their common plan. Sennacherib, for example, Babylon's impious despoiler, was also a keen gardener. Outside the walls of Nineveh, he converted tracts of uncultivated land into a hunting park. A tributary river was dammed to hold the annual inundation and feed the orchards of cypress from the Lebanon and sissoo trees from India. Inside the high walls he built 'a garden like Mount Amanus' – that is, like the high range of mountains that feeds the magnificent fertile vale around the Lake of Amik, outside Aleppo, these being the first lush fields and lakeside the Assyrians armies would have seen after their regular 300-hundred-mile march across the Syrian desert from Nineveh to the Mediterranean seaboard. To make a model of a mountain on the dry wide plain of Nineveh, a model large enough to hold a royal garden, was a considerable work of engineering. Not surprisingly, the theme of the manufactured mountain range continued in the king's choice of plants, 'like those of the mountains and the hills', with wild vines and olives and cotton plants and trees assembled from the corners of the empire.

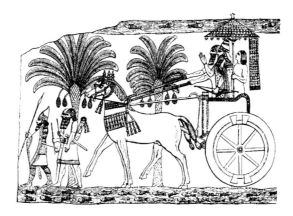

King Sennacherib rides through his gardens at Nineveh. From Layard, *Nineveh*, 1867

Through several such descriptions, then, a single pattern slowly emerges. There is wild land outside the garden walls, and a single powerful water source that, on entering the garden, divides into smaller streams, traditionally four in number. Much of the garden stock is foreign and exotic – from cooler climates – and requires special care on the hot river plains of Mesopotamia. High walls, the trees' own shade and careful watering would keep such gardens from being scorched – the cool moist climate that this system would produce often being described as one of the gardens' main delights. Such environments would have required an abundance of water at high pressure. This implies considerable landscaping, as the texts suggest, usually taking the form of large embankments – and these, in all probability, are the 'mountains' made for Nebuchadnezzar's queen.

Just as the Assyrians had done before him, Nebuchadnezzar collected foreign plants and gardeners in his wars. His Hanging Gardens too, their 'very high walls, supported by stone pillars', must also have supported powerful irrigation schemes to make the necessary humid forest on the hot wide plain where, as the text describes, 'lofty stone terraces, made a vista as if of mountains and [were] planted [with] all sorts of trees' in imitation, once again, of a foreign land; 'because his wife, who had been brought up in the area around Media, wanted mountain scenery'.

This then is the real landscape of the Hanging Gardens. We may imagine a steep artificial hillside with a high wall running around it, and a hunting park outside. Inside the walls, all is trees and fruit and shade. Water is running melodiously down through the steep-sided orchards, and a fine cooling mist from the fountains, scented, lingers in the sunlight until the heat burns it away.

The exact phrase Berosus uses to describe the Hanging Gardens is that they were a 'hanging paradise'. This word 'Paradise' is Persian. It first appeared after King Cyrus the Great and his court and armies came down from their ancient uplands, the lands of the Median princess, and took Assyria and Babylon from Nebuchadnezzar's dynasty, to create the vast empire that Alexander would take for himself. In Old Persian, *paradeisos*, meant 'hunting park', an enclosed area that could be filled with game for sport; the park outside the walls. After they had settled in the ancient cities of the plain, though, the word was also used to describe the formal pleasure gardens built beside the cities, and this is where Berosus finds the word. The prophet Nehemiah tells us that Paradise was the park of the Persian king; the beginning of the Book of Esther gives us a picture of the King of Persia and his court engaged in an enormous drinking party in the paradise of Susa.

> In the third year of his reign . . . the king gave a banquet for all the people present in Susa the capital city, both high and low; it was held in the garden court of the royal pavilion and lasted seven days. There were white curtains and violet hangings fastened to silver rings with bands of fine linen and purple; and there were alabaster pillars and couches of gold and silver set on a mosaic pavement of malachite and alabaster, of mother-of-pearl and turquoise. Wine was served in golden cups of various patterns: the king's wine flowed freely as befitted a king . . .

Xenophon, a philosophically inclined Greek mercenary who fought in the armies of a Persian Prince, is the first Greek whom we know to have used the word paradise. This then is how paradise, that perfumed dream, came into Europe. Xenophon tells an old soldier's tale about this Persian prince, named Cyrus after his famous ancestor, and the Spartan general Lysander walking together through a royal garden at the city of Sardis, which the prince's ancestor had taken from the Lydian kings.

Lysander was amazed at the paradise: the trees were so beautiful – they were planted at even intervals, their rows were perfectly straight, and all the angles were just right – and as they walked, different sweet smells accompanied them. In his amazement at all these things he said, 'I am truly amazed at all these things, Cyrus, because of their beauty. But I am more struck by the man who measured out and arranged each tree for you.' Cyrus was pleased at the compliment and replied, 'I did all the measuring and arranging, Lysander, and I also did some of the planting.' Lysander looked at Cyrus and saw the beautiful clothes he was wearing, and noticed his perfume and the necklaces and anklets and jewellery he was wearing, and said, 'What do you mean, Cyrus? Did you really plant any of these trees with your own hands?' Cyrus replied, 'Does that surprise you, Lysander? I promise you, by the Sun-god, that, when I am fit and well, I never sit down for dinner until I have sweated from some military or agricultural exercise, pursuing some highly honoured activity.'

Xenophon, *Oeconomicus* IV, 21–4 (*c.* 362 BC)

For the Greeks, the novelty of the tale lay in the richest monarch in the world working like a common slave. Prince Cyrus, on the other hand, must have gained amusement at the thought of scandalizing this quick-witted mercenary from the hard poor lands beside the bright blue sea.

'The Persian gallants', reported the redoubtable Sir Thomas Browne from Norwich in 1658, 'maintained their Botanicall bravery. Unto whom we owe the very name of Paradise: wherewith we meet not in Scripture before the time of *Solomon*, and conceived originally *Persian*. The word for that disputed Garden, expressing in the Hebrew no more than a Field enclosed. While many of the Ancients do poorly live in the single names of Vegetables, all stories do look upon Cyrus, as the splendid and regular planter. According whereto *Xenophon* describeth his gallant plantation at Sardis.'

Just as Xenophon's blimpish tales have appealed to Western teachers and soldiers down the ages, so Cyrus' Botanicall braveries, bearing all the imagery of the magical eastern garden, have softly and continuously permeated the West's imagination since ancient times. In the medieval age, Eden's Garden, watered and quartered, ran through the Holy Bible and even the worrisome apples of Paradise, one suitably bitten, could be viewed in a church in a suburb of Cairo. At the time of the Renaissance, however, the older myths were told again, and almost as much about the Seven Wonders of the World was known then from the works of Strabo and Josephus as is known today. The dream of the Hanging Gardens greatly affected the most modern gardens of those days, just as it has done ever since. There is a direct line of transmission here, from Eden in Babylon to Italy and from there to all the modern world. The continuing story of the Hanging Gardens, then, is a rich seam in the modern imagination. And that, perhaps, is why of all the Seven Wonders it is the one that everybody knows best.

The splendid walled gardens of the Villa Lanté at Bagnaia, were built originally for the bishops of Viterbo, at the edge of a grand hunting park. A single massive aqueduct already carried water to the top of the sloping hillside above the park, where it split into various separate streams. In 1573, a massive wall was built at one side of the park and the greater part of the water diverted to run down its steep hillside. The Villa, arranged in two separate wings, was designed by Vignola and built for Cardinal Giovan Francesco Gambara. Its formal gardens carefully and deliberately followed the patterns of the world's most ancient gardens, taken from classical texts and the words of the Bible. Fountains and statues were filled with classical images representing the first Golden Age, the age of innocence before the fall, when wine had been invented, men lived on acorns and trees had fruit without end. And just as at the end of the first Golden Age came the Flood, so at Bagnaia the Fountain of the Deluge stands above the formal gardens, where the waters of the aqueduct divide. Though outside the walls of the formal garden nature dominated, inside, the trees are terraced, set in lines and carefully tended for their fruit. Here, the Cardinal's wine was cooled in the waters of paradise, a musical stream carried in a long stone-lined water channel, a design as old as the East herself. Here, though, the deluge of rivers does not split into the Tigris and Euphrates, but into the Tiber and the Arno, each guarded by a stony bearded god, their waters cradled in stones bearing the cardinal's device – a *gambero*, a crayfish. More stone deities, Flora and Pomona, guard the Cardinal's estates that were nourished by these symbolic waters. Statues of gods and flowers and food display the bounty to be served at the Cardinal's table. All this, of course, shows erudition, a learning planted with the vines and roses. The round island in the pool at the centre of the garden, quartered by four paths, was taken from an antiquarian's reconstruction of a text describing an ancient Roman aviary. The four paths are like the streams of paradise, the lines dominating and measuring all the garden. And high behind them, on the natural hillside, behind the Cardinal's two palaces, shaded by great trees, is a mountain from which springs the Deluge. This then is a plan similar to the Hanging Gardens that Nebuchadnezzar made for his mountain queen. And wouldn't the Cardinal have been pleased if you had quoted such texts to him, such careful bookish symbolisms!

> Were I to choose the most lovely place of the physical beauty of nature in all Italy or all the world that I have seen with my own eyes, I would name the gardens of the Villa Lanté at Bagnaia.
>
> Sacheverell Sitwell (1949)

Along with a select handful of other houses, the Villa Lanté soon became an ideal of earthly paradise, and its influence quickly spread through Europe. Paradise, that most potent image of the ancient East, had come to Italy, as did all things Greek, by way of ancient Rome; initially from stories such as Xenophon's tale of Cyrus and Lysander, and then, after the conquest of Macedonia and the sack of Corinth, as Rome filled with slaves and courtesans, the fine foods and flowers and fruits of Hellenism. Though archaeologists have never found the Hanging Gardens and the streams of Eden, though Babylon has crumbled and the world is now a very different place, the vision stays; a vision of a walled and scented garden filled with shade and trees and tumbling water. It truly is the root of Paradise.

ACADEMY AND OLIVE GROVES

Alexander's ancestors had been transhumant shepherds, their lives governed by the routines of milking and spinning on the rich plains of central Macedonia. Dynastic legend tells of a king and queen who live in modest accommodation, the queen baking, the king caring for his goats and sheep alongside his retainers. The Delphic Oracle told them to found the capital of Macedonia 'where you see shiny-horned snow-white goats recumbent in their sleep'. This they did, and so the city where Alexander buried his murdered father before setting out for Asia was called Aegeae, which is Greek for 'goat-town' or, more onomatopoeically, 'bleaters'. Alexander not only inherited a powerful and experienced army, but, unlike the Greek states to the south, the notion of hereditary kingship and a powerful clan system that served to cement and stratify his army.

In contrast, most of the countryside of coastal Greece to the south, where the great cities had grown up, is marginal agricultural land; rainfall is sporadic, there is a diversity of microclimates. The decision to cultivate one rocky hillside as opposed to another is based on delicate calculation; such thin soil requires intelligent and labour-intensive farming, and usually, in such stony valleys, the hillsides need terracing even before planting can begin. Such land was completely different from that which supported the settled estates on the fertile flood plains of the Middle East, and it would not sustain the enormous slave farms that evolved later on in the Roman era. Classical Greece, the Greece that Alexander's father conquered, consisted largely of cities supported by small farms producing the then fairly novel combination of oil, wheat and wine; three remarkable, rich staples from such a poor hard land. In the cities, wheat, slaves and cash were the premier commodities, and this made for a hard, spare people. Plato's Academy, where the Athenian state officers were trained, had started as a simple olive grove on the outskirts of the city. Later a gymnasium was added and a group of tall plane trees, where the scholars and pupils walked and talked. This is the environment in which many of the philosophical dialogues that have such influence in the modern world are set. It was also the garden of the Greeks.

In Alexander's time, it has been said, three main forces moved society and so prompted the beginnings of the modern world: first the invention of coinage; secondly the adoption of a true alphabetic script; and thirdly a revival of international trade. Though Alexander, the catalyst of this diffusion, was a Westerner, all three of these forces were born in the East. By raiding and part colonizing that ancient world, Alexander became a bridge by which the products of the East, everything from bullion to Buddhism, came to the Mediterranean.

The Seven Wonders were made of the age when this newly aggressive West first looked at its Eastern neighbours, made a careful stock-taking, took what it wanted, and then named the foreigners as barbarians. At the time that the list of Seven Wonders was compiled – this being part of the notion of appraisal of the world – the Hellenistic cities affected to regard the Orient with wry humour and disgust. Its great legendary rulers, Sesostris, Cyrus, Ninus and Nebuchadnezzar, were portrayed as weak perfumed despots, a reaction that obscured the fears and envy of a brash new barbarian order set on taxing the oldest cultures of the world. As they had walked through the East, however, Alexander and his generals had rediscovered – perhaps sensed would be a better word – a shared heritage, a common root. Everything from the language that they spoke to the gods they worshipped and the herbs they used to heal themselves shared common ancestry with the ancient world through which they travelled. Though richer and brighter, underneath the veneer of foreignness, everything was strangely familiar. Not surprisingly, Alexander easily took to the notion of Middle Eastern monarchy; its gestures, rituals and the very language of the court were echoes, if greatly magnified, of his own childhood. He had come home.

Paradise, that Persian word, was a part of the West's first dream of the East. In search of it, and the richly perfumed monarchies who lived in it, Alexander took his armies through Afghanistan to India. At the new-made court of Alexander, with his officers and camp followers, contact with these old sophisticated cultures changed the Westerners' traditional idea of 'nature'. As he moved through the great empire, Alexander walked in many of these paradises, from Babylon with Nebuchadnezzar's 200-year-old gardens, to the 'hunting parks of Samarkand' and perhaps the lost estates of Asia and India beyond. In Persia, the heart of the conquered kingdom, he visited the royal palaces at Susa and Persepolis, which he destroyed, and the pavilions of Parsagadæ close by Persepolis, where great King Cyrus lay in a fine stone tomb.

Today, King Cyrus' garden palace in the flat plain of Parsagadæ, with its watercourses and pots for shrubs, is, as far as can be told, the oldest Eastern garden known to have survived. In this low well-watered valley the king planted pomegranates and mountain cherry, roses, irises and lilies; some of the most beautiful flowers of the northern uplands and trees as well. The carefully cut stone-lined watercourses that sustained the park still run between the remaining stonework of the royal pavilions, and drop less than an inch on their way through the gardens. The plan and disposition of this, the stone pavilions marvellously made by captured Greek masons brought from Sardis, the garden paths and stone bridges, the finely graded beds and terraces, are entirely Persian and are part of another gentler gardening tradition, one we know of from the 16th century gardens of both Persia and India. Here, the word 'Paradise' begins, and you can easily imagine why the great king was buried here, beside his garden palace, surrounded by his trees and plants.

Before arriving at Parsagadæ to view the coffin of the king, Alexander and his army had plundered the vast coffers of the Persian empire. The largest single treasure that the world had ever seen was moved from a bullion store and tipped into the aggressive economy of the eastern Mediterranean. Close behind it followed more immediate treasures: sugar, cotton, peaches, cherry trees and apricots. And with them, a new and richer agriculture entered the Mediterranean basin; better mills with professional millers, high-pressure olive presses, a more subtle understanding of crop rotation, iron ploughshares, ox-driven water wheels, camels too, and velvet, silks and satins – all the plundered detritus of a long and elaborate civilization.

Out of Persia too, with the gardens and the gold, came a range of mystic wisdoms, astronomies and alchemies and the crafts of carpet-weaving that held, so it was said, the eastern garden in colours made by alchemists who learnt their arts in Babylon. And then these dreams of perfumed gardens were taken east to India, to Shalimar and Amber, Kashmir and Shrínagar; and way beyond the dusty roads that Alexander walked, to the palaces and courts of other yet more distant empires.

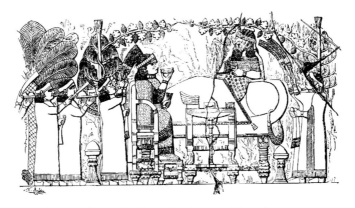

King Ashurbanipal in his garden bower at Nineveh, *c.* 650 BC,
from the *Illustrated London News*, 3 November, 1855

Chapter 6

THE TEMPLE OF ARTEMIS AT EPHESUS

THE DISCOVERIES AT EPHESUS

The Temple of Artemis at Ephesus is the only house of the gods. Whoever looks will be convinced that a change of place has occurred: that the heavenly world of immortality has been placed on the earth. For the Giants or the sons of Aloeus who attempted an ascent to heaven made a heap out of mountains and built not a temple but Olympus.

Philo 6, 1 (*c.* 225 BC)

The arts of Greece and the wealth of Asia had conspired to erect a sacred and magnificent structure. It was supported by a hundred and twenty-seven marble columns of the Ionic order; they were the gifts of devout monarchs, and each was sixty feet high. The altar was adorned with the masterly sculptures of Praxiteles. Successive empires, the Persian, the Macedonian, and the Roman, had revered its sanctity and enriched its splendour. But the rude savages of the Baltic were destitute of a taste for the elegant arts, and they despised the ideal terrors of a foreign superstition.

Edward Gibbon, *The History of the Decline and Fall
of the Roman Empire* (*c.* AD 1776)

The end of antiquity saw most of the great Hellenistic cities left high and dry, and drained of wealth and population. Huge shifts in economic status and political power and disasters, natural and man-made, first damaged then finally obliterated most of the great cities, among them Ephesus, the city of the goddess Artemis. For more than 1,000 years, the temple of that goddess, the most celebrated shrine of classical antiquity, completely disappeared from view.

The vision of it was never lost, however. In Gibbon's day, though no one had seen stick or stone of the building for a millennium, his description of that pagan tabernacle had all the enthusiasm of the recounting of a long-held dream; that European vision of antiquity, whose ending people like Gibbon took as evidence of the workings of morality in human history. More than any other ancient monument, the temple of Artemis came to stand in that other Eden, that lost classical paradise, that same paradise which, in its enthusiasm and ever-growing wealth, the rapidly industrializing North thought it could re-enter and retake for itself. The temple of Artemis at Ephesus therefore was the first monument of the ancient East that Europeans and their governments went out to find with spades and shovels, even before Heinrich Schliemann went to dig at Troy and Mycenæ and in so doing, at a stroke, brought archaeology to the notice of both traditional scholarship and the public. Schliemann, indeed, visited Ephesus shortly after the temple of Artemis had been refound, and as he stood upon its ancient marble steps, he asked its discoverers how he too might obtain the permits from the Imperial Administration of Turkey to allow the excavations he wanted to conduct at Troy.

The man who went looking for Artemis' great temple was an English architect working for the company that was building the first railway lines through south-western Turkey, the Smyrna and Aydin Railway Company. A modern man, straight from a fashionable, if underworked, architectural practice in central London, John Turtle Wood was not a great archaeologist (in his day indeed there was really no such thing), nor was he well-organized or clear-headed, yet he had endless determination and enthusiasm for the work, and a great kindness, too. An unlikely man, perhaps, for such a labour, yet at the same time he was a member of the most powerful nation in the world, a nation with sufficient cash to finance such dreamers, to thrill to their enthusiasms and discoveries and to provide funds for their further delectation.

For the first five years of his Turkish adventure, from 1858, Wood lived in Smyrna, at the centre of the west coast of Turkey, traditionally the hometown of the poet Homer, and still in Wood's day the centre of Greek life in that country. Five years' work and travel in the rich surrounding countryside changed Wood's life for ever. In 1863, at the age of 46, after reaching an agreement with the trustees of the British Museum by which they obtained the necessary permit for his excavations and retained the antiquities he found, Wood resigned from full-time employment and, financing himself entirely with his own savings, started to dig at Ephesus, looking for the great temple.

There was little enough to show where to begin. The ancient city was virtually abandoned, mile upon mile of enbrambled ruins which, until the fame of Wood's work spread and cruise boats began to stop at nearby fishing ports to send carriages of tourists to inspect the city, was visited only by shepherds and small parties of travellers. The richer of these itinerants might stop at the small town of Seljuk, clustered around the base of a picturesque fortress that guarded the land entrance to the coastal plain where ancient Ephesus had stood. Though the railway, Wood's former employer, slowly brought a measure of prosperity to the area, the desolate malaria-ravaged region remained relatively inaccessible until the laying of hard-surfaced roads after the Second World War. In Wood's day it was wild bandit country, with a few pretty, settled villages and a very beautiful hemisphere of hills around it. At the ancient site, there was not a fragment of the temple of Artemis to be seen.

How to find this temple, then? No one had ever attempted such a thing before, and Wood had to make his own plan of action. His sole source of information about the building was the classical authors, well known enough then, and taught in every middle-class school in England. However, when it came to describing the temple's location, the venerable texts seemed contradictory. Wood therefore sifted through them all, separated a handful which he felt might be more reliable than the rest, and started to dig at sites that caught his fancy, all the while unearthing statues and fragments of ancient architecture. Above all, he was searching for something to link the topography of the buried city that he and his workmen were disinterring with the written descriptions of the living city in the ancient texts. This combination, he thought, would lead him to the legendary shrine which for more than five centuries was held to be the greatest holy wonder of antiquity.

Like the pattern of his excavations, Wood's extraordinary account of this work, which continued at Ephesus for more than 20 years, has little plan. Frequently, his book is repetitious, the events placed confusingly out of sequence. Once teased out from the text, however, his story is perhaps the single greatest tale of early archaeology. With its melange of anecdote and observation, it holds in it the gritty reality of this strange adventure, the day-to-day experience as well, that slowly built in him the expertise he needed to narrow down his hunt, and, finally, to bring about the renaissance of an ancient wonder by excavating the temple of great Artemis herself.

On arriving at Ephesus, and studying the ground in every direction outside the city, I found a long strip of land standing several feet above the general level of the plain between the city and the sea. At the western end of this strip an open space is reached, which would have been of all others the best possible site for the Temple. There it would have been a most conspicuous and beautiful object from nearly every house in the city, as well as from the suburbs, and from the sea. I lingered about this spot and looked about me, though in vain, for a promising mound. Seeing none, I sank some trial holes in the highest land I could find. At the same time I tried some cross trenches, but in none of them did I find anything except the substructures of some monuments and tombs, and the thin brick walling of Roman and Byzantine buildings.

I had only five Turkish workmen, whom I found unemployed at the station at Ayasuluk [Seljuk] on the first day of my arrival. These men, who had just been discharged by the railway officials, I at once engaged. Shouldering their picks and shovels, with their bread and

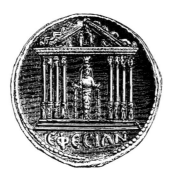

Wood's illustration of an Ephesian coin showing Artemis in her temple. From Wood, 1877

water for the day, they followed me down to the open plain beyond the ruins of the city. Turks have the reputation of being very grave and sedate, and so they are generally; but of these five men, one was a jester, and he kept the others in roars of laughter, till our arrival at the place, when I commenced work.

The excavations had been very much impeded by an accident, which prevented my visiting Ephesus during the month of September. This accident befell me in the cause of science. I had promised Dr Birch, of the British Museum, before I left England, that I would try to obtain a cast, or a copy of some kind, of the bas-relief of Sesostris, which is carved on the perpendicular face of a white marble rock at Nif [now Kemalpaşa]. Returning home alone at night, I missed my road. My horse fell with me into a dry ditch; my collar bone was broken by the fall, and I was otherwise injured . . .

These excavations were undertaken under many disadvantages. They were begun in May, when the hot season sets in, and when, as I afterwards learnt, they must be suspended. The spot where I began operations was more than three miles from the village of Ayasuluk; and my workmen had to walk this distance for their daily supply of food. They lived at that time in a tent, which was kindly supplied by the Turkish military authorities at Smyrna.

I had at that time no house at Ephesus, but lived alone at the hotel at a village a few miles from Smyrna. I had to walk a mile and a half to meet the train, which started from Smyrna at six o'clock in the morning, and took me up at Paradise station. The fifty miles between Smyrna and Ayasuluk occupied nearly three hours and a half . . . The six hours and a half which elapsed between the arrival of the train at Ayasuluk and its return in the afternoon, I spent in walking to and from the place where my men at that time were working, in searching about the plain and studying the ground, and superintending the workmen. Often I took to digging, myself, during the men's dinner hour, as well as at other times, when I was impatient at the slow movements of the men, or their unskilful mode of going to work. I had further to take notes and measurements, and make drawings of everything that was found. Then there was the return journey by railway, and the walk home. I was sometimes so over-excited by the hard day's work, that I ran most of the distance between the station and the village. The whole day's work occupied between fourteen and fifteen hours.

As I could not afford to increase the number of my workmen beyond eighteen or twenty, the work of exploration proceeded very slowly, and more than five months passed before I felt quite satisfied that the site of the Temple was not to be found between the city and the sea. I had approached nearer to the city, and had even tried a large mound on the north side of the City Port, as well as a considerable tract of land to the north of the city.

When I first began my excavations I used to wander about the plain seeking for mounds or other indication of the site of the great Temple. In so doing I encountered all sorts of people, who were often of an unprepossessing appearance.

One day a tall, earnest-looking Greek overtook me, and eagerly asked me if I would consent to dig, or allow him to do so in certain places which he would point out to me. He had dreamed, he said, of treasure which lay buried many feet under ground, and he had distinctly seen in his dreams certain subterranean passages, which led to the door of the chamber containing the treasure. I refused to dig myself on this man's account; but as I had some hope of his striking accidentally upon the wall of some building, or hitting upon some inscription of interest, I so far humoured this dreamer of dreams as to promise him the protection of my firman, in any excavations he might make amongst the ruins of Ephesus, which should be subject to my control or approval, though not at my own expense. With this understanding he set a few men to work, and sank a number of shallow trial holes about the Serapeion and elsewhere in the city, thus betraying the fact that his dreams had not clearly defined the situation of the treasure.

On exploring the ground in the Forum in front of the great Gymnasium, I found a large Hall, the walls of which were built of brick. Small columns of marble, and niches for statues, adorned it on every side. Amongst the debris were found small marble statuettes of Aphrodite and Hermes. It was while the workmen were employed in clearing out this Hall, that I had my first warning to be more careful than I had hitherto been. I had been in the habit of going down into all the trial holes without hesitation, but one day, on approaching this particular excavation, I paused for a moment. As I did so, the whole fell in with a tremendous crash, the debris consisting of large bricks which had formed part of the vaulting of the chamber. From that day I became more careful in the method of sinking trial holes, for my own sake as well as for that of my workmen. In the course of the explorations which I made outside the city, I found that the whole plain of Ephesus had been silted up to the average height of 12 feet within the last fifteen centuries.

By the close of the year 1863, I had dug seventy-five deep holes. I had also dug many other trial holes, and many long trenches in mounds, which it was necessary to cut through without interruption. In my perplexity I remembered that I had, years before, seen at Venice a church, the front of which was decorated with pilasters on pedestals, upon which pedestals were carved, if I remember rightly, the plans of Cyprus, Rhodes, and two other cities. It then occurred to me that, although I might not find in any of the ruins of the public buildings in the city of Ephesus, similar bas-reliefs, there was just a chance of finding some idle scratching, which might indicate the direction, if not the exact position, of the Temple.

The great Theatre, and the Odeum, or Lyric Theatre, seemed the most likely buildings to commence with, especially as in them would most probably be found sculpture and inscriptions, which would encourage the trustees of the British Museum to recommend the necessary advances for the excavations. I applied, therefore, to the trustees, in the first instance, for the small sum of £100, to commence the exploration of the ruins of the great Theatre. The grant was voted, not, however, to explore the great Theatre, but the Odeum.

I commenced work at the Odeum about the middle of March 1864, with as large a gang of workmen as my funds would allow. I engaged a Greek named Spiro as ganger to superintend the workmen in my absence, as I was at that time practising as an architect in Smyrna, and could not, therefore, go out to Ephesus every day of the week. To assist the ganger in carrying out my instructions more readily, I now made a plan of the Odeum from the data at my command, which enabled him during the intervals between my visits, to conduct the work without much difficulty; but many small objects found in the excavations were, I fear, at that time appropriated by both ganger and workmen.

During the time I was exploring the Odeum, I did not fail to study the ground outside the city in search of the Temple, and from time to time put one or two men to open up any suspicious-looking mound which attracted my attention.

The Smyrna and Aydin Railway Company had this year provided first-class carriages on their line. The journey, therefore, between Smyrna and Ayasuluk was made with greater comfort; but it still took fully three hours to traverse a distance of scarcely fifty miles. There are ten intermediate stations between Smyrna and Ayasuluk.

Sometimes, on holiday occasions, large groups of Greeks from Kirkenjee visited the ruins to see what was going on. These were chiefly composed of women and children in charge of one or two old men. Sometimes a young man would accompany them, who was probably the betrothed of one of the young women. The women were remarkable for the unconstrained ease and grace of their movements, as well as for their pretty costume of many colours; and the children were generally, healthy-looking and beautiful.

In the month of April 1865, H.R.H. Prince Arthur visited the ruins of Ephesus, accompanied by Major (now Colonel Sir Howard) Elphinstone. I had afterwards the honour of joining the suite of His Royal Highness, and accompanied him in a cruise to Mytilene, Pergamon, and Assos. At Assos the Turks were removing the marble seats of the theatre, and conveying them to Constantinople, where a large palace was in progress. On our return to Smyrna, I was honoured by an invitation to accompany the Prince on another cruise, returning to Assos, and onward to Mount Athos; but as Mrs. Wood was dangerously ill with bronchitis, I was most kindly excused accepting the invitation.

During the months of June, July, and August the excavations were almost entirely suspended, the ganger, as well as the men, finding the weather much too hot for work among marbles which reflected so much light and heat. The few men who might have been hired, notwithstanding the heat, asked as much as fifteen piastres a day, their ordinary wages being only ten piastres.

While the works were suspended, I made copies, and took paper pressings, of all the inscriptions I could find on the surface and elsewhere; but the strong wind which set in from the sea made it very difficult to make good impressions, and it seemed always to rise as I placed the paper against the marble. This may be accounted for by the fact of my generally beginning this part of my work about the time that the sea breeze sprung up. Towards the end of August I engaged a fresh ganger, a Catholic, named Joseph; and, with a fresh set of workmen, I resumed my exploration of the Odeum, and at the same time put one or two men on the large mound covering the ruins of the proscenium of the great Theatre.

One day, while my men were all at work in front of the Great Theatre, I went into the building alone to take some dimensions of the proscenium. I at once smelt a very unpleasant odour, which I attributed to the decomposition of some dead beast. I made no remark at the time to anyone, although this smell compelled me to leave my work undone. In the evening my ganger Vitalis came to my room, and with a solemn and mysterious manner asked me if I had not smelt a 'dreadful smell' in the Theatre, and whether I had seen anything. On my replying that I had smelt something, but seen nothing, he said, 'It's a dead man, Sir!' . . . One of our Turkish labourers, named Osman, the only man of the whole seventy, then in my employment, who was regular at his devotions, had that morning told my ganger that on the previous Tuesday (four days before) he had assisted some of his fellow-workmen to bury the body of a man at the Theatre, and that they had threatened to kill the Greeks, if they told me or any of the authorities.

The ganger had feared to tell me of this when he first heard of it, feeling sure, he said, that I might incur danger by investigating the matter. I ordered him to be in readiness in the morning with a gang of half-a-dozen men for the purpose of exhuming the body for examination. At sunrise, the police then lighted the torches they had brought with them, and some of my workmen proceeded to exhume the body of the murdered man. This was no easy task, for the body had been deposited five or six feet below the surface, and large stones had been heaped upon it. Two good hours were spent in getting at it, and when it was taken out, its advanced state of decomposition left the exact manner of his death as much a mystery as before.

In the month of February 1866, having obtained the necessary advances from the Trustees, I began in good earnest the exploration of the Great Theatre, which is one of the largest in Asia Minor. By my computations this vast theatre was capable of seating 24,500 persons. It is built on the western slope of Mount Coressus, and from the upper seats may be seen a long strip of blue sea. Its diameter is 495 feet, and like most theatres of this description, it is of a horse-shoe form. The stage, or pulpitum, was nearly 22 feet wide. A large archway on the north side of the outer wall of the auditorium is of the period of Augustus. The proscenium, built almost entirely of white marble, was adorned with granite columns and highly enriched entabletures of fine white marble, in two tiers. All these, having fallen upon the stage, remained there undisturbed. I proceeded to remove as many of the blocks of marble as was necessary to clear a portion of the stage for its whole width. I then turned over and carefully examined the remainder, and took all the inscriptions and sculpture that were worth sending to England.

There was, however, a much greater prize awaiting my discovery, for I found that the whole of the eastern wall of the entrance was inscribed with a series of decrees, chiefly relating to a number of gold and silver images, weighing from three to seven *potrods* each, which were voted to Artemis, and ordered to be placed in her Temple, by a certain wealthy Roman, named C. Vibius Salutarius. On a certain day of assembly in the Theatre, viz., May 25, which was the birthday of the goddess, these images were to be carried in procession from the Temple to the Theatre by the priests, accompanied by a staff-bearer and guards, and to be met at the Magnesian gate by the Ephebi or young men of the city, who, from that point, took part in the procession, and helped to carry the images to the Theatre. After the assembly, the statues or images were taken back to the Temple in the same order of procession. The intention was evidently to make as complete a circuit as would enable the inhabitants of the city generally to see the images as they passed along.

This inscription, then, gave me the clue, and confirmed me in the resolution already formed, to search for one or two of the city gates and open up the roads leading from them, choosing the most worn road as the one likely to lead to the Temenos of the Temple of

Artemis. As I had obtained leave to spend a portion of my grant from the Trustees in continuing my search for the Temple, I employed about twenty men in sinking trial holes outside the city, eastward and, before the close of the year I had succeeded in finding the Magnesian Gate, one of the two gates named in the long Salutarian inscription from the Great Theatre.

Having found the Magnesian Gate, which I found had three openings, one of which was for the use of foot passengers, the other two for chariots and wagons, I set as many men to work as I could spare from the great Theatre to clear a large space to open up the road leading from it, and I had to clear a distance of 140 feet outside the gate, before I reached the point where the road bifurcated, one branch of it leading around Mount Coressus towards Ayasuluk, the other towards the Ephesus Pass and onward to Magnesia ad Maeandrum. It was this latter road that gave the name to the gate.

I soon determined which of these two roads was more likely to lead to the Temple. The road leading to Ayasuluk, thirty-five feet in width, and paved with immense blocks of marble and limestone, was very deeply worn into four distinct ruts, showing the constant passing and repassing of chariots and other vehicles. The road leading to Magnesia, on the other hand, showed little or no wear, the marks of wheels being scarcely discernible. In opening the road towards Ayasuluk, I found at first only a few large marble sarcophagi, inscribed with the names of the occupants; and none of these were of special interest. The discovery of them was occasionally announced by the English ganger, who informed me in quite an excited manner, 'They've found another sarcopalus, Sir!'

Looking now from the Magnesian Gate in the direction of the road which I had selected as the most likely to lead to the Temple, I could see no ground within six hundred feet which could possibly be the site; yet this appeared to be the length of the Stoa or Portico of Damianus described by Philostratus as uniting the Temple with the city. I determined ultimately to set aside for a time the question as to the exact length of this portico, and to bestow all my means and energy in opening up as great a length of the road as I possibly could, with the balance I had then in hand, before the hot season should set in. I therefore opened up the outer side of the road around the mountain, in search of a road which led away from it towards the open plain, where I thought the Temple must inevitably be found and I succeeded in exploring five hundred yards of the road in this manner by the time my funds were exhausted. At this distance from the gate I found the stone piers of a portico which must have been that of Damianus. I now concluded that this portico was of great length, and that the six hundred feet of it mentioned by Philostratus as having been built of stone, was of a more ornate character than the remainder. The clouds had begun to disperse, and the difficulties to lessen.

But above all, there was the fear of failure for want of funds to continue the excavations. This caused me constant anxiety at that time. In my less sanguine or hopeful moods, I would sometimes wish for a great earthquake to open up a chasm, and reveal the secret; but if this had happened, I should have lost the credit of finding the Temple. During my stay in England, the Trustees of the British Museum determined to proceed with the works, and Mrs. Wood accompanied me on my return to Smyrna towards the end of October.

On our arrival at Ephesus I set to work immediately with the few men I could get together on the spot, beginning from the point where I had suspended work in May, and continuing to open up the road leading towards Ayasuluk. The trenches remained open up to the time of my leaving Ephesus, and no one had applied to have them filled up. The average depth of the excavation along the road traced from the Magnesian Gate was about 12 feet. Tombs of every description, but chiefly sarcophagi of white marble, of the third, fourth, and fifth century of our era, were found on both sides of the road. As the tombs and sarcophagi along the main road were placed side by side as closely as possible, I opened up the outer side of the road with a continuous trench, always looking for the road, which I thought must lead to the Temple.

The fear of failure now cost me many a pang, as I looked over the smooth plain of Ephesus, with its gentle uninterrupted incline towards the sea, and without any mound to indicate the site of such a building as the Temple of Artemis. I continued opening up the road however, and by now sinking my pits less frequently than before, I very quickly explored another 600 feet of road. This brought me nearly opposite an ancient road, or bridle-path.

A great and apparently insuperable difficulty now presented itself. The whole plain of Ephesus had that year been sown with barley, and as we were then in the month of April, it had grown up to nearly its full height. Barley in Asia Minor grows high enough to conceal a man on horseback. I could not venture to cut the barley, as I had not the means to compensate proprietors or occupiers of the land, and the admission of their claims might have brought upon me a large number of demands for holes and trenches left open in the ground already explored. I took advantage of a modern boundary between two barley fields, to trace the road for several hundred feet. Looking onward in the direction which it took, I found it pointed towards some large olive trees which grew by the side of a modern boundary, more than half a mile distant, where I had before sunk a trial hole without any satisfactory result, the sand and stones having fallen in before the hole had been sunk to a sufficient depth.

I determined now to venture the small sum total of my balance in hand. I put a dozen men to dig one or two large trenches near the olive trees, and a few others to dig as many trial holes, in the ground between them and the foot of the mountain, wherever the boundaries between the fields permitted, in order to trace the direction of the road leading to the Temple. In a few days we found in the large trench a thick wall, built with large blocks of stone and marble, which I hoped would prove to be the peribolos wall [the enclosure wall] of the sacred precinct of the Temple.

I now carefully studied the ground in the immediate neighbourhood of the morsel of wall found near the olive trees. I observed that the wall took the same direction as that of a modern boundary which formed an angle near the trench I had dug. Suspecting that the modern boundary might mark the position of an ancient wall, I cut another large trench and hit most fortunately upon the angle of the wall into which were built two large stones, equidistant from the angle, with duplicate inscriptions in Latin and Greek, by which we are informed that this wall was built by order of Augustus in the twelfth year of his Consulate and the eighteenth year of his Tribunitian power in 6 BC, and that it was to be paid for and maintained out of the revenues of the Artemisium and the Augusteum. This was therefore, without doubt, the peribolos wall of the Temple of Artemis.

The great question as to the whereabouts of the Temple was now decided. Six years had elapsed since I had first begun the search. This seems a long time, but the actual time devoted to the search did not extend over more than twenty months, and the cost of the work did not exceed £2,000. The discovery of the peribolos wall and the inscriptions built into it occurred early in May 1869, and it was at that time that I had several narrow escapes of being taken prisoner by the same band of brigands which, soon after I left Ephesus that year, succeeded in taking Mr. Alfred Van Lennep, on his father's farm, not many miles from Ephesus.

Eager to obtain more inscriptions, I opened up the peribolos wall each way from the angle, and at the distance of eighteen feet found on each face another inscription, giving the width of the roads and streams. The wall itself was a most disgraceful piece of work, probably contract work! If I had not found the inscriptions built into it, I never could have believed that it had been built in the time of Augustus. After having traced the direction of the wall for 1,000 feet northwards and 500 feet eastwards, and thus fully proved, with the inscriptions, that the peribolos wall of the sacred precinct had been discovered, we left for England towards the end of May 1869.

I now felt convinced that, as I had found the sacred precinct of the Temple, I should have no difficulty in obtaining a further grant for the renewal of the excavations. I therefore left everything in preparation for my return in the autumn. The discovery of the peribolos wall sufficed, as I had hoped, to induce the Trustees of the British Museum to continue the excavations; and having recruited my health for a fresh campaign, we returned to Smyrna towards the end of September.

I soon got a small gang of men together and at the same time sank a great number of trial holes over the whole area which at that time was defined as being within the sacred precinct. I thus hit upon the front wall of some Roman buildings; which I traced for seven hundred feet in a straight line running eastward and, which I suppose, were the dwellings of the priests. In a number of cross trenches I found some mosaic pavements. One of these represented a triton, with a dish of fruit, and crooked stick; an attendant dolphin carries his trident. This mosaic, which is well executed and remarkably rich in colour, is now safely lodged in the British Museum; but it was with great difficulty taken up from its original position, in which it had remained undisturbed for about eighteen centuries.

Towards the end of October I had the misfortune (as it appeared at the time) to injure my foot so severely that I lost the use of it for some weeks, but as it led to a change in my life at Ephesus, which added greatly to my comfort, I have since regarded it as one of the fortunate accidents of my life. Having suffered so much from fever myself, I had such a dread of exposing my wife to the risks which I had to encounter, that I had hitherto gone alone to Ephesus, while Mrs. Wood remained in Smyrna. We were thus alone for five or six days every week; but when this accident happened, and I needed assistance, it was arranged that we should both go out to Ephesus together. I went on horseback to the works, while my wife accompanied me on foot.

The men were at that time chiefly occupied in digging trial holes within the sacred precinct, searching for the pavement, or other remains of the Temple, which would reveal the secret of its site. Mrs. Wood saved me all useless labour by examining the holes, and reporting to me what might be seen in them. As the holes were in many cases from twenty to twenty-four feet deep, it was neither a pleasant nor an easy task for a lady to approach their edges, amongst the loose earth, stones, and debris, and, stooping over, to examine them thoroughly on all sides to their lowest depths. For many days, however, when I was unable to leave the house, Mrs. Wood went to the works, accompanied by a kavass and made the necessary inspection of the trial holes, and even gave instructions to the workmen. My lameness was accompanied by fever and general ill health; but the prolonged test to which our new mode of life was subjected served only to prove the advantages as well as the pleasantness of the new arrangement, and from that time Mrs. Wood was my constant companion at Ephesus. This made our little home there pleasant, not only for myself, but for visitors, during the last five years in which excavations were carried on.

December 1st is marked in my journal as a red-letter day, for on this day I have recorded that at last we found part of the base of the column. On December 9th, we found one of the capitals, which, although much mutilated, gave a good idea of its boldness and grandeur. What building could this be but the great Temple of Artemis? On the last day of the year 1869, the marble pavement of the Temple, so long lost, so long sought for, and so long almost despaired of, was at last actually found at a depth of nearly twenty feet below the present surface of the ground. One of the workmen, who had been put to sink a number of deep holes, in one of the most likely fields of the group in which I was working, struck upon a thick pavement of white marble, which I at once concluded must be that of the Temple. It was the first thick pavement I had found within the sacred precinct. The next day was the first of the Turkish feast of Bairam, but I persuaded the man who found the pavement to work for two or three hours in the morning, before he left for his three days holiday. On New Year's Day 1870 this pavement proved to be Greek, and eventually it was found to be that of the last Temple but two. It consisted of two layers, the upper one of rubbed white marble 9 inches thick, the lower one, roughly tooled, of grey marble 15 inches thick.

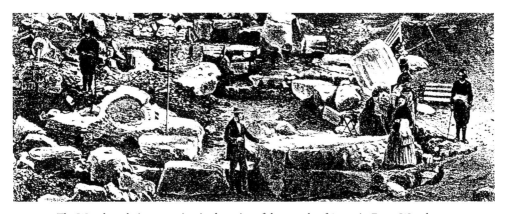

The Woods at their excavation in the ruins of the temple of Artemis. From Wood, 1877

The thirty days' fast of Ramadan, during which the Turks allow nothing, not even a cigarette or a drop of water, to pass their lips from sunrise till sunset, had now begun. The Mudir of the district, hearing of marvellous discoveries at Ephesus, came down from Kirkenjee, where he was quartered, and paid me a visit. Being a good Turk, he refused coffee, but accompanied me to the works to see the 'wonders' he had heard of. On my showing him the drums of the large columns, and the capitals, he asked me to what building they had belonged. I told him they were the remnants of an ancient mosque or church in the time of the ancient Greeks, when they did not worship the one true God, but had many gods, male and female, and that this church was dedicated to the worship of a female, whose statue, forty or fifty feet high, was set up inside it. 'Ah,' said the Mudir, as if a new light had broken in upon him, 'they were Protestants.' I did my best to undeceive him, and to make him understand that we Protestants were not worshippers of idols, but he evidently did not understand how Protestant worship could be anything but idolatrous, since we had not Mahomet as our prophet, and the whole thing remained a mystery to him.

December 16. This day the celebrated Dr. Schliemann, the discoverer of Troy, visited the excavations. He was kindly enthusiastic in his congratulations when he planted his foot upon the 'veritable' pavement of the Temple. He had been digging in the Troad, but had been stopped by the Turks, and he now asked my opinion, whether he could get a firman to dig in the Troad in search of the city of Troy. I expressed my doubts, as the Turks had made known their determination to grant no more firmans for excavations. He said they might have what was found, as he was anxious only to prove by excavations his own theory about the position of Troy, and being a rich retired merchant, he could well afford to spend out of his income ten thousand francs a year.

The excitement caused by this discovery and the hard work to which I was then subjected, were too much for my health. By a note in my journal on the 3rd of January, I find I had been writing that day from 9 am. till 10.45 pm., and that I had suffered from fever every night for three weeks. I did not, however, give in, but I continued my work without relaxation. Before the close of the year I had removed about 4,000 cubic yards from the large excavation, besides sinking a number of pits over the site of the Temple. We had unusually hot weather, slight shocks of earthquake, and rumours of a band of brigands at Ephesus, towards the close of this month.

Twenty days after Schliemann's visit to the temple, Charles Newton of the British Museum arrived from England and was, Wood says, delighted that the temple had been found. There was every possibility now of Wood receiving constant funding from the Museum to investigate the temple, which clearly covered an enormous area. Just as Newton himself had done at Halicarnassus, Wood arranged for the purchase of the land under which the temple lay. Though the weather was very bad, the railway lines broken and Wood was suffering from his usual combination of falls and fevers, he none the less managed to ship some of the finest pieces of the temple's architecture back to the Museum within a few months, where they were put on immediate exhibition and received wide publicity. Wood's discovery, indeed, caused quite a stir in Europe. Every educated person had known of the fabled temple since their schooldays, and now it had been found. Wood soon found himself acting as guide to rich and royal holidaymakers, as they visited the temple in the course of Mediterranean cruises. Unlike Newton or Schliemann, however, he did not attempt to capitalize on his hard-won success and simply kept at work, digging deeply in the temple precincts, year after year, until he had opened a vast hole some 20–30 feet in depth and nearly 600 feet long.

Once again, however, as at the Mausoleum, ancient wrecking gangs had quarried the temple away. Ominous limekilns were found standing on the ruined steps. All the sculptures were severely damaged, and just one of the famous column drums, one of which, so the ancient texts say, had been made by Scopas himself, was found in a good enough condition to allow its casual perusal in the public galleries of the British Museum. So large was this column block – one of 127 equal-sized blocks, according to Pliny's description – that Newton spent months moving it to the docks and crating it for shipping. Fifteen men, he records, were only able to pull it 50 or so paces every day down to the distant waterfront and the hold of HMS *Terrible*. The work continued for several years; coin hoards were found, and much damaged sculpture. All this time, though, a high water table and seeping water prevented the excavation from reaching into the lower levels of the temple.

In 1872, Wood was lecturing in England and seeking more money to continue the work in the temple. In 1873, the year he first published a set of the temple's plans, he also discovered that there had been three temples, one above the other standing on the same site. This was, as one newspaper put it, 'one of the so-called wonders of the world which, for architectural design, the excellence of its sculptures, and the interest of its associations, is not surpassed by any of the existing remains of antiquity'. Wood's site, the better part of the temple enclosure, was enormous and the greater part of it unexcavated. Clearly, its potential easily outstripped that of the Mausoleum that Newton had excavated in the 1850s. Even though the older buildings that surely lay underneath the remains that Wood had so far excavated were inaccessible, the random pits that they had excavated before Mrs Wood had hit upon the temple steps showed that there was an enormous and vastly interesting area of priestly houses and many other buildings too, all set inside the sacred area of the temple.

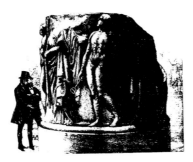

A column drum from the last temple of Artemis 'sent home by Mr Wood', observed by two gentlemen at the British Museum, from the *Illustrated London News*, 22 March, 1873

Yet 1874 began, as Wood says, with 'vexation and disappointment'. Newton reached Ephesus direct from England and immediately closed down the excavations, 'even before visiting the works'. Wood arrived on the morning train to find large numbers of his workmen waiting disconsolately on the station platform. After consultations with Newton, Wood paid all but 20 of them off, and they parted affectionately enough, if somewhat sadly after all their years of effort. Newton now wanted the ancient drains and wells cleared in a search for gold and statues, but none were found in them. He then asked to examine the venerable mosques of Ayasuluk for portions of ancient relief, such as he had found in the fortress of St Peter at Bodrum, but the imams would not let him do so. Then the British Museum withdrew.

With a small civic pension and grants awarded by individuals and professional institutions, Wood continued working at the temple. In 1877 he published his book *Discoveries at Ephesus including the Site and Remains of the Great Temple*. He spent his last season working there in 1884: 'We had the most lovely weather for our work during the month of January, which is one of the most pleasant months in the year in Asia Minor. The annual feast, Courban Bairam, took all my men away from their work for several days. The month of February opened with continued cold weather, and found us still at work . . .' He died a few years later, at the age of 70, in Worthing, of a heart attack.

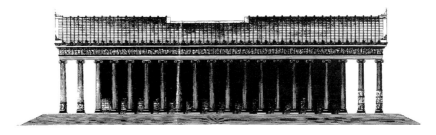

Wood's reconstruction of the last temple of Artemis at Ephesus. The huge open light-well breaking the line of the roof is probably mistaken. From Wood, 1877

THE GODDESS SMILES

Xenophon finished his epic Persian campaign around the year 394 BC and immediately embarked on an equally hazardous adventure in Greece, fighting alongside his friend Agesilaus, the Spartan king, against the armies of his native Athens. He was still carrying his share of Persian plunder with him, gold from the sale of slaves and booty, and this he wanted to secure before taking to the battlefields once more. Ten per cent of the sum he dedicated at the little treasury of Athena at the holy site of Delphi, whose oracle had advised him to undertake his Persian trip. Another 10 per cent, some 50 talents, so he says (though as a talent was considered to be the reasonable load for an adult to carry, this is rather hard to credit), he put on deposit with the head priest of Artemis, the Megabyxus of the great Temple of Ephesus; with the provision that if he did not survive this next campaign, the sum would be directly offered up to Artemis.

The choice was apt. The temple, revered by Persians and Greeks alike, was seldom plundered and the goddess moreover had a particular affinity with money; the first gold coins in the world, stamped with the symbols of Artemis-Kybele, had been made 150 years before out of metal taken from the River Pactolus at Sardis, a little to the north. It seems that, ever since the invention of money, the Megabyxus and his predecessors had had many dealings with the sacred coins of Artemis, for large amounts of them, some claimed as the oldest ever found, have been retrieved by archaeologists from cracks and corners of the temples' broken floors.

Xenophon fought his war, and later met the Megabyxus at the Olympic Games, and there his treasure was restored to him. Once again he consulted the gods as to what he should do, for he was in a difficult situation, Athens having, understandably, sent him into exile. The gods, and probably his Spartan friends as well, told him that he should buy a large estate near Olympia at a place called Scillus, where, he noted:

> By chance the river that flowed through the site was the River Selinus. At Ephesus, too, a River Selinus flows past the temple of Artemis. In both rivers there are fish as well as mussels. In the plot at Scillus, what is more, hunting of every type of wild animal is possible.
>
> Xenophon, *Anabasis*, v, iii, 8

Xenophon, a great hunter and devotee of Artemis, goddess of the hunt, would have liked that. So he bought the estate and built a house for himself and his family, and there he made a rare thing for the Greece of those days: a small garden grove, an orchard such as those he must have seen during his Persian adventures, and in it he built a little temple, a copy of the Temple of Ephesian Artemis. As was his habit, Xenophon now offered a tenth of the produce of his estate to the goddess Artemis. Every year, all the workers and inhabitants of the neighbourhood of Scillus joined in a country festival, with a feast of barley meal, bread, wine, and sweetmeats in honour of great Artemis, and shared the game taken from the estate of the goddess by Xenophon and his two sons; wild boar, roe and red deer, running on the land of Artemis.

> The place is on the road from Sparta to Olympia, about two miles from the temple of Zeus at Olympia. In the sacred precinct is meadow land and hills covered with trees so pigs, goats, cattle and horses can graze, and there is enough even for the yoked animals, which bring people to the festival, to feast on. Right around the temple an orchard of fruit trees has been planted which yield dessert fruit at the right times in the year. The temple, small as it is, resembles the big temple at Ephesus, and the image of the goddess, although made from Cypress wood, is like the gold one at Ephesus. Near the temple stands a tablet, bearing the following inscription: 'The precinct is sacred to Artemis. Whoever lives here and reaps the harvest must offer up a tenth in sacrifice every year, and from what remains must look after the temple. If these things are not done, it will be a matter for the goddess.'
>
> Xenophon, *Anabasis*, v, iii, 11–13

Artemis, worshipped under a variety of names and titles in both Europe and through Asia, was the city deity of Ephesus. Goddess of wild beasts, guardian of untamed lands, Artemis is virgin because she is not dominated by a male god. She is then, as a fertility figure, a mother who avoids marriage, a virgin mother. Artemis also held a threat; many such ancient gods offered danger rather than the promise of salvation, so as to encompass sudden unexpected deaths in childbirth, from disease, plague and war. Sometimes, then, the Great Goddess stands high upon a lion, a ferocious symbol of sudden death stretching back millennium upon millennium, as did in Xenophon's day her common symbols, bees, that too were imported from Anatolia with the goddess. At Ephesus her priestesses were called Melissae – 'the honey bees' – while the name of the chief priest, the Megabyxus, was literally the 'drone'. This priestly name Melissa, however, hardly suggested a sacred virginity of itself: 'You do everything, Melissa, that the flower-loving bee does . . . you drop honey from your lips when you sweetly kiss, and if you ask for payment, you sting, quite unfairly.' So runs an epigram of one Marcus Argentarius.

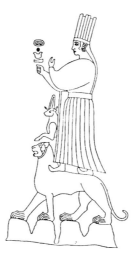

The ancient Anatolian goddess Hepat standing, as did her successors, on a lion. Part of a relief in the Hittite rock shrine of Yazilikaya, mid-second millennium BC, after Akurgal, 1985

Imagine, then, this vastly impressive city of Ephesus, the wealthiest in Asia Minor, its citizens all out of doors and in procession, honouring their goddess whose annual circuit of the city finished the sacred winter month of Artemesion, named in the goddess's honour. These were dazzling affairs; poor Wood caught a hint of them in the text of Caius Vibius Salutarius, the city councillor who left a great memorial inscription on the triangular south wall of the city's theatre. Still in Salutarius' day, four centuries after Xenophon, the processional splendour of the goddess continued. Indeed, the care and detail of these decrees show how important the town council and the provincial government thought the procession to be. Salutarius left a fortune for the manufacture of a large number of gold and silver images to be carried in this procession, each one specified by its lavish weight (never less than three pounds), which were to be kept in the vestibule of the great temple, where they would be seen by visitors and pilgrims. As well as this, Salutarius also left capital to finance the temple ritual and its annual processional by payment of interest at 9 per cent per annum, all this couched in terms that show that the temple priesthood had long experience of book-keeping, from the calculation of rates of interest to changing money and charging adequate commission. The interest on Salutarius' legacy was to be paid annually to specially selected citizens and members of the temple administration – hierophants and choristers and 'gold wearers' – on the birthday of the goddess, on the sixth of Thargelion; that is, in late May. Considering that Salutarius' heirs also had use of this capital provided that they paid the annual rates of interest to the goddess, it seems to have been a sensible provision that the Proconsul of Asia himself, one T. Aquillius Proculus, set punitive fines for neglect of these payments; a decree that fixed a sharp eye on the state of the goddess' pension fund.

The route of the luxurious procession is completely described by Salutarius and this it was that enabled Wood to retrace the path of Artemis and find her temple. It must have been one of the sights of the ancient world on those warm and poetic days, the skies a lucid azure blue, the great stadium standing high above the flashing marble city and the population waiting for the passing of their goddess. Democritus of Ephesus wrote two books, now lost, 'On the Temple of Ephesus'. Surviving fragments boast of the Ephesians' love of luxury and bright parade:

'The clothes of the Ionians are dyed violet, purple and yellow, woven in lozenge shapes, and the tops are decorated at equal intervals with pictures of animals. And there are *serapeis* robes which are yellow, purple and white, and also *halourgeis* robes; there are *kalarseis* robes, long ones, made in Corinth – some of these are purple, others violet, others crimson and you can get hold of them in flame-orange or sea-green. There are also Persian *kalasireis*, which are the most beautiful of them all. One might also see,' he [Democritus of Ephesus] continues, 'the so-called *aktaiai*, which are the most expensive Persian robes. This is closely woven to make it strong and light, and all over it there are gold beads which are each attached at the centre with a purple cord which leads to the inside of the robe.' He says that the Ephesians use all of these garments, so dedicated are they to luxury.

Athenaeus, *The Deipnosophists*, XII, 525c-e (*c.* AD 200)

As well as his bank, the Megabyxus also controlled large estates, an elaborate staff and an enormous choir, amongst the most celebrated in the ancient world, and a large number of musicians too, for the temple was especially famous for its sonorous bronze horns. Musicians, indeed, felt especially comfortable with the goddess Artemis. One man who had spent years perfecting the design of a lute had visited Ephesus especially to hang the finished instrument inside her temple. Now though, surrounded by the city marshals and officials, with the young men and women of the town and all the priests and priestesses in their solemn dress and splendid decoration, accompanied by precious statues, Artemis Ephesia, the veiled goddess with gilded lips, amidst clouds of incense, shadowed wisps of smoke in the bright sun, was borne in sacred circuit round her holy city.

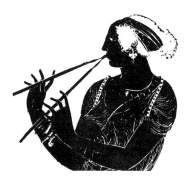

Flute player, from a south Italian red figure vase by the Karneia painter,
late fifth century BC, from Taranto

After the coming of Christianity, when the goddess's temple was torn down and buried
deep and the cross of salvation was chiselled on every wall and pavement, the bishops
of the church met at Ephesus in general conclave. There, after long and fierce delibera-
tions, they declared Mary, Jesus' mother, who was believed by many to have lived at
Ephesus in later life, to be 'Theotokos', god-bearer. So in one way or another, Ephesus
held to its ancient identity as the city of a mother goddess until its ending. The city, it
was said, had been founded around a shrine of Artemis. In ages long before the time of
Xenophon, when a Persian army attacked, the Ephesians tied a rope around the city wall
and tied its end onto the wooden columns of the goddess's temple and claimed the sanctuary of that most holy place. Later, generations of criminals and fleeing and unseated
rulers also came to Artemis' temple to claim the right of that same sanctuary – a sanctuary confirmed and broken by various commands of Alexander. Not surprisingly, the
land around the sacred temenos was holy too, as were its birds and animals and fishes.
The gilt-headed bream, which still live in the nearby river estuary with golden crescents
on their heads and two gold spots upon their cheeks, were once considered sacred, and
a good meal too:

> Do not leave out the fat gilt-head fish from Ephesus which people there call 'the Ioniscus'.
> Catch a young one from the river Selinus, wash it properly, then bake it whole and serve
> it, even though it is fifteen feet long.

Athenaeus, *The Deipnosophists*, VII, 328b

Bright and lazy lives then, filled with feasts and epigrams and resplendent priests. And
great processions joined by all the townspeople and their slaves and servants. Powdered
boys and girls dancing round the veiled lady, weaving down through stout arcades built
by wealthy townsfolk, named after their wives and built so that the goddess and her
admirers would not get wet when it rained upon a feast day. Artemis then, was borne
along on general admiration, accompanied with the wealth of her temple, the donations
of foreign emperors and kings and local magnates, gold and silver and precious woods
and silks, and jewels beyond imagination.

'Let us go to the temple of Aphrodite,' sings another short sharp poem, 'and see how finely worked the golden statue is. Polyarchis made it after she enjoyed the benefits of a large amount of trade from the beauty of her own body.' This poem is Hellenistic, from the age when Alexander's cities and their temples first invested something of their civic potency in cold hard cash. The temple of Artemis where Xenophon had left his gold half a century before was built in an archaic and more innocent age. It had been the first marble temple to have been built in the Greek manner. Wood found small bits of it in his excavations, marvellously worked pieces of Ionic architecture, some of them fragments of decorated column drums, inscribed in both Lydian and Greek telling that part of the building had been presented to the goddess by King Croesus, Sardis' legendary golden monarch. The temple had been colossal, a true wonder of its age and an appropriate enough dwelling for a deity the Romans identified with Diana, the goddess of the hunt. For the building was forested with columns; columns that stood two deep right around the central sanctuary, in 14 pairs along each side, and six along each end with a long central passageway of columns, a veritable hypostyle hall, leading in to the vestibule and on towards the central shrine that housed the image of the great goddess. In comparison with the Parthenon of Athens, the temple was bigger, broader, taller, and more elaborately decorated with gilded, exaggerated detail, like the fitments of a baroque altar. When Xenophon had left his money with the Megabyxus, the temple was a century and a half old, and considered as a fit model for all later temples.

This archetypal monument was designed by a Cretan architect and his son who, so the great hall of columns leading to the sanctuary would suggest, had visited Egypt and had been impressed by its gigantic standing temples with their halls of columns. 'The overall length of the temple is four hundred and twenty-five feet, its width two hundred and twenty-five feet,' writes the Roman Pliny.

> . . . Chersiphron was the architect in charge of the work. The most amazing thing about it is that architraves of such mass could be lifted. He managed this with bags filled with sand: he made a gentle slope leading up to the top of the columns, and gradually emptied the sand from the bags at the bottom to ensure that the structure slowly settled into its position. But his biggest problem was with the lintel itself which he was trying to place on top of the door. That, you see, was the heaviest block and it did not settle in its proper place. The artist grew distressed and decided in the end on death. The story goes that as he was thinking this, as he slept in a state of exhaustion one night, he saw the goddess for whom the temple was being made, right in front of him, and that she encouraged him to live, saying that she herself had put the stone in place. The following morning this appeared to be the case. By its own weight it seemed to have righted itself.

> Pliny, *Natural History*, XXXVI, 95–7

As well as designing temples, deciding upon their precise proportion and architectural detail, Greek architects also kept a sharp eye on the quality of the carved decoration – many of them were well-known sculptors in their own right. These same architects were responsible too for the temples' day-to-day construction, the sheer size and novelty of which, in the case of Artemis' great temple at Ephesus, seem to have given the architect Chersiphron many sleepless nights. However, as is the case with most architects working before the last few centuries, engineering was a considerable part of their trade. Even as they designed lavish and complex buildings, every one of them worked with the knowledge that their personal skills of engineering and organization would be called on to realize their plans; that they and their assistants would control both the labour and the machinery by which those plans would be accomplished. This it is perhaps that gives so many ancient buildings their special unity, a tension, a pride of accomplishment even, that much larger structures built by people other than their designers completely lack. Thus, though Chersiphron's name is now linked indelibly with one of the Seven Wonders of the World as its architect, in his own time he was far more than its designer.

The only complete treatise of architecture that has survived from classical antiquity, Vitruvius' manual lays out the ancient job of architects, both as the makers of the classical city and as the builders of the homes of their gods. Vitruvius' work is dedicated to the Emperor of Rome, whose 'divine will and intelligence' and 'power to command the world' was the earthly instigator of all Roman building. To the modern mind, the book divides between theory and practice. There is a chapter on the movement of the heavens, followed by a chapter on moving quarried stones across the earth. To the Roman Vitruvius, and to the Greek Chersiphron before him, the distinction would have been less important – success in the latter was dependent upon a correct understanding of the former. So chapters on the theoretical origins of architecture and its materials follow naturally on chapters dealing with the winds, on finding water, and on erecting buildings that reflect the character of the gods they were to house. Just as the great gods, both male and female, filled the world with power and substance, so their great temples, those buildings at the heart of the ancient world, gave style and proportion to all the other forms of civic architecture. Major architects such as Chersiphron ensured that the temple, the yardstick of the city, was fine and splendid and in harmony both with the gods it housed and the land it decorated. Ideally, it enabled people to feel at home and in their proper place upon the earth, at one with the movements of the heavens and their fellow beings too.

Clearly, the materials of such a temple were most carefully chosen, not only for the strength and availability of the stone, but also for what today we call aesthetic considerations. In this ancient universe such things were part of the whole. The look of a stone was part of the assurance of its sanctity and suitability. The fine white marble for Artemis' temple was found, in true mythic fashion, by a shepherd boy. Appropriate to the sensitivity of ancient architects, Vitruvius gives us a full account of the event:

> I will set down how the quarries were discovered . . . When the Ephesian citizens were thinking about building a marble temple to Diana [Artemis] and were debating whether the marble was to be got from Paros, Proconessus, Heracleia or Thasos, Pixodarus [a local shepherd] drove his flock to that very place and was pasturing them there. Two rams

charged at each other and missed, but one of them crashed into a rock with his horns and chipped off a bright white fragment of the rock. So, the story goes, Pixodarus left his sheep on the mountain and ran with the piece of marble to Ephesus, when the debate about the marble was at its most intense. Straightaway, therefore, the citizens decreed him honours and changed his name. Instead of 'Pixodarus', he was to be called 'Evangelus' [Greek for 'the bringer of good news']. Even today the magistrate goes there monthly and performs a sacrifice to him, and if he does not, he is punished.

Vitruvius, *On Architecture*, x, ii, 15

A suitable stone having manifested itself, Chersiphron could now start building.

He wanted to bring the shafts of the columns down from the quarries to the temple of Diana at Ephesus, but he did not put his trust in carts – he was afraid that the wheels would sink in because of the size of the load and the soft country lanes. So this was what he tried: he put four pieces of four-inch timber into a frame, put two horizontal pieces, of the same length as a column-shaft, across between them, and dove-tailed them together. He then leaded iron pivots (just as one leads dowels) on the tops of the column-shafts. Then he attached sockets in the frame to receive the pivots and tied the tops to wooden posts. Thus the pivots in the sockets moved frictionlessly. So when yoked oxen drew the frame, the shafts rolled constantly, through the turning of the pivots in the sockets.

When, however, they had carried all the column-shafts in the way described, and were beginning to tackle the problem of the transportation of the architraves, Metagenes, the son of Chersiphron, applied the method of conveying the column-shafts to the transportation of the architraves. He made wheels of about twelve feet in diameter, and put the ends of the architraves into the middle of the wheels. By the same rationale he put pivots and sockets on top of each architrave. Thus, when the frames were drawn by oxen, the pivots that were held in the sockets turned the wheels round, and each architrave was held in like an axle in a wheel and, by the same principle that was used in the conveyance of the shafts, soon reached the building-site.

An example of the method is the way in which rollers make the walks in the exercise area level. This would not have been possible unless (a) the distance was small (for it is no more than eight miles from the quarries to the temple), (b) there was no slope (there is an uninterrupted plain).

Vitruvius, *On Architecture*, x, ii, 11–12

The soft ground of the river estuary, a typical site of such temples in Asia Minor, was a constructional hazard at the site of the temple itself, and one solved by the usual ancient mix of sensitivity and ingenuity. 'They built it on marshy ground,' relates Pliny, 'so that it would be immune to earthquakes and not endangered by subsidence. But to avoid placing such massive foundations on a squelchy, unstable base, they first laid trodden charcoal and then fleeces of wool underneath.'

Though the brutal work of manipulating such colossal stones was accomplished with the skilful organization of large gangs of slaves, and afterwards with the accomplished chisels of some of the classical world's finest sculptors, the entire city was engaged in some way or another with making the new house for the goddess. So when Croesus of Sardis, who had captured Ephesus and razed the city to the ground, commissioned famous sculptors to decorate the brand-new marble temple, he was engaging in an astute act of piety that today we would call good politics – a fact he celebrated on the bases of elegant archaic columns in inscriptions written in both Greek and in his native Lydian, texts that emphasize, if emphasis were needed, the true sophistication of what we now call 'Greek' art. Though decorated with the finest reliefs that Greeks sculptors of the day could make, the column bases of the marble colonnades were ringed with figures in the manner of ancient Anatolian monuments. Fragments found by Wood show that these figures were about lifesize. A single surviving face shows their extraordinary quality; this was the finest archaic art, a face with a serene smile as old as human time itself, an Asian face perhaps, but a local face as well, one seen in other nearby early temples at Didyma and Samos. As you entered this great temple, alongside Xenophon clutching his gold, as you walked into the presence of the goddess in procession, you would have joined rows of these beautiful calm figures on the temple's column drums, whose eyes, at human height, met yours, in an endless friendly, sightless, marble gaze; a sort of procession in themselves, winding through the sacred grove of column shafts towards the goddess in the sanctuary.

It is particularly suitable that this ancient building standing so beautifully in the golden haze of legend was burnt down on the very day, so it was said, that Alexander of Macedon was born. Burnt down, that was, in 356 BC by a man named Herostratus who wished, in a most modern manner, to be famous. It is usually assumed that, for the destruction to have been so extensive in a marble building, Herostratus must have fired its enormous timber roof. In one way or another, the philosophical incendiary secured his immortality. Later Greeks used the epithet 'herostraton' to denote notoriety, others though have called him mad, 'a wicked and deborsht fellow'. Yet Herostratus' act of taking the fame of this extraordinary building to himself has the same directness as Croesus' archaic columns; unfortunately, it lacked their subtle sensibility.

PERICYNTHION

I saw the wall that chariots drive along at lofty Babylon, and [the statue of] Zeus by the Alpheios, and the Hanging Gardens, and the Colossus of Helios, and the huge labour of the sheer Pyramids, and the enormous tomb of Mausolus. But when I saw the palace of Artemis, stretching as far up as the clouds, the rest faded into insignificance, and I said 'Look, apart from Olympus, the Sun has not yet looked on anything that compares with this.'

Antipater, *Palatine Anthology*, IX, 58

When Alexander came to Ephesus, aged 22, and just a few months away from his first great victory against the Persians, the rebuilding of that first great temple was well underway. His offer, in the manner of Croesus, to be its royal patron was politely rebuffed; it was not fitting, the Megabyxus is supposed to have said, for one god to honour another. And so Alexander and his army passed down the coast, to Halicarnassus, to Egypt, Alexandria and the pyramids. It was said however that Alexander's visionary architect Dinocrates subsequently came to work upon the temple, so it is likely the Megabyxus' shrewd reply was written in a later age to demonstrate the power of Artemis over all men, even Alexander. If the story of Dinocrates is true, he must have supervised the upper sections of the building, for before Alexander had arrived the first plans had been laid by two architects from Ephesus: Paionius and Demetrius, the latter termed a slave of Artemis, and probably therefore owned by the goddess and controlled by the Megabyxus.

> Real admiration for Greek magnificence can be found in the surviving temple of Diana at Ephesus, built by the whole of Asia over a period of 120 years.
>
> Pliny, *Natural History*, XXXVI, 95

Most ancient people were in general agreement with Pliny; the new temple was certainly held to have been more magnificent than its predecessor. Not novel in any way at all, however. Temple designing was a conversation in a very small language, a dialogue for the informed, with a vocabulary consisting of columns, capitals and all the other elements that made the standard pitch-roofed temples of the Greeks.

> There are four sorts of column. Those whose height is six times the diameter at the bottom are called 'Doric'. Those in which the proportion is nine to one are called 'Ionic'. Those in which the proportion is seven to one are called 'Tuscan'. Corinthian columns have the same ratio as the Ionic, but they are different because the height of Corinthian capitals is the same as the diameter at the bottom of the column, and they thus appear more graceful. The height of Ionic capitals is, you see, a third of the diameter at the bottom.
>
> There was an ancient theory that the width of a temple should be three times as long as the height of the columns. In the temple of Diana at Ephesus, which was built earlier, bases were placed under the columns for the first time, and capitals were added. They decided that the diameter at the bottom of the columns ought to be one eighth of their height, and that the height of the bases should be half the diameter at the bottom of the column, and that the diameter at the bottom should be bigger than the upper diameter by a seventh.
>
> Pliny, *Natural History*, XXXVI, 178–9

The art of temple designing, then, was more like performing Shakespeare than composing acts of experimental theatre. Everything was dependent on nuance and allusion and above all on a precise presentation of the hallowed forms which at the same time as preserving their proper order continued the equally ancient tradition of minute design experiments. Overall, the art is best described, as Vitruvius puts it, as one of architectural decorum:

Decorum is found when magnificent interiors are made to match similarly elegant entrance-halls. For if the interior looks elegant, but the way in is unimpressive or discreditable, there will not be decorum. Similarly, if dentils are carved on the cornices of Doric entablatures, or if triglyphs are applied to voluted capitals or Ionic entablatures, i.e. what is proper to one style being applied to another, then visually we are offended because the separate conventions for each style were set up long ago.

Vitruvius, *On Architecture*, I, ii, 6

Though the forms of the Ionic order had been changed slightly from Croesus' time to that of Alexander's, Greek decorum had led to a precise refinement of the older forms, a near-perfect craftsmanship and a dazzling use of fine materials. At Ephesus, where the scale and scheme of the earlier temple was completely preserved, the result of this rich conservatism was, so it is said, a building with detail so beautiful that it was considered to have equalled, if not surpassed, the Erectheum at Athens and, being neither as complex nor as disjointed as that extraordinary building, but cast in the basic design of all Ionic temples, was consequently the apogee of Ionic style, the largest, most magnificent temple the Greeks had ever made.

The single departure from the overall architectural design of the earlier building had been that the new temple was set upon an extra plinth of ten grand marble steps. Following their long experience of Croesus' Temple, they gave the new building almost 9 feet of extra elevation, and thus endowed it with a new size and majesty. As with Pheidias and his Zeus, the basic notion, the drive to perfection and a single end, had resulted in continuous sensitive refinements.

The architect loosened the bottom of the underlying ground, then dug out trenches to a great depth and laid down the foundations underground. The quantity of masonry expended on the structures below the ground amounted to whole quarries of mountains. He ensured its unshakeable steadiness and, having previously set Atlas under the weight of the parts that would support the building, first he set down on the outside a base with ten steps, and on that base he raised . . .

Philo 6, 2

From the city behind it and above the plain, you would have seen the form of this great high marble building shining over the walls of its enclosure. From the sea, as you came into port, you would have seen the straight figure of Artemis herself, standing in a central window on its western pediment, a simple mummiform figure carried over from the most ancient East where kindred goddesses in ivory and marble smile from the decorations of everything from chairs to tomb façades. In Egypt, the priests took similarly posed effigies of Osiris onto temple roofs in annual processions to show the farmers and the land around that the mysterious power of fecundation was still held inside their sacred shrines. In the Hebrew Bible, the Old Testament, in the tragic ending of Jezebel the pagan queen, we see Israel taking terrible revenge upon this pagan image with its paint and powder as Jezebel is thrown down from her window at the palace and trampled under the hooves of Jehu's cavalry. At Ephesus, Artemis looked down upon a sacrificial altar, a great columned building with stalls for 20 oxen, a grandiose slaughterhouse, that was later echoed in the architecture of the altar on the hill of Pergamum. Here all the city's meat was slaughtered under the eye of the great goddess, the altar being carefully aligned to take the evening sunlight, shining alike upon the bloody stone and the gilded lips of the smiling statue high above.

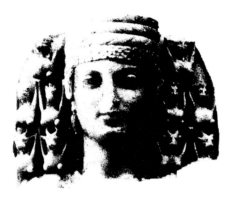

Artemis of Ephesus, from an alabaster statue in Ephesus museum

All that is left of this today, the temple and the altar both, is a pleasant field, with a fine view, a single re-erected column with a stork's nest on the top and, when the ground water does not turn Wood's great rectangular pit into a bright green lake, the trim trenches of modern archaeology. It is difficult even to make out the outline of the temple's famous platform with its extra steps. The white stones that lay all about in heaps are smashed and broken, many of them so reworked in later ages that their original surfaces have gone. Walk through the little town of Seljuk, near Ephesus however, and you may find fragments of the last great temple, pieces of column and temple moulding embedded in a Byzantine aqueduct, or superb slabs from the altar and the temple's dark interior placed in the bright walls of mosques or in the ancient church upon the hill of Ayasuluk. Wood also found a great many fragments of the architecture on site, and shipped the best of them to London. He proved the basic dimensions of the building given by Pliny and amplified them too. He also proved that the temple had indeed been cast in the Ionic order typical of south-western Turkey, ancient Ionia, not the more solid Doric, nor the taller, thinner Corinthian. Ancient depictions of the temple – small models and the designs on Ephesian coins – give yet further detail. Add all of this together and you may obtain a fairly good idea of what Pliny saw in the first century AD as he walked into the sacred enclosure of the goddess Artemis of Ephesus.

This was a building with sophistications and enrichments that austere older temples had not matched. It was much larger than the Parthenon, for example, with thinner, more open colonnades and shadowed galleries, all sitting grandly on its high-stepped podium. It was also much more to the taste of most ancient people than the older temples. The Parthenon, after all, does not figure on a single ancient list of wonders; that it is so much to modern taste reflects a common tendency within the West to overvalue the monuments in modern Greece at the expense of those in Italy or Asia Minor, in short, to archaize and Westernize the ancient Greeks themselves.

Glimpses of Artemis' lost charms can still be had at Didyma, 50 miles to the south of Ephesus, where there is a part-preserved temple virtually the same width as the Artemis Temple and just 7 feet shorter. The temple at Didyma stands on average, to a height of 10 feet or so, and most of these portions are very well preserved. Despite differences in temple design – Didyma was dedicated to Apollo, not Artemis, and had a unique central area and staircases for an oracle – there were strong similarities in the two temples, some individual architects, indeed, are recorded as having worked on both of them. First impressions at this temple are of surprise at the reality of such colossal stones and fine craftsmanship. First and most obvious is the impressive bulk of the columns and the walls. Then the powerful lines of the temple walls and column bases, all superbly decorated, enriched with wonderful detail: detail, it may be noticed, as small and precious as a jewel. Tiny figures of sea gods riding dolphins ring a column base, wreaths of crisp leaves spin around another, and similarly, many other areas of tiny precise decoration allow the warm marble of the massive column bases a surprisingly human scale. Though the building is for Apollo, a cold cruel god, the temple is human-sized and friendly. Here you walk with Apollo, as once at Ephesus you would have walked with Artemis.

At Ephesus, though, there were yet more things to fill the visitors with earthly delight. Beside the golden statues of C. Vibius Salutarius, there was a host of other donations brought from all around the Middle East, and these were famous throughout the classical world. A great art gallery indeed, as Pliny says:

> The artists who are most highly praised competed with each other despite being born in different eras, because they had made [statues of] the Amazons. When these were dedicated in the temple of Diana at Ephesus it was decided that those of the artists who were there should themselves choose which one was most commendable. It turned out that the statue which won the vote was the one which they had each judged to be second to their own: that of Polycleitus, second came that of Pheidias . . .

Natural History, XXXIV, 53

The story was that some wounded Amazons, that dauntless race of female warriors from a kingdom at the very edge of Earth, had taken refuge during their war with Hercules in the compound of the goddess Artemis at Ephesus, and that the gods had sanctioned their action and so proved the validity of the temple sanctuary. In Pliny's day, there were many famous Amazon statues standing by the temple, some of them still known to us from Roman copies. They were much beloved of the Ephesians, who made drawings of them in the marble reliefs inside the city, in panels on the walls of the theatre and other public buildings. These exotic beings, embodiments of alluring dangerous Asia, also stood for all the foreign pilgrims who visited Artemis' shrine with offerings for the great goddess.

There were also famous paintings at the temple; Apelles, the greatest painter of antiquity, who is said to have lived in Ephesus in the time of Alexander, left a painting of the young king there. Another story tells that Alexander appointed Apelles as his personal portraitist, together with the sculptor Lysippus, and the gem-cutter – and therefore coin die-maker – Pyrogoteles, and that these three between them fashioned the heroic image of the young king that has endured until today. Suitably enough, Apelles' picture in the temple of Artemis was said to show Alexander seated like Zeus, king of the gods, upon a throne. When Apelles first showed him the picture, it is said that Bucephalus, Alexander's horse, immediately recognized the likeness and gave a friendly whinny while Alexander himself was still puzzling over the thing: '"King," said Apelles, "the horse seems to have a better sensibility for art than you do"', which, though it might well have been true, showed a lack of understanding of what Alexander wanted of the images his artists were making for him.

The greatest treasures at the temple, though, were generally held to be the new set of decorated column drums standing along the processional entrance to the innermost part of the temple. Wood excavated the fragments of some of these and shipped them home to London. The biggest of these, the great drum that he had so much trouble transporting to the docks, tells us a great deal about this new temple. Though one of these same drums was said to have been made by Scopas, that sculptor of tremendous reputation who was also said to have worked upon the Mausoleum, it seems unlikely that the London drum is it, for it is hardly a great work of art and is certainly far inferior to the few fragments to have survived from the columns that Croesus donated. Here the processing god and goddess seem curiously and deliberately stiffened; their drapery too, is drawn in an intentionally old-fashioned way as if the sculptor was remembering older styles. It is hardly the ground-breaking work of Lysippus; instead, it looks back to an earlier age and to our eyes it suffers in comparison, a rather careless stylistic mixture; sub-Parthenon stuff. On the other hand, it is Hellenistic Ephesus to a T. The city was never as austerely avant garde as were the cities of Greece; simply richer, happier and less embattled, it wore its heritage lightly, and with great delight.

THE LATE ENDING OF THE WORLD

But the rude savages of the Baltic were destitute of a taste for the elegant arts, and they despised the ideal terrors of a foreign superstition.

Edward Gibbon, *The History of the Decline and Fall of the Roman Empire*

Operating from seaports in the Crimea, Gothic fleets sacked and plundered Ephesus and fired Artemis' great temple in AD 262, a decade after the same tribes had annihilated a Roman army and killed the emperor. Like the city, the temple was rebuilt, the walls of the innermost sanctuary that held the image of the goddess being remade with stones taken from the sprawled ruin of the great façades. A pavement was also put down that sealed many fragments of the devastated treasures and the broken statues in the earth beneath. In the fourth century, the building was shaken again, this time by earthquakes. Finally, in 401, the rebuilt treasury and shrines were plundered by St John Chrysostom, a pious and most learned man, the Patriarch of Constantinople. At the same time, a limekiln was set up on the temple's steps to render the building's marble into mortar to serve the Christian city's grand rebuilding programme. Block by block, Artemis' great temple was absorbed into this new city, its stone quarried and recut and reused in churches, roads, aqueducts and fortifications. Though even in the sixth century there was still enough of the vast temple left standing for one of Justinian's ministers to busy himself in sending some of its surviving statuary off to Constantinople to join the collections that also held Pheidias' noble Zeus. He took a gigantic gorgon's head from Ephesus, the one, so it was said, that had filled the centre of the temple's eastern pediment. Even then, after all this savage stripping, for many Ephesians the sacred precinct still held the aura of their great goddess. Christian writers contemptuously describe these 'Hellenes', as they called them, digging around in the ash and rubble and venerating the fragments of the ancient cult they found there.

Christian accounts of the unthroning of the goddess, though mostly compiled at a later date than the events they describe, give a nervous picture of the end of Artemis, for the new Christians were very frightened of the goddess and her ancient power; this picture, however, is confirmed by archaeology. St John it was, the pseudo-gospels tell us, that brought the Word to Ephesus. Cast up by the sea and Divine Providence in a field by the city, he walked to a city gate and onto the ground of Artemis, and from the careful topography of the tale, this was certainly the Magnesian Gate that Wood excavated 18 centuries later. At the gate, John found that the incense from the Festival of Artemis was so thick that it veiled the sun. And there too he saw a painted statue of the goddess with gilded lips, a veil over her face, and a lamp burning before her image. He took up work, it is recorded, in that pagan abomination, a public bath house built close by the gate – just where, in fact, a fine small public baths has recently been excavated. Like many early Christians, we may assume John eschewed bathing and kept 'his soul crisp for God'; certainly he would hardly have appreciated the bath's delicious humidity – especially as its steam veiled the fornications of the Ephesian *jeunesse dorée*. A common Christian belief was that many pagan public buildings were haunted. John's baths were said to be the den of a demon that occasionally strangled the unwary; the saint cast it out, and showed the young the error of their ways. Suitably impressed, their parents converted to Christianity and then called a meeting in the theatre to discuss the fate of Artemis – the same great theatre where, the Book of Acts tells us, the city tradesmen, who earned their money making and selling models in the image of the goddess and her temple, had rioted, and shouted 'Great is Artemis of the Ephesians' in protest at the preaching of St Paul. Now, though, a Christian audience filled the theatre's hemisphere and looked down in scorn at the Artemis Temple in the Valley. Then, it is said, the priests of Artemis blew their horns, lit the lamps around the holy statues, and opened the great bronze temple doors. Standing at the back of the theatre, on the highest row of seats, John blessed the Ephesians and baptized the entire theatreful. This, then, was the final fatal contest.

Three days later, John took up residence in a small hut built on the slope of the hill of Ayasuluk, high above the temple. From there he watched the great Festival of Artemis, which on this occasion served to so enrage his converts that they swarmed into the temple, whereupon the pagans foolishly scored an own goal by casting stones which were miraculously deflected onto the figure of the goddess. Ropes were tied around the cult image, and it was pulled down. John then drove the demon Artemis out of Ephesus by prayer and the converts set about pulling down all the pagan images in the city, burning them, and setting up crosses on the city gates and building a church for holy worship. John then left for Patmos. When he later returned to Ephesus, it is said he found the pagan statues and the temples quite collapsed.

The pseudo-gospels also say that John then settled once again into his house upon the hill, in the company of the Virgin Mary. Here it was that Peter and Paul came to persuade him to write his Gospel, a task he accomplished, it is recorded, in a single hour. He died finally at the age of 120 and was buried on this same hill, overlooking Artemis. Or rather, he sleeps upon his hill, for some short lines of John's own Gospel may be interpreted as saying that he will not die until the Second Coming. For many centuries, those who visited the churches built above his tomb saw his breathing sending little puffs of dust up into the air, manna it was called; it cured all ills, and an international trade developed, one not scorned by St Augustine, who observed that it had been given credence by several serious people.

Archaeologists have found that by the fourth century AD, the name of Artemis was chiselled from all public buildings in the city. Christian records also tell that the Artemis statue that had always stood at the centre of the city was taken down about this time and a cross put up in its place: 'Demeas took down the deceitful image of the god, Artemis, and put up the sign of truth. He honoured the god who drives away many idols, and the Cross, the immortal, victorious symbol of Christ.' So frightened were these converts, though, living in the great city of the goddess, that almost every pavement stone, every decorated column top and shaft was carved with some kind of Christian symbol, usually a cross, and these were also carved on the foreheads of the statues. The pull, the power of Artemis was strong – she appears in the Book of Revelations as part of a sort of anti-Seven Wonders, while Ephesus itself is known as one of the seven cities of Christian Asia. Archaeologists, though, have discovered that the Ephesians never quite managed to part themselves completely from their great goddess. Two beautiful stone statues of her cult image, carefully laid in fine red sand, were buried underneath the Christian city hall, and found there in excavations in the 1960s.

It was in the fourth century too that the Third General Council of the Church – the First Council of Ephesus – was held in the city's cathedral, a converted grain store down on the ancient dockside, within sight of the ruined temple of the great goddess. Though the harbour was silting badly, and the town hardly what it was, at that time Ephesus and the surrounding landscape was still rich and fertile, and the city remained an important port upon the ancient sea roads.

> Asia . . . has countless cities. Indeed she has very large cities and many of them by the sea. We must mention two of these: Ephesus which reputedly has a remarkable harbour, and similarly Smyrna, which is also a splendid city. But the whole area is huge and yields harvests of all fine things: varied wines, oil, grain, quality purple dye and spelt. It is a most marvellous region, and it is difficult to praise it too highly.
>
> Anon, *Expositio Totius Mundi et Gentium*, XLVII, *c.* AD 360

In AD 614, however, the city was half-destroyed in an earthquake and at this same time a marauding Persian army roamed the area, prompting the remaining citizens to retreat to St John's hill which they heavily fortified, often taking stones, as they had always done, from the ruins of Artemis' great temple.

So the city of the ancient goddess was deserted, its quays and harbours left to fill with the silt that the River Cayster has always carried and which had always required the most careful and persistent dredging if the port was not to fill completely. As at Olympia, Ephesus' river now brought yet larger quantities of yellow silt down from the untended farmlands of the abandoned interior. This clogging silt first closed the ancient port that had been the city's artery, then forced the sea to retreat out of the bay for several miles well beyond the ancient quays and thus sealed the final fate of Ephesus. By the 10th century, the temple was so deeply buried that there were houses built upon the silt above it, with fields and wells, and with a graveyard too. Until Wood appeared digging his endless 12-foot trench, the temple had entirely disappeared.

The Third General Council of the Church, however, had made a distinctively Ephesian mark on basic Christian doctrine. For this council it was that bestowed the title of 'Theotokos' or 'God-bearer' upon the Virgin Mary as part of the solution to a bitter continuing debate about the nature of Christ, which in an empire ruled and run as a mirror image of the order of heaven had strong political as well as theological significances. The assimilation of a female principal into Church theology was not accomplished without a great deal of argument. Bishops arrived from all over the empire with veritable armies of supporting monks and wide and disparate traditions of religious experience. At Ephesus, imperial counts operating as policemen favoured one delegation over another; delegations were locked into their houses and the Ephesian churches, even the tomb of John, were barred to some of them. The Ephesians themselves took an active part in the Council, which sometimes degenerated into urban warfare. Rioters sometimes filled the city marketplaces or attacked the houses of different delegations, all of them carefully marked and designated according to the parties they supported. Bands of imperial troops roamed the streets with clubs and manifestoes. Some bishops were kept under house arrest so that the voting in the council would run one way or another. As they were variously deposed, condemned or promoted, great shouts of joy and rage roared round the city. Triumphant processions then paraded through the town, accompanied by lamps, incense and young men and women. This ferment continued for years, some delegates ran out of money and were ruined, some took to drink, some died of hunger, heat and wounds. Eventually, though, notwithstanding differences of translation and the myriad perceptions of the precise nuance of this sacred principal, the notion of 'Theotokos' eventually united all the warring factions.

THE DECLARATION OF JOHN OF ANTIOCH, JUNE 431

The holy synod, assembled at Ephesus by the grace of God and the command of the most pious and Christ-loving Emperors, made the following declaration: We prayed that the synod should take place peacefully, according to the canons of the holy fathers and according to the command of our most holy and Christ-loving Emperors. But since in rashness, in confusion and with a heretical frame of mind you held a council among yourselves, although we were just outside the room in accordance with the command of our most holy Emperors, and since you filled the city and the holy synod with utter confusion in order to prevent discussion of the important matters – of the false beliefs and the impious activities of the Apollinarians, Arians and Eunomians – and did not wait until the holy bishops had arrived from every country, . . . know, you Cyril of Alexandria and you Memnon of this city, that you are cast out and no longer part of the episcopate, absolved of your ecclesiastical duties, because you were the commanders and ring-leaders of all the disorder and lawlessness and because you were responsible for trampling on the commands of the Fathers and of the Emperors' ordinances.

CYRIL OF ALEXANDRIA TO JOHN OF ANTIOCH, APRIL 433

May the heavens rejoice and the earth be glad . . . we enjoyed the conference . . . We are now fully assured that the quarrel between the Churches was altogether excessive and inappropriate. Bishop Paul, most dear to God, brought us a document containing an unexceptionable admission of faith, which was, we hear, composed at the approval of Your Holiness and the most reverent Bishops there . . .

. . . *We agree that the holy Virgin is Theotokos, on account of the fact that God the Word was incarnate and was in man, and from the same conception united the temple taken from her with himself* . . .

On reading these holy words of yours, and finding that we too think this, . . . we glorified God, the Saviour of the world, and we rejoiced with each other that our churches and your churches have converged on a faith [which agrees] with the divinely inspired scriptures and our inheritance from the Holy Fathers. But when I discovered that some of those who love to criticise were buzzing around, in their customary manner, like fierce wasps, spitting out rude words against me (as though I had said that the holy body of Christ had been carried down from heaven and was not from the holy Virgin), I thought that I ought to say something to them on this subject:

'Foolish men, insulting is the only thing you know how to do. How did you reach such a state of unintelligence? How do you come to be infected by such silliness? For you ought, *you ought* to know well, that practically the whole of our argument about the faith was based on our assertion that the holy Virgin is Theotokos. But if we say that the holy body of Christ, Saviour of us all, was born from heaven and not from her, how would "Theotokos" be understood? Who was it, in short, that she bore, if it is not true that she gave birth, physically, to Emmanuel?'

So let those who have spoken this nonsense about me be mocked . . .

THE JEWELS OF ARTEMIS

The British Museum returned with water pumps to excavate Artemis' great temple in 1904–5. The low-lying area underneath the central shrine, by its constant water seepage, had foiled the best efforts of John Turtle Wood. There, deep in the bottom of Wood's enormous excavation, they found the remains of temples far older than those of Croesus' or Alexander's day. And there too, amongst these modest ruins, they found surprising quantities of precious objects from the ancient cult: small ivories, much pottery, some golden jewels and statuettes, and coins so ancient that they were generally held to be the oldest in the world. As with most important discoveries, though, the work raised as many questions as it solved and so in the 1980s a team of Austrian archaeologists returned to work in this same area. This time they not only re-excavated the ancient temple sanctuaries but went down beneath them, right back to Artemis' beginnings on the long wide plain.

The ancient Ephesians had always said that the oracle of Apollo had told them to build their city 'where a fish shall show them, and a wild boar shall lead the way'. Some fishermen, the story went, had been cooking their midday meal by a spring on a lonely beach when a fish and a coal had fallen from their grill, started a fire in a thicket and startled a boar. As the animal had run off towards the mountain he was brought down by a javelin. Even before the Austrians started work at the central shrines, their earlier excavations had made it clear that these stories were an uncanny reflection of archaeological reality. To the west of the Artemis temple, beside the foundations of its enormous altar, they had excavated the ancient beach of Ephesus, its firm sea sand buried now under deep grey river silt. They also found a small freshwater spring upon this beach, an unusual combination, but a prerequisite of a good landing place for sailors. Beside this spring had been a footpath, and by that, a small square sacrificial altar. Nearby, cut in the top of the ancient beach, where the classical Greeks had built their enormous sacrificial altar, the Austrians even excavated a thick layer of charcoal that, just as Pliny described, had been laid down under the ancient foundations. Pottery found around this area suggests that Mycenaean boats had put in on this beach, that is, in the second millennium BC, a long time before the foundation of the city. Here then, by this little shrine and altar set on a seashore with a spring, lay the beginnings of the city. In the course of centuries, through half a dozen temples, massive floodings and several conflagrations, this modest haven also came to house the cult of Artemis Ephesia and that, mythologers had long suggested, had always been known and venerated throughout the most ancient East.

Suggestions that there once had been a vast continuity of myth, from India to Ireland, from Varuna to Romulus, from Diana to Kybele and the White Goddess, had raised many a scholarly eyebrow, as well they might. Modern sensibilities, after all, are entirely different from ancient ones; our sense of place and time, the very way we think, is unique to today and the connections that we make therefore may well just be our own. On the other hand, Greek and Roman travellers had easily recognized their national gods in foreign lands, gods perhaps with completely different names and costumes, but with personalities and attributes they also held in fond memory from their earliest days. Now, from these new Austrian excavations at the very heart of Artemis' great temple came proof that such intercultural connections really existed very early on at Ephesus; that in those times there had been a deep and widespread commonality of faith throughout the ancient East. Lying all around the goddess's most ancient shrines, Dr Anton Bammer and his team have found offerings from Egypt, Anatolia and Greece, from central Asia, Phoenicia and Palestine, many of them holding the signs and symbols of goddesses who, in the context of their own cultures, held similar significance to Artemis. At Ephesus, it clearly did not matter whether the goddess that you honoured at your home was Artemis or Kybele or Wanax; Tausert, Bes, or Ma; Astarte, Diana or Kubaba; the people who came to this temple and left these offerings understood that their own deities were linked in some way to the deity they called Artemis at Ephesus.

The archaeologists have not yet reached the bedrock of this work, and there may still be a millennium of earlier remains lying in the soggy silt beneath the present trenches. Much of what has been found so far is difficult to place in time and origin, especially as many of the objects may have been moved from earlier to later buildings, as still occurs in churches, where precious offerings are carefully preserved and often moved from older buildings into newer ones. The astonishing collection of objects found around these various ancient shrines of Artemis are best seen therefore as a single group, a single ancient bridge between the goddess Artemis and humankind's most ancient faiths. This is the real wonder here at Ephesus, the real power of Artemis: that she was so many things to so many different peoples. Though the precise identity of many of these things may always be difficult to determine, and many of them come from cultures hardly known today, here Artemis is their coherence. They speak with one voice.

There were ivories lying in these temples that had been brought from Syria, ivories such as the Bible's prophets railed at, and used as evidence to denounce the godlessness of kings. Ivories like those that decorated the thrones of Syrian princes and rooms of the royal palace at Samaria. From Egypt, or perhaps from Egyptianizing artists working on the Phoenician coast, there were more ivories too, of a style typical of the last phases of ancient Egyptian art. And here as well, as if to emphasize the broad continuing theme of the goddess as a mother, were faience images of Bes, the Egyptian deity who for millennia upon millennia had presided over childbirth. Bes, the little bandy-legged god who danced and banged a tambourine, offered up at Ephesus as though he was Artemis' midwife. There were figures too, in ivory and solid gold, of ancient priests and priestesses, hard-staring long-robed men and women with eyes that look as if they might come from a Persian book illumination; that stared as well from the darkness of the most ancient Mesopotamian temples of the fourth millennium BC. And dazzling ivories in the form of spoons and boxes, bearing the most ancient patterns; designs found on fragments of the palace furniture from right across the ancient world, from Nimrud, Carchemish and Zinjirli. Fragments too of scenes set in those most ancient gardens, such as Gilgamesh walked through in delight, at Uruk and Babylon. And there were winged griffins, those ancient demons of the night fixed upon the walls of the palaces of Ashur and the towers of Babylon, and later on the columns of the Persian palaces that Alexander burnt.

Some of the little griffins offered up to Artemis are made of ivory, others are cast as small portable bronzes by the mobile cultures that came from the plains of central Asia. There were other bronzes, some of them, those small beguiling artifacts so beloved of collectors in the West, from Luristan, whose strong linear designs echoed the most ancient cults of Mesopotamia and in later centuries, diffused, on horse trappings and the decorations of their swords and bucklers, appear in lands from China to Iceland. Many of the same images and decorations also appeared much earlier in Anatolia, in the second millennium BC with the Hittites of the central plains. And these too are found as offerings at Ephesus, carried along many different routes. The story of these patterns curls like the designs themselves, snaking back and forth in time.

Another powerful image offered to the goddess is of a woman, a priestess perhaps, or the goddess herself, standing on a lion, and this in turn is reminiscent of some of humankind's most ancient images. At Ephesus, the lady on a lion is given to Artemis in exquisite ivory. That lion, though, is the same lion that roars on the first coins from Sardis, and there she is the lion of Kybele. These coins are also found here amidst the cracks of Artemis' early temples.

From Greece came bears' teeth, drilled to form splendidly curved barbaric necklaces, offered here to Artemis. There were modelled heads of little warriors also made in Greece and Cyprus and sent as offerings, and fine fragments of Greek pottery, from the sixth and eighth century BC. In return, these Western Greeks took elements of these Eastern images for themselves. The great gorgon of the temple pediment which Justinian's minister had taken back to Constantinople to use as decoration began as an Asian design; similarly the running swastikas seen in so many Greek temple decorations had also started on the plains of Asia. And those Asian griffins, offered to Artemis at Ephesus, the classical Greeks adapted as designs for waterspouts to decorate their temple roofs. Ultimately, though, the mixed reality of this ancient world renders such labels futile. For this period of these early temples is the age when Greek culture was itself in the process of formation. Artemis' ancient temples were one of the crucibles in which the Greeks themselves were forged.

In their own way, the later Greeks did not forget this. The wounded Amazons of Pheidias and all the other sculptures that stood in competition in the compound of the later marble temples were an echo, a subtle memory, of ancient wars fought against fierce migrating tribes. Yet here at Ephesus in Artemis' early temples these same peoples who had devastated most of Asia Minor offered up works of bronze and ivory alongside those of the Greeks.

At first glance, these ancient temples that once underlaid the marble edifices do not seem to amount to much. None the less, the area is an archaeological treasure, the kernel of a residue of a thousand years of sacredness sealed under river silt and the waters of a spring. The oldest of these temples found so far seems to have been built around 850 BC. The forms of these jumbled buildings, alternatively flooded and destroyed by fire, each one made of pieces of the others, are difficult to separate. The only continuity indeed is that each new temple was raised upon another, just as the temple of Alexander's day was raised above the earlier one of Croesus' time. It was Croesus' pious rebuilding of Artemis' temple, following his armies' destruction of Ephesus, that partly ensured the preservation of the holy treasures underneath the extensive marble pavements of his new building. For here, under that once fine marble temple, are the simplest of all column bases, rough shaped rows of stones set in the earth to stop the wooden columns sinking into the ground. Once they surrounded an oblong central shrine: together, they are the oldest example known of the typical Greek temple, the ancestor of the Parthenon and all those other later wonders. Amidst all this diversity, then, a great part of Greek culture began and with it a part of modern culture too. This treasure is best held on plans and paper, the reality in the silty soil is hard to see as standing architecture. One can say, though, that the beginnings are modest enough, clear and plain and quite symmetrical.

Quite another prize, however, was waiting in the mud at the ancient centre of the temple. This area had been anciently flooded, covered with silt, and never touched again. In the silt, the excavators found part of a bellows, like those from the gold refineries at Sardis. And you may wonder then if the goddess here was making coins like Kybele's at Sardis. Close by the bellows, astonishingly enough, they found the jewels of Artemis herself, thousands upon thousands of them; beads and precious ornaments and all the myriad trappings of the goddess's statues, the necklaces, the bracelets, the golden clasps that held the goddess's robes, the gold rosettes that once were sewn upon them, and her great bronze buckled belts that gathered the cloth together at her waist. All those things, previously known from carved representations of them on the sculptures of the goddess, those strange mummiform images of deity with clustered breasts and heavy jewellery. Once, perhaps, an ancient cult image of the goddess had fallen here and been buried in the mud. If it was a wooden image, it would have swiftly rotted in the soft wet earth. This holy area was deliberately sealed by the succeeding generation of architects as they made the later shrines. Eventually, then, the great cult statues of the marble temples stood right above this spot, on ground quite literally studded with precious images from the most distant past, many of them carried right across the ancient Indo-European world.

The broadest themes of the goddess's cult were carried on into Artemis' own decoration. The great bronze belts have buckles typical of designs from the European north; the goddess's amber too, a host of beads, was carved by Greek craftsmen working Baltic ambers. Her glass beads, some of them shaped into little faces, were made in Phoenicia to the south. Here, too, the archaeologists suggested, was a clue to the origin and significance of those extraordinary rows of breasts that decorate the later statues; Artemis Polymastica, copious Artemis of the flowing milk, a continuity of cult, perpetuated locally at Ephesus perhaps, in a lonely valley cave above the ancient city, where there resides a force that provides nursing mothers with the milk they need. Centuries before Artemis Polymastica was carved, however, these small amber beads shaped like hips and haws and poppy heads, aubergines and pomegranates, were threaded into bulky necklaces and thrown across the breast of the archaic statue. These seem like Artemis' breasts in miniature, the fruits and pods of flowers and shrubs. The varying interpretations of these simple forms perhaps show changing archaeological tastes down through the ages, from breasts to ostrich eggs, the testicles of slaughtered bulls to little bags of gold.

The wonder of this great temple in the marsh was not just the last marble building made for Artemis, nor even the last two splendid temples, but the idea of her universal cult. Just as the cathedral of Chartres was a great shrine of the Virgin Mary before the present church was made, and to the faithful will remain so even though the present church may fall, so Artemis' temples too rose through fire and plunder on this single spot. The wonder, then, was in this continuity of sacredness.

In the age of the Seven Wonders, large amounts of the ancient past were discarded and forgotten. Underneath this brave new world, however, there remained deep continuities. Later visions of the Artemis Temple, the Hanging Gardens and the Mausoleum may have been inaccurate and fanciful, but they tried to keep faith somehow with Philo's intuition of wonder as a sort of religious fear, a true amazement. This sense of wonder it was that led the ancient world to honour their gods, just as later it led Alexander and his successors to elevate and honour the works of humankind. The Seven Wonders act as a conduit, a conduit of ancient sacredness, a sacredness held, not in the dogmas of religion, but in their greatest images; images that link that most sophisticated lady of Ephesus both to the most ancient deities of Anatolia, and to the modern world as well.

Chapter 7

THE PYRAMIDS AND THE RISE OF WONDER

THE BIRTH OF WONDER

Whilst it is impossible to build the pyramids in Memphis [today], it is marvellous to describe them. Mountains have been built on mountains. The sheer size of the squared masonry is difficult for the mind to grasp, and everyone is mystified at the enormous strength that was required to prize up such a weight of material... The ascent is no less long or tiring than a road journey. Standing on the top and looking down, one can only dimly see the bottom . . . The whole polished work is joined together so seamlessly that it seems to be made out of one continuous rock . . . To one's astonishment is added pleasure, to one's admiration respect, and to its lavishness splendour . . . it is through deeds such as these that men go up to the gods, or that gods come down to men.

Philo 2, 1–5

Of all the Seven Wonders, the pyramids of Egypt are the only ones still on everybody's all-time list of wonders; they are the oldest, largest, most accurate stone buildings ever made and the only Wonder of all the Seven to have survived more or less intact. The pyramids are also the only Wonder to have been made in that most distant age when the gods, not humankind, were seen as the earth's true wonder-makers. This then is where it all began, that long journey of the human imagination that has reached down until today.

In Philo's day, the greatest of the Egyptian pyramids, those grouped around the ancient capital city of Memphis on the Nile close by Cairo, were almost three millennia old. All that Philo, the Alexandrian Greek, could suggest by way of explanation of their venerable grandeur was that fortune boasted that 'with its extraordinary expense it can touch the very stars'. Three centuries later, the elder Pliny, that most sensible of Romans, thought the venerable pyramids to be but 'a tedious and foolish ostentation of the wealth of kings.' Though the age of the Seven Wonders was hardly averse to extravagant architectural folly of its own, it none the less considered the vast expenditures of national resources obviously required to build the pyramids to be but a shameful indulgence on the part of unknown despots. Like Pliny, the inhabitants of the Hellenic cities were rather frightened by the hubris of these ancient rulers who had ordered the construction of such astonishing monuments. And still for most of us today the pyramids, those stupendous tombs, are merely memorials to human vanity. But while it is true that the pyramids were indeed built as tombs for kings as every literate citizen of classical antiquity well knew, to their ancient builders and to the ancient Egyptians of most later ages too, they stood for many other things as well. Indeed, even the simple notion of the pyramid as royal tomb is by itself confusing. Many pyramids have more than a single burial chamber in them, some kings have more than one pyramid and, on the only occasion that a sealed royal pyramid was opened and examined, that of the archaic Pharaoh Sekhemkhet, the closed sarcophagus did not hold the body of the monarch. In the age before the pyramids, indeed, the kings of Egypt had more than one tomb prepared for them and this may also be true for the era of the pyramids themselves. These great stone monuments then, are complex symbols.

> The scribe Nashuiu came to the district of the Pyramid of Teti, beloved of Mut, and the Pyramid of Djoser, discoverer of stone working. He says: 'Be gracious, O King . . . to all the gods of the West of Memphis; may I be near you, for I am your servant!'

Nashuiu wrote his quick graffito in the July of 1246 BC, when some of these same pyramids, already more than a thousand years old, were undergoing pious restoration. Of all the pyramids, King Djoser's stepped pyramid at Sakkara, the first ever constructed and the first stone structure of any size to have been built anywhere, was especially revered; as more inky graffiti written on the limestone walls of one of its ancient courtyards still show:

> Year 47, second month of winter, day 25 [January, 1232 BC], the treasury scribe Hadnakht, son of Sunero and Tausert, came to take a stroll and enjoy himself in the West of Memphis together with his brother Panakht, scribe of the Vizier. He said: 'O all you Gods of the West of Memphis . . . and glorified dead . . . grant us a full lifetime in which to serve you and a goodly burial after a happy old age, like yourself . . .

For these ancient Egyptians of much later ages, the old smooth-sided buildings standing in the clean desert sand at the wilderness' edge, confirmed that the state which they served, that in their own words 'gave them life', was set for all eternity. For it followed that if the state of which they were part was truly joined to the eternal gods and to the ancient ancestors, then they too could live in proper order in their green and pleasant valley. For these rich scribes the pyramids were a physical expression of the state that they served; the first expression, indeed, of what the nation could achieve when organized upon a national scale. As they had built their pyramids, the Egyptians had literally built their state as well. These pyramids, therefore, the residue of a stupendous process, are the first expression of national solidarity in the history of the world. For ancient Egyptians they stood as memorial and celebration of the founding of their state: a stony row of triangles set on the plateau of the desert's edge signifying a hard-earned compact with the gods. The pyramid makers had indeed reached out to touch the stars and, as Philo had surmised, fortune had smiled upon them and their fertile land.

166

PYRAMIDOGRAPHIA

. . . in an hour or two, we saw the Pyramids. Fancy my sensations; two big ones and a little one: ! ! ! There they lay, rosy and solemn in the distance – those old, majestical, mystical, familiar edifices.

from William Thackeray's Notes of a Journey from Cornhill to Grand Cairo, *performed in the steamers of the Peninsular and Oriental Company,* London, 1846

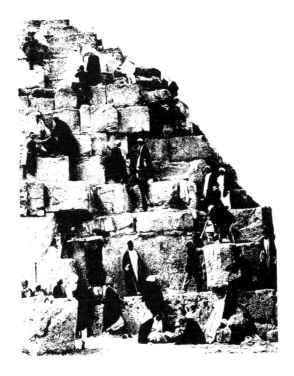

Climbing the Great Pyramid, from a photograph by Félix Bonfils, *c.* 1875

With its three regal pyramids, each with their attending Brobdingnagian courts of nobles' tombs, the plateau at Giza close to Cairo is the pyramid site par excellence; from a distance ! ! ! just as Thackeray described them in the journal of a cruise he took in the winter of 1844. A unique quality of these great buildings is that their tops are several hundred feet back from the line of their foundations and this unsettles all normal expectations of perspective. For most of the day, it renders their shadow insignificant and this also unsettles the expectations of the eye, which normally anticipates a large dark mass of shadow for objects of such tremendous size. Pyramids, then, often appear peculiarly weightless and unreal, their size and scale both difficult to grasp. At Giza, for example, even the smallest and prettiest of the grand trio is in fact enormous. Originally some 228 feet high, it was made in the reign of the pharaoh Mycerinus and finished almost exactly 2,500 years before the time of Christ. It is the equal of any of its eighty or so successors, while the two other monuments at Giza – Thackeray's ! and ! – the pyramids of the two pharaohs Cheops and Chephren, are but half of a titanic quartet of near-500-foot-high pyramids, the other two standing lonely in the desert some 12 miles to the south. All four of these stupendous monuments were made within 75 years of each other. To this day, they remain the largest and most accurate stone buildings ever made, a feat achieved within a century of the first use of cut stone as a major building material.

The Greek historian Herodotus who visited Egypt in the middle of the 5th century BC, also tells us some amusing details about the Giza pyramids, just as Thackeray does. He tells us of unlikely ancient inscriptions recording the quantities of onions, radishes and garlic the ancient masons ate and relates too a risqué tale of how the pharaoh Cheops, for whom the Great Pyramid, the biggest of them all, was built, 'when he was short of cash, he installed his daughter in a brothel and commanded her to charge a certain quantity of money . . . She charged that amount and, intending to leave a memorial behind, she asked each of the men that came to her to give her a stone.' By Pliny's time, Herodotus' tale, which vaguely expresses those same Roman sentiments of indignation at the demands of such apparently cruel rulers, had been transformed into a fantasy in which Mycerinus' pyramid stood in a sort of sepulchral red light zone: 'The smallest of the pyramids, but the one that is most highly praised was made by the prostitute, Rhodopis. She was once a fellow-slave and concubine of Aesop, the philosopher of fables, and we are even more amazed that such expense was met by the earnings from prostitution.' Roman Pliny, then, opts for lust and cruelty as the two great pyramid powers. As Philo had remarked two centuries earlier, 'The sheer size of the squared masonry is difficult for the mind to grasp, and everyone is mystified at the enormous strength that was required to prize up such a weight of material.'

To the west of Giza high on another desert plateau above the village of Abu Roash, we may leave the enigmas of the finished pyramids of Giza behind and see an unfinished pyramid still in the rough process of its manufacture. For here it was, in the years 2566 to 2528 BC, that the pyramid of the Pharaoh Djedefra, who ruled briefly between the Pharaohs Cheops and Chephren, was intended to be built. The king, however, died too soon to have a finished pyramid – it often took more than 20 years for the Egyptians to complete that royal monument.

The Egyptians were very traditional people. The first thing they did as they began work on Djedefra's pyramid was to cut a huge rectangular chamber and the sloping passage that led down into it, deep into the limestone plateau. They had cut just such square-chambered tombs in the desert rock for the Egyptian kings for five centuries and more before they ever thought of building pyramids of stone above them. They had also built the tombs for those archaic kings at perfect pyramid locations, right along the western horizon at the desert's edge. Indeed, the pyramid's very form, that tall advertisement, was probably partly developed out of an impulse to build a tomb to loom above the archaic mud-brick sepulchres that fringed the desert skyline and notched the setting sun.

Today the gigantic cutting of Djedefra's burial chamber stands as solitary evidence of the true beginnings of a pyramid. In its present state, anciently stripped of its granite lining stones and half-filled with drifting sand, it is possible to see that the design of the burial chamber pit appears to have been harking back to the dimensions of the archaic tombs. This burial chamber is out of proportion to the pyramid outlined above it in just two rows of giant limestone blocks. If it had ever been finished, lined in granite, furnished with a great sarcophagus and covered by a completed pyramid, it would have been the biggest royal tomb chamber ever set beneath a pyramid.

The hard stone blocks designed to line Djedefra's burial pit were quarried from granite hills some 450 miles to the south in Upper Egypt. They were shipped down the Nile on barges right to the docks of Memphis and a canal that ran close to the pyramid. At this same time, tens of thousands of workmen were opening other quarries across the Nile from Memphis to procure the fine white limestone that would eventually have faced the finished monument. More quarries near the pyramid itself were also being opened to supply the coarser blocks of stone that served to fill the pyramid's bulk. As at Giza, such local quarries were worked with care, and in the process, the area around the monument itself was landscaped with subtlety. Ramps of stone were left to provide access to the pyramid that was rising on the high plateau. With great organization and concentration all these various blocks of granite, limestone and filling stone, some of them amongst the largest men have ever moved, were being slowly dragged to the plateau by the work gangs and placed around the shadowed rectangle of that burial pit.

How on earth did the Egyptians move such enormous stones? For the first two thousand years of the pyramids' existence, no one would ever have needed to ask that question because so many nations were trundling around just such great blocks for their own purposes, and knew quite well how it was done. To them, only the scale, the size of the pyramids, would have seemed exceptional. But then the ancient monument builders died, and another world came into being. Practical knowledge was replaced with conjecture; observing these gigantic stones, some of the early Eastern Christians could only suppose that they had been transported by the power of prayer. Similarly, in medieval times, rabbis taught that Moses had moved the great stone blocks, working with slave gangs of ancient Israelites. In the 19th century, British archaeologists explained that the pyramids were made by gangs of coolies working under the same firm governance that the British themselves were then providing for their empire. Later, in the age of the Sputnik, the pyramids were said by some to have been built by an alien race of spacemen. Nowadays, modern science having moved much quicker than the dull imaginings of the 1960s, it is amusing to read the different versions of these theories that picture visitors from space at ancient monuments, sitting in the poses of Yuri Gagarin and John Glenn as they were strapped into their capsules, waiting to be shot into the outer atmosphere. Keeping up with the times, though, there is today a brand new crop of ecologically ingenious solutions for how the pyramids were made, many of them derived from what are loosely termed Third World technologies. Nowadays, to their great bemusement, skilled Egyptian craftsmen are employed to demonstrate these brand-new 'primitive' technologies by building little bits of instant brand-new pyramid on the Giza sand. The unfortunate truth is that all these varied and fanciful explanations have started from the same dubious and arrogant premise: 'How could such ancient primitives have made such wondrous things?'

The question sets its own agenda and poses a problem largely of the questioner's own making. Take the pyramids at face value, grant that the ancient Egyptians did construct them, indeed accomplished that labour more efficiently than we could do today, and the problem largely disappears. And so it should, for these pyramids are not the residue of an ingenious lost technology. The wonder here is of yet more subtle skills that have today entirely disappeared.

If, in 1962, John Fitzgerald Kennedy had announced that the United States would take thirty years to send an astronaut to the moon and that the cost of the journey would entail the whole national economy for that same period, his electors would have roared in disagreement. As it was, he had more realistic ambitions. What we now consider to be possible and practical holds unspoken restrictions of both time and money; these, though, are both restrictions that the ancients never knew. Yet most modern theorists attempting novel explanations of how the Egyptians moved the stones and made their pyramids, base their calculations on similar parameters of practicality and efficiency, explanations more appropriate to today than to a vanished race of people of five thousand years ago. Despite their professional expertise, most modern scientists and engineers have precious little experience of organizing huge numbers of people or of the value of collective ingenuity and enthusiasm. Seldom do we even consider the potential of the simple technologies that the pyramid builders used.

There is a tale told by archaeologists of a foreign excavator of a century ago who found a huge sarcophagus lying at the bottom of a shaft in the desert. Time and again his workmen broke their tackle in their attempts to lift the dead weight to the surface. Just as the archaeologist had abandoned his attempt to carry off his trophy, some local villagers asked if they could try to lift the great block from its narrow pit. Greatly amused, the archaeologist negotiated a price for work he thought that they would never accomplish. The next day, the village women came to the trench with ropes and sticks and baskets and were lowered down beside the granite box. Sitting there together and talking all the while, they gently tapped sand under the great stone and slowly, inch by inch, it rose up towards the surface of the desert.

Apocryphal or not, such tales should give us pause. Certainly, the large blocks that lie today on the plateaus of Giza and Abu Roash can actually be moved by far fewer people than one might imagine. With such tasks, method is all. Some years ago, using information derived from Egyptian wall paintings, a group of elderly egyptologists pushed an enormous block of concrete along the high street of a French town to show what could be done with thought, care, slick mud, wooden rollers, and a commonality of effort. At Abu Roash, the work gangs came with centuries of experience of just such tasks, directed by a royal court involved for generation after generation in organizing the national population as a single work force.

The pyramid builders routinely employed hundreds of thousands of people, welded them into a single enterprise and focused them on a single point. Though they employed the simplest rope and roller methods, they maintained an organization of astonishing complexity and efficiency, one that kept the giant stones moving up the ramps onto the desert plateau and up to the pyramid day after day, week after week, year after year. For modern engineers and scientists concerned largely with time and money and all those other things that are termed 'practical' such continuities are completely unattainable. Perhaps the nearest this century ever came to a similar situation were the Chinese work forces employed in dam construction during the Great Leap Forward of the 1960s. We find the making of the pyramids so mysterious, so difficult to comprehend, because it embodies the absolute reverse of our modern situation.

The pyramid age, then, inhabited an entirely different economic universe to ours today. It was also, it should be emphasized, a quite separate universe to that inhabited by Greek Herodotus and Roman Pliny too, and all the other people of the age of the Seven Wonders. Just like ours today, their prime reaction to the pyramids was either to mock such ancient enterprise – the pyramids may owe their present name to the Greek word for a bread roll – or alternatively, to profess horror at the barbarity of the rulers who were buried in such piles. In the age of the Seven Wonders, an age of slavery, the ancient pharaohs could only appear as the greatest slave masters of all time, an especially frightening image for the Romans, who had aspirations to that same title. The reality however was that the pyramids were built neither by slaves nor free men – both these states are closely linked – but by a skilled work force operating with an extraordinary intensity of effort and with techniques and attitudes to work that have now vanished from the larger cultures of the planet.

We may never be able to explain entirely the apparent sudden flowering of expertise, both in masonry and in management techniques, that underpinned the building of these mighty pyramids, that sparked the genesis of the world's first stone buildings. Part of the puzzle revolves around the nature of stone itself. Though other materials tend to disappear, cut stone, even from the most distant past, usually survives. So these grand surviving blocks of stone serve to exaggerate the sudden power and richness of the state that quarried them. All that such relics really tell us is that at a particular moment in its history this state had sufficient resources to employ its surplus population in cutting stone. It does not mean, however, that in the years before it took up masonry, the Egyptian population was not prosperous or well governed. The sudden expansion of the state required to make the pyramids was surely grounded in long experience. Certainly, the efficient unification of the state was a prerequisite. From the Nile's delta by the Mediterranean to the first cataract of the river in the south at Aswan, all the national resources of the day would have been engaged in the enterprise of making the royal pyramid. Anthropological theory has proposed declining harvests and the rise of greater social differentiation in the Nile-side communities as a prerequisite for unification. At all events, the sudden appearance in history of the imperious line of pyramids above the Nile at Memphis need not imply an economic or political miracle by itself but, rather, that in the preceding unknown decades the Egyptians slowly moved away from building royal monuments in perishable materials, while at the same time re-organizing their government on a truly national scale. Once these two factors were in place – and, as those Ramesside tourists to the pyramids well knew, this event occurred precisely in the reign of the pharaoh for whom the first stone pyramid was made, King Djoser, the discoverer of stone-working – the novelty of building for eternity seized the imagination of the court, and Egypt was fused into a single work force, a single national unit, to make these extraordinary stone abstractions.

A Pyramis is a solide figure contained under many playne superficies set upon one playne superficies, and gathered together to one point.

Billingsley's Euclid, 1570

I made a Voyage to Grand Cairo, on purpose to take the Measure of a Pyramid.

Joseph Addison in *The Spectator*, 1711

The pyramids are not merely the world's first grand stone structures, nor just the largest either: they remain the most accurate stone buildings ever made. They represent far more than a nation pushing blocks of stone around. These pyramids are set precisely on the four points of the compass, their discrepancies measured only in the minute fractions of a degree. Their corners too, are near-perfect right angles. Similarly, the lengths of their four sides are virtually the same: in overall dimensions of 600 and 700 feet and more, the common maximum error of these enormous structures is a matter of inches. All this precision was achieved with trenches filled with water to maintain a level, with the stars and dripping water clocks employed to find true north, with subtle geometries of ropes and string determining the building lines; everything relentlessly maintained at an aston-ishing level of exactitude and control. The accuracy of the pyramids shows their builders' determination to keep upon their chosen path without a jot of deviation. So great was their success that such tiny errors as are present in these buildings remained undetected until the surveyors and map-makers of the last century arrived and used these seemingly quite perfect objects as the fixed points from which the land of Egypt could be measured. For most of their history though, for all intents and purposes, the pyramids seemed to be perfect structures. Strange silent things that had stood in the sand for all eternity, manufactured by unfathomable means.

Like the people of the age of the Seven Wonders, but unlike us today, the people of the pyramid age could never free themselves from the processes of nature in which their lives were utterly enmeshed. The earliest known records made by humankind, tens of thousands of years before the pyramids were ever built, describe in lines and dots the changing phases of the moon. Similarly, all the Seven Wonders, whether Babylonian, Greek or Egyptian, were judged as successes or failures by their contemporaries for the extent to which they embellished and harmonized the lives of people with the gods that drove the natural world. Ultimately, such things were not decorations to human life, nor mere utilities. As this extraordinary complex of pyramid builders worked together in their intricate interlocking system of supply and manufacture, that vast community formed into the world's first nation-state. And the offices created for this enormous enterprise, foreman, mason, manager, provisioner, scribe and supervisor, became the titles of the offices of government. Philo, on the Seven Wonders, tells the truth: to individuals, the pyramids gave order and meaning; to their societies, they gave identity.

It is often said that the first leap forward made by humankind was the consolidation of those slow and silent processes by which the major crops that we still use today were first identified and cultivated, when the farm animals we still employ and eat were gathered up and set to live next to people, when the first metals of the world were smelted and cast in useful shapes. In short, during that long age of experiment and innovation that took place before writing and stone architecture was invented. In a sense, the pyramids are the summation of that extraordinary process, the time when all those imaginative innovations were collected and placed inside a social structure to give humankind a potential that it had never known before. The pyramids are a sort of celebration of a new-found power, the power of government and state that would not be explained in abstract words until the Greeks appeared millennia later. That, perhaps, is why these yellow buildings in their distant desert still float weightless and mysterious within the modern mind: they are the shape of our beginnings. The real wonder of these pyramids, then, is why they were made at all.

A thousand years ago, the historian Abu'l Hasan Ali al Mas'udi recorded the then-current Egyptian explanations of the pyramids as part of his thirty-volume history of the world. While repeating the old stories about the methods of construction, Mas'udi also answers our question by placing the pyramids in an imaginary context that at least gives them a force and reason beyond that of empty pomp and modern functionality.

The reason for building the Pyramids was the following dream, which happened to one of the kings of Egypt, Surid Ben Shaluk, three hundred years before the flood. It appeared to him that the earth was in chaos, its inhabitants laid prostrate and the stars which were wandering confusedly from their courses were clashing together with tremendous noise . . . Soon after, in another vision, the king saw the fixed stars descend upon the earth in the form of white birds, seize the people and enclose them in a narrow cleft between two great mountains . . . and he awoke in great consternation, and went to the Temple of the Sun and with great lamentation, prostrated himself in the dust.

In the morning he assembled the chief priests from all the provinces of Egypt, a hundred and thirty in number . . . and he related his first and second vision. After the interpretation announced 'that some great event would take place', the high priest, whose name was Philemon, also spoke, 'Grand and mysterious are thy dreams, O king, and your visions are not deceptive, for your majesty is sacred . . .'

Then the king directed the astrologers to ascertain by taking their altitude, whether the stars foretold any great catastrophe. The results announced an approaching deluge . . . a flood to overwhelm the land . . . The king then inquired if the earth would again become fruitful . . . and they answered that its former fertility would return. The king then demanded what would happen next, and was informed that a stranger would invade the country, kill the inhabitants, and seize their property; and that afterwards a deformed people, coming from beyond the Nile, would take possession of the kingdom

Then the king ordered the Pyramids to be built, and these predictions to be inscribed upon columns and their large stones. And he also placed within the pyramids his treasures, and the bodies of his ancestors. He also ordered the priests to deposit within the pyramids written accounts of their wisdom and acquirements in the different arts and sciences. Subterranean channels were constructed to convey to the pyramids the waters of the Nile. The passages were filled with talismans, with idols and with the writings of the priests, containing all manner of wisdom, the names and properties of medical plants and the sciences of arithmetic and of geometry; that they might remain as records, for the benefit of those, who could afterwards comprehend them.

The King ordered pillars to be cut, and an extensive pavement to be formed. The stone came from the neighbourhood of Aswan. The three Pyramids were all built in this way. Leaves of papyrus inscribed with certain characters, were placed under the stones cut in the quarries, and upon their being struck, the blocks were moved at each time by one hundred and fifty cubits and so, by degrees, arrived at the Pyramids . . .

When the building was finished, the people assembled with rejoicing around the king, who covered the Pyramids with coloured brocade, from the top to the bottom, and gave a great feast, at which all the inhabitants of the country were present. The king then offered up sacrifices to prevent the intrusion of strangers to these pyramids, and . . . caused the following text, in Arabic, to be inscribed upon them. 'I, Surid, the king, have built these Pyramids, and have finished them in sixty-one years. Let him, who comes after me, and imagines himself a king like me, attempt to destroy them in six hundred. To destroy is easier than to build. I have clothed them with silk; let him try to cover them with mats.'

PYRAMIDOLATRY

The city wherein I was born is called Memphis; my father's name, and mine also, is Calasiris. As touching my trade of life, I am now a vagabond, who was not long ago a priest . . . when I heard there was a certain city of Greece sacred to Apollo, which was a temple of the gods and a college of wise men and far from the troublous resort of the common people, I went thither, thinking that a city which was dedicated to holiness and ceremonies was a meet place for a man being a prophet to resort unto. Now Grecian ears are wonderfully delighted with tales of Egypt. In a word they leave nothing that appertaineth to Egypt unsearched . . . and I told them what I knew, and was written in the holy books, and was lawful only for priests to read and know . . .

. . . certain of the civilest sort fell in talk concerning the Nile, and asked me whence his sources came . . . and some would ask after what fashion we Egyptians honoured our gods . . . others enquired of the structure of the pyramids and of those winding shafts in which our kings are buried. This was no natural work, but dug out by Egyptian hands very artfully to keep their spoils. It was made after this sort. It had a dark narrow entrance and was shut with privy doors, so that even the threshold was instead of a gate, when need required, and would open and shut very easily. The inner part was countermined variously with divers slanting ways, the which would sometimes run along by themselves artfully for a while and sometimes would be entangled like the roots of trees; but in the end they all led to one level place which received a dim light from an opening made at the edge of the pool.

Abstracted from *Aethiopica*, Book 1; *An Aethiopian historie written in Greeke by Heliodorus, no lesse wittie than pleasant, englished by Thomas Underdowne.* (Heliodorus, a Syrian Greek, flourished AD 220–250; Underdowne's translation appeared in 1587.)

The Greeks, the people of the Seven Wonders, frequently wrote about their debt to Egypt. They said that geometry itself had come from the land beside the Nile. Many of the cleverest Greeks, they said, had visited that country and lived with its priests, the traditional holders of the ancient wisdom. As if in confirmation, a great deal of classical art shows an obvious debt to Egypt. The great flowering that occurred within the cities of Greece in just a few short centuries was founded on millennia of previous experience gained in other regions of the world. The basic forms and language of Greek temple architecture, the pose and craftsmanship of classical sculptures, were established millennia before the Greeks took them over and transformed them. The debt to Egypt, though, was entirely practical. Despite their interest, neither the Greeks nor the Romans who conquered them, ever really understood the Egyptians. Unlike them, the Egyptians had little use for abstract thought. They had created their nation-state neither by dialectic nor abstract speculation, but by building pyramids, by carrying stones and pushing blocks onto the high plateau above their valley. Almost nothing of the subtle product of this process was outlined in written words until, in just the same way that Greek writers turned Egyptian religion into a dozen simple stories, so the Greek philosophers began their literary conversations about the nature of the state.

In consequence, the Greeks and Romans regarded the Egyptians in a manner similar to that with which the West has traditionally regarded the Chinese: as inhabitants of a wise and ancient kingdom set in an unfathomable alien universe. Some, like the Roman poet Juvenal, an ancient Evelyn Waugh, joked about this fusty race of foreigners who seemed so ill-fitted to the classical environment, others mystified it to produce sensual synthetic faiths based upon its ancient rituals. For the most part though, old Egypt was left to lie in tumbled ruin, obliged to provide wheat for the imperial mills, the odd exotic queen, and phyles of nimble-minded soothsayers. The matchless pyramids, however, endured, standing proof of the efficacy and impenetrability of an extraordinary culture, even if, in Greek and Roman times, the apparent uselessness of those great monuments served mainly to illustrate a damning vision of an elderly and stupid nation ripe for colonization.

Today, perhaps, we are less in need of such self-serving evidence and many people try to penetrate the ancient mystery, to discover something of this nation that laboured long and hard to make these pyramids. The very range of our explanations, though, shows just how nonplussed we all still are, and how difficult it is to regain even the smallest corner of that most ancient world.

Some grasp at the simple observation that rays of sunlight shining on the Giza plateau first provided inspiration for the form of the pyramids: a theory that bypasses all consideration of the relationship of the ancient Egyptians to such transient phenomena as sunbeams, and invites us to view the ancient Egyptians as a race of romantic landscape artists. Others suggest that the Egyptians expended centuries of effort making perfect pyramids especially to place them in patterns that, from an aeroplane or helicopter, roughly resemble small sections of a modern star chart.

Whatever the explanations are, though, and there are very many more of them, one thing is certain: the pyramids have certainly kept the world wondering all these years. To the medieval Arabs, they were known as pharaoh's mountains. 'Man fears time,' they popularly asserted, 'but time itself fears the pyramids.' Many thought that the pyramids were especially made to measure time, a belief shared by numbers of European astronomers and mathematicians. To some it seemed that the ethereal simplicity of the pyramids was perfect form made concrete, an idea which gave the ancient stones a theological significance. 'The notion or idea of God is no more arbitrarious or fictitious than the notion of a cube or tetraedrum or any other of the regular bodies in Geometry', asserted Professor Henry More, an eminent Cambridge divine of the 1650s. And what finer tetrahedrons were there in the world indeed, than those 'bodies geometricall', the golden pyramids standing in the ageless sand of Egypt. After the first modern survey of the Giza pyramids was published in 1648 by a learned Oxford professor, numbers of European mathematicians, Jesuit encyclopedists and Protestant astronomers took to analysing the measurements of the architecture of the largest of them, the Pyramid of Cheops, in an attempt to discover the metric unit that had governed its design. More accurate than the contemporary field apparatus that measured them, with hints of magical geometries held in their anonymous precision, the stripped and battered pyramids appeared as if they had once been perfect things, crystallizations of the universal order, allied both to time and space. The general notion of a universal standard unit of measurement was a common preoccupation of the time – even the aged Galileo was involved in correspondence with some of the pyramid researchers on the subject. More ardent pyramid theorists maintained that if the basic units of measurement used in the pyramids could be detected then their inscrutable architecture could be linked to other absolute number systems too – the seasons and the years, the movements of the stars, the verses of the Bible and the histories of its kings. In old age, great Newton himself searched long and laboriously amongst such figures, and wrote books and papers on the subject.

Through following centuries too, many other eminent scientists have been impressed by the precision and geometry of the pyramids and plied their various modern trades upon them. To many people, it seemed that there were hidden wisdoms, vanished technologies, powerful secrets held in these ancient stones; a wisdom more wonderful perhaps precisely because the professionals who specialized in studying ancient Egypt seemed to be completely disinterested in such things and had, in consequence, quite failed to find anything at the pyramids beyond a few innocuous inscriptions. Though random fragments of its original outer facing still adhered to it beneath the drifted sand, most of the fine stone of Cheops' pyramid had been entirely stripped away by generations of Cairene masons, a fact that allowed these esoteric theorists to reconstruct the pyramid as a completely perfect form. In truth, however, there is no way of knowing precisely where this missing outer casing lay, not, that is, with sufficient precision to provide the minute measurements these investigators needed for their work. For true believers, such measurements as these could hold the mark of God in them, as did the Holy Bible. If this were so the smallest measurements that bound these ancient stones might, like the Book of Revelations, hold details of the future in them. Such researchers thought the Great Pyramid to be the relic of an unknown race of ancient seers, a sort of molecule of cosmic DNA that held within it the stony calendars of past and future time.

During the 19th century, the greater part of these theories focused on the interior architecture of the Great Pyramid, all the near-contemporary monuments having been somewhat irrationally excluded from the game. The vast labyrinth of rooms in Cheops' pyramid was the result of three changes in the ancient plan for the location of the royal ritual of entombment. Just as Cheops' father, Sneferu, had built three huge separate pyramids, each with their own burial chambers, so his son had made three great burial chambers, one above the other. Together, these rooms and corridors form a complex architecture of their own.

The first of Cheops' burial chambers had been cut into the rock under the centre of the pyramid in the traditional way at the beginning of the work, just like the burial chamber of his successor Djedefra at the unfinished pyramid at Abu Roash. The king's second burial chamber was built later on above this excavation, amid the great rough blocks of the lower courses of the pyramid, then still standing in the sunlight. Years later, as the pyramid rose, a third and final burial chamber was built high at the pyramid's heart, at the end of a wonderful, unique corridor, now called the Grand Gallery, an architectural masterpiece in its own right with magnificent granite corbelling and an extraordinary precision of construction and design. Standing in the Grand Gallery today, it is easy to feel how such wonders can breed mystery, and mystery may breed mystification. Walking through these strange warm corridors might be likened to the experience of members of an Amazonian tribe on their first walk through the turbine tubes of a silent power station. The twists and turns, the angles, hazards and strange spaces of these interiors are silent and mysterious. From egyptologists to conservationists, from fundamentalists to tourists, for pyramidologists too, the dark glass of the granite walls reflects the images of our imaginings.

The Planet Earth, and its measures, is specifically mentioned by the Creator of Earth, who is also the Architect and Designer of the Great Pyramid, in direct connection with a pyramid form of building in the inspired Book of Job, chapter 38, verses 1 to 7. Therefore, a huge-shaped pyramid, the cubical bulk of which agrees with the cubical bulk of the earth, either bulk for bulk, or by some recognised and harmonious mathematical proportion, can be reasonably accepted as the basis for the calculation.

In sentences as complex as Cheops' corridors, Morton Edgar, a Scottish noncon-formist, lays out his rationale for his examination of the Great Pyramid. His book *The Great Pyramid*, published in Glasgow in 1924, provides a view of ancient monuments that takes wonder far away from pagan Greece and Rome, and Alexander.

Counting out the years from the Bible's story of Creation, Edgar and many of his fel-low researchers variously measured out the corridors and chambers of the Great Pyramid, counted through the ages of Adam and the Patriarchs, through the Prophets and the Kings and the life of Jesus, and climbed up to the doorway of the highest burial chamber which, Edgar claimed, marked the year 1914 – the same year, it seemed to most Westerners of the time, that had witnessed the beginning of the greatest tragedy the world had ever seen.

There is one possible time-indication in the Great Pyramid which ought not to pass unno-ticed [he notes for us] but as it is partly of a date yet in the future, we can only draw atten-tion to it by presenting the calculations which seem to support it as reasonable. Part of this time-measurement has already been fulfilled in accordance with the interpretation we give it, and because of this it is not impossible that the future part may be fulfilled.

Measuring upward from . . . the first Ascending Passage, adding, as shown, an exact 100 inches to this measure, we arrive at that place in the Pyramid's passage-system which marks the date of our Lord's death and resurrection, 33 AD . . . This south wall of the Grand Gallery is vertically in alignment above the north wall of the rock-cut Subterranean Chamber, which chamber is symbolical of the destruction into which the nations of Christendom entered when the great war was precipitated upon the unsuspecting world in Autumn of 1914 AD . . . If we continue the interpretation of the first low passage to the second low passage, this second passage could be held to represent the final trouble upon the world, and upon the Lord's children (1 Thessalonians 5: 1-6).

That the south wall of the Ante-Chamber, which is also the north-beginning of the low granite passage leading to the King's Chamber, should mark the date 1928 AD may be regarded as appropriate enough . . . for this point also marks . . . the date 1878 AD. Between these two dates is a period of 50 years, just as there was a period of 50 days between the parallel date to 1878 AD., namely, 33 AD, when our Lord rose from the dead, and the great Pentecostal day when God poured out his Holy Spirit upon his waiting Church (Acts 2: 16-18).

For Morton Edgar, standing in the warm gloom of those ancient passages, the future of the world suddenly seemed to lie in the room ahead of him, in King Cheops' final burial chamber. History's secrets held in a ruler! Back home in Glasgow, he measured out the years as they approached that final Pentecost, the 'seventh Sunday of the seventh

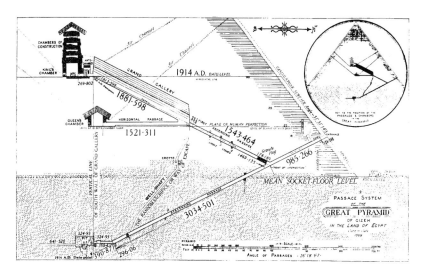

The Great Pyramid Chart of the Ages, from Edgar, 1924

day', the ending of the world – in 1928. And that, perhaps, is why poor Edgar and his theories are derided by more modern pyramidologists – unthinkingly, he brought their sacred science into ridicule. In a strange way, though, researches such as Edgar's share something of ancient mentality.

Consider Cheops' third great burial chamber. The simple granite box of the royal sarcophagus is just a little wider than the deep low doorways that give access to the room from the Grand Gallery below. The sarcophagus, then, was put in place within that beautifully proportioned room before the granite blocks that make up its roof were set in place: nine great slabs, between them weighing close to 400 tons. Beyond them, high above this colossal ceiling, are five more granite chambers supporting the tapering weight of the pyramid itself. Vast harmonious fitments designed to stand for all eternity and still more suited to this task perhaps than any other building ever made.

Two air shafts in this same vast chamber run up through the fabric of the pyramid out to its surface, their small square outlets perfectly cut in its enormous granite walls. Both of these shafts were placed in careful alignment with major stars. That the pyramid's designers were trying to lock their building into heaven is further underlined by the precision of the alignment of the four faces of the pyramid, set exactly on the four points of the compass. The design of the pyramid, too, has its own absolute integrities; an extraordinary geometry. Its triangles and squares are held inside a web of mathematical relationships, some of them based on the subtly simple device of the 8:5 triangle, whose angles render right angles and whose numbers are part of the charmed ratio called the Golden Mean. Such careful numeration does not occur by chance; indeed, similar numeric series were used repeatedly by Egypt's temple builders. The pyramid makers, then, caught hold of all the absolutes they could, the durability of stone, the power and harmony of numbers and the very stars of heaven, to lock their building into the natural universe.

Egypt's priests sometimes told visiting Greeks that their country was the temple of the world: in other words, the natural elements of their fertile valley were set on the compass of the universe. In this bright oasis, the life-giving river flowed from south to north, the sun bisected it each day, and the kings and priests both joined with these powers in endless rounds of ritual. If he were ever buried in his pyramid, King Cheops would have lain at the heart of this perfect and harmonious kingdom, in precise alignment with the heavens and at the very heart of Egypt. Reaching out to join such harmonies, Egypt made its rulers' tombs as hard as diamonds and as perfect as they could, to last for all eternity.

This is the simple reason why the Egyptians worked so hard to build their pyramids and state. The people who made pyramids, as all the Seven Wonders, were bound by the forces and rhythms of the natural world. Initially, human wonder was a reaction to the energy and mystery, the alien life they sensed inside their universe. These ancient people worked hard to harmonize themselves with those forces; to communicate with the gods that embodied them. The main agents of this communication operating through rite and ritual, sacrifice and offering, were priests and kings. The arts, everything from potting to pyramid building, were the media by which the ritual harmony was sensed and joined.

For the Egyptians, pharaoh's mountains proved that even the dangerously unique event of human death could be absorbed as part of this astonishing pact that joined earth onto heaven. Whilst later civilizations marvelled at the oddness of the pyramids and invented endless silly stories about their purpose and significance, to the Egyptians, they were standing proof of the value of their state; that it was, indeed, set in interface with heaven.

JOSEPH'S GRANARIES AND NOAH'S ARK

Each new age makes its own idea of wonder; chameleon-like, the pyramids have generally managed to survive as wonders simply by changing their identity and purposes. At various times, King Cheops' tomb has been the Ark of Noah, the universal calendar and Joseph's granaries. Philo, who wrote the oldest list of Wonders that we know of, thought them to be a wonder of construction, a wonder made by human beings to impress other human beings. Three of the ancient Wonders on his list of seven – the Pyramids, the Zeus statue, the Hanging Gardens – show an inquiring age reassessing the ancient past, an important part of establishing themselves within a brand new universe, the beginning of the modern world. The Seven Wonders, then, a kind of cosmic stock-taking, have become wonderfully picturesque markers of the largest single transformation the human race has ever undergone.

Philo lived in Alexandria in the late 3rd century BC. He was a member of an illustrious school of ancient engineers, in reality perhaps more librarians and scholars than practising members of a profession. Ctesibius, the son of an Alexandrian barber, had been the founder of this school in the generations before Philo. These 'pneumatic parlour magicians', as they have been called, took the broad theoretical approach of earlier Greek scientific writers and used their theories to make everything from automatic toys

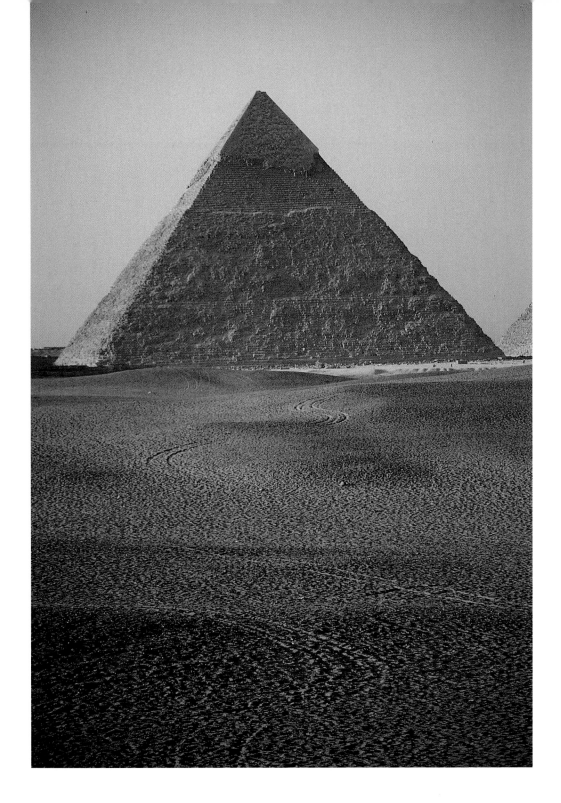

24. The Pyramid of Chephren at Giza. Retaining part of its outer casing in its upper reaches, the pyramid of Chephren is the most complete monument at Giza. Sited higher than its two neighbours, it appears to be the largest of the group; in fact, it was once ten feet shorter than its close neighbour, the Great Pyramid. Should you wish to construct a wall of stone cubes one foot square around the surface of our planet, the stones of this monument would supply almost two thirds of the material required – so Napoleon himself once calculated

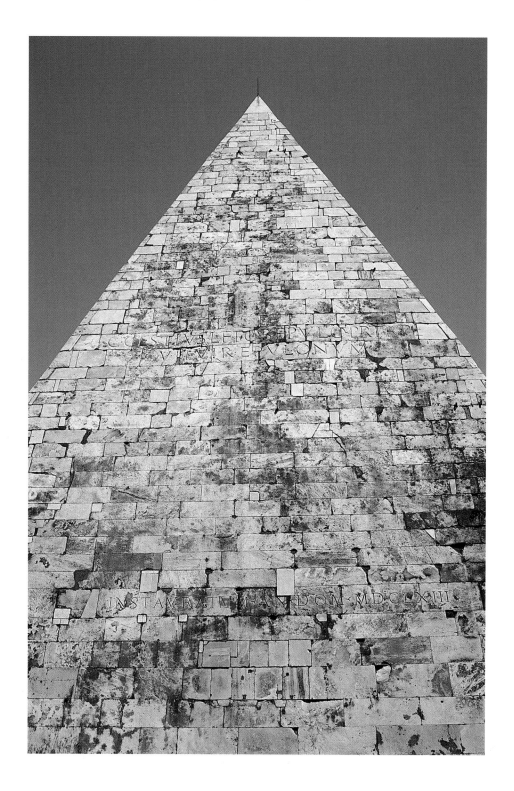

25. The Pyramid of Cestius at Rome. The sole survivor of two modest pyramids built at Rome, this is the tomb of Caius Cestius Epulo, a wealthy Roman tribune who died in 12 BC. The two Roman monuments made such an impression upon the first European travellers that most early Western drawings of the Giza pyramids mistakenly show them as possessing the same steep angle as the Roman pyramids. This steep angle may also have contributed to the common belief that there was little distinction to be drawn between pyramids and obelisks – hence Rome with all its obelisks was seen as a city filled with pyramids

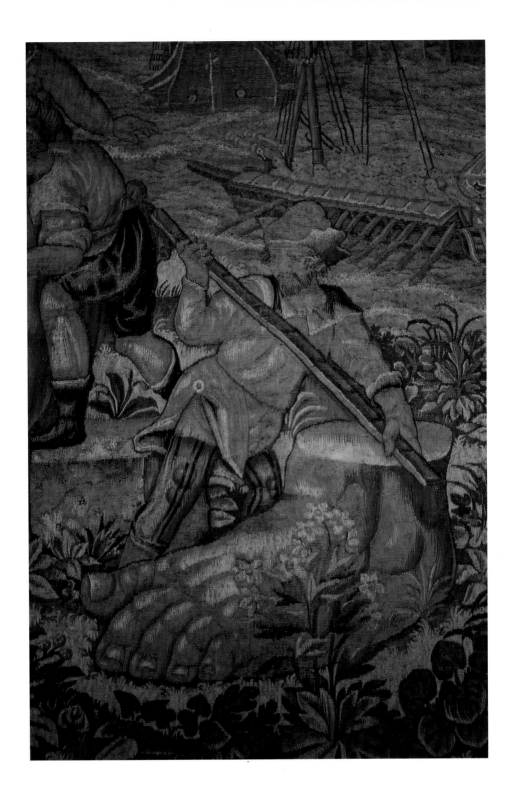

26. Measuring the Wonders; a detail from a baroque tapestry. This small conceit, part of a grand set of 17th-century Brussels tapestries of the Seven Wonders now in the Musée Réattu at Arles, shows an antiquarian Turk taking the measure of the foot of the Rhodian Colossus. Many Renaissance artists had been similarly intrigued by the surviving remnants of colossal antiquity, and measured and drew them so that they might re-use the antique designs in their own work

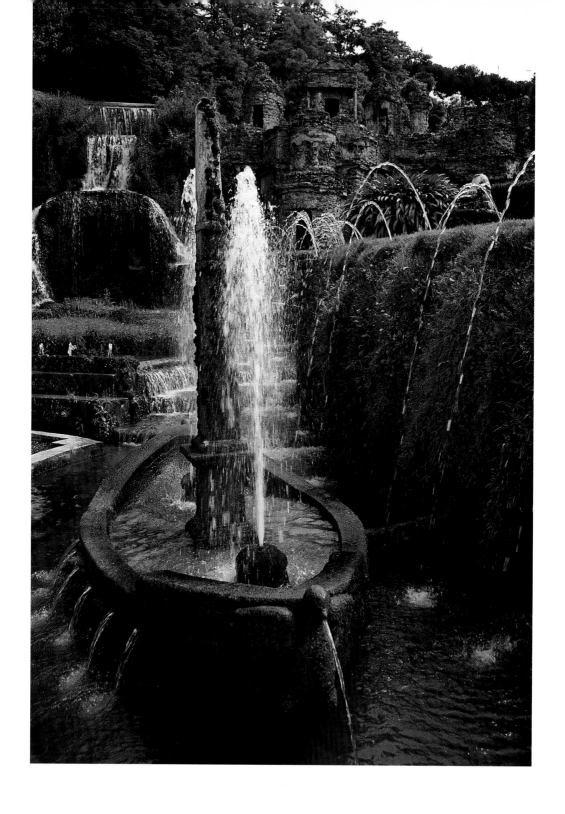

27. Pirro Ligorio's model of Rome at the Villa d'Este, Tivoli. As well as designing the great Artemis (*see* plate 16), Pirro also built a charming model of ancient Rome in the gardens at Tivoli, to symbolize civilization. Its ruins echo the Seven Wonders which, Pirro imagined, once stood in ancient Rome. His miniature Tiber holds a stony boat filled with an obelisk, a design that Pirro took from his own restoration of the quays on the ancient Island of the Tiber at the heart of Rome

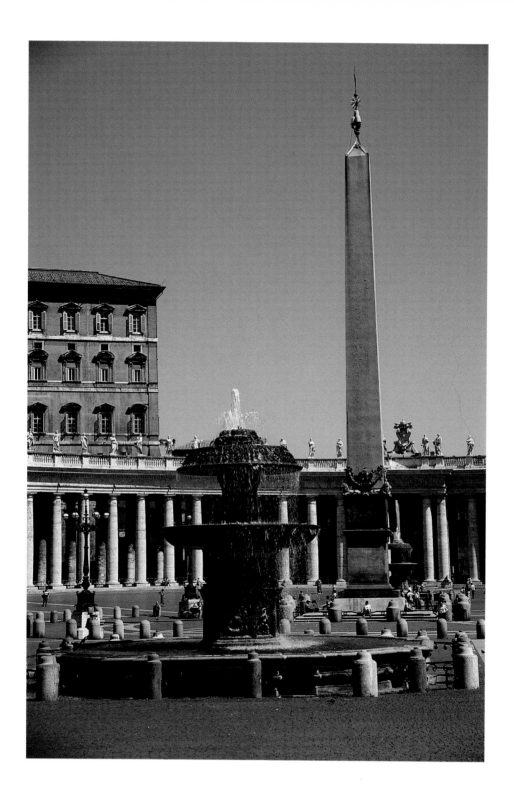

28. Piazza San Pietro at Rome. Pirro's modest designs seem to have had great influence upon the later planners of baroque Rome. Even the Piazza of St Peter's echoes his drawings of the port of ancient Rome, with an obelisk, a Colossus and a Pharos. The obelisk of the Piazza San Pietro marked the traditional location of St Peter's crucifixion. For many years, the gilded ball above the star upon its top was believed to hold the ashes of Julius Caesar

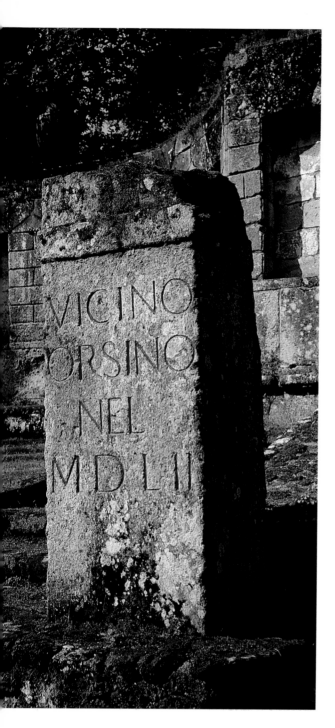

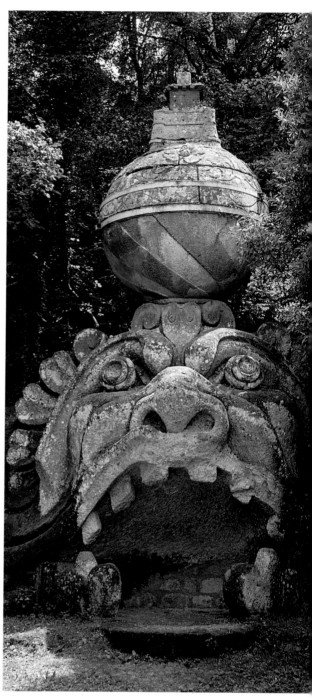

29. (*Left*) Orsini's inscription in his garden at Bomarzo. Member of a great medieval Roman family and long-serving Papal mercenary, Prince Pier Francesco 'Vicini' Orsini, proudly claims his eccentric garden close by his summer palace at Bomarzo, north of Rome

30. (*Right*) The Pharos of Bomarzo. Although Orsini's garden sculptures do not readily conjure up the antique wonders, they often quote those seven vanished monuments as symbols in a silvan dream. The Light of the World, which Orsini has perched uneasily on the head of a monster, is derived from Pirro Ligorio's reconstruction of the Pharos of Alexandria

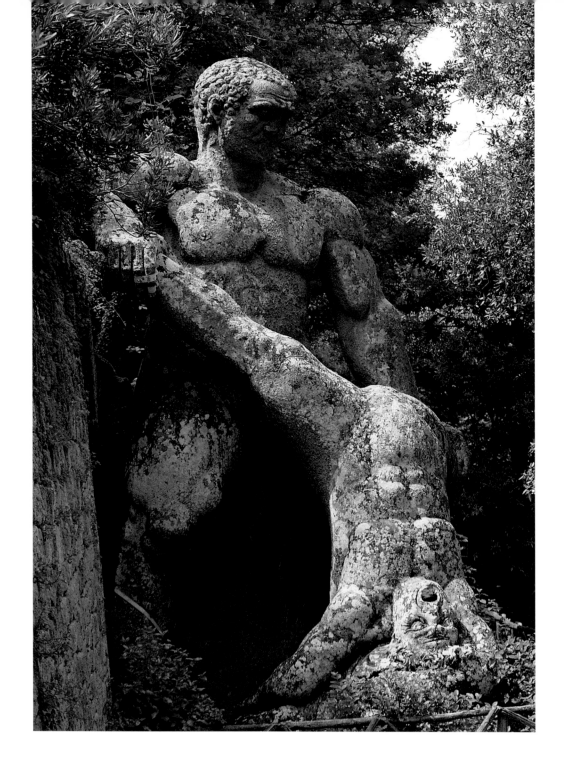

31. The Colossus of Bomarzo. 'As Rhodes once took pride in its Colossus, so by this one, my wood is also glorified ...'
So reads Orsini's inscription set beside this ferocious statue. Here, the antique Colossus has been transformed into the mad
hero of Ariosto's poem 'Orlando furioso', and is literally tearing his opponent into pieces

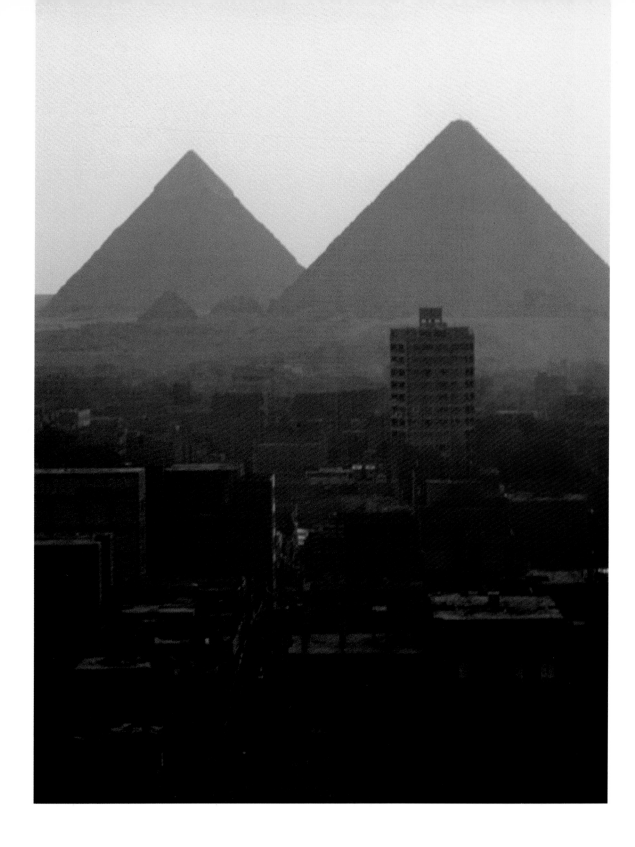

32. The Great Pyramid of Giza at sunset, the sole survivor of the Seven ancient Wonders. The Pyramids are the oldest, largest, and most accurate stone buildings ever made: the one true universal wonder of the world

like mechanical birds and drinking dragons to miniature turbines and water organs that sounded eerie notes as the tides rolled back and forth on the rocks of Alexandria's harbour. Like the casting of the Colossus of Rhodes and the building of the pyramids, these more modest feats of engineering were also seen as wonders. The celebrated literary works of men like Hero and Philo which describe them made up an important section of the library of the ancient world, one which, when born again in various epochs of Western history, helped to produce those periodic spurts and bounds of progress that we sometimes call a renaissance. Also preserved along with these writings was this specifically Greek notion of wonder, wonder as something to be made, explained and understood, wonder as human achievement.

Like Philo, many of these antique scientists worked at the great library of Alexandria which had been initiated in the first days of the city by King Ptolemy I. At its height, this library held close to half a million volumes. Book buyers working for the Alexandrian library combed Athens and Rhodes where the best second-hand book shops were to be found. Other libraries too, were often asked to lend their manuscripts so that copies could be made. All ships entering Alexandria harbour were required to surrender any books that they carried that were not already represented in the city library. These were catalogued and labelled 'from the ships' and the captains of the vessels were given copies in exchange. So the great library, which was open to all literate people, was also a sort of editorial house. Over the centuries, the staff of the library standardized a system of punctuation and accents and even developed a recognizable literary style of their own. Later Ptolemies proudly boasted that they owned copies of every known book; the library contained all the wisdom in their world and was a beacon for the city that burned more brightly than the Pharos. Not only did the library hold a powerful catalogue of all known wisdom, it also represented the conscious conservation of the literary heritage of Greece, which for the next 15 centuries would come to stand as the symbolic root of Western wisdom.

As one might expect, the senior librarians of this extraordinary institution were often celebrated authors in their own right, producing plays, encyclopedias, poetry and many other works, drawing on the extraordinary resources of the library. One of these luminaries, Eratosthenes, a chief librarian and royal tutor who was of the generation before Philo might well have compiled the first list of Seven Wonders. The surviving traces of his works, sometimes little more than tantalizing titles, deal with everything from a universal theory of political history to mathematical and geometrical problems (Eratosthenes' 'sieve' is still used for testing computers), from musical theory to the measurement of the earth, philosophy and plays. Unlike Philo of Byzantium, whose works suggest his being a follower of the Alexandrian school rather than an initiator, Eratosthenes had the originality, the curiosity, and the ability to synthesize, and was poet enough to have invented the concept of the Seven Wonders of the World.

Whether or not he conceived the notion of the Seven Wonders, Philo certainly seems to have compiled the text we now call his, a text that with all its ambiguity, may be traced as Denis Haynes has said, 'to a good Hellenistic source' (see p. x). After the invasion of the Arabs in the seventh century and the final dissolution of the Library, copies of Philo's text were preserved at Constantinople, where so many ancient wonders had been phys-ically gathered (see pp. 22 ff.) and whose own geometricians and engineers, direct inher-itors of Philo's great tradition, had made some of the finest ancient buildings in the world. Philo's list first appears in Byzantium in the fourth century, in the speeches of Bishop Gregory of Nazianzus, the famous preacher who ruminated so movingly upon the Mausoleum (see pp. 99–100). Later commentaries on Gregory's sermon even include a Byzantine miniature of one of Philo's seven ancient wonders, showing the Mausoleum standing by the sea. In this same illustration, a nearby statue standing on a plinth across some water may even represent the great Colossus of the isle of Rhodes – which, at the time this scene was painted, had long since fallen and been broken up for scrap. In the rather practical vein of Philo and other ancient commentators like the Roman Pliny, who also thought the pyramids to be impractical (see p. 165), Gregory listed the Seven Wonders as abstract types of monument 'a wall, a statue, gardens, the pyramids, a tem-ple, another statue, a tomb' – a short list of civic monuments which is still a part of almost every modern city.

The oldest surviving manuscript of Philo's essay dates from the ninth century, a stout vellum codex carefully written in brown Byzantine ink, copied out at the time when the prominent Byzantine scientist known as Leo the Mathematician was prompting one of those periodic miniature renaissances of science which sometimes occurred within Byzantium. A well-known teacher, Leo's fame spread from the court of the Caliph of Baghdad even to the desolate empire in the west of Europe. Drawing on the writings of the ancient school of Alexandria, Leo even made some celebrated wonders himself, won-ders in which the Emperors of Byzantium made regular appearances, to the amazement of visiting foreign envoys:

A gold-plated bronze tree stood in front of the emperor's throne, and the branches of the tree were filled with birds of different sorts, similarly made of bronze. The birds squawked according to the species of bird each was. The throne of the emperor was made in such a way that it seemed now to be low, now higher, and then very high. The throne was very big, and whether it was made of bronze or wood is not known. But lions, covered with gold, acted as guards in a manner of speaking – they beat the ground with their tails and, open-mouthed, tongues lolling, they let out a roar. Here, leaning on the shoulders of two eunuchs, I was led for an audience with the emperor. On my approach the lions roared and the birds screeched in the manner of each of their species, . . . so I prostrated myself three times in deference to the emperor, I raised my head, and the man whom I had just seen sitting slightly above the level of the ground, I then saw wearing a different outfit, sitting just below the ceiling of the palace. I could not work out how this had happened... But at that point he said nothing to me because, even if he had wanted to, the great distance between us would have made it unseemly to do so.

Bishop Liudprand of Cremona, Ambassador of the King of Italy and the
Holy Roman Empire, *c.* AD 950, *Antapodosis*, VI

Philo's 1,200-year-old essay would certainly have appealed to a man who made all that; it is clear, moreover, that the inspiration for his automata were the writings of the School of Alexandria to which Philo had belonged. A century later, during another resurgence of interest in scholarly and scientific writing, the Byzantine Emperor Constantine Porphorygenitus was himself writing on some of Philo's Wonders and their later history. Clearly, these ancient Alexandrian works were still accessible in Byzantine libraries, and occasionally, Philo's Wonder list was enumerated and copied, and taken up again and used as inspiration.

In 1436, during the early years of the Italian Renaissance, Philo's ancient musings were taken to western Europe, part of a fat vellum volume stowed in the baggage of a Dalmatian cardinal. The volume also included a dozen other unique texts written over the course of seven classical centuries: an account of an ancient voyage to west Africa undertaken in the fourth century BC; a treatise on bronze casting by a well-known Hellenistic sculptor who had worked at Pergamum; a history of the first eight centuries of the Olympic Games; a handful of poems; a collection of myths and some saucy stories especially designed by Virgil's teacher for use in epic poems; a Greek grammar and a lexicon and some letters of eminent Greeks and Romans, all translated into Greek along with a tale about a wondrous island called Panchaea, a magic, mystic place whose enlightened inhabitants, without education, wealth or ambition, wore golden jewelry, clothes of down and oyster shells and 'buried their dead in the sea at low tide'. In short, some of the wonders of a lost and ancient world.

After passing a quiet century on the shelves of a monastery at Basle in Switzerland, the Philo manuscript found a new home in the house of the great printer Frobenius. There its precious texts were carefully studied by a number of scholars including perhaps, the great Erasmus himself, who at that time was old and ill and living in nearby Freiburg, from where he visited Frobenius to supervise the first printing of the holy works of Bishop Origen of ancient Alexandria. Long before its publication in the 17th century, then, Philo's list had already entered the emerging world of Western scholarship and is a vital link in the trail of ancient wonder from the pyramids until today – part of the history of the modern imagination. It is not however the entire history of the Seven Wonders. The idea of them had never left the West but, fractured from its classical past and ancient scholarship by war and poverty, the list had changed. Wonder itself had been transformed.

At the time of its decline imperial Rome was completely penetrated by the Christians, who had come quietly into the West and worked right through the structures of that merciless pagan empire. The Christians shunned pagan things. For them, all true wonders were the works of God, and pagan writings were part of a wicked, old illusion. So, as classical civilization crumbled in the West, Philo's Seven Wonders seemed to disappear. In western Europe for example, for close on a thousand years, even the mighty pyramids entered a discreet oblivion. For the pyramids are not so much as mentioned in the Bible, and the Bible, the main source of knowledge of eternity and God and all the wonders of his world, gave Christendom its reason and significance.

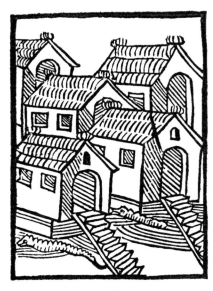

Joseph's Granaries, complete with snakes, from Sir John Mandeville's *Travels*, 1482

Despite this antagonism, despite a reluctance to even notice pagan things, half-memories of the ancient wonders still flickered in the West's imagination. The pyramids especially, those enigmatic perfect objects, still stood blankly in their desert, and many travellers and pilgrims still walked astonished through the sand to see them. For explanation and identity, however, such wonders now required a kind of Biblical validation, and so the pyramids were named the Granaries of Joseph, the pharaonic storerooms of the Book of Genesis, built to stock the grain of Egypt and feed the nation in the seven lean years of famine, as prophesied by Joseph in the Bible's book of Genesis.

Now I will speak of another thing that is beyond Babylon, above the Nile, towards the desert, between Africa and Egypt; that is, of the granaries of Joseph, that he caused to be made, to keep the grains against the dear years. And they be made of stone, full well made of masons' craft; of the which two be marvelously great and high, and the others be not so great. And each granary has a gate to enter within, a little above the earth; for the land is wasted and fallen since the granaries were made. And within they be all full of serpents. And above the granaries without, be many scriptures of diverse languages. And some men say that they be sepultures of great lords, that were sometime, but that is not true . . . for ye may well know that tombs and sepultures be not made of such greatness, nor of such highness; wherefore it is not to believe that they be tombs or sepultures.

The Voiage and Travayle of Sir John Mandeville, Knight
written in Bruges in the 14th century

For most travellers, it really did not seem to matter that even the most cursory inspection of the pyramids showed them to be completely solid and therefore not really suitable for storing corn; the extraordinary ancient wonders were absorbed into

Christendom as Joseph's granaries, antique and mystic structures which, it was believed, cast no shadow and might even aid alchemists to make pure gold.

This reticence to call a pyramid a pyramid had already appeared at the time of the first records of Western pilgrims journeying through the empire of Byzantium to visit the Bible lands. Today, the first surviving record of this journey is the lively and inquisitive account of a traveller called Egeria, who left Bordeaux with her retinue in AD 333, bound for Egypt and the Holy Land. Apparently, the indefatigable Egeria obtained her information from local people – evidently the notion of Christian tourism was already well developed in her time. The citizens of Byzantium were eager to show these curious visitors from the north the sites of Bible stories and show them, too, the order and service of their church. Extracted from a later compilation of several such accounts, part of this rare text describes a visit to pharaoh's granaries.

> Heliopolis is twelve miles from Babylon [a Roman fortress close by modern Cairo]. In the middle of this city is a large flat area where the Temple of the Sun is, and where Potiphar's house is too. Between these two is the house of Asenath. The inner wall inside the city is rather old and made of stone, like the temple and the houses of Asenath and of Potiphar. There too is the garden of the sun where there is the lofty column, called Bomon, the column on which the Phoenix perched after 500 years.
>
> Memphis is twelve miles from Babylon. There are many pyramids there which Joseph built for storing corn in.

Peter the Deacon, Appendix ad Itinerarium Egeriae

Two centuries after Egeria's pilgrimage 'Joseph's granaries' are again mentioned in a peroration by one Julius Honorius. By that time, we may assume that this identification had generally gained acceptance at least in Julius' circles; that is, in Rome, at the very heart of the West. That the alias was always understood to be a pious circumlocution, a modest avoidance of paganicity, similar to that displayed by many non-Western people today, is clearly shown in the writings of St Isadore, a Bishop of Seville of the early seventh century. Isadore, a busy writer, composed treatises on grammar, mathematics and medicine, on the doctrine and practice of the faith in Spain, and he also wrote a history of the world from the Creation to his own day, AD 615 – encyclopedic volumes which, in their own dry way, list a great part of the knowledge that was then available in the West. For this reason alone, St Isadore's works were much prized during the following centuries and both quoted and plundered by many later scholars. For him, as for the encyclopedists who followed in his footsteps, 'pyramids' were two quite separate things: geometrical figures and the tombs of powerful, ancient people. The word, so Isadore tells us, is derived from the Greek word for fire – pyr – and like fire, he says, they rise to a point. In a hint that emphasizes the pyramids' nature and their wonder, he adds the old alchemical belief that they cast no shadows; a statement based partially, perhaps, upon observation: the sloping sides of the pyramids produce far less shadow for the building's size and bulk than the human eye, used to vertical buildings, usually expects (see p. 167).

As far as Christian pilgrims were concerned, however, both piety and propriety kept the pyramids' identification as Joseph's granaries, and this was even true of such inquisitive scholars as the Irish monks who came to Egypt in the eighth century and made the first survey of those wonders since the days of the ancient Greeks and Romans.

Then, after a long journey up the Nile, they saw from the distance seven granaries (seven, to match the number of years of plenty), which Saint Joseph had made, and they admired the mountain-like structures, four in one place and three in another.

As they approached the group of three granaries, they came across a lion and eight people – men and women – dead, next to the granaries. The lion had overpowered them. They had killed it with their spears and swords; for both places in which the seven granaries had been built were in the desert.

After this, we carefully inspected the three granaries and once again marvelled at their being built completely of stone from their lowest foundations to their very tops. Right at the top they have a slender point. Then the brother whom I mentioned above measured one side of one of the granaries from corner to corner and it came to four hundred paces.

Then they embarked on their boats and sailed along the river Nile as far as the entrance to the Red Sea. From that harbour over the Red Sea to the eastern land, to the path of Moses, is only a short way. The man who had measured the side of the granary wanted to go as far as the harbour where Moses and his people had entered the sea. He wanted to go not only so that he could enter the harbour but also to see the traces of the chariots of Pharaoh and the ruts that the heels had left. But the sailors did not agree. He estimated the width of the sea there to be six miles.

The journey of Brother Fidelis and 'some Irish clergy and monks who were in Jerusalem for the purpose of prayer', recorded in Dicuil's *De Mensura Orbis Terrae*, 6, 13–18 (compiled about AD 760)

In common with their predecessors, the Arab rulers of Egypt in the days of Brother Fidelis, took little practical interest in the pyramids. When they wrote about them, they were generally content to paraphrase the information of the Greek and Roman authors. The travelling monks, however, shared the common universe of most northerners of their age, a universe peopled by Bible characters and haunted by the enigmatic force of half-remembered legend. Their account of their fearful yet aggressively practical investigation of the pyramids shows the beginnings of a new and very different vision of antiquity, and a different attitude to wonder, too. For though the pyramids are never called anything but granaries in the West, and this for many centuries after Brother Fidelis' day, the response to this frightening marvel is to investigate, and even on occasion, measure. And this is the beginning of an attitude that is still within the modern world, an attitude born of a powerful mix of fantasy and preconception coupled with a desire to understand and, even, to take a part of wonder for ourselves.

Not all of Brother Fidelis' apprehensions stemmed from his fears of hell fire and damnation. After Arab armies had conquered Egypt in AD 642, it was often difficult and dangerous for Westerners to visit Joseph's granaries. Yet the memory of them flickered brightly in the Christian imagination and Joseph's distant granaries were often pictured on the walls and windows of churches. In lengthy contact with both the Arabs and the Byzantines, the merchants of Venice, especially, collected fine fragments of the ancient vanished world through which they moved and traded. Still today, as you approach that beautiful city on the sea, as your boat ties up beneath the architraves of the Piazza Grande, you can enter something of the medieval universe of wonders. Bobbing brightly between the East and West, the sights of Venice are a collection of magic things, an urban *bricolage* of Eastern wonders.

Set high upon its ancient column in the grand piazza, even St Mark's great lion is a Hellenistic sculpture, one made in the epoch of the Seven Wonders and probably removed from a great funeral monument like the Mausoleum. Maybe it once had the statue of the Mother Goddess standing on its back, just as it appeared sometimes in ancient Anatolia, and in Artemis' great temple too, far away in Ephesus in Asia Minor. Today, in many Italian churches, you can see that ancient sacred lady, transposed now into the Holy Virgin, still standing on a lion.

Standing beside St Mark's great church are further wonders carried from the East; columns of Egyptian porphyry, like those, it was said, that stood by Solomon's great temple, which in medieval lists of wonders sometimes replaces the image of Artemis' great monument at Ephesus. And there are other columns too: brilliantly wrought marbles brought from Byzantium, wonderful works, measured and collected by the plundering crusaders whose army had been taken to that ancient city by the fleet of Venice, and had devastated the Byzantine Empire in 1204 during the Fourth Crusade. The four bronze horses on St Mark's façade were also from the plunder of Byzantium. Along with the bronze lion of St Mark standing on its column top, these, too, once formed part of a larger Hellenistic monument, one from the age of the Seven Wonders. Originally these four horses formed part of a quadriga, a statue group of a chariot similar to the marble sculpture that had topped the Mausoleum. Venetian sailors had even tried to remove Pheidias' great marble horses from the Parthenon sculptures but their ships' ropes had snapped and sent the sculptures tumbling to the ground – a loss that later proved Lord Elgin's gain.

The gilded equine bronzes of St Mark's possibly also reminded the Venetians of another legendary ancient wonder – a statue of Alexander's horse Bucephalus which reportedly had once hung in the air over Smyrna, suspended by giant magnets. Alexander himself, the king of wonders, is also carved upon the side of St Mark's. He is shown flying up to heaven in a basket carried by four eagles. In medieval times, the stories of the great king's explorations had not stopped at India, and extended into fantasy.

Inside St Mark's, the mosaic images of Christ still echo Pheidias' ivory statue of great Zeus, which had stood in similar darkness at Olympia. And there, in a little half-round dome, is another of Philo's wonders: a marvellous mosaic of Joseph's granaries, a row of pointed pyramids standing in a golden desert. All around the pyramids people set up sheaves of wheat as provision against the Bible's famine. There is the Pharos, too, drawn out in golden tesserae on the arch of a small vault. The great lighthouse of Alexandria, its three stages accurately recorded by artists who could well have seen the antique original, is depicted as the prized possession of its later Arab harbour masters; all carefully maintained, with a small mosque upon its top. In the mosaic, a sailing boat brings the Apostle Mark to the city of his legendary martyrdom (see p. 54).

Amongst the sights of Venice, then, are a collection of ancient marvels, half-remembered memories of wonder culled from the Bible and from the distant, dangerous East. There are no Babylonian walls, nor Hanging Gardens, but outside the great cathedral is another half-memory of Alexandria. Set between the church and the quay, the huge brick campanile holds within it echoes of the Pharos, the ancient lighthouse past which the relics of St Mark sailed on their way to Venice from Alexandria, when, some eight centuries after Christ, the city's patron saint was smuggled away to grace the watery city. This trip was elegantly reversed within the last two decades, when an ecumenical Pope returned some of the ancient bones, escorted by a squadron of the Italian navy. At Venice, the remaining relics of the saint are still carried past that great brick tower each time they appear in procession. Venice, then, appears as another Alexandria, rich in gold and wisdom, in ships and spears, proud and learned, and filled with as many wonders as its medieval memory can hold.

At the fortress given the name of Pharma is the beginning of Egypt. And about two days journey to the west is Tamiathin, a great fortress which was the place of Christ's exile. Four days journey to the west of it, is the city of Alexandria. There lies buried Saint Mark the Apostle and Evangelist, Athanasius the Great, Saint Troilus, and Saint John the Eleimon and Saint Peter, the last of the Martyrs, Apollinarius the Orthodox, Holy Vitalios and the five Virgins who proved to be like the five Wise Virgins.

And at the harbour of Alexandria stands the tower called Pharos, the first wonder: it is jointed with lead and glass and is 300 rods high. And to the west of Alexandria, about nine miles away, lies buried holy Menas. Another nine miles further on lies Saint Theodora who changed her name to Theodore, who was also condemned. And to the south of Alexandria, six days' journey, lies buried Saint Macarius the Great, who came near to Paradise: that monastery contains a thousand fathers and a thousand cells, and it is a solitary fort.

About four days on from Saint Macarius are the Granaries of Joseph, thirty-six of them. And from the things there you cross the River Phison on a bridge supported by eighty boats. From there one enters Babylon the Great and the Palace of Pharaoh. And to the east of Babylon, about six miles away, lies buried Saint Arsenius the Great. Four days to the east of him lies Saint Antony . . .

from the *Pilgrimage of Epiphanius the Monk* an eighth to tenth-century compilation of journeys to the Holy Land

WONDER AND THE WEST

For most people living in the European Dark Ages, richness, plenty, wonder and the Bible lands were all a long way off. Isolated from the East by the Arab invasions of the sixth and seventh centuries, disconnected from Byzantium and the heritage of classical culture by the schism between Eastern and Western Christendom, the very idea of wonder changed, not only shifting nearer to the Bible's word, but also moving into landscapes nearer home as well. The records of the long, dark centuries that followed the dissolution of classical civilization in the West are scarce and often unreliable. Yet even when all knowledge of Philo's ancient list in faraway Byzantium seems to have gone, the path of wonder, the abstract notion of a list of seven ancient monuments, can still be traced within the mind of Western Europe. Indeed, the idea that there were also other wonders in the world, and some of them not man-made but natural, already occurs in the last centuries of classical civilization. In third-century Provence, Julius Titianus, the teacher of the children of the ill-fated soldier-emperor Maximian, listed four Sicilian volcanoes as wonders, whilst another schoolteacher, Lactantius, who taught some of the emperor Constantine's numerous offspring, wrote of the wonder of the phoenix, a mythical bird who regularly made a funeral pyre of fire and rose up Christ-like from its ashes. St Hilary of Poitiers too, who had studied and travelled in the distant East and knew his Greek, tells us of a hot spring at cold and mountainous Grenoble that seemed to him to be a real wonder. And who, sitting in his draughty Bishop's palace, could ever have disagreed with him?

So even without the benefits of Eastern libraries or Philo's list, some Western writers had taken to writing out their own ideas of wonder in lists quite unlike that of Philo's yet still shaped in that magic number seven. Seven, the number of days in the Babylonian weekly calendar, somehow retained a special place in Christianity. In the following centuries there were found to be Seven Deadly Sins, Seven Virtues, Seven Works of Mercy, Seven Sacraments, Seven Holy Deacons of the Church, Seven Gifts sent from the Holy Ghost. The Virgin too bore Seven Sorrows in her life, and the Last Words spoken from the Cross, were seven in their number.

These, then, are the Seven Wonders of the World according to St Gregory, Bishop of Tours, who listed them in the second half of the sixth century, the next known list of Wonders from western Europe: the Hanging Gardens, the Pharos and the Colossus, the Mausoleum, King Solomon's Temple, the Capitol at Rome and a Theatre at Heracleia that was formed, so it was said, of a single block of stone.

Four of Philo's Wonders still feature in Gregory's list. As for the others, the legendary theatre at Heracleia today has no known pedigree, whilst the Capitol of Rome is clearly a pious nod towards the centre of Western Christendom, just as the inclusion of Solomon's Biblical Temple is another nod towards the Bible. By this time, the centuries-old device of calling pyramids granaries, has had the effect of excluding them entirely from the list, while, for the first time, the Pharos of Alexandria is named as a Wonder. This, perhaps, is because it was the only ancient monument of any real size regularly seen by Western travellers to the ancient lands of the Middle East.

A fine list, yet, Gregory comments in his essay, all these wonders are merely monuments made by human hands and are therefore subject to decay. True wonders, our saint observes, are those that 'destruction cannot touch, the Wonders that God himself has given to the world'. And they are seven also, but of a different pedigree to those of Philo: 'the first being the daily movement of the ocean sea', the sun and moon, the germination of plants and seeds, the mystic phoenix, a Sicilian volcano and St Hilary's warm fountain at Grenoble, 'from which flow fire and water in alternation'. In true Gothic fashion later scholars took Gregory's speculations and fashioned them into elegant formal lists, a symmetrical analysis of the elements and humours that governed God's creation, all carefully crossed with the account of the Creation in the book of Genesis.

Before these works of scholarship, however, another Dark Age scholar wrote out a widely influential list of ancient wonders; he was the Venerable Bede, working in his scriptorium at Jarrow Monastery in the north of England. Bede was a seventh century polymath, and the library he used at Jarrow was sufficiently stocked with books obtained by way of the Roman trips of his Bishop, Ceolfrid, to enable the scholar-monk to write works of tremendous value and significance for the Western European monasteries of the day.

> I beg you to copy and send me some of the treatises from the works of the scholar Bede whom divine grace has recently endowed with spiritual understanding, so we hear, and has allowed to shine in your country, and whom we too enjoy like a candle, which the Lord has generously conferred on you . . . I beg you to acquire and be good enough to send us any of the books that the elder, Bede of blessed memory, wrote to console us in our exile . . . Perhaps I demand a lot, but I do not ask a great deal for true affection.

So runs a series of letters written in the latter half of the eighth century by the archbishops of Mainz, attempting to obtain copies of Bede's work from English churchmen. And the Bishops of Jarrow of the generations that succeeded Bede coped as best they could, for working conditions at Jarrow were wretched, with Viking raids, bad living conditions, plagues and illnesses sometimes sending the community's numbers down into single figures.

> Now indeed, since you asked for something from the works of the blessed father, I together with my boys have prepared, as far as strength allowed, what I could for your enjoyment . . . I would gladly have done more if I could have. Because the weather last winter most cruelly oppressed our people's island with cold, ice, and persistent and widespread gales and storms, our scribe's hand was delayed from completing most of the books . . . But with respect to the minor works of Bede of blessed memory, of which you still do not have copies, I promise that I will help you in your request, if we survive.

Such were the rigours of Dark Age scholarship. None the less, in a halting procession of leather-bound vellum tomes packed and tied to the backs of mules, Bede's works were sent down through northern Europe to the Alps, and then beyond. The tomes included, in all probability, his pretty list of the Seven Wonders of the World, part of a brief treatise on the beginning of human history, revised and later edited by other scholars. Famous throughout Western Europe, with his writings greatly in demand in the learned communities of the monasteries, Bede's list of wonders was of greater influence than that of Gregory, whose text the Northumbrian monk clearly had at his disposal in his library.

Bede based his Seven Wonders on the books at Jarrow. Amongst many other important ancient texts of Saint Augustine, Ambrose and Jerome, the library also contained a copy of Vitruvius' manual on building and construction in which, although the Seven Wonders of the World are mentioned as a group of monuments, as they are in some of the writings of the saints, the constituents of Philo's list are not all individually named. Vitruvius of course assumed that his ancient audience would have known what the Seven Wonders were. Bede, however, living in another time and place, did not have such information. He proceeds, therefore, by listing those wonders that Vitruvius does name and makes up the remainder of the list himself, usually by copying those wonders already nominated by St Gregory of Tours a century earlier. Unlike Gregory, Bede did not include the Hanging Gardens in his list – perhaps the venerable monk could not bring himself to believe that sinful Babylonia, which he knew only through the words of the Bible, could have made and housed a Wonder of the World. He did, however, include Gregory's mysterious nomination of the Theatre at Heracleia. He seems also to have used an unknown source for he nominated, for some now-unaccountable reason, the statue of Alexander's horse which hovered magnetically in the air above the ancient city of Smyrna. Bede also lists, again from an unknown source, another distant Eastern wonder, the 'Baths of Tyana', presumably a mirage of a great classical bathing hall whose ingenious design, so it was later said, permitted its waters to be boiled by a single candle. At any rate, no one would want to deny this most comfortable wonder to Bede and his frozen-fingered monks working in the cold, damp northern winters, though one must notice with the slightest smile the esteem in which these pious men still held the clever pagan empires that had gone before them.

Quite possibly these two last, extraordinarily abstruse, wonders on Bede's list were extracted from another now-lost text. Alternatively they may have arrived at Jarrow by word of mouth, brought perhaps by some visitors from Rome, who, it is recorded, had been sent to the distant monastery to teach the English monks the proper order of a Roman service. A yet more intriguing possibility is that Bede and his monks learned of those Eastern *mirabilia* from the tales of a Byzantine Greek. Judging by the few illustrations that have survived from Bede's scriptorium, at least one Greek-educated artist seems to have worked at Jarrow, illustrating the vast bibles that the monks produced.

Underlining the direct connection with Gregory's earlier Wonder list, Bede also places the Pharos in his list of seven and so further stresses the new significance of the tantalizing tower, still standing at that time in distant Arab Alexandria and memorialized in a dozen pilgrim stories. This innovation took root in Bede's time: today, the Pharos is the only one of our modern list of Seven Wonders not to appear in any of the ancient Greek or Roman lists. Philo had filled his list of seven magic monuments by including the fabled walls of Babylon beside the Hanging Gardens of that same city as a separate wonder in its own right (see appendix).

Bound with texts of Isadore and Aristotle and the Fathers of the Church, the Wonder lists of Gregory and Bede became part of a grand tradition of wisdom that persisted in the West for centuries. At the Gothic schools of Chartres and Paris, there remain from the 12th century alone, almost a dozen examples of these Wonder lists, bound together with catalogues of miracles and travellers' tales of journeys to Rome and Jerusalem. By this time, though, the Seven Wonders had become as fantastic as the illuminations on the manuscripts, marvellous mixed images of fact and fiction which, subsequently, the pellucid texts of Greece and Rome and the later works of the scholars of the Renaissance would completely replace. Throughout the Gothic centuries, however, there flourished images of an ancient wonder world furnished with a dozen different tombs in which, in magic splendour, Etruscan kings and Persian emperors were laid. Monuments too, that Semiramis, and the Queen of Babylon, and Mausolus' sister, Artemisia, commissioned to be made, along with Solomon himself and Joseph, Daedalus, Ctesiphon and Hiram, king of Tyre. In this magic world, Solomon's Temple is piously confused with Artemis' great pile at Ephesus, the Pyramids become the Ark of Noah, and Pheidias' great idol of immortal Zeus is utterly abandoned.

Both Gregory and Bede, however, included the monuments of pagan Rome upon their lists, so acknowledging the sacred supremacy of the ancient city in the Northern church, a supremacy first promulgated by the ancient Caesars. Similarly, the ancient Romans had already begun to move the Seven Wonders to the West; an epigram of the poet Martial boasts that the wonders held in his beloved Rome were far greater than those a foreigner could build. In these later lists, Rome herself, the entire city, is sometimes counted as a wonder; as are individual monuments, especially the square of the Capitoline, the centre of the medieval city.

In the days of Gregory and Bede, however, the stark reality was that the once-grand Imperium of Rome had become an impoverished ruin divided by warring tribes of noblemen living in fortresses made from the ancient stones of the vanished city. Abandoned by its emperors in the fourth century, Rome took a thousand years to recover something of its former splendour. Yet the Popes of this dilapidated ruin were still counted as major figures in the church, the equal of the Patriarchs of Alexandria, Antioch and Constantinople. And surely too, the ghosts of wonder hung about its melancholy stones. To claim, as Christians often did, that all the ancient gods had been destroyed, was merely boasting, shouting in the dark. The temples had indeed been closed and sacked and burnt, their priests were gone as well, the sacred statues of the gods and goddesses carried off to Constantinople or the limekilns. But the gods themselves still stood inside most people's consciousness. The signs of the zodiac, the magic numbers, seven high amongst them, were still all known and their magic well appreciated. Despite the efforts of the church to displace the ancient signs and relics with stories from the Bible, texts such as Egeria's, which stressed Christian learning at the exclusion of all pagan thinking, remained a careful, rather self-conscious, exercise in piety. Neither the vengeful Christian emperors nor the prayers and deeds of pious monks and pilgrims had wholly changed the way that people felt and thought. The humours and temperaments of the ancient world were still the sensitivities of daily life. The very names of the ancient gods marked the daily calendar, the planets and the constellations still controlled people's lives. Even the churches were set in alignment with the heavens, and the priests celebrated the sacred offices around the year in concert with the sun and moon. Each ancient city had its pagan protectors too, its founders and its ancient heroes, all of them part of that permanent starry universe, that visible eternal world of endless certainty that was as inviolable as the ancient pyramids.

At Rome, the pagan past had part-fused with the holy city of the Popes. To northerners, Rome seemed filled with wonders. It became a city of the saints, a new Jerusalem, the earthly city of the Lord of Heaven. Pilgrim maps show the growth of this mythical city, the *Urbs Mirabilis*. The sides of the first encampment at the site of Rome were said to be set facing the sea and the mountains, and were bounded by an iron fence. At its centre, they said, stood the Capitol 'once the head of all the world, where the consuls and senators abode to govern the earth. Its face was covered with high walls and very strong, rising high above the top of the hill and covered with glass and marvellous carved works': thus the unknown author of the *Mirabilia Romae*, Roman Wonders, addresses the pilgrims to his city. Just as there were Seven Seas and Seven Virtues, Rome had seven hills. And like ancient Babylon had been, Rome was thought to have been built according to cosmological criteria, in astronomically significant numbers, its walls shaped in the image of Leo, the zodiacal lion. Now Rome, not Babylon, was filled with stars and zodiacs, a magic city surrounded by a wall of iron, with seven hills standing for each of the six days of creation, and one for the Creator's rest. And there were three hundred and sixty-five squares at Rome, three hundred and sixty-five streets, three hundred and sixty-five palaces for the popes, and each palace had three hundred and sixty-five steps, and each step was covered with bread enough to feed the world. It was, needless to say, a dream of poor people imagining a legendary past of endless wealth and wonder.

Fragments of wonder were scattered through the ancient wreckage of the city: colossal statues of stone and bronze, with distant echoes of Rhodian colossi and the gods of Greece and Rome. Egyptian obelisks brought to the city by the Caesars and left standing in rock-strewn fields were considered to be pyramids. Two tombs of noble families, private Roman funerary monuments made in imitation of Egypt's distant tombs, were thought to be the sepulchres of Rome's twin founders. The halfway point between the Pyramid of Romulus near the Vatican and the Pyramid of Remus was thought to mark the holy spot where St Peter had been crucified, set upside down at his request, so as not to imitate the pose of Christ. Along with pyramids and saints and martyrs, Rome also had its Mausoleums and its Hanging Gardens. The tomb of the Emperor Hadrian, the Castel San' Angelo as it is known today, had been called the 'Mausoleum' from the time of its building. Along with the similar if smaller monument of the Emperor Augustus across the River Tiber, these two great terraced tombs planted with trees were seen as hanging gardens. In the Renaissance, smaller imitations of them would be built as garden decorations, little Hanging Gardens made for cardinals. Gregory, Bede and their successors had moved the Seven Wonders to the West, and Rome, as much as Babylon or the Egyptian desert, now become the landscape of the dream.

A RENAISSANCE OF WONDER

One evening, late in November 1507, Pope Julius II declared that he could no longer abide the sight of his fearful predecessor Pope Alexander VI peering at him from a portrait frescoed on the wall of his private study in the Vatican at Rome. He ordered his entourage to move into temporary quarters on a higher floor. Decorators and painters were engaged to renovate the papal apartments and the celebrated 25-year-old artist Raphael was commissioned to decorate the three rooms that ran off the pope's bedroom: an audience chamber, a separate reception hall and the pope's own library. The paintings that he made changed the face of European art.

Raphael started in the library, more properly Julius' *studiolo*, or little study. One of the windows in this room opened on to a fine view of a hill, which Julius would have seen when he sat at his desk. In ancient times this hill had been sacred to Apollo. Raphael drew a mountain top above the window and decorated it with a gathering of gods and artists, everyone from Homer to Dante, all seated on Mount Parnassus listening to Apollo playing a contemporary violin, a small detail that announced one of Raphael's most novel intentions for this work. For Raphael took the familiar gothic schemes that were traditionally placed in such important apartments and filled them with a vivid contemporary air and a wonderful liveliness of painting. On the rear walls of the room, above the papal book shelves, he painted a semicircle of figures that could well have been placed by a sculptor or mosaic artist of ancient times: a depiction of the fathers of the church earnestly disputing its central mysteries. On the lower levels of the scene, however, Raphael added contemporary figures, popes and cardinals and the ubiquitous Dante, painted in a beautifully fresh manner that, in its day, before a thousand imitations had been made, would have seemed startlingly new and quite extraordinary. On the facing wall, Raphael reconstructed in magnificent detail the enormous cavern of the ancient Roman baths, whose ruins so intrigued him in his frequent walks through Rome. In these baths, though, perhaps the first true glimpse of grand antiquity since ancient times, Aristotle walks with Leonardo da Vinci, the young sons of Raphael's patrons listen attentively to Ptolemy and Euclid, and even Raphael himself peeps out proudly from the wall, confident of his position in the extraordinary company he has assembled.

While Raphael decorated the pope's rooms, Michelangelo was painting in the Sistine Chapel and close by, under the direction of Bramante, the new St Peter's, with scaffolds in its nave, was slowly rising. The city, too, was gradually filling with scores of brand-new palaces and churches. Julius had assembled one of the greatest gatherings of Western artists that the world would ever see. At the pope's urging, Raphael and his contemporaries, using the city's venerable images, were bringing ancient wonder back to life in

Rome; all the ghosts and wonders of the ancient capital assembled to serve in a grandiose re-enthronement of Rome as Christendom's mother city. After centuries of poverty and papal exile, Julius set the great ghosts of the past walking through a reborn Rome.

In this brave new world, the notion of recreating ancient wonder played a major role. Inspired by the stories of Vitruvius, Lysippus and all those ancient wonder-makers who designed the Mausoleum and planned ancient Alexandria and the other ancient mythical monuments, Michelangelo, Raphael, Bramante and their followers were building in the ruins of a fabled past. And now it seemed as if the sheer size of those ancient fragments was serving to put them on their mettle, to enlarge their vision, and allow them to compete with the ancient monuments. Though few of these great artists ever referred directly to the seven ancient wonders, their distant images formed part of the air they breathed, part of that astonishing renaissance, that grasping for heroic scale, the redrawing of humanity that made the shape of modern man.

With the passing years, architecture, the grandest and most public of the visual arts, became the focus of Raphael's attentions and he came to realize that the physical ruins of the great old city, the fount of the designs for this extraordinary papal propaganda, were the keys to the grand new world that was being made in Rome. He became concerned for the still largely unconsidered ruins and spent increasing time upon their study and their measurement and also, finally, on their preservation. At the same time, whilst succeeding popes and their cardinals were quarrying the ancient monuments for stone for their churches and palaces, they too came to share something of Raphael's passion for the ruins of the ancient city.

In 1514, Pope Julius' successor, Leo X, also turned his attention to conservation, requesting Raphael to prepare a report for him upon the standing monuments of Rome, the first modern attempt at the conservation of the Western past. Leo had already procured the services of diverse architects who were working at St Peter's to make measured drawings of many ancient stones and monuments. Now Raphael engaged various friends, amongst them some celebrated writers, to help in the work. 'Consider the divinity of the antique spirit,' they advised Pope Leo. 'Look at the near-corpse of this noble city, mother and queen of the world, so piteously mangled . . . how many Pontiffs have allowed the ruin and defacement of ancient temples, statues, arches, and other buildings, the glory of their founders! How many have suffered their foundations to be undermined for the mere sake of quarrying *pozzolana*, whereby in a short time the buildings themselves have fallen to earth. How much lime has been made of statues and other antique decorations! I should not hesitate to say that the whole of this new Rome which now meets the eye, great as it is, and fair, and beautified with palaces and churches and other buildings, has been cemented with lime made from antique marbles.' They mourned especially the continued mining of the ruins for their multicoloured granites and marbles, stones the ancient empire had gathered in the city at such vast cost to the subjects of their empire, and they also mourned the demolition, as part of a papal scheme of road enlargement, of the little pyramid close to the Vatican, long held as the legendary tomb of Romulus, a founder of the city.

In reply, the pope decreed that henceforth no one should remove from the ruins stones with ancient inscriptions cut upon them and instituted heavy fines for breaking the new ordinance. After centuries of neglect and savage superstition, scholars and artists were now caring for the ancient stones again. Up to the last weeks of his short life, Raphael enthusiastically continued the papal survey of the city, walking through its varied quarters observing the tumbled ruins with his friends, and sketching all the while, envisaging a vast project to rebuild the ancient city. Then, suddenly and unexpectedly in 1520, at the age of 37, he died and was buried by a grief-stricken pope, in a tomb built in the ancient Roman temple of the Pantheon, surrounded by the finest ancient marbles.

Without its champion, Raphael's gallant project died with him. One man, though, who had been caught up in its excitement, eventually saved something of the dream – an elderly professor from the northern city of Ravenna, who specialized in the translation of Greek medical texts and the teaching of geometry, one Marco Fabio Calvo. When Raphael painted his tremendous image of ancient philosophers mingling ghost-like with his patrons and his friends, it was said that he had painted Calvo as the Greek Diogenes, a visual counterpoint to the brooding Michelangelo, the two men seated on a flight of steps, both occupied in solemn musing. Raphael had invited Calvo, his elder by close on half a century, to come to Rome to live in his great palace workshop and help him in his study of Vitruvius, that ancient architect whose treatise meant so much to the high Renaissance. So Calvo had gone to Rome, and sat with Raphael and his books; today their cribs are still preserved for us, with the young artist's notes written in their margins. In the first flush of dismay at Raphael's death, the 83-year-old Calvo had gone home to Ravenna, but he could not forget their work together and returning to Rome he occupied himself with a great plan of the ancient city, a simpler realization of what, in the hands of Raphael, would have been a marvellous vision filled with ancient wonders. Housed now in a hovel in a poor quarter of the city, living on a pension from a cardinal and renowned as much for his waspish stoicism as for his written works, old Calvo became an important part of Roman intellectual life. Now he was nicknamed Diogenes, after the philosopher who lived inside a barrel and had told King Alexander to get out of his way. Following the advice of Galen and the other ancient doctors whose works he had translated, Calvo lived, so it was said, on beans, and gave most of the cardinal's stipend to his neighbours. Now, old Calvo carefully considered the ancient Seven Wonders of the World. Not, however, in the manner of someone thrilled with the information as though it were new, but as a schoolteacher might repeat the list for the information of his pupils:

> The Seven miracles are these: the Temple of Diana at Ephesus, another in Cyzicus, and also the Sepulchre of Mausolus in Caria, and the Colossus of the Sun in Rhodes, and the Capitol at Rome another, the theatre of Heraclea in Pontus, the pyramids of Egypt, the walls of Semiramis in Babylonia, the monuments of Thebes of a hundred gates in Egypt.

He includes however, some brand-new wonders. By this time, the phrase the 'Seven Wonders' had itself become a kind of title for a gathering of wondrous things – Calvo lists at least nine 'Seven Wonders' without so much as pausing to notice the contradiction. Five of them came from the ancient list of Philo of Byzantium; two, the theatre at Heracleia and the Capitol of Rome, from the list of Bede, whilst the remainder, a temple at the town of Cyzicus, and the monuments of Thebes in Egypt, also appear on near-contemporary Byzantine wonder lists, and probably originated from a now unidentifiable Eastern source. On the whole, Calvo gives us a conservative gathering of largely unseen wonders, a list, however, of practical possibilities. There are no magic flying horses here, nor impossible feats of hot-water plumbing, but things that could be made anew, just as the great nave of new St Peter's was rising up again to the accompaniment of calculations that listed the ancient monuments whose size it would surpass. Calvo's ancient wonders, then, were wonders that could improved upon.

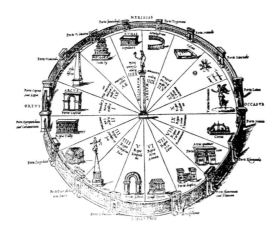

Fabio Calvo's schematic map of ancient Rome, *urbs quatuordecim regionum*, from the *Simulachrum*, Rome, 1527

In April 1527, when in his nineties, Calvo published a large folio volume *Antiquae urbis Romae cum regionibus Simulachrum*, containing 24 maps of ancient Rome all laid out schematically, a pale shadow of Raphael's original plans. Like alchemical Alexandria, Calvo's Rome was focused on a single central point, a pyramid, an obelisk in fact, of vast proportions that governed the size of each and every quarter of the city. All the city's measurements were made of sacred numbers, and, like the admonitions of Vitruvius and the Greek doctors, were set to accommodate favourable winds. Each of its sixteen quarters had its gate, and each its symbolic building: pyramids, obelisks, hanging gardens, mausolea, whose measurements were culled from surveys of the ruins. Some of these surveys, though, still dealt in legends. Medieval pilgrims, for example, had thought that Noah had sailed the Ark to Rome and beached it at the centre of the Roman forum. There, as everybody knew, stood the ruins of an Ark, a Roman arch: ARCA NERVAE, an inscription spelled. To the pilgrims this was clearly Noah's Ark. The Bible says the Ark was built under divine command and to exact sizes and proportions, and carried all earthly life within it. When Raphael and Calvo and their friends walked through Rome and measured up its monuments, as they drew a tape over the venerable *Arca Noè*, they measured more than ancient monuments.

Calvo's book and maps eventually went into several editions and had tremendous influence upon all later plans of Rome and the history of the Seven Wonders, too. Printing played a major role in this history, by diffusing knowledge of the ancient wonder lists and in pictorial form showing Western Christendom something of the scale and nature of the rebirth of ancient architecture. Even before young Raphael arrived in Rome in 1508, over 5,000 printed books were already in circulation throughout Italy, many of them translations of ancient texts. Vitruvius' manual, *De architectura*, was very popular, the first edition being printed in Rome itself in 1488. In Raphael's time, a Roman cardinal subsidized a society especially for the study of Vitruvius' manual; the study that is, not of its practical concerns, of materials and techniques, but of its system of mathematics, of harmonies and proportions and ratio, which in their closed perfection and absolute abstraction seemed to many people of the age to contain something of the nature of the universe, something of the trace of God, just like the *Arca Noè*. Raphael himself had used one of these early editions, compiled by a friend, in his studies with Fabio Calvo. For the first time, ancient wisdom was available to anyone with cash enough to buy a book.

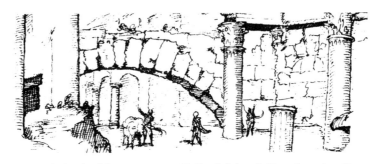

Heemskerck's sketch of the Roman *Arca Noè* buried deep in Nerva's ancient Forum.
A detail from his Roman sketchbooks, *c.* 1535

Prompted by Vitruvius' frequent mention of the Seven Wonders of the World, several of these early editions produced footnoted lists of wonders in their commentaries and translations, in an attempt to supply the full list that Vitruvius had not bothered to complete. Of all these speculations, by far the grandest and most influential accompanied a translation of Vitruvius first published in Como in 1521, the work of Cesare Cesariano, a pupil of Bramante. Cesariano's list of seven starts with Philo's list transmitted through the lines of the ancient Roman poet, Martial, and adds two pretty confusions at its ending, combining the classical labyrinth on Crete with the mythical tomb of an Etruscan King:

> To talk a little on the Seven Spectacles of the world: the Temple of Jove – Ammon written about by the astute poet Martial, who also recommends Domitian's Amphitheatre. The

same commentator also talks of the barbaric pyramids, and Caesar's obelisk in Rome, which no man can now raise up. Neither could they make the colossal walls and statues of Egypt and Babylonia and Greece or the other nations of the world about which we read in the clear and elegant writings of the ancient people, as well as the ruins that still fill our memories, like the Labyrinth of King Porsena.

Cesariano not only listed the Seven Wonders, but illustrated several of them too as part of a superb series of architectural woodcuts, some of which, it has been suggested, were inspired directly by Leonardo da Vinci. Cesariano's lively engraving of the Mausoleum seen, as Philo would have said, 'in his mind's eye', shows it as a great Renaissance pile, a Bramante-esque church shaped like a Greek cross, standing by the lapping sea and topped by a northern knight, a fine St George, in shining armour. It is a robust drawing, the first modern illustration of one of the Seven Wonders of the World, and just as its successors would be, entirely cast in terms of its own time. None the less, Cesariano has carefully followed the ancient descriptions of the Mausoleum. Cesariano's Mausoleum then, is a half scholarly fantasy; a monument of its age.

Martial's epigram, which so handily paraphrased Philo's ancient Wonder list, had been known to a small group of Italian scholars ever since its rediscovery in the previous century by Boccaccio, the author of the famed *Decameron*. The account of his astonishing discovery in a precious volume kept at the ancient library of the Monastery of Monte Cassino, underlines how fragile was the transmission of these ancient documents, on what slender threads the edifice of modern scholarship rests. It should also be borne in mind however that Boccaccio may have stolen some of these manuscripts and that this romantic story, told by Benvenuto Ramboli da Imola, is possibly his excuse:

I will tell you what my revered teacher, Boccaccio of Certaldo, so amusingly related. When he was in Apulia, he was attracted by the celebrity of the convent of Monte Cassino, of which Dante spoke. Wanting to see the collection of books, which he understood to be a very choice one, he gently asked a monk, for he was always most courteous in his manners, to open the library, as a favour for him. The monk answered stiffly, pointing to a steep staircase, 'Go up; it's open.' Boccaccio went up gladly, and he found that the place that held such great treasure was without a door or key. He entered, and saw grass sprouting on the windows and all the books and benches thick with dust. In his astonishment he began to open and turn the leaves of first one tome and then another, and found many different volumes of ancient and foreign works. Some of them had lost several sheets, others were snipped and pared all round the text, and mutilated in all sorts of ways. Lamenting that the toil and study of so many illustrious men should have passed into the hands of such abandoned wretches, he burst into tears and sighed. Coming to the cloister, he asked a monk why the books had been so disgracefully mangled and the monk answered that to gain a few *soldi*, they were in the habit of cutting off sheets and making psalters from them, which they sold to boys. The margins too they manufactured into charms, and sold to women. So, O man of study, go to and rack your brains; make books that you may come to this.

This manuscript of Martial's Epigrams, the one that Boccaccio rescued, was probably the principal path of transmission of Philo's ancient list of Seven Wonders during the exciting period when Rome was rising up again.

> May foreign Memphis keep quiet about the miracles of her pyramids. Let not Assyrian toil boast of its Babylon. Let not the soft Ionians be praised for their temple. May the altar of many horns keep its Delos a secret. Let not the Carians unrestrainedly praise to the sky the Mausoleum, hanging in mid-air. All toil yields to the Amphitheatre of Caesar. History shall speak of this one work, not the rest.
>
> At the place where the celestial Colossus sees the stars from a closer vantage point, and where high scaffolds rise up in the middle of the road, the loathsome palace of a fierce king used to shine.
>
> Martial, late first century AD, *Epigrams* 1; 2, 1–4

No one now knows why Martial added the many-horned altars of the isle of Delos to Philo's list; clearly it had been his pride in Rome that led him to praise the Colosseum by belittling the Seven Wonders, and in so doing inadvertently preserving the myth that the colossal statue of Helios which had stood beside the giant amphitheatre, was none other than the Rhodian Colossus itself, brought to Rome. In the 15th century, the old story led to the christening of this great amphitheatre itself as the Colosseum, in honour of the lost Colossus. Martial's rediscovered praise of the Colosseum had a further effect upon the wonder lists, for Renaissance antiquarians had long since realized that the Capitoline was not the centre of ancient Rome, merely a medieval market place. After the discovery of Martial's poem they were happy to ignore the Venerable Bede's listing of that piazza as one of the Seven Wonders, and replace it with the Colosseum, the most impressive fragment of antiquity remaining in the city.

Not only were Western antiquaries digging deep into Europe's ancient libraries, but for a century or so, they had also been travelling through the Mediterranean lands, writing, drawing and sometimes even measuring the ancient monuments themselves. In 1436 the pyramids of Egypt were visited by Ciriaco Pizzicolli, or Cyriacus of Ancona as he is known. Cyriacus who once said he visited such things to 'wake the dead', is the first Westerner of whom we know, who refers to pyramids as pyramids, rather than that age-old genuflexion, the 'Granaries of Joseph'.

> At last [came] what I had longed for, the *raison d'être* of our journey over such a wide river – to see the marvels of the pyramids at Memphis . . . On the fifth of September we arrived at the pyramids themselves, and when I saw the spectacular size of the structures from a distance, I thought that they outdid all other antiquities . . . For they were so huge that I would never have believed that man could raise on the earth a work of such size. The length of any side at the widest was almost 400 yards, and its height 2,000 yards. We saw the sides rising up to a point at the top, in the shape of a pyramid. At the very top we

observed a very old epigram in Phoenician characters, a language indecipherable to men nowadays.

Cyriacus, (1391–1452), *Commentaria Rerum Antiquarum*, Iter Aegypticum 3–20

Cyriacus was especially interested in the seven ancient Wonders. Around 1435, he annotated and part-copied a Greek wonder list, that of Gregory of Nazianzus, for the amusement of the Bishop of Padua. The text was carefully placed in the Bishop's library, bound with a copy of a text of the ancient geographer Pomponius Mela. Cyriacus was a famous traveller in his day and his notebooks were widely circulated during the following century. His list of wonders, then, was probably known to Fabio Calvo, who, like Cyriacus, not only includes the monuments of Egyptian Thebes in his list, but the Temple of Cyzicus as well. At this time, no one in the West except Cyriacus and his sailors had ever seen or heard of Cyzicus; today, indeed, this vast forgotten Roman temple, built by Hadrian to the south of Byzantium on the Proconnesus, is still a low mound of rubble waiting to be excavated. When Cyriacus visited the site, however, a great part of the temple was still standing, a huge ruin not much smaller than the temple of Artemis at Ephesus. Cyriacus sketched its rows of standing columns, which at 70 feet in height exceeded even the gigantic columns at Baalbek in the Lebanon.

These, then, were the beginnings of our knowledge of the wonders of the ancient world, images inspired by Raphael and Calvo and their near-contemporaries in the belief that the ancient past would rise again within the Western mind. It was in this first enthusiasm of scholarship that the finest images of the ancient Seven Wonders were created, at that magical juncture when scientific study had begun, yet all the ancient memories and myths, the sorceries of the Dark Ages, were still alive.

In 1532 a Dutch artist, Martin van Heemskerck, a talented young man from a small town on the sand dunes by the North Sea, travelled down to Rome and was completely overwhelmed by it. Well-trained in northern studios, like most other artists of his day Martin regarded Italian painting as the best and in turn was sufficiently well regarded by the Romans to find employment, painting scenes for the decorations erected to welcome the Emperor Charles V on his great triumphal entrance to the city in 1536. The contemporary painter and publicist-biographer of his profession, Giorgio Vasari, gleefully informs us of the young Northerner's progress in the work:

Martin, who excelled in grisaille, did some battle-scenes of the greatest vigour and with fine invention, conflicts between Christians and Turks. The quickness and carefulness of Martin and his men were marvellous for they finished the work in time and never left it for they were given a continual supply of drink. They were always drunk, but warmed by the good Greek wine and the enthusiasm of work, they performed wonders.

Years later, back in his native Holland and seeing Rome again as through a golden haze, Martin produced a set of drawings of the Seven Wonders, dreams of wonder

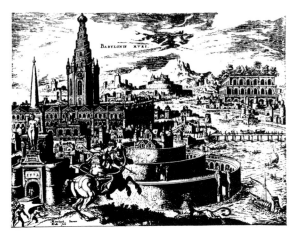

Heemskerck's *Babylonis*, with the Walls and the Hanging Gardens,
from the *Octo Mundi Miracula*, Anvers, 1572

that placed the mythic monuments inside a blend of travelogue, nostalgia and half-remembered Roman myths. So successful were the prints made from these drawings that they were famed from Italy to Sweden and were copied and recopied time and time again over the centuries. Elaborated and enlarged by other artists, painted onto pottery and porcelain, woven into fabrics and traced on countless canvasses, Martin's joyfully naive visions became the Wonders of the World that everybody knows. So computer artists working at reconstructions of the ancient wonders who wish to endow their visions with a popular validity, still utilize Martin's drawings, or those of his imitators. For Heemskerck fixed the size and scale of wonder. Taking his cue from earlier German artists, Martin viewed the Seven Wonders from the same line of sight that we still recognize today; he made the stage of wonder. Though modern archaeological techniques may recover the ancient reality of the Seven Wonders, though computer animation may resurrect them on a television screen, the stage on which all this is set is usually Martin Heemskerck's.

In many of their manifestations, Martin's wonders are peopled by great lords and nobles, half Turks, half Romans, half biblical kings like Solomon, half chivalrous ladies like Queen Artemisia, and all of them accompanied by the panoply of Roman popes out with their sons and daughters. Splendours inspired perhaps by the entourage of Holy Roman emperors like the one whose triumph Martin decorated, trotting through the Roman sunlight on caparisoned horses together with their knights and trumpeters. The wonders that these nobles visit are often filled with workmen measuring blocks and hewing statues, building an alchemy of gilded temples and great monuments – tapestries woven from facts and fictions richer than anything Hollywood has ever made, yet part of that same tradition of document and fantasy that so effectively breathes life into the past. Here is part of the beginnings of the Western imagination: Raphael's grand designs combined with clumsy northern earnestness and half-remembered texts and stories, a synthesis of myth and archaeology and grand ambition.

Does it really matter then if Martin's temple for the goddess Artemis bears strong resemblance to the house of a northern burgher, that the goddess herself sometimes looks like a Dürer *hausfrau*? Modern scholars are often dismissive of such scenes, patronizing even: 'This sixteenth century idea of the temple of Artemis bears no resemblance to the evidence of the coins, although Maerten van Heemskerck's engraving is very imaginative.' Yet Martin's images, too, have had great effect. So does it really matter that he conflates pyramids and obelisks, a common wordplay of the day, or that the angle of his pyramids is that of Remus' monument at Rome; is it important that his Egyptian desert holds an alchemical furnace in it and gold is transmuted under the eye of a mannerist pharaoh served by an heraldic eagle carrying the royal sandals in his beak?

A century after Heemskerck's death some of the finest weaving studios of Brussels used his designs as the basis for sets of enormous tapestries, wondrous golden images of the Seven ancient Wonders that, in their day, cost more than original paintings by Raphael or Titian. Such great cloths were truly an extravagance of kings, wonders of their own time. These are Martin's drawings encrusted now with Northern Gothic fantasies and a nagging preoccupation with the warring Turks (see plates 6 & 26).

Though not originally conceived by Martin, the single most abiding image of his drawings is surely the great Colossus standing astride the harbour gate at Rhodes. He took the single figure designed by Jean Cousin the Younger (see p. 27) and set it in a real Eastern harbour, with workmen quietly polishing the giant head and Chares himself standing by, looking at his drawing tablet. On the Brussels tapestry, his Rhodian harbour has been invaded by the Turks, just as Europe had been. While local people pray

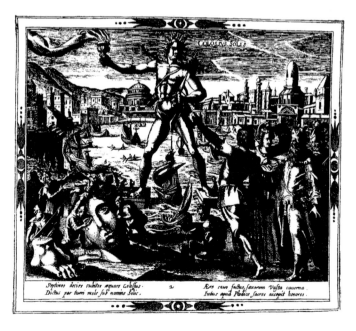

Closely following Heemskerck's work, Martin de Vos' design of the Rhodian Colossus is part of a set of Seven Wonders published in 1614. De Vos' prints were widely copied by Flemish tapestry weavers

to the Colossus for salvation, Christian galley slaves pull their great feluccas in to raid the town, and alien workmen break up the great bronze head for scrap.

Similarly, in the many tapestry images of the Temple of Artemis at Ephesus, Gothic master masons chip away at unfinished columns. There is a suitably Gothic confusion here as well, for Artemis is conflated sometimes with Jehovah, King Solomon's temple with that of Ephesus, in the same way that some Italian artists, the great Uccello and Ghiberti amongst them, employed images of those perfect geometric objects, the pyramids, for their renditions of Noah's Ark.

Interestingly enough, the imaginations of those Brussels weavers went far beyond Martin and his pictures. All around the edge of Martin's great set pieces, in little scenes set in the borders of the tapestries, there are yet more wonders of the world, and some of these derive from Bede and the Dark Ages; 'What are these seven wonders compared to those of God who moves the oceans and fructifies the earth, who sends sinners to the fiery inferno, who made the sun, the moon, the stars, the phoenix, Etna, and the hot springs of Grenoble?'

No grand visions here, but a common world of magic, the world of the Brussels weavers themselves, liberated from their grand designs, making play inside the borders. Confused with the legendary phoenix, the pelican pecks her breast to feed her young, Mount Etna spews eternal fire, and a salamander strolls unharmed – you may sin like a salamander went an ancient saying, and still live for all eternity in the fire of God's great wrath, for the animal was fireproof. The Hanging Gardens are here as well, walled northern orchards now, sheltered from the east wind. Even the hot springs of Grenoble are shown in these borders, gushing water for a grateful group of local gentlemen. First identified a thousand years before by the saintly Bishop Hilary, this specific ancient wonder was revived by a group of Renaissance humanists at Lyon who, in their turn, compiled for us the Seven Wonders of the French Dauphiné.

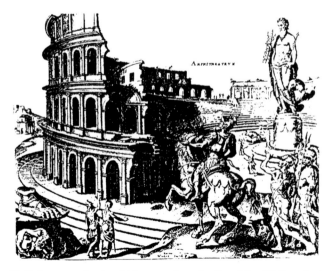

Heemskerck's Colosseum: the *Amphitheatrum* from the *Octo Mundi Miracula*, Anvers, 1572

Like Calvo, Heemskerck did not confine himself to merely Seven Wonders; Rome's own Colosseum is his last, the eighth, the only one of all of them the northerner had seen. A Latin text beneath the print tells us that the poet Martial first added this immortal monument to the list (see p. 204), and though Heemskerck still calls it the Amphitheatrum, he stands the eponymous Colossus right at its centre. Heemskerck seems to have had especial affection for this shambling monument; a self-portrait shows him, bearded, handsome, quizzical, peering from a canvas half-filled with its crumbling terraces. In Heemskerck's day, many people still believed that the Colosseum had been a Temple of the Sun with a great gilded statue at its centre and a roof like the Pantheon under which Raphael lay, its great domed ceiling covered with the sun and moon and stars.

THE DARK ALTERNATIVE

In 1527 one of the armies of the Holy Roman Emperor, a mixture of Spanish and German mercenaries, assaulted Rome and sacked it. At the Castel San' Angelo, the fortress made from the Emperor Hadrian's antique Mausoleum, Clement VII melted down the papal regalia, paid off his soldiers and surrendered to the imperial generals. At the Vatican, in the pope's apartments, thieves drunkenly scratched Martin Luther's name in gothic script into the bright plaster of Raphael's frescoes. Aged and penniless, expelled from his Roman studio because he could not pay the occupier's head tax, wandering alone through the Campagna, Fabio Calvo died of hunger in a deserted farm house. Just three copies of his folio, his *Simulachrum* of ancient Rome, survived the burning of the Roman libraries. The great epoch of the Roman Renaissance, that astonishing, febrile mix of grandeur and perversion, was gone.

> The Ephesian walls and the ivory idol,
> Babylon, Memphis, Rhodes and Pharos,
> the most chaste sepulchre of Caria,
> are no more, even though once sublime.
> Their fleeting disposition lasts but a day
> nature transforms them,
> returns them to earth, water and air,
> as the fallen kingdoms of Porsena and Turno.
> But the edifices founded by the greatest architect,
> are unmoved by ungrateful and bitter time
> for they are not made of the four elements
> but of virtue and perfect desire,
> eternal love, angelic jasper.

This earnest musing, from a collection of devotional tracts, was composed by the Roman noble, Luca Contile, in 1560, when Rome had been restored, if not to her earlier heights then at least to a wiser and more sober city than before. Contile's poem uses his description of the Seven Wonders to point a moral. He considers how vain it was to make those seven vast edifices that time has now reduced to nothing; this, after all, is the age of the Counter-Reformation. In the second half of his poem, Contile tells us to build on the words of Christ, who builds eternity in the souls of the righteous and who has made another world for us, a palace of happiness and peace. At the Vatican, the pope's workmen were building the drum of the vast dome of St Peter's which Michelangelo now intended to serve as the greatest refuge of the faithful on this earth.

At the same time, though, successive popes were also building splendid small pavilions for their earthly repose, little pagan palaces in the gardens of the Vatican. Many Romans maintained small villas at the city's edge, where they stayed when the summer's heat inside the city was insupportable. Following the Sack of Rome, many of Rome's richest families began to build much larger villas on estates further away from the city. In the late 1550s, one of the most successful papal *condottiere* of the day, Pier Francesco Orsini, called 'Vicino', perhaps because of his close relationship with Pope Paul III, retired from Rome completely and returned to live on the family estates where he had spent his childhood and the years of his marriage, close to the village of Bomarzo. A drawing of him shows the old soldier simply dressed, clutching a heavy pair of riding gloves; he looks older than his years and like Michelangelo, is broken-nosed. He walked, so we are told, with a pronounced limp. When he was young, Orsini had planned to make changes at Bomarzo, especially to the great high castle that loomed over the village. His wife Giulia, who died whilst he was away fighting for the pope, had supervised some Roman architects, building new churches in the village and fitting fine Renaissance balconies and new apartments in amongst the castle's battlements and vaults. Now, between this castle filled with memories and the hills of the surrounding landscape, Orsini transformed the traditional image of the Seven Wonders, changing those most admirable icons of ancient splendour to images yet more pessimistic than those of Contile's pale sonnet. In the gullies of Bomarzo, in the long shadow of the castle, the Seven Wonders came to fill a wood with arcane footnotes, paradox and terror.

On two wide terraces overlooking the great green gorge, Vicino Orsini had three inscriptions carved out in spidery roman letters: EDE, BIBE, ET LUDE: POST MORTERA NULLA VOLUPTAS (eat, drink and be merry, after death, no pleasure); SPERNE TERRESTRIAL: POST MORTERA VERA VOLUPTAS (spurn the world, after death, true pleasure); and, halfway between the two, MEDIUM RENUERE BEATI (blessed are they who hold the middle way).

Such dissonances, such riddles, were part of the stuff of contemporary conversation. A popular motto, one adopted by poor Pope Clement, indeed, was *Festina Lente,* 'hurry slowly', two words often accompanied by images of a tortoise and a butterfly. In similar vein, soldiers like Orsini might meditate on the notion of deadly lead shot flying through the warm caressing air, whilst the lyric poet Ariosto might eulogize the soldiers of d'Este armies, once the embodiment of knightly chivalry, now engaged in mowing down their opponents from a distance using brand-new guns. Perhaps Orsini's retreat to Bomarzo was a personal response to such contemporary paradoxes, for he was a chivalrous man yet had fought in many bloody wars. In another poem, Contile gives the old heroic image of ancient Babylon and its many wonders a twist, so that it appears like Rome before its dreadful sacking; for many people like Orsini, the grand adventure, the brave new Rome, seems also to have turned to dust. At Bomarzo at any rate, he kept his spirits up by entertaining his many friends and in undertaking a lively correspondence with a variety of cardinals and noblemen.

> You ask what I am doing . . . the harvest which, since I have no hope of selling the grain, is unpleasant . . . looking after my offspring, both he and she, both great and small . . . looking after my whores of whom, thank God, being now forty, I have more than one (for I am resolved that I want no more Roman gentlewomen, but will be content with my shepherdesses in the shade of a fine beech) . . . putting the fountains in my wood in order . . . but now that the earth has produced its flowers and done its duty, the heavens disagree and thwart everything, and I am in despair because I cannot enjoy the spring madness of my little wood.

In April 1561 Orsini wrote to Cardinal Alessandro Farnese, to whom he was related by his marriage to Giulia. The cardinal was staying nearby in his palace at Caprarola, perhaps the greatest of all these Roman summer villas.

> I spend my time down in my grove to see if I can make it appear as marvellous to you as it does to the many simpletons who come here. But that won't be possible since wonder born of ignorance cannot affect you. Well, in any case, the poor little grove, knowing that it is to receive your Eminence this summer, is doing itself up as best it can, and with this I kiss your hand.

Unlike Caprarola's magnificent formal gardens, the like of which have influenced most of the later formal gardens of the Western world, the garden grove Orsini built was unique; a shadowed wood, a dark and rocky valley lying underneath his castle filled with bizarre and broken statuary, with esoteric texts chiselled on the stones.

Not surprisingly, the sad remains of this extraordinary garden have become the happy hunting ground of cultural historians, many of them bent on finding the key to unlock Orsini's abstruse messages. Was the garden a wordplay in stone, an erudite collection of sayings and allusion scattered through a forest, or was it merely an amused sarcastic comment on the formal gardens that his neighbours were engaged in making? In a sense, the questions and their answers are irrelevant; like all good paradoxes, the wood may not be explained by spelling out its parts like answers to a crossword puzzle. Bomarzo is something like a dream, and like a dream it shows us something of the sensibility and limits of its age. Something, too, of the progress of the Seven Wonders in the modern mind. For those old familiar images haunt these gardens just as they have come to haunt most modern cities; here, though, they have become sarcastic comments upon aspiration and competition, part of the ambiguous role that history itself will play within the modern world, where history is presented as a lost ideal.

In the carved inscriptions and in the subject matter of its sculptures, erudite Orsini quotes many literary works inside this wood. The setting of all these fables, however, the mood of this dark forest, is that of a Venetian dream book the *Hypnerotomachia Poliphili*, named by its 16th-century English translator as *The Strife of Love in a Dreame*. The soul's true destiny, the *Hypnerotomachia* tells us, is the union of love and death through the sacred marriage of pleasure and pain, drastic sentiments expressed as a lovers' ecstatic journey through a dreaming forest filled with naked nymphs and sacred gardens, shattered temples and all the decorations and devices used by the artists of the day. Here, though, all this art and style is not yet glossed with the genteel varnish of scholarship, but holds the fresh excitement of a violent sexual dream. Such ghosts as these haunt our modern cities too; dreams that first found concrete form within the West in this Italian wood.

Despite the acrostic given in the first letter of each of the chapters of the *Hypnerotomachia*, POLIAM FRATER FRANCISCUS COLVMNA PERAMVIT, 'Friar Francesco Colonna desperately loved Polia', the true author of this extraordinary text is still disputed although the candidates for the honour form a splendid cast of 15th-century Venetian monks and priests. One thing though is sure, the *Hypnerotomachia* was one of the first few thousand books to be printed in Italy and enjoyed immediate and immense popularity, selling thousand upon thousands of copies in various editions and in all the languages of Europe. Its success was based on a device that would be taken up again by several later historians, especially those of the 19th century, who also breathed life into the quiet forms of classical antiquity by projecting intensely personal emotions into them. If nothing else, the *Hypnerotomachia* celebrated passion.

> . . . sitting thus together among the sweete flowers and redolent roses, I fastened mine eies upon this heavenly shape of so faire and rare a proportion, where unto my sences, were so applied, drawn and addicted, that my hart was overwhelmed with extreeme delights, so as I remained senceles, and yet cast into a curious desire to understand and know what should be the reason and cause that the purple humiditie in the touch of hir bodie, in the smoothnes of hir hand should be as white as pure milke: and by what meanes that nature had bestowed in hir faire bodie the fragrant sweetnes of Arabia. And by what industrie in hir starrie forehead, pampynulated with threds of gold aptly disposed, she had infixed the fairest part of the heavens, or the splendycant Heraclea . . . Alas most delighted Polia, at this present to die by thee is a thing that I desire, and my death if it were effected by these thy small, slender and faire hands, the ende thereof should be more tolerable, sweete and glorious unto me . . .
>
> English translation of 1592, by 'R. D.'; probably Sir Robert Dallington of the 'famous Universitie of Cambridge'

Beside its dashing text, the *Hypnerotomachia* also displayed a series of superb woodcuts that not only gave birth to the genre of European ruin painting (see p. 93), but also, by their architectural renderings of Fra. Francesco's fantasies, gave most splendid form to several of the Seven Wonders in their finest Renaissance clothing. Heemskerck, for example, knew and used this book.

The very first illustration in the *Hypnerotomachia* shows the errant friar dreaming underneath a tree: *Hypnerotomachia Poliphili*, Polias's erotic-dream-war, 'Wherein he

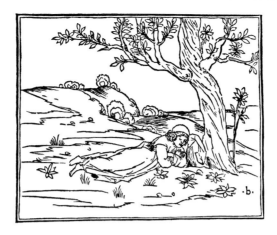

The dreaming friar, from the *Hypnerotomachia*, Venice, 1499

showeth, that all humaine and worldie things are but a dream, and but as vanitie itselfe. In the setting forth where of many things are figured worthie of remembrance.' The monk awoke unsatisfied, the text says, on May Day, 1467.

At Orsini's wood, two sphinxes guard the entrance to the path. One bears the following inscription: TV CH'ENTRI QVA PON MENTE PARTE A PARTE . . .

> You who enter here, think a little
> and tell me then, if so many marvels were
> made to trick you, or for art.
> Even he with furrowed brow and narrowed lips
> could not leave this place
> before admiring the Seven ancient Wonders of the World.

Orsini is riddling us with one of Petrarch's famous sonnets, where the 'furrowed brow and narrowed lips' are the results of unsatisfied love, as in the *Hypnerotomachia*. The garden, then, is to be the antidote of such irritations. Its entrance is a weirdly tilting building, a sort of Renaissance time lock whose twisted rooms are so unbalanced that they may produce in visitors a sense of disassociation similar to sea sickness. Walk down through its twisted halls and you enter the garden of the dream; a garden where the Seven Wonders have become a set of riddles in a sacred grove.

CHE PEL MONDO GITE ERRANDO VAGHI DI VEDER. MARAVIGLIE ALTE ET STUPENDE, VENITE QVA. DOVE SON FACCIE HORRENDE, ELEFANTI, LEONI, ORSI, ORCHI ET DRAGHI

(You who have travelled the world to see great and stupendous marvels, come here, where there are horrendous faces, elephants, lions, bears, orcs and dragons.)

All the while, Orsini stands at your elbow, his inscriptions talking to you as if you were in conversation. And there they all are indeed, just as he promises, a grove of stony monsters, a life-sized elephant at their centre, modelled so it is said, on a real elephant named Hannibal, an ominous present for the pope given by the King of Portugal. Here too amongst the dragons is a giant vase, exactly copied for some unknown reason, from an ancient original at Rome. And everywhere in the garden, there are fine strong-featured statues of majestic women, as grand as Picasso's classical nudes, though here they are at least twice as large as life. And here too a jewel-like temple, a beautiful Renaissance structure in the manner of a Roman church, built, so it is said, by Orsini as a memorial to Giulia, his wife.

Turn the path again, and you meet a travesty of wonders. SE RODI ALTIER. GIA FV SVO COLOSSO . . . 'If Rhodes took pride from its Colossus, so by this one my wood is glorified, I can do no more than I have done,' Orsini tells us in another of his gnomic texts, this one cut into a cliff beside a colossal statue group. Here the Sun God has become a madman tearing an opponent right in half (see pl. 31). Though there is still something here perhaps of the underlying fear that many people felt when they saw ancient statues, the agonized face of the splitting warrior must have been a familiar vision of Orsini's, who had conducted massacres for his popes. At all events, the old soldier shows us a darker side of valour, the paradox of war. A parody as well of ancient Rhodes and Hercules and all the tumbling heroes of that stupendous antique world that Raphael and Michelangelo worked so hard to manufacture. At the same time, however, he wishes to appear as an educated gentleman, so the mad Colossus also illustrates a passage from Ariosto's epic poem, *Orlando furioso*, that describes the madness of a perfect chivalrous knight.

Lower down in the gorge there is a small brook where, Orsini says, he liked to sit and listen to the water. Here he had some of the great grey water-worn boulders carved into yet more fantastic sculptures – a colossal tortoise marching slowly into the jaws of hell with, butterfly-like upon its back, the Roman figure of victory, that light, elusive lady stamped on thousands of ancient coins. A figure too, copied directly from the *Hypnerotomachia*, where it forms part of an elaborate and influential reconstruction of the Mausoleum. The *Hypnerotomachia* tells us that the original of this figure which topped the Mausoleum was called Occasio and made of gilded bronze. The trumpets that Occasio carried served as a wind vane and sounded as they spun. For the agonized friar, they were the cries of unfulfilled desire.

> . . . letting fall mine eies towards hir pretty feete, I beheld them inclosed in red leather cut upon white, fastened upon the instep with buttons of gold in loopes of blew silke. And from thence I returned upward my wanton regard to hir straight necke compassed about with a carkenet of orient pearle striving but not able to match with the whitenes of the sweet skin. From thence descending down to hir shining breast and delitious bosome, from whence grew two round apples such as Hercules never stole out of the garden of Hesperides. Neither did ever Pomona behold the like to these two standing unmooveable in hir roseall breast, more white than hils of snowe in the going downe of the sunne. Betwixt the which there passed downe a delicious vallie, wherein was the delicate sepulcher of my wounded hart, exceeding the famous Mausolea.

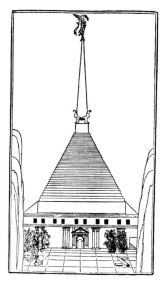

The 'Mausoleum' of the *Hypnerotomachia*, Venice, 1499

Another of the *Hypnerotomachia*'s woodcuts showed the friar and the eternally pursued Polia walking through the ruins of an ancient city in a forest. Orsini made a brand-new ruin in his wood; a ruined tomb cut from a single rock, a copy of a late Roman monument that stood beside a nearby town. In another grove, set high upon a rocky base, a great winged Pegasus, heraldic emblem of the family of Orsini's wife, suddenly appears like Bede's vision of the magnetic horse of Smyrna. Close by there is a celebrated sculpture of the medieval mouth of hell bearing Dante's now-ominous imprecation 'Abandon thought ye who enter here'. It is tall enough for you to walk through, just like a real entrance.

CEDAN ET MEMPHI ET OGNI ALTRA MARAVIGLIA . . .

Memphis and every other marvel
that the world has held in praise
all yield to the Sacro Bosco
that resembles itself and nothing else.

So boasts Orsini, but here you look in vain for Memphis' pyramids until you realize that for Orsini, as for Heemskerck and indeed, for Martial and Livy too, in ancient Rome, a 'Pyramis was a steeple in times past.' Here then, Memphis' marvels are obelisks, like those on which Orsini signed his name (see pl. 29).

At last, perhaps, at the very bottom of the garden, is hope. Here, Orsini built the Light of the World, a model of the Pharos of Alexandria, another of the Seven Wonders, standing atop the earthly globe. Orsini's world, however, is barely balanced on the monster Glaucus' head, and the dark green grove in which it stands is filled with Janus' busts of four-faced gods.

GHOSTS OF WONDER

Famous only briefly, the garden grove of Bomarzo died with Orsini when his estates passed into the hands of more orthodox landlords. The intricate theatre of ideas was soon overgrown and tumbled, the standing sculptures that remained to show where it had been were barely noticed and very little known. Local historians thought that they might be the work of ancient Etruscans; certainly, they had no role at all in that pretty aesthetic vision of 'The Renaissance' that 19th-century writers conjured so effectively and it was not until the 1950s that Orsini's gardens were rediscovered and identified. By that time most of the pathways that would have showed the garden's order and direction had disappeared and to this day, no excavation has taken place to tell us of the garden's plan. Yet even in its present condition Bomarzo holds extraordinary residual power; clearly a great artist gave Orsini's dreams this wild extravagant reality, and traces of the guiding hand remain. Bomarzo's finest sculptures, for example, bear close resemblance to those in other Roman country gardens made by Orsini's contemporaries. Several of these gardens along with others at Rome itself were partly decorated and designed by this same man, he who had also made the drawing of Orsini's Pharos for him: the Neapolitan architect-antiquarian, Pirro Ligorio. Not only was Ligorio personally fascinated by the ancient Seven Wonders of the world, he was also one of the greatest garden-makers that the West has ever known.

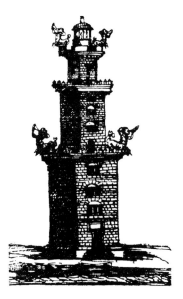

Pirro's Pharos, after Madonna, 1976

Pirro is best known today as a scurrilous forger of antiquities and for being the architect in charge of St Peter's who was sacked for attempting to change Michelangelo's designs. Pirro, whose name means 'fiery', and who sometimes signed himself 'Meisopogniro', the hater of the wicked, did not worry overmuch about making enemies and even did a turn in jail. Certainly, he seems to have cared very little for the aged and respected, not to say revered, Michelangelo. Even when the great Florentine was still working at St Peter's, planning its great dome, Pirro is supposed to have said that the old man was in his second childhood, and that he could provide nothing more than 'the ignorance of a poor councillor'. What had annoyed Pirro, apart from his impatience to succeed to the old man's post, was that one of Michelangelo's designs had called for the transformation of an antique statue of the god of the Tigris into a statue of the god of the Tiber, and that this changling had been set up at the Capitoline itself as part of an architectural scheme that underlined the medieval notion of the Capitoline as a world wonder, as the centre of Rome and the centre of the world. 'Babylon resurgent', Pirro called the plan. He was a scholar. For him, every old statue had individual identity and significance. He regularly advised cardinals and noblemen on the restoration of antiquities. Some of these restorations had led to his reputation for forgery but he believed he was merely restoring their ancient identities. The difference was vital. God, thought Pirro, was a practical scientist, and had left him many clues. All the works of the ancients, from books like those of Vitruvius to statues like the god of the Tigris, held part of the key to an understanding of the order of that golden Roman age that had been broken by Gothic invasions, and medieval poverty.

Along with Fulvio Orsini, Vicino's contemporary and an illegitimate member of that same great Roman family, Pirro founded the learned Academy of Virtue to study Rome and its ancient wisdom. Throughout his adult life, he wrote ceaselessly about antiquities. More than 50 fine quarto volumes remain, all written in Pirro's exquisite calligraphic hand in brown transparent ink on light blue paper, the text accompanied by the most delicate of line drawings. Scholars of earlier generations usually conjured up their visions of the past from books alone; even the 24 plates of Calvo's *Simulachrum* owed more to ancient texts than contemporary archaeology. Pirro, however, saw the fragments of the past as if they were all parts of an airliner that had crashed and been strewn across the landscape. With the aid of texts, Pirro studied all these pieces and tried to reconstruct them. The greater part of the antiquities that he describes in his 50 volumes, everything from altars to copper coins, from the inscriptions on leaden drainpipes to the most celebrated statues, came from Rome. Pirro measured and translated them all and wrote commentaries on them as sensitive as his drawings. At the same time, Pirro was a sufficiently eminent architect to be appointed as Michelangelo's successor as architect in charge of St Peter's. Despite all this, perhaps indeed because of it, Pirro was little appreciated by the Renaissance's most celebrated hagiographer, Giorgio Vasari. Pirro after all was a broad-accented sharp-tongued Neapolitan. Vasari, on the other hand was a very proper Tuscan who worshipped his 'divine' Michelangelo. So Pirro got short shrift. Yet this was the man who designed the most beautiful of all the papal pavilions, most gracefully set amidst the gardens of the Vatican, and planned as well the magnificent gardens of Ippolito d'Este, Cardinal of Ferrara, gardens of such fame today that the very name of Tivoli, the town in which they stand, has been taken and used by other pleasure gardens all around the world. At Tivoli, Pirro's profound obsession with antiquity and with the Seven Wonders found popular advertisement. And partly by this means, the images of those seven ancient things have flowed deep into the modern city.

The seat of Cardinal Ippolito d'Este's family, the north Italian city of Ferrara, had long been surrounded by great houses with fine gardens, and these the cardinal had already reproduced on a smaller scale beside his Roman palace. Plunging dramatically through the rocky gorges of the town, Tivoli's roaring cascades of river water must have presented an irresistible challenge for the enthusiastic gardener-cardinal from the flat plains of the River Po, for his water gardens – a series of fountains and waterfalls set running through high stone terraces – decorate and regularize this splendid natural phenomenon. Working erratically through the decades after 1550, in which year the cardinal first obtained the land, an entire hillside was fashioned to accommodate these cascades, and an elaborate system of aqueducts and reservoirs was cut into the rocky hillside around the town above. At the same time, vast quantities of earth were moved into the lower sections of the valley, transforming the ancient city walls into an enormous terrace that held four great green orchards, four enormous fish tanks, and four garden mazes.

In the manner of Hero and Philo at ancient Alexandria, the water's pressure in the gardens gave voice to water organs, whose ethereal music hung in the spaces between the rows of giant fountains and the architectural façades that frame them. Now the façades remain in silence, the organs having been quietened by time. The fountains, though, still explode in the sunlight and form patterns like the lilies of the cardinal's emblem, the devices of their splashings decorate statues and grotesques. Even at the summer's height, the garden is scented, green and pleasant. It is shaded too, for the cardinal planted hundreds of trees in it; local chestnuts, firs, elms and laurels, and imported citrus. The four square mazes that once stood at the gardens' ending had hedges of two complementary perfumed species: orange and myrtle; cherry and honeysuckle; pine and thyme; spruce and *fiorella*.

The architect of the villa, who also laid out the overall plan of the estate, was, like his cardinal, from Ferrara. However, the garden's design, its symbolic meaning and all its details, was drawn up and supervised by Pirro who at that time was serving both as the cardinal's personal archaeologist and as a papal architect. In consultation with the cardinal, he shaped the water paradise into a visual parable, a model of the universe, but a human-centred universe, filled with echoes of the Seven ancient Wonders. When it was new, before the great dark trees grew up, Pirro's design – every bit as literary as that of Bomarzo – must have been overwhelming: a vision exceeding even Babylon's great Hanging Gardens. Several monumental fountains, one with a Neptune, stood for the wild oceans and the seas. There were representations of natural rivers, filled with stony gods and water spouts, all running through the garden of wild nature. Ancient Artemis of Ephesus was resurrected as the goddess of this natural garden. Her tall figure was made in the Eastern, many-breasted image of the cult statue of her ancient temple (see pl. 16 and Chapter 6) and fashioned by the same craftsmen who had cut the classical goddesses of Bomarzo. She presided over the careful ordering of the garden's living contents, everything that was, from the fish in the great square tanks to the flowers and fruit trees and the models of owls and song birds which, like those of Leo the Mathematician of Byzantium, chirruped their song to their amused beholders. Pirro stood his Mother Nature at the centre of a vast fountain shaped like the ending of a Renaissance temple; Artemis Polymastica, whose breasts streaming water 'spinning out lyke silver twist' says the *Hypnerotomachia*, fed all creation.

Art would bring this wild nature garden into civilization. Another section of the garden was made in the image of Parnassus, the home of Apollo and of all the arts. At its centre stood a statue of a leaping horse, Pegasus, looking much like its Bomarzo twin. Facing Parnassus, formal gardens laid out in careful lines showed the benefits of 'nature improved and transformed' by art. The climax was a garden containing a model of ancient Rome, Pirro's particular obsession, symbolizing the height of man's manipulation of the natural world. There were moral lessons, too, within this great green universe. Tivoli was also the Garden of the Hesperides where Hercules had laboured for the golden apples of Temperance, Chastity and Prudence. A subtle choice this, for the cardinal proudly counted Hercules as his ancestor – such pagan stories were employed by artists and writers of the time to illustrate the Christian virtues. So Pirro's Hesperides was also another Eden, offering a choice of paths, just as had been offered to both Eve and Hercules. Pirro broke the garden's careful symmetry of pathways especially to make a grand diversity of choice.

Tivoli had been a Roman resort long before Cardinal d'Este took up residence there. A celebrated Roman temple still stood within the city, and on the plain below were the ruins of the Emperor Hadrian's huge country villa, in reality a fair-sized town, whose lakes and fish tanks had all been supplied from Tivoli's cascades. In its day, Hadrian's villa had also been filled with wonders, made apparently in celebration of his travels through the empire. Egypt, Greece and Mesopotamia were all represented in buildings of extraordinary extravagance. For the signs and symbols of his water gardens, then, for the essential clues informing the learned of all its underlying meanings, the cardinal did not have to carve the natural rock with spidery inscriptions as Orsini did, but simply plunder the ruins of Hadrian's ancient villa for stones and statues which, for people of erudition like himself, would nicely underline the message. The cardinal enjoyed statuary and ancient architecture every bit as much as Raphael and he had collected up a great deal of it. One of Pirro's first tasks for Cardinal d'Este had been some archaeological excavations at the villa and the restoration of d'Este's vast collection.

From the red earth and ruin of this ancient villa, Pirro recovered many of the most celebrated monuments to have survived from ancient Rome; extraordinary quantities of statuary, jewels and cameos, and architectural detail, in stone, plaster and mosaic. Many of these discoveries had immediate impact on the artists of the day. The garden statue of Artemis at Tivoli, for example, made to Pirro's own design, was based on an antique original excavated at the villa. For men like Pirro, these fields filled with buried broken wonders hinted at a past both immeasurably rich and incredibly wise. Beside all their other meanings, the great Renaissance gardens like those of Tivoli and Bomarzo can also be considered as re-creations of those magical fields of ruins. The crumbling brick and stucco held strange and powerful logic in them, a mysterious buried order that ran deep inside the earth itself. The presence of this buried antique past haunts all the great gardens of the West.

The first thing that Pirro excavated at the villa was an enormous open court strewn with fallen statuary, such as is reproduced in miniature in the dark wood of Bomarzo. Close by, he also found some fine marble reliefs of sea monsters, just like the dappled beauties that still stand in Orsini's silvan dream. Indeed, all the elements of the garden at Bomarzo – its squares and stairways, rooms and buildings – fit together in a similar manner to the plan of Hadrian's great villa, a jumbled series of rectangular courts and spaces linked asymmetrically to make an endless round of entertaining walks without a single central point or axis. Orsini's upside-down world is the exact reverse of Tivoli's majestic certainties which are grouped symmetrically along a single central line: the two gardens, then, are opposites.

Dozens of classical fragments, many of them collected up by Pirro, still litter the cardinal's great garden at Tivoli. Even those marble sea monsters that he found at the ancient villa in the plain below were brought up the hill to decorate the miniature Rome. Here they form an important visual element of Pirro's model of civilization, alongside Romulus and Remus and the suckling she-wolf, and a seated figure of a goddess that, to British eyes looks just like King Charles' favourite mistress, as seen on copper coins, posing as Britannia. Behind this small statue field, Pirro built a lovely model city and by its side a tiny river Tiber, with a gated bridge which, in generations after Pirro, was designed to douse you with water as you pulled it open. In the middle of this model river stands a small stone barque with an obelisk standing upright at its centre; a little boat-shaped fountain squirting its water as hard as its copper jets allow. Sadly, most of the miniature Rome was bombed during the last world war, although enough has now been rebuilt to sense its pretty size and scale, and understand something of its influence on real Rome as well.

Like Martial before him, Pirro thought that Rome itself had been the greatest wonder of the world; unlike Martial, such wonder held many different meanings for him, each ruin had its own tremendous symbolism. A symbolism that, in nearly forty years of

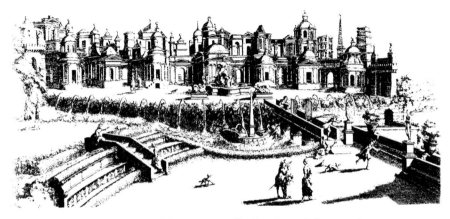

Pirro Ligorio's model Rome at Tivoli, after Venturini's engraving

effort, Pirro tried to penetrate and explain in his encyclopedic volumes of antiquities. In this, the Seven Wonders played a vital role. Just as he had made Tivoli a model of the universe, so he saw the Seven Wonders as a vital set of symbols in the ancient world, essential points of reference on the path of human evolution – a phrase first used in Pirro's time, and used of course to signify humankind's moral growth through time.

References to the Seven Wonders are scattered right through Pirro's books. Like most of his ancient predecessors, he seems to assume that everyone knew what they were and understood their great significance. He surmises, for example, that if the pyramids really had been granaries, they had also served as astronomical observatories in order to count the Biblical spans of seven lean and fat years. He notes that the Hanging Gardens had been a superb forest, filled with spoils and trophies, just as Tivoli was planned, symbolic of both chivalry and good fortune. He was especially interested in the Pharos of Alexandria, and the symbolism of its light. He conducted so much research into the subject that he knew almost as much about it as we do today. He knew the name of Sostratus, its supposed architect, and from ancient coins he made a fairly accurate reconstruction of it, which served as the model for Orsini's lighthouse at Bomarzo. Pirro also made drawings of a sea-borne Pharos that stood on the deck of a Roman warship, in a manner similar to the boat-shaped fountain he built within the cardinal's model Rome at Tivoli. He knew that in ancient Roman times there had been an island in the Tiber shaped like a boat and that at its centre had stood an obelisk. Obelisks, pyramids and lighthouses were fairly interchangeable, both as words and wonders, too.

Pirro wrote widely on the Colossus of Rhodes, identifying portraits of the sun god Helios, and collecting together all the ancient writings and relics of the god that he could find. He thought that, like the Hanging Gardens, the Mausoleum and the Colossus had served to symbolize 'war and good fortune'. From Vitruvius, he knew that the Mausoleum had stood beside a palace at a port, and that one of the harbours of this port had been secret. Working from Vitruvius' description of Halicarnassus, Pirro tried to penetrate the significance of this entire group of buildings, a single complex half hidden, half public; it seemed to him to have deep esoteric meaning. Similarly, in his interpretation of Artemis' Temple at Ephesus, he viewed it as something more than a temple jammed with treasure. For Pirro, it had been the house of a supra-national deity, the goddess of all Asia, whom he calls Diana, as does the Bible. Pirro knew all her ancient stories; Diana, whose decorated statue he had found at Hadrian's Villa; Diana, queen of the virgin priestesses, who appeared ritually in yearly festival at the sacred window of her temple. Artemis Polymastica, Tivoli's central image of living, fecund nature with a million breasts, became a central preoccupation, a vital part of Pirro's notion of the '*gran macchina del mondo*', the great machine of the world. All the delicate engravings on her statue that he had so carefully drawn and studied pointed to this vital role; they showed that Diana employed the zodiac, the sun and moon, to order everything in its season, to aid and succour all humanity. Pirro's Seven Wonders symbolized the perfect balance of humankind and nature; sometimes, his prose rises like a great poem to these mystic symbols and the forces that, it seemed to him, they all embodied.

Like the scheme of his great garden, Pirro's Seven Wonders also held Christian truths within them, in the tales of their builders' pride, tenacity and vanity, in their builders' aspirations and their longings. In their Christian role, Pirro called them the seven 'works of virtue'. Following Vitruvius and Gregory of Nazianzus, he observed that the Pyramids were the largest buildings ever made of stone; the Walls of Babylon, the largest structures built of brick; the Colossus, of bronze; the Zeus, of chryselephantine; the Artemisium and the Mausoleum, the finest examples of the integration of sculpture and architecture; the Hanging Gardens, the finest example of the integration of man and nature. So Pirro's Pharos was also a transmitter of salvation, his pyramids and obelisks united the soul with heaven; the Zeus and the Colossus were great images of the hidden and revealed God. Pirro's Seven Wonders, then, held an astonishing range of wisdom in them. They were things whose imitation would bring virtue and good fortune to their builders, and the city where they stood; the Seven Wonders were steps on a pathway up to God.

Pirro detected his Seven Wonders all over ancient Rome, the centre of the World. Following Calvo's *Simulachrum* he made a series of maps of the ancient city, showing it stuffed with models of the Seven Wonders. To make his maps, Pirro surveyed the city and carefully counted out its ruins, as Raphael and Calvo had done before him but he worked in much finer detail. Employing Calvo's maps as his model (see p. 197), Pirro sectioned his map of Rome into sixteen *quartieri* like a giant pie sliced from a central point. Each of these quarters he filled with monuments of his own design, partly based on the surviving fragments and ancient descriptions of the city, all with reference to the Seven Wonders, each one a necessary part of the great machine. Although it was still an antiquary's map founded on other maps, Pirro's plan of Rome was filled with the results of personal study and observation of the standing monuments and relics; a work of great intensity and seriousness. Pirro was entirely convinced that with the Seven Wonders and the ancient authors as his guide he could entirely recreate the past. But it was a task which even fiery Pirro could not finish in a single lifetime:

> I was moved to write of the Antiquities of Rome and to include everything worthy of record about them, not only describing them in words but also drawing them and placing them before the eyes in pictures. But having devoted many years to these studies, burning much midnight oil and putting an intolerable strain on my fortune, I now find the task more difficult and protracted than I first anticipated. . . instead I have thrown together in a little book a few of the more notable monuments of Rome and other places, these monuments being misunderstood by people today. And I have called the book 'Paradoxes' since it is written in opposition to current opinion. For I do not wish to employ my wit to prove what is false, but rather to demonstrate the truth.

The climax of Pirro's works, however, was not his 'Paradoxes,' but the 16-sheet map engraved and printed in 1561, a wonderful image of ancient Rome. To Pirro it embodied a beautiful and perfect balance of man and nature. Here, were a multitude of Wonders; 7 x 70 of them Pirro affirmed. In this Rome the pyramids were not merely symbolic Biblical granaries, but were monumental stores holding the wealth and wisdom of the human soul. Similarly, his Roman lighthouses not only guided people through the streets and down the rivers, but on the journey of life itself, to the paths of righteousness. The Hanging Gardens, high stepped palaces and tombs, held valour and honour in their terraced groves.

Though Pirro was arguably the most advanced archaeologist of his time, his Rome was still essentially a medieval wonder world, the city's walls a sacred enclosure where the tents of Abraham, the Ark of Noah and the temples of Solomon and Artemis had all once stood. Rather than working from the standing ruins, or even Calvo's *Simulachrum*, he often starts his reconstructions from the symbolism that he had invested in the Seven Wonders, crossing this with descriptions culled from ancient texts. Thus Pirro's reconstruction of the ancient port of Rome has all the seaside wonders of the ancient list within it; ancient Rome would surely need such virtues at its grandest harbour in order to bring it honour and good fortune. Here there is a vast Colossus holding the earth's globe in its hand, a statue similar to many that ancient texts attribute to countless ancient Roman harbours. Pirro's port also has a Pharos, a *Torre Pharaglione* he calls it, a great lighthouse to enable the wheat barges to sail into the Eternal City in the hours of darkness. This is an echo of the tower which, as Pirro well knew from several ancient texts, had stood inside the ancient port of Ostia by Rome. Pirro, though, also calls his Pharos an 'anti Babel', a beacon of rationality to guide souls across the sea of ignorance into civilization's harbour. Ancient texts described the port of Rome as having a series of gigantic linking quays; Pirro drew them as sets of vast arcades, embracing not only the sailors and the port but all the savage souls who would visit Rome for their enlightenment.

The plan of this port, notes Pirro, has beauty and great practicality. Its extraordinary size, its rigorous construction and precise technology produced far more than spectacle. This is Pirro's grand machine at work, a harmony of sign and symbol, of practicality and wonder. It is also the summation of these literary reborn Wonders, in many ways more wonderful than their lost originals.

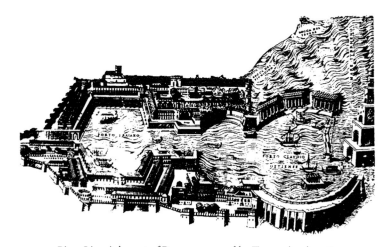

Pirro Ligorio's port of Rome, engraved by Tramezino in 1561

Pirro died at Ferrara in his eighties in 1583, still in the service of the d'Este family, still writing up antiquities in his great blue quarto tomes. A fellow Neapolitan, the stormy poet Torquato Tasso, also long in the service of the d'Este, had derived a great deal of inspiration from Pirro's work which he often celebrated in his poetry, writing for example, of an enchanted wood like the grove at Bomarzo. Now he wrote his friend a sonorous requiem:

> Pirro is dead! And the high and holy ruins
> that he brought to light now crumble,
> fall into shadow and are again encumbered.
> Rome weeps, that prey of all the universe
> who has seen her best things taken from her.
> Rome weeps, as do her shadowed fountains,
> weeps and cuts her long hair.
> Stone Niobe hands back the Augustan dream,
> marble statues brilliant with tears,
> eyes full of teardrops.
> All antique glory was put to earth
> with the art that was extinguished,
> when his hand became cold.

Fortunately, this was not true. Almost a century after Pirro's death, his magic port was born again in Rome itself, in the Piazza of St Peter's beside the Vatican. Not that the genius Bernini, who designed its swinging colonnades, necessarily knew of Pirro's sketches of the ancient port but none the less he employed, in all high seriousness, Pirro's signs and symbols. Just as Pirro's Ostia had been a port of faith, with its Colossus and a Pharos light, so once again the ancient wonders were assembled as elements in Bernini's plan. The great Egyptian obelisk at the centre of the piazza, which Pirro would have called a pyramid, is crowned, exorcised and decorated with a golden cross. On marble slabs of paving set in a circle around its base, Calvo's 16 quarters, the quarters used by Pirro to define his map, are carefully laid out, marked with the Vitruvian winds. Here, the centre of Calvo's city has been moved to become the centre of the faith; the centre of the world. With its surrounding colonnades, it is also the port, the haven of the faithful. And Pirro's harbour is decorated now with colossal statues of the saints, and his Pharos has become the lantern on St Peter's dome, sending the light of faith into the darkness of the world, shining out across the sea of ignorance. Inside the church, set behind St Peter's throne and framed by a soaring baldachino, is a small triangular image of the Holy Dove in golden yellow glass, the climax of Bernini's tremendous scheme: Jupiter is reborn and hovers over the ancient imperial throne.

Bernini did not simply pick this extraordinary complexity of images out of the blue. Pirro's notion of Rome as a symbolic machine was originally medieval. Some of the greatest artists of Pirro's century had also used individual images of the Seven Wonders

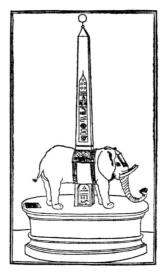

The elephant and obelisk, from the *Hypnerotomachia*, Venice, 1499

in their work. Raphael had employed a pyramid proportioned like the Roman monuments to stand for death and immortality. Giulio Romano, his assistant, had designed a splendid, stepped tomb for a friend at Mantua in the image of a miniature Mausoleum. Even Michelangelo had played with a similar notion in the early stages of his plans for the tomb of Pope Julius II, while Bernini himself had set splendid fountains in the streets of Rome, and put a Pharos on a boat inside a fountain, just like Pirro's model in the gardens of the Cardinal d'Este. Following a design from the pages of the now-venerable *Hypnerotomachia*, Bernini had even set a real Egyptian obelisk upon a stony elephant's back. Pirro Ligorio had simply gathered and refined such symbolisms, and his Roman maps, highly influential and widely copied, were their fullest expression.

It is apparent in very many of Rome's other monuments that the symbolism of the Seven Wonders was still in common use in Bernini's day. When the architect Francesco Borromini designed the spire of the church of St Ivo da Sapienza as a corkscrew tower just like the images of Heemskerck's Pharos, he drew upon the same source as Pirro had, yet this beacon was a beacon of knowledge, the church of the University of Rome. By Borromini's day, such spiralling towers were also linked with images of Solomon's temple, seen as a source of knowledge and wisdom. These age-old symbolisms now changed their forms and image as swiftly as reflections flashing and dissolving in the waters of the Roman fountains, yet the grand underlying messages remained. Street by street, square by square, all Rome was filled with these distant dreams of wonder. Haunting visions of antiquity, of Alexander, elephants and Pharos; of pyramids and mausoleums, of magic kings and queens and vast vaunting temples. Ancient ghosts of wonder.

The grand underlying image is of Rome herself, the mother of the church, the mother of all wonder. Rome the centre of the world, where all ancient civilizations had once been gathered up as if they were the figures of Bernini's fountains, giant gods, enchained, entrapped. And always that enormous sense of scale, that competition with those unseen ancient wonders that Raphael had felt and Michelangelo attempted to surpass. Huge ambitions and baroque images spilling out across the Western world.

So the gardens of a Roman mercenary and a cardinal became the gardens of the Palaces of Schönbrunn and Versailles, all of them haunted with images of ancient wonder. The vast royal palace of the Escorial in Spain was planned by a Jesuit according to his vision of the Temple of Solomon, and he too wrote out a list of Seven Wonders. In 1666, to honour the Sun King, François Dubois designed a lighthouse chapel shaped like an Egyptian pyramid to stand in the central courtyard of the Louvre in Paris, as I. M. Pei's glassier memorial does today. Now too, the temple of Artemis has become the headquarters of numberless banks and stock exchanges, the Mausoleum has spawned a multitude of Masonic temples, the Pharos, a thousand churches.

Wonder then, was born again and flooded right through Western Christendom, to every modern city of the world. The wonders of Pirro's Rome have become the wonder at the heart of every city, the celebration of their power, excitement and their vanity. They are simply a part of what a city is.

THE MOST RATIONAL OF WONDERS

An Austrian finally brought the Seven Wonders down to earth. At the end of a long career designing baroque Vienna following the triumphant defeat of the Turks, the great court architect Johann Bernhard Fischer von Erlach produced the West's first work of art history, *Entwurff einer historischen Architektur*, made, he said, so that artists 'can see that nations dissent no less in their taste for architecture than in their food and clothing.' Published in Vienna in 1721, his book is a fine folio with some ninety line engravings opening on double pages, panoramic amusements with grand images of the architectural wonders of the world. Most of these wonders, of course, were European buildings; the majority of them, indeed, were Fischer von Erlach's own designs. But he also included ancient Egyptian, Chinese and Islamic buildings, and the ancient Roman

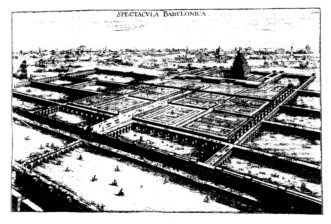

Fischer von Erlach's *Spectacula Babylonica*, with walls and gardens in the baroque manner. From the Seven Wonders of his *Entwurff*, Vienna, 1721

works that served to provide the Austrian architect with much of his inspiration; everything in fact, in which he detected 'certain general principles of architecture', from ancient times to his own.

The classic Seven Wonders begin the story. The overall conception is still Martin Heemskerck's; their stage, a manipulation of perspective taken from Albrecht Altdorfer and the like, with the eye line carefully chosen for the grand panoramic view. The Colossus still spans the harbour entrance, the statue of chryselephantine Zeus is still decorated by a high arch halo-like around his head. But Fischer von Erlach has also taken into account the work of antiquaries like Pirro, so for the first time his reconstructions of the Seven Wonders use ancient images of them found on coins and medals. This is, in fact, the beginning of scholarly veracity, 'the latest reconstruction based on scientific principles' that we expect today.

Despite their energy and exoticism, Fischer von Erlach's pictures now seem thin and cold. Martin's magic world has gone. For these are not the Seven Wonders as marvels and miracles, but the Seven Wonders as process. Underneath the baroque decoration is the vision of an engineer. Fischer von Erlach takes us back to Roman principles, to Gregory of Nazianzus' list that treated the Seven Wonders as a collection of techniques and materials. His plate of the Hanging Gardens, for example – a marvellous aerial vision of Babylon – shows the entire walled city on a great flat plain laid out as carefully as Fischer von Erlach's designs for the great palace of Schönbrunn at Vienna. It shows precisely how the Hanging Gardens could be irrigated, how they were placed, and gives footnoted references to the ancient authors who described them. He also notes that if the dimensions given by the ancient authors are correct, the walls of Babylon were the largest brick constructions ever made. Similarly, at the Egyptian pyramids, which he sets calmly in a real desert next to a diminutive Sphinx, Fischer von Erlach makes the point that these are the biggest stone buildings in the world. At Olympia, though, he is not merely interested in showing us the biggest chryselephantine statue ever created, but is greatly concerned to show how this prodigy could have been accommodated inside an ancient temple. He provides us with careful sectioned drawings to show how it was done, a drawing that contemporary archaeologists could claim was 'wrong' because his vault is Roman and not Greek. This, then, is a modern man thinking about modern wonders. In competition with the ancients, Fischer von Erlach wants to work out how, precisely, it was done; his Pharos not only describes the tower and the light but also the logistics of their construction. Just as he used the standing monuments of ancient Rome for inspiration in his own work at Vienna, so his illustrations are the meditations of a competitive working architect, his text a dialogue with other specialists. The Seven Wonders have been transformed from miraculous visions to rational structures.

It is but a short leap from Fischer von Erlach's book to the classic modern Western 'wonders'. Structures like Brunel's bridges, Sullivan's skyscrapers and the Eiffel Tower all sound precisely the same triumphal note as Fischer von Erlach's baroque palaces. The 19th century's triumph was not over the Turks – the international exhibitions that prompted so many of these strange extravagances had already put non-western cultures

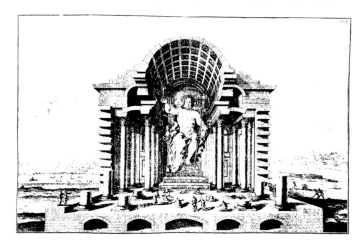

Fischer von Erlach's eminently practical, if ultimately erroneous, solution to the problem of housing the Zeus, from the Seven Wonders of his *Entwurff*, Vienna, 1721

into harmless small side pavilions of their own – their triumph was what is still sometimes called the triumph of man over nature:

1. Golden Gate Bridge
2. Mount Rushmore Presidential Portraits
3. The Astrodome
4. Statue of Liberty
5. Hoover Dam
6. Disney World
7. Gateway Arch at St Louis

Seven Wonders of the USA,
from a 1974 poll conducted by the US travel service

Looking ahead in an hour or two, we saw the Pyramids. Fancy my sensations, dear M . . . two big ones and a little one: ! ! !

There they lay, rosy and solemn in the distance – those old, majestical, mystical, familiar edifices. Several of us tried to be impressed; but breakfast supervening, a rush was made at the coffee and cold pies, and the sentiment of awe was lost in the scramble for victuals.

Are we so blasé about the world that the greatest marvels in it do not succeed in moving us ? Have society, Pall Mall clubs, and a habit of sneering, so withered up our organs of veneration that we can admire no more ? My sensation with regard to the pyramids was, that I had seen them before: then came a feeling of shame that the view of them should awaken no respect. Then I wanted (naturally) to see whether my neighbours were any more enthusiastic than myself – Trinity College, Oxford, was busy with the cold ham: Downing Street was particularly attentive to a bunch of grapes: Fig Tree Court behaved with decent propriety; he is in good practice, and of a conservative turn of mind, which leads him to respect from principle *les faits accomplis*; perhaps he remembered that one of them was as big as Lincoln's Inn Fields. But, the truth is, nobody was seriously moved. And why should they, because of an exaggeration of bricks ever so enormous ?

I confess, for my part, that the pyramids are very big.

from William Thackeray's *Notes of a Journey from Cornhill to Grand Cairo, performed in the steamers of the Peninsular and Oriental Company*, London, 1846

Long before the Eiffel Tower was made, Thackeray had foreseen the death of Heemskerck's modest wonders; Fischer von Erlach's Schönbrunn Palace could happily accommodate most of that ancient list. Today, most large cities have anonymous high rises similar in height to the pyramids of Egypt. None the less, despite the fact that hardly anyone today can name more than two or three of the ancient Seven Wonders, the notion of their unseen excellence persists. Democratically we participate in newspaper competitions to decide upon modern septets of wonder; novel lists that still make moral lessons of the wonders, just as Pirro once had done. This, for example, is an account of a competition organized by *The Times* newspaper of London in September 1991.

Eight-year-old Richard Pratt chose the winning list of seven wonders . . . his list was drawn up only after careful family discussion in his home at Hove, Sussex . . . 'We thought very hard about all the countries of the world, and all the places where you could go and stare and say: "Wow!",' he explains.

Richard's choice of Disneyland was one of the factors which led Simon Jenkins, editor of *The Times*, to pick his entry out of the hundreds submitted . . . 'There was a remarkable agreement on the leading wonders,' he said . . . 'Richard [though] . . . put the modern wonder of the world he most wanted to see – Disneyland – at the very top of his list of seven. Now he will soon be seeing Disneyland for himself.'

Richard's winning wonders were slightly different from the overall list, compiled from all the entries in the competition:

1. Disneyland
2. Aswan Dam
3. Panama Canal
4. Golden Gate Bridge
5. Apollo 11 (first man on moon)
6. Sydney Opera House
7. Empire State Building

The Times readers' top modern wonders:

1. Sydney Opera House
2. US Space Programme (Apollo, Cape Canaveral, Space Shuttle)

3. Concorde Airliner

4. Aswan Dam, Egypt

5. Empire State Building

6. Golden Gate Bridge

7. Channel Tunnel

8. Disneyland/Disneyworld/Epcot

9. Panama Canal

10. Mount Rushmore

Surprisingly, the Sydney Opera House is now the classic modern wonder. It is on every modern wonder list, a folly as beloved as Concorde, an unexpected triumph, one might suppose, for an opera house too small to stage grand opera and a building that in itself is rather passé as a work of modern architecture. What does it matter then if, as one wag has put it, the Australian national opera is forced to put its 'stage in Sydney and its orchestra in Melbourne'. The story that this modern wonder took three years of computer processing to calculate the concrete curves the young Danish architect Jorn Utzon had sketched upon his pad, vies with the ancient tale that tells that the goddess Artemis herself emplaced the vast marble beams of her temple's architrave; the information that titanium and resin hold the Opera House together hints of technologies as innovative as Chares' work at the Colossus. In common with the Greeks, Utzon was also in the business of making wonderful things. Climbing up inside his opera house is much like climbing up inside the pyramids, a journey through the scenery, back to the most ancient ghosts of wonder.

Yet, on the face of it, these modern lists of wonders make odd collections. Few of their components are still the biggest, the tallest or the fastest: a sixties opera house, an old high rise from which King Kong fell in a movie; various obsolete aeroplanes, some dams and bridges, most of them rather rusty now. These none the less are the things that people want to see before they die. Things that fill them with wonder. And indeed, arriving at Sydney by boat is much like arriving at Alexandria in Egypt; there is still a seaside wonder, the Opera House, standing like a ship in full sail. In general, what is wonderful to us, is what was defined as wonderful by the Ptolemaic Greeks of ancient Alexandria.

On November 26, 1922, Howard Carter and Lord Carnarvon concluded their six-year search for the tomb of King Tutankhamun, discovering what has been called the greatest archaeological find in the history of the world.

On December 18, 1993, Luxor Las Vegas once again opened the doors to the tomb of King Tutankhamun, continuing the drive for diversified entertainment in Las Vegas, and adding culture to the Las Vegas Strip.

Press release from 'The Next Wonder of the World', the Luxor Hotel, Las Vegas

The Luxor is a pyramid at the end of the main runway of Las Vegas International Airport. People play inside the Luxor, they are cooled and warmed and entertained by it. Eleven acres of glass clad its darkly shimmering sides. From its tip shines the world's largest beam of light, some 40 billion candle power; sufficient illumination, its press officers will tell you, to read a newspaper ten miles up in space. At the Luxor everything is a wonder and the connection with the ancient world is expensively and most carefully sought – even the light beam is named Re, after an Egyptian god. And, of course, it all works. Every year, millions of people walk the Strip to peer at just such brassy wonders. Yet this is not antiquity revived. This is only temporary. The great god Re will certainly be switched off the minute tastes change; similarly the Luxor pyramid, like the Sydney Opera House, has a calculated lifespan, a built-in obsolescence. Quietly now, for two centuries and more, the real nature of wonder has been changing.

Some modern wonders, for example, have sell-by dates stamped on their packets:

1. The Microchip
2. The Pill
3. The Telephone
4. The Jumbo Jet
5. The Gullfaks C North Sea Oil platform
6. The Hydrogen Bomb
7. Man on the Moon

Wonder list from the *Economist*, 25 December 1993

Three of these wonders are patented, one is top secret, another, the Moonshot – a carefully created televisual opportunity – is now history, and a wonder so intangible that *The Times* was obliged to put a bracketed explanation by its side when it was included in its wonder list. Philo of Byzantium never had to do that. Further confusion surrounds Walt Disney's entry on that same *Times*' list; their three locations span a continent – a single wonder then, soldered by a trademark. Similarly, four of the *Economist*'s wonders are regularly replicated on production lines and only one of them is a single unique structure, a good old-fashioned colossal oil platform.

One dire result of this strange shift of wonder has been to change the way we view the wonders of the past. We who are used to replication and the production line and indeed consider some of these products to be wonderful, no longer automatically assume, as did all ancient people, that each and every object in the world is unique. Break one telephone and you may buy another – an attitude that tends to make us careless with the remaining fragments of the past, especially if it consists of rows of standing temples or entire cemeteries of ancient tombs or 'mass housing for the workers'. Now it is difficult for us to see the individual qualities of things, the odd integrity of all the remnants of the past, and they are suddenly vulnerable.

This change has occurred since Fischer von Erlach's day. Before that time, most Western societies had hardly altered since ancient times. A Hellenistic courtier, say, from ancient Alexandria would have had little difficulty understanding the court protocol of Fischer von Erlach's Vienna or King Louis' Versailles. From that time onwards, the West organized human knowledge into a single academic system and planned and parcelled up the world itself. Before the 18th century, humankind had lived inside a limitless uncontrolled and unencompassed nature. Pirro's designs at Tivoli were gentle processes of manipulation of this great grand nature, a carefully laid out model of the universe. Such ancient palaces and gardens, those tombs and temples and all the other wonders were merely points of reference in the lavish natural wilderness, prisms marking and shaping the domain of humankind.

From the 18th century, though, this boundless world has been continuously mapped out and parcelled up. Everything from railway lines to fibre cables now run right round the planet. That great grand world in which humankind had lived since time's beginning, the world in which the Seven Wonders were once built, has gone forever. Unlike Philo's Alexandria or Renaissance Rome, modern cities no longer need great grand centres in them. No need soon for architectural urban spectacles either, for social reference points, or local wonders. Electronic cities, with their wiry nerves, occupy quite different public spaces. In these new cities, all that will be left from the age of the Seven Wonders is something of its gathering excitement, the social order and ambition of the ancient cities. The slaves have gone and only the ambitions of their owners, freedom and the pursuit of happiness, remain.

Already, there has grown up a new world of wonder makers. Ansel Adams' photographs of Yosemite, as carefully composed as Heemskerck's drawings of the ancient Wonders, made with a sensibility that is now absorbed into the root of a vast media industry, have transformed the natural rocks of a wild place into familiar forms that most Californians would consider of more significance than the ancient Pharos or the Mausoleum. How new the change is, may be seen by the fact that modern San Francisco still houses many old-style wonders: the clock tower of the Embarcadero on the harbour is based upon the Pharos; there is a prestigious pyramid inside the city, a Hanging Garden in a grand hotel; a temple too, like that which houses Martin Heemskerck's Zeus. Now, though, many recent wonder lists are just lists of natural wonders, as they were in Gothic days, when Philo's Wonders all but disappeared from view and wonder itself was given back to God. Lamenting the passing of 'grand nature', many people attempt its temporal re-creation at wonder spots like Yosemite, set now between the roads and wires. So we would make the world a garden. With such a lordly sense of nature's place and people's position in it, the 18th century would surely have approved of us.

Yet this lordly viewpoint is not quite as it was. It has moved away from Martin Heemskerck's perspectives, to pictures gained from space or from electron microscopes. What Captain Cook once saw as a terrifying hidden hazard on a voyage of discovery has now, by virtue of underwater photography and satellite surveillance, become another wonder of the world. The Barrier Reef, the world's largest living organism, is as large as the state of California, with 400 types of coral, 1,500 fish species, 400 molluscs and a host of larger animals like whales and turtles. Fly over the reef and it appears like a chain of opals lying in the sea; and only a microscope will show you the symmetric beauty of the coral polyps that make it all.

The paradox is that at the same time as we move away from the ancient images of wonder, we are moving closer to the sensibilities of the ancient world that made them. It is commonplace to point out that the skyline of Las Vegas and even its great god Re depend upon power generated from the collected waters of a man-made lake; this is merely an everyday manipulation of natural laws. With all his science though, Philo of Byzantium would not have understood the trick because it has no obvious natural manifestation which would explain it. We, however, regularly deal in things we cannot see, or even properly explain. Like 19th-century engineers, of course, Philo would have been suitably impressed by the great blue lake behind the concrete dam, and by the dam itself which is larger than the Egyptian pyramids. For us, it probably looks less impressive from the dusty roadside than it does on TV. We no longer wish to decorate grand nature with great gleaming wonders, human signposts, as Philo's generations did. We trust in theories concerning basic natural laws, and we extend these laws and put the results to work for us. Our culture now depends upon these processes. These then are the new wonders: wonders of nature invisibly manipulated.

To visit the pyramids today, you fly through time zones, see the beauty of the flight path, the lights of modern cities, all those strange evolving modern landscapes. Beneath the pyramids, in modern Cairo, people are looking at TV, playing with cards and computers, and talking to each other as ever people did. Now though, the people of the Nile manipulate their natural environment on a scale far larger than the builders of the pyramids could manage. The sacred Nile is checked and channelled to provide electricity and year-round irrigation, and Cairo is part of that vast complex of processes that link all cities.

Ancient people judged their wonders as they judged their whole existence; on the extent to which they failed or succeeded to harmonize with their gods and the elemental forces they embodied. Though we may no longer sense it, we still live on this same precarious interface between the hidden powers of nature and the order and well-being of society. Just as the Egyptians made their pyramids in a vast unvoiced attempt to join in harmony with the most elemental forces, so we now also operate with what we consider to be hidden elemental power. We deal direct with nature in something of the same way the ancient wonder makers thought they did. The difference is that ancient people fell in line with nature: we on the other hand, manipulate it, secrete its power, change its structures. As for the past, we consider ancient cultures like those that made the Seven Wonders to have been a series of separate systems each working inside their own laws; our modern system we hold as universal, working with universal laws. None the less, ancient things and ancient places still hold their wonder for us, perhaps because they hold within them something of the still and subtle balance that their makers so carefully created and maintained; maintained on precisely that same dangerous interface that moves up upon us now, and touches us again.

APPENDIX

PHILO OF BYZANTIUM
ON THE SEVEN WONDERS

Translation by Hugh Johnstone

✦   𝕗ίλωνⲟⲥ ✤ ⲃⲩⲍⲁⲛⲧίⲟⲩ   ✦
ⲡⲉⲣίⲧⲱⲛⲉ̄ⲡⲧⲁ̄ⲑⲉⲁⲙάⲧⲱⲛ

INTRODUCTION

(1) Everyone has heard of each of the Seven Wonders of the World, but few have seen all of them for themselves. To do so one has to go abroad to Persia, cross the Euphrates river, travel to Egypt, spend some time among the Elians in Greece, go to Halicarnassus in Caria, sail to Rhodes, and see Ephesus in Ionia. Only if you travel the world and get worn out by the effort of the journey will the desire to see all the Wonders of the World be satisfied, and by the time you have done that you will be old and practically dead.

(2) Because of this, education can perform a remarkable and valuable task: it removes the necessity to travel, displays the beautiful and amazing things in one's very own home, and allows one to see those things with one's mind if not with one's eyes. If a man goes to the different locations, sees them once and goes away, he immediately forgets: the details of the works are not recalled, and memories of the individual features fail. But if a man investigates in verbal form the things to wonder at and the execution of their construction, and if he contemplates, as though looking at a mirror image, the whole skilful work, he keeps the impressions of each picture indelible in his mind. The reason for this is that he has seen amazing things with his mind.

(3) What I say will be shown to be reliable if my words make a clear description of each of the Seven Wonders, and persuade the listener to acknowledge that he has got an idea of the spectacle. Of course, only the Seven Wonders are commonly described as praiseworthy, in so far as other sights can be seen just as much as these, but the admiration provoked for the Seven Wonders and for other sights is different. For beauty, like the sun, makes it impossible to see other things when it is itself radiant.

(1) HANGING GARDEN

(1) The so-called Hanging Garden with its plants above the ground grows in the air. The roots of trees above form a roof over the ground. Stone pillars stand under the garden to support it and the whole area beneath the garden is occupied with engraved bases of the pillars.

(2) Individual beams of palm trees are in position, and the space separating them is very narrow. The wood from palm trees is the only kind of wood which does not rot. When they are saturated and under great pressure, they arch upwards and nourish the capillaries of the roots [of the vegetation], and admit into their own crevices roots that are not their own.

(3) On top of these beams a great amount of earth is poured to quite a depth. On top grow broad-leaved trees and garden trees, and there are varied flowers of all kinds – in short everything that is most pleasing to the eye and most enjoyable. The area is cultivated just as happens on ground level. In much the same way as on normal ground, it sees the work of people who plant shoots: ploughing goes on above those wandering through the supporting colonnade.

(4) While people walk along the top, the land on top of the roof is motionless and, as in the most fertile regions, remains pure. From above, aqueducts carry in running water: along one way the stream follows a wide downhill course, along the other way the water runs up, under pressure, in a screw; the necessary mechanisms of the contraption make the water run round and round in a spiral. The water goes up into many large receptacles and irrigates the whole garden. It dampens the roots of the plants deep in the earth and keeps the earth moist. This is why the grass is always green and the leaves of the trees grow permanently [?], nourished by the dew, on tender boughs.

(5) For, free from thirst, the roots suck up the permeating water and form roaming entanglements among themselves below the ground and, as a unit, preserve the developed trees safe and sound. The masterpiece is luxurious and regal and it breaks the laws of nature to hang the work of cultivation over the heads of spectators.

(2) THE PYRAMIDS IN MEMPHIS

(1) While it is impossible to build the pyramids in Memphis [today], it is marvellous to describe them. Mountains have been built on mountains. The sheer size of the squared masonry is difficult for the mind to grasp, and everyone is mystified at the enormous strength that was required to prize up such a weight of material.

(2) A four-cornered base was set down, and hewn stones make up the foundations which are of the same dimensions as the height of each structure above ground. Gradually the whole work was brought up into a pyramid, tapering to a point.

(3) Its height is 500 feet and the distance around the base is 3,600 feet. The whole polished work is joined together so seamlessly that it seems to be made out of one continuous rock. But in fact different colours and types of stone have been used in its construction: here there is white marble, here there is black African stone. Then there is also what is called 'the blood red stone' and a stone of variegated translucent green, brought, so they say, from Arabia.

(4) The colours of some of the stones are a dark glass-green, others are almost quince-yellow, while yet others have a colour that is likened to the purple in conch-shells. To one's astonishment is added pleasure, to one's admiration respect, and to its lavishness splendour.

(5) The ascent is no less long or tiring than a road journey. Standing on the top and looking down, one can only dimly see the bottom. Royal wealth has woven extravagant expense alongside a pleasing array of colours. May its fortune boast that it believes that with its extraordinary expense it can touch the very stars, for it is through deeds such as these that men go up to the gods, or that gods come down to men.

(3) OLYMPIAN ZEUS

(1) Cronus is the father of Zeus in heaven, but Pheidias is the father of Zeus in Elis. Immortal nature was the parent of the former, but the hands of Pheidias of the latter; those hands alone were capable of begetting gods. Blessed is that one person on earth who saw the king and had the ability to show the Thunderer to others.

(2) But if Zeus is embarrassed to be called the son of Pheidias, skill was the mother of his representation. Nature produced elephants and Africa abounds in herds of elephants just so that Pheidias could cut the tusks of the wild animals and work the matter with his hands into the form that he intended.

(3) Whereas we just wonder at the other six wonders, we kneel in front of this one in reverence, because the execution of the skill is as incredible as the image of Zeus is holy. The work brings praise, and the immortality brings honour.

(4) Those were the good old days for Greece! When her wealth in the world of the gods surpassed any other people's wealth at any subsequent time; when she had an artist who was a creator of immortality unmatched by any that later ages produced; when it was possible to show men how the gods looked – appearances which it was never to be possible for other ages to see. Certainly, Pheidias is the champion over Olympus for the longest time, just in the same way as facts are better than guess-work, knowledge better than enquiry, and sight better than hearing.

(4) THE COLOSSUS AT RHODES

(1) Rhodes is an island in the sea. It had been hidden below the sea for a long time, but then Helios revealed it, and requested of the gods that the new island be his own. On this island stands a Colossus, one hundred and twenty feet high and representing Helios. The statue is recognizable as being of Helios because it has his distinctive features. The artist used a quantity of bronze that might have exhausted the mines, for the molten image of the structure was the bronze-work of the world.

(2) Perhaps Zeus poured down marvellous wealth on the Rhodians precisely so that they could honour Helios in spending it on the erection of the statue of the god, layer upon layer, from the ground up to the heavens. The artist secured it firmly from the inside with iron frames and squared blocks of stone, of which the horizontal bars exhibit hammer-work in the Cyclopean fashion. The hidden part of the work is bigger than the visible parts. Further questions strike the admiring spectator: what kind of fire-tongs were used, what size were the bases of the anvils, with what workforce was such a weight of poles forged?

(3) A base of white marble was laid down, and on this he first set the feet of the Colossus up to the ankle-bones. He had already conceived in his mind the proportions in which the one-hundred-and-twenty-foot god was going to be built. Since the soles of the feet on the base were already at a greater height than other statues, it was impossible to lift up the rest and set it on top. The ankles had to be cast on top and, just as happens in building houses, the whole work had to rise on top of itself.

(4) And for this reason, in the case of other statues, artists first make a mould, then divide it into parts, cast them, and finally put them all together and erect the statue. But the artist of the Colossus cast the first part and then moulded the second part on the first and, when the second part had been cast in bronze, built the third part on top of that. He used the same method of construction for the remaining parts. For it was not possible to move the metal parts.

(5) When the casting had been done on the earlier worked parts, the intervals of the bars and the joints of the frame-work were taken care of, and the structure was held steady with stones that had been put inside. So that throughout the construction he might retain his conception unshaken, he continually poured an immense mound of earth round the finished parts of the Colossus, hiding what had already been worked on underground, and carried out the next stage of casting on the flat surface of what was underneath .

(6) Little by little he reached the goal of his dream and, at the expense of five hundred bronze talents and three hundred silver talents, he made his god equal to *the* god. He produced a work outstanding in its boldness, for on the world he set a second Helios facing the first.

(5) THE WALLS OF BABYLON

(1) Semiramis was rich in royal inventiveness. So when she died, she left a treasure of a wonder behind: she laid down foundations forty-one miles long and walled Babylon. The perimeter wall is

long enough to exhaust a long-distance runner. The wall is striking not only on account of its length, but also on account of the solidity of its structure and of the width of the recesses inside it. For it is built from baked brick and bitumen.

(2) The wall is more than eighty feet high and four four-horsed chariots can simultaneously ride along the width of the circular track [on top]. There are consecutive multi-storied towers [along the wall] which are capable of housing a whole army. The city is, thus, the advanced fortification of Persia. From the outside you would not guess that it encloses within itself a habitation.

(3) Thousands and thousands of men live inside the city's round wall! The size of the land outside the walls which is farmed is hardly bigger than the built up area in Babylon, and the farmers outside the walls are as foreigners to those people living within the wall.

(6) THE TEMPLE OF ARTEMIS AT EPHESUS

(1) The Temple of Artemis at Ephesus is the only house of the gods. Whoever looks will be convinced that a change of place has occurred: that the heavenly world of immortality has been placed on the earth. For the Giants or the sons of Aloeus who attempted an ascent to heaven made a heap out of mountains and built not a temple but Olympus. The result is that the work exceeds the enterprise in boldness and, likewise, the skill exceeds the work.

(2) The architect loosened the bottom of the underlying ground, then dug out trenches to a great depth and laid down the foundations underground. The quantity of masonry expended on the structures below the ground amounted to whole quarries of mountains. He ensured its unshakeable steadiness and, having previously set Atlas under the weight of the parts that would support the building, first he set down on the outside a base with ten steps, and on that base he raised . . .

[The next page of the manuscript has been lost, and so the rest of the account of the Temple of Artemis at Ephesus no longer exists, nor does the description of the Mausoleum at Halicarnassus, which will be the seventh Wonder in Philo – see his introductory paragraph.]

SELECT BIBLIOGRAPHY

This bibliography is not exhaustive. It contains works that are fundamental to their subject, works specifically referred to in the text and recent publications that offer an overview of their subject and up-to-date bibliographies.

GENERAL WORKS

Ashley, M., *The Seven Wonders of the World*, Glasgow, 1980
Clayton, P. and Price, M. J., (eds.) *The Seven Wonders of the Ancient World*, London, 1988
Dinsmoor, W. B., *The Architecture of Ancient Greece*, (3rd rev. ed.), London, 1950
Ekschmitt, W., *Die Sieben Weltwunder*, Mainz, 1984
Green, P., *Alexander to Actium*, Berkeley, 1990
Hammerton, J. A., (ed.) *Wonders of the Past*, New York, 1924
Jones, A. H. M., *The Greek City from Alexander to Justinian*, Oxford, 1940
Pollitt, J. J., *Art in the Hellenistic Age*, Cambridge, 1986
Psicon, *Rivista Internazionale di Architettura*, 7, III, 1976
Robertson, M., *A History of Greek Art*, Cambridge, 1975

INTRODUCTION

Diller, A., *The Tradition of the Minor Greek Geographers*, Lancaster PA, 1952
Mittler, E., (ed.) *Bibliotheca Palatina*, Heidelberg, 1986
Starace, F., 'L'architettura e il senso del meraviglioso – Il trattato sulle sette meraviglie del costruire nel codice Palatino Greco 398', Naples, 1974
Stevenson, H., *Codices Manuscripti Palatini Graeci Bibliothecae Vaticanae*, Rome, 1885

CHAPTER 1: THE STATUE OF ZEUS

Ashmole, B., and Yalouris, N., *Olympia*, London, 1967
Ashmole, B., *Architect and Sculptor in Classical Greece*, London, 1972
Barnett, R. D., *Ancient Ivories in the Middle East*, Jerusalem, 1982
Breckenridge, J. D., *The Numismatic Iconography of Justinian II*, New York, 1959
Cook, A. B., *Zeus: A Study in Ancient Religion*, Cambridge, 1940
Curtius, E. and Adler, F., *Die Ausgrabungen zu Olympia*, 5 vols., Berlin, 1875–81
Honour, H., *Neo-Classicism*, London, 1977
Liegle, J., *Der Zeus des Phidias*, Berlin, 1952
Mallwitz, A. and Schiering, W., *Die Werkstatt des Phidias in Olympia*, Berlin, 1964
Mango, C., Vickers, M. and Francis, E. D., 'The Palace of Lausus at Constantinople and its Collection of Ancient Statues', *Journ. Hist. Coll.*, 4, 1, 1992
Morgan, C. H., 'Pheidias and Olympia', *Hesperia*, 21, 1952
Pater, W., *The Renaissance. Studies in Art and Poetry* (Library Edition), London , 1910

RICHTER, G. M. A., 'The Pheidian Zeus at Olympia', *Hesperia*, 35, 1966

RICHTER, G. M. A., revised R. R. R. SMITH, *The Portraits of the Greeks*, Oxford, 1984

SCHWABACHER, W., 'The Olympian Zeus before Phidias,' in *Arch.*, 14, 1961

SWADDLING, J., *The Ancient Olympic Games*, London, 1980

VOGELPOHL, C., 'Die Niobiden vom Thron des Zeus in Olympia', *Jahrb. D. A. I.* 95, 1980

WALDSTEIN, C., *Essays on the Art of Pheidias*, Cambridge, 1885

CHAPTER 2: THE COLOSSUS OF RHODES

GABRIEL, A., *La cité de Rhodes*, 2 vols, Paris, 1921–3

GABRIEL, A., 'La construction, l'attitude et l'emplacement du Colosse de Rhodes', *Bull. Corr. Hellen.*, 56, 1932

HAYNES, D. E. L., 'Philo of Byzantium and the Colossus of Rhodes', *Journ. Hellen. Studies*, 77, 1957

JACOPI, G., 'Monumenti di Scultura del Museo Archeologico di Rodi II' in *Clara Rhodos* v, pt 2, 1932

KLIBANSKY, R., PANOFSKY, E. and SAXL, F., *Saturn and Melancholy*, London, 1964

KOLLIAS, E., *The City of Rhodes*, Athens, 1988

LENDLE, O., 'Antike Kriegsmaschinen,' in *Gymnasium*, 88, 1981

LOJACONO, P., 'La Chiesa Conventuale di S. Giovanni dei Cavalieri in Rodi,' in *Clara Rhodos* VIII, 1936

MARYON, H., 'The Colossus of Rhodes', *Journ. Hellen. Studies* 76, 1956

MAIURI, A. and JACOPICH, G., 'Rapporto Generale' in *Clara Rhodos* I, 1928

RIEMSCHNEIDER, M., *Rhodos, Kultur und Geschichte*, Vienna, 1974

SCARFÌ, B. M., (ed.) *Il Leone di Venezia*, Venice, 1990

CHAPTER 3: THE PHAROS OF ALEXANDRIA

BRUCE, J., *Travels to Discover the Source of the Nile* (3rd ed.), Edinburgh, 1813

BURSTEIN, S. M. (ed. and trans.), *The Hellenistic Age from the Battle of Ipsos to the death of Kleopatra VII*, Cambridge, 1985

BUTLER, A. J., *The Arab Conquest of Egypt*, 2nd ed., ed. Fraser, P. M., Oxford, 1978

CARY, M. and WARMINGTON, E. H., *The Ancient Explorers*, Harmondsworth, 1963

COSSON, A. DE, *Mareotis*, London, 1935

CRESWELL, K. A. C., revised ALLEN, J. W., *A Short Account of Early Muslim Architecture*, Cairo, 1989

FORBES, R. J., *Studies in Ancient Technology* VI, 1958

FORSTER, E. M., *Pharos and Pharillon*, London, 1923

FORSTER, E. M., *Alexandria: A History and a Guide*, London, 1961

FRASER, P. M., *Ptolemaic Alexandria*, Oxford, 1972

GARIN, E., *Astrology in the Renaissance*, London, 1983

GOLDBERGER, P., *The Skyscraper*, London, 1981

GOODCHILD, R. G., 'Helios on the Pharos', *Ant. Journ.*, 41, 1961

GRANT, M., *The Visible Past*, London, 1990

HANDLER, S., 'Architecture on the Roman Coins of Alexandria', *Am. Journ. Arch.*, 75, 1971

IBN BATTUTA, *The Travels of Ibn Battuta* ed. Gibb H. A. R., 2 vols., London, 1956, 1962

JACOB, C. and POLIGNAC, F. de, (eds.), *Alexandrie III siècle av. J. –C.*, Paris, 1992

LEWIS, N., *Greeks in Ptolomaic Egypt*, Oxford, 1986

LUXOR, H., *Egypt for Yachtsmen*, Cairo, 1987

OTERO, M. L. and ASIN, M. DE, 'The Pharos of Alexandria', *Proc. Brit. Acad.*, 1933

POXON, R. L., 'Facts about United States Paper Money' in *Selections from the Numismatist*, Am. Numis. Acad., 1960

SCOTT, W., *Hermetica*, Oxford, 1924–36

SEMPLE, E. C., *The Geography of the Mediterranean, its relation to ancient history*, London, 1932

STEVENSON, D. A., *The World's Lighthouses*, London, 1959

THIERSCH, H., 'Griechische Leuchtfeuer', *Jahrb. D. A. I.*, 30, 1915

THIERSCH, H., *Pharos antike Islam und Occident: ein Beitrage zur Architekturgeschichte*, Leipzig and Berlin, 1909

VEITMEYER, L. A., *Leuchtfeuer und Leuchtapparate*, Munich, 1900

CHAPTER 4: THE MAUSOLEUM

ASHMOLE, B., 1972, *op. cit.*, Ch. 1

BAEDEKER, K., *London and its Environs*, (7th ed.), Leipzig, 1889

BARKER, F., *Highgate Cemetery, Victorian Valhalla*, London, 1984

BEAN, G. E., *Turkey beyond the Maeander*, rev. ed., London, 1989

BLUNT, A., *Artistic Theory in Italy*, Oxford, 1940

BUSCHOR, E., *Maussollos und Alexander*, Munich, 1950

CARTER, J. C., *The Sculpture of the Sanctuary of Athena Polias at Priene*, London, 1983

COLONNA, F., *Hypnerotomachia Poliphili*, Venice, 1499, ed. by Pozzi, G. and Ciapponi, A., Padua, 1980. ('Hypnerotomachia, the strife of love in a dream', English translation, by 'R. D.', London, 1592, reprinted, with Introduction by Lucy Gent, New York, 1973)

COLVIN, H., *Architecture and the After-life*, New Haven, 1991

COOK, B. F., 'The Mausoleum Frieze: Membra disjectanda,' in *Ann. Brit. Sch. Athens*, 71, 1976

DETIENNE, M. and VERNANT, J-P., (eds.) *The Cuisine of Sacrifice among the Greeks*, Chicago, 1989

DRERUP, H., 'Pytheos und Satyros,', *Jahrb. D. A. I.*, 69, 1954

HAVELOCK, C. M., 'Round Sculptures from the Mausoleum at Halikarnassos' in *Studies presented to G. M. A. Hanfmann*, Mainz, 1971

HORNBLOWER, S., *Mausolus*, Oxford, 1982

Illustrated London News, 1857–1861

JEPPESEN, K., *Patadeigmata*, Aarhus, 1958

JEPPESEN, K. and STRONG, D., 'Discoveries at Halicarnassus', *Acta Archaeol.*, 35, 1964

JEPPESEN, K., 'Explorations at Halicarnassus', *Acta Archaeol.*, 38, 1967

JEPPESEN, K., HOJLUND, F. and AARIS-SORENSEN, K., *The Maussolleion at Halikarnassos. 1. The Sacrificial Deposit*, Aarhus, 1981

JEPPESEN, K. and LUTTRELL, A., *The Maussolleion at Halikarnassos, 2. The Written Sources and their Archaeological Background*, Aarhus, 1986

MCNICOLL, A., 'The development of urban defences in Hellenistic Asia Minor,' in Ucko, P. J. *et al.* (eds.), *Man, Settlement and Urbanism*, London, 1972

NEWTON, C. T., *A History of Discoveries at Halicarnassus, Cnidus and Branchidae*, London, 1862

NEWTON, C. T., *Travels and Discoveries in the Levant*, London, 1865

PANOFSKY, E., *Tomb Sculpture*, (new ed.), London, 1992

SACK, R. H., *Images of Nebuchadnezzar*, Cranbury, N. J., 1991

SCHEDE, M., *Die Ruinen von Priene*, Berlin, 1964

SMITH, A. H., *A Catalogue of Sculpture in the Department of Greek and Roman Antiquities in the British Museum*, London, 1900

STEPHEN, L., *Mausoleum Book*, Oxford, 1977

WAYWELL, G. B., *The Free-standing Sculptures of the Mausoleum at Halicarnassus in the British Museum*, London, 1978

WAYWELL, G. B., 'The Mausoleum at Halicarnassus' in Clayton 1988, *op. cit.*, General

CHAPTER 5: THE HANGING GARDENS

'ALWAN, K., 'The Vaulted Structures or the So-called Hanging Gardens,' in *Sumer*, 35, 1979

ANDERSON, J. K., *Xenophon*, London, 1974

FINKEL, I., 'The Hanging Gardens of Babylon' in Clayton, 1988, *op. cit.*, General

GRAVES, R. and PATAI R., *Hebrew Myths: The Book of Genesis*, New York, 1963

GRIMAL, P., *Les jardins romains*, Paris, 1984

HALL, E., *Inventing the Barbarian*, Oxford, 1989

HEIDEL, A., *The Gilgamesh Epic and Old Testament Parallels*, Chicago, 1946

KOHLMEYER, K., *Wiedererstehendes Babylon, Eine antike Weltstadt im Blick der Forschung*, Berlin, 1991

KOLDEWEY, R., *The Excavations at Babylon*, London, 1914

MASTROROCCO, M., *Le Mutazioni di Proteo, I giardini Medicei del Cinquecento*, Florence, 1981

McCRINDLE, J. W., *Ancient India*, Calcutta, 1877

MOYNIHAN, E. B., *Paradise as a Garden*, New York, 1979

NAGEL, W., 'Where were the "Hanging Gardens" located in Babylon?' in *Sumer*, 35, 1979

PRITCHARD, J. B., (ed.) *Ancient Near Eastern Texts*, Princeton, 1950–1955

ROMM, J. S., *The Edges of the Earth in Ancient Thought*, Princeton, 1992

ROUX, G., *Ancient Iraq*, Harmondsworth, 1980

SANDARS, N. K., *The Epic of Gilgamesh*, Harmondsworth, 1964

STRONACH, D., *Parsagadae*, Oxford, 1978

THACKER, C., *A History of Gardens*, Princeton, 1979

WARNER, G. F., *The Buke of John Mandevill*, London, 1889

WETZEL, F., *Die Stadmauern von Babylon*, Leipzig, 1930

WISEMAN, D. J., 'Mesopotamian Gardens,' *Anatolian Studies*, 33, 1983

WISEMAN, D. J., *Nebuchadnezzar and Babylon*, London, 1985

WOLKSTEIN, D. and KRAMER S. N., *Inanna, Queen of Heaven and Earth*, London, 1984

CHAPTER 6: THE TEMPLE OF ARTEMIS AT EPHESUS

AKURGAL, E., *Ancient Civilizations and Ruins of Turkey*, Istanbul, 1985

BALMUTH, M. S., 'Remarks on the Appearance of the Earliest Coins' in *Studies presented to G. M. A. Hanfmann*, Mainz, 1971

BAMMER, A., *Die Architektur des jüngeren Artemision von Ephesus*, Wiesbaden, 1972

BAMMER, A., 'Recent Excavations at the Altar of Artemis in Ephesus', *Archaeology*, 27, 1974

BAMMER, A., et al., *Führer durch das Archäol. Museum in Selcuk-Ephesos*, Vienna, 1974

BAMMER, A., *Das Heiligtum der Artemis von Ephesus*, Graz, 1984

BAMMER, A., 'A Peripteros of the Geometric Period in the Artemision of Ephesus', *Anat. Studies* XL, 1990

BAMMER, A., 'Ivories from the Artemision at Ephesus,' in *Ivory in Greece and the Eastern Mediterranean from the Bronze Age to the Hellenistic Period*, ed. Fitton J. L., London, 1992

FOSS, C., *Ephesus after Antiquity*, Cambridge, 1979

GHIRSHMAN, R., *Persia from the Origins to Alexander the Great*, London, 1964

HANFMANN, G. M. A., et al., *Sardis*, Cambridge, Mass., 1983

HANFMANN, G. M. A. and WALDBAUM, J. C., 'Kybebe and Artemis,' in *Archaeology*, 22, 1969

HOGARTH, D. G., *Excavations at Ephesus, The Archaic Artemisia*, London, 1908

Illustrated London News, 1873–1875

LETHABY, W. R., 'The Earlier Temple of Artemis at Ephesus', *Journ. Hellen. Studies*, 37, 1917

MUSS, U., *Studien zur Bauplastik des archaischen Artemisions von Ephesos*, Bonn, 1983

PLOMMER, H., 'St John's Church, Ephesus', *Anat. Studies* 12, 1962

ROBINSON, E. S. G., 'The Coins from the Ephesian Artemision Reconsidered', *Journ. Hellen. Studies*, 71, 1951

SCHABER, W., *Die archaischen Tempel der Artemis von Ephesos*, Waldsassen, 1982

TRELL, B. L., *The Temple of Artemis at Ephesus*, New York, 1945

WOOD, J. T., *Discoveries at Ephesus*, London, 1877

WOOD obit., *The Builder*, 12 April 1890

CHAPTER 7, PART ONE: THE PYRAMIDS

ARNOLD, D., 'Ritual und Pyramidentempel', *Mitt. D. A. I. K.*, 33, 1977

BADAWY, A., *Ancient Egyptian Architectural Design*, Berkeley, 1965

BALL, J., *Egypt in the Classical Geographers*, Cairo, 1942

BOBER, H., 'The Eclipse of The Pyramids in the Middle Ages' in *Pyramidal Influence in Art*, Dayton, Ohio, 1980

EDGAR, M., *The Great Pyramid*, Glasgow, 1924

EDWARDS, I. E. S., *The Pyramids of Egypt*, 1st edn, London, 1947, and many subsequent

IVERSON, E., *The Myth of Egypt and its Hieroglyphs in European Tradition*, Copenhagen, 1961

KITCHEN, K. A., *Pharaoh Triumphant*, Warminster, 1982

LAUER, J-P., *Observations sur Les Pyramides*, Cairo, 1960

MENDELSSOHN, K., *The Riddle of the Pyramids*, London, 1974

PETRIE, W. M. F., *The Pyramids and Temples of Giza*, London, 1883

THACKERAY, W. M., *Notes of a Journey from Cornhill to Grand Cairo*, London, 1864

VYSE, H., *Operations carried on at the Pyramids of Giza in 1837*, London, 1840

WILKINSON, J., *Jerusalem Pilgrims before the Crusades*, Warminster, 1977

WILKINSON, J., *Egeria's Travels to the Holy Land*, (rev. ed.), Warminster, 1981

CHAPTER 7, PART TWO: THE RISE OF WONDER

ARMANI, E. P., *Perin del Vaga: l'anello mancante*, Genoa, 1986

Arup Journal, 8, 'Sydney Opera House Special Issue', London, 1973

BOCCACCIO, G., *Opere Latine Minore*, ed. Massèra, A., Bari, 1928

BRETT, G., 'The Seven Wonders of the World in the Renaissance,' *The Art Quarterly*, 12, 1949

COFFIN, D. R., *The Villa d'Este at Tivoli*, Princeton, 1960

COFFIN, D. R., *The Villa in the Life of Renaissance Rome*, Princeton, 1979

COFFIN, D. R., *Gardens and Gardening in Papal Rome*, Princeton, 1991

COLONNA, F., *Hypnerotomachia Poliphili*, op. cit., 1980, Ch. 4

DARNALL, M. J. and WEIL, M. S., 'Il Sacro Bosco di Bomarzo; its 16th-Century Literary and Antiquarian Context', *Journ. Garden Hist.*, 4, 1984

DUCLAUX, L., 'Dessins de Martin van Heemskerck', *Rev. Louvre*, 5/6, 1981

FISCHER VON ERLACH, J. B., *Entwurff einer historischen Architektur*, Vienna, 1721

GEANAKOPLOS, D. J., (ed.) *Byzantium*, Chicago, 1984

GENT, L., Introduction to Hypnerotomachia, 1973, op. cit., Ch. 4

GREENHALGH, M., 'Fantasy and Archaeology,' *Arch. Rev.*, 145, 1969

HAAN, H. DE and HAAGSMA, I., *Architects in Competition*, London, 1988

HARRISON, J. C., *The Paintings of Maerten van Heemskerck. A catalogue raisonné*, Charlottesville, 1988

HAUPTMAN, W., 'Luceat Lux Vestra coram Hominibus: a new source for the spire of Borromini's S. Ivo,' *Journ. Soc. Arch. Hist.*, 33, 1974

JACKS, P., *The Antiquarian and the Myth of Antiquity, the origins of Rome in renaissance thought*, Cambridge, 1993

KENNET, W. and YOUNG, E., *Northern Lazio*, London, 1990

KING, E. S., 'A New Heemskerck', *Journ. Walters Art Gallery*, VII–VIII, 1944–5

MADONNA, M. L., 'Septem mundi miracula come templi delle virtù Pirro Ligorio e l'interpretazione cinquecentesca delle meraviglie del mondo' in *Psicon*, 1976, *op. cit.*, General

MADONNA, M. L., 'L' 'Enciclopedia del mondo antico di Pirro Ligorio', *Quad. Ric. Sci.*, 106, 1980

MADONNA, M. L., 'Il Genius Loci di Villa d' Este. Miti e Misteri nel sistema di Pirro Ligorio' in *Natura e Artificio* ed. M. Fagiolo, Rome, 1981

MANDOWSKY, E. and MITCHELL, C., *Pirro Ligorio's Roman Antiquities*, London, 1963

MOSSER, M. and TEYSSOT, G., *The History of Garden Design, the Western Tradition from the Renaissance to the Present Day*, London, 1991

NASH, E., *Pictorial Dictionary of Ancient Rome*, London, 1968

NORDHAGEN, P. J., *The Codex Amiatinus and the Byzantine Element in the Northumbrian Renaissance*, Jarrow, 1977

PANOFSKY, E., *Renaissance and Renascences in Western Art*, New York, 1969

ORMONT, H., *Les Sept Merveilles du Monde au Moyen Age*, Bib. L'Ec. des Chartres, 43, 1882

PARKES, M. B., *The Scriptorium of Wearmouth-Jarrow*, Jarrow, 1982

PFEIFFER, R., *History of Classical Scholarship from 1300 to 1850*, Oxford, 1976

PRAZ, M., 'I mostri di Bomarzo,' in *Il Giardino dei sensi*, Milan, 1975

RIGGS, T., *Hieronymus Cock, Printmaker in Antwerp*, Yale, 1971

SCHOTT, H. A., *De Septem Orbis Spectaculis*, Ansbach, 1891

STANDEN, E. A., *European Post-medieval Tapestries and Related Hangings in the Metropolitan Museum of Art*, New York, 1985

THEURILLAT, J., *Les Mystères de Bomarzo et des Jardins Symboliques de la Renaissance*, Geneva, 1973

TRACHTENBERG, M., *The Statue of Liberty*, London, 1976

VELDMAN, I. M., *Marten van Heemskerck and Dutch Humanism in the Sixteenth Century*, Dublin and Amsterdam, 1977

WILLIAMS LEHMANN, P., and LEHMANN, K. *Samothracian Reflections*, Princeton, 1973

INDEX

Compiled by Ian D. Crane